W9-DCF-756

THE DOCTRINE OF SALVATION
IN THE FIRST LETTER OF PETER

The prevalence of salvation language in the first letter of Peter has often been acknowledged though rarely investigated in depth. Martin Williams presents a new account exploring the concept of salvation in this theologically rich letter. He brings together the disciplines of hermeneutics, New Testament studies, systematic and historical theology in order to explore the language of salvation which resonates within the text. The book also elaborates on a methodological level the segregation which has arisen between biblical studies and theological studies. In doing this, Williams identifies a basis for how there can be interaction between these two different viewpoints. This book will be a valuable resource for students and scholars interested in the exegesis and theology of 1 Peter, the doctrine of salvation and biblical interpretation.

MARTIN WILLIAMS is a minister in the Presbyterian Church of New Zealand. His research interests include the Catholic Epistles, Greek grammar, hermeneutics, the doctrine of salvation and the Reformation and Puritan era and its theology.

SOCIETY FOR NEW TESTAMENT STUDIES

MONOGRAPH SERIES

General Editor: John M. Court

149

THE DOCTRINE OF SALVATION

IN THE FIRST LETTER OF PETER

SOCIETY FOR NEW TESTAMENT STUDIES

MONOGRAPH SERIES

Recent titles in the series:

127. Matthew's Trilogy of Parables
    WESLEY G. OLMSTEAD
128. The People of God in the Apocalypse
    STEPHEN PATTEMORE
129. The Exorcism Stories in Luke-Acts
    TODD KLUTZ
130. Jews, Gentiles and Ethnic Reconciliation
    TET-LIM N. YEE
131. Ancient Rhetoric and Paul's Apology
    FREDERICK J. LONG
132. Reconstructing Honor in Roman Philippi
    JOSEPH H. HELLEMAN
133. Theological Hermeneutics and 1 Thessalonians
    ANGUS PADDISON
134. Greco-Roman Culture and the Galilee of Jesus
    MARK A. CHANCEY
135. Christology and Discipleship in the Gospel of Mark
    SUZANNE WATTS HENDERSON
136. The Judaean Poor and the Fourth Gospel
    TIMOTHY J.M. LING
137. Paul, the Stoics and the Body of Christ
    MICHELLE LEE
138. The Bridegroom Messiah and the People of God
    JOCELYN McWHIRTER
139. The Torn Veil
    DANIEL M. GURTNER
140. Discerning the Spirits
    ANDRÉ MUNZINGER
141. The Sheep of the Fold
    EDWARD W. KLINK III
142. The Psalms of Lament in Mark's Passion
    STEPHEN P. AHERNE-KROLL
143. Cosmology and Eschatology in Hebrews
    KENNETH L. SCHENCK
144. The Speeches of Outsiders in Acts
    OSVALDO PADILLA
145. The Assumed Authorial Unity of Luke and Acts
    PATRICIA WALTERS
146. Geography and the Ascension Narrative in Acts
    MATTHEW SLEEMAN
147. The Ituraeans and the Roman Near East
    E.A. MYERS
148. The Politics of Inheritance in Romans
    MARK FORMAN

The Doctrine of Salvation in the First Letter of Peter

MARTIN WILLIAMS

CAMBRIDGE UNIVERSITY PRESS
Cambridge, New York, Melbourne, Madrid, Cape Town,
Singapore, São Paulo, Delhi, Tokyo, Mexico City

Cambridge University Press
The Edinburgh Building, Cambridge CB2 8RU, UK

Published in the United States of America by Cambridge University Press, New York

www.cambridge.org
Information on this title: www.cambridge.org/9781107003286

First published 2011

Printed in the United Kingdom at the University Press, Cambridge

A catalogue record for this publication is available from the British Library

Library of Congress Cataloguing in Publication data
Williams, Martin.
  The doctrine of salvation in the first letter of Peter / Martin Williams.
    p.   cm. – (Society for New Testament studies monograph series ; 149)
  Includes bibliographical references and index.
  ISBN 978-1-107-00328-6 (hardback)
  1. Salvation–Biblical teaching.   2. Bible. N.T. Peter, 1st–Criticism,
  interpretation, etc.   I. Title.
  BS2795.6.S25W55 2011
  234–dc23   2011020308

ISBN 978-1-107-00328-6 Hardback

To my wife
Jeong Ho (Joy)
συγκληρονόμος χάριτος ζωῆς (1 Peter 3:7)
and

my children
Jonathan Edwards
Hannah Grace
Sarah Joy
ταύτην εἶναι ἀληθῆ χάριν τοῦ θεοῦ εἰς ἣν στῆτε
(1 Peter 5:12)

CONTENTS

Preface   *page* xi
List of abbreviations   xiii

Introduction   1

PART I: METHODOLOGY   9

1   Theological-critical exegesis   11

PART II: LITERAL SENSE EXEGESIS   41

2   Chosen for salvation: election in 1 Peter   43

3   The provision of salvation: the atonement in
1 Peter   81

4   Rebirthed unto salvation: the new birth in 1 Peter   127

5   The expectation of salvation: salvation as a
future event   149

6   Salvation as future victory and vindication   188

PART III: INTERCATHOLIC CONVERSATION   227

7   Divine election   229

8   The atonement   254

Conclusion   273

Bibliography   280
Index of names   300
Index of references   303

PREFACE

The impetus for this project began in Cameroon, West Africa, where in the course of teaching New Testament theology and exegesis at the Faculté de Théologie Evangélique du Cameroun (2000–2004) questions arose about the nature of salvation in general and the eternal state of those Africans who had died without ever being exposed to the message of salvation in particular.[1] It was with respect to the latter that the interpretation of 1 Pet. 3:19 (with its reference to Christ's proclamation to the spirits in prison) and 4:6 (with its reference to the preaching of the gospel to the dead) and its implications for the African church became acute. At the end of my second academic year at the Faculté I devoted the three months of my 'summer' holidays to an in-depth study of this entire passage (3:18–4:6). The first letter of Peter acquired fresh relevance in that context, and the questions simmered during the next two years of teaching (which incorporated a study of this passage).

When my missionary contract for West Africa ended, opportunity to explore the passages more fully came with doctoral studies at the University of Otago, assisted by a very generous University of Otago postgraduate scholarship, for which I am very grateful. In the course of my research I have accrued a number of other debts. My supervisor, the Revd Dr Paul Trebilco (Professor of New Testament at the University of Otago), offered steady advice, rigorous criticism, and generous friendship. He always struck the right balance between offering excellent advice and fostering independence. This, coupled with his enthusiastic encouragement and support, made my time of research at the University of Otago a real pleasure. I also wish to acknowledge the valuable contribution of my second supervisor, Dr Ivor Davidson (Professor of Systematic Theology), whose critical comments and theological insight made those theological

---

[1] For some useful reflections on 1 Peter and the challenges of communicating its message of salvation into an African context see Wendland, '"Stand Fast in the True Grace of God!" A Study of 1 Peter', 68–78.

portions of this work much better than they otherwise would have been. If this book suggests any significant contribution, it will be due in large part to their skilful and insightful supervision. The superb facilities of the University of Otago library were made accessible by competent and courteous staff. Moreover, I could never have accomplished the depth of research without the valuable assistance of the interloan library staff at the University of Otago, who tracked down my many (and at times obscure) interloan requests, and who helped render distance an illusion.

In revising this dissertation for publication, I eliminated about 30,000 words, comprising some longer word studies, plus a chapter on baptism (1 Pet. 3:20–1) and a theological chapter on regeneration. These chapters can still be found in the original thesis.

I am very conscious of how much my work owes to the love, support, and generosity over many years of family and friends. They are too numerous to name, but without their contribution in so many different ways my research on 1 Peter would never have seen the light of day. In particular I extend my thanks to those many friends and family who have provided funds to meet some of my expenses. I could never have completed this project without the very generous financial support of four very special friends: in South Korea, Dr Chun Bae Lee and his wife Dr Youn Soon Cha, and in Switzerland, Beat and Susanne Meier, to whom I am very grateful.

My own family has been a loving and supportive context in which to carry out this project, one which has kept me firmly anchored in the reality of contemporary life. To my wife Jeong Ho (Joy) I want to say thank you for all that we have done together, including this book. Thank you for providing all of the personal encouragement, support, and love I have needed. I also want to express my thanks to my children, Jonathan Edwards, Sarah Joy, and Hannah Grace, not just children, but fellow strangers with me in this world and pilgrims to the next (1 Pet. 1:1; 2:11) – a truth we have all learned as we have shared Peter's First Letter and John Bunyan's *The Pilgrim's Progress* together during our evening devotions. To you I dedicate this book.

I would also like to express my thanks to all the kind people at Cambridge University Press for their editorial expertise, warm encouragement, and valuable assistance in formatting the text for publication.

Finally, to Jesus Christ I acknowledge infinite indebtedness. From the time I came into being, I have gone deeper and deeper in debt to Christ, and will continue to do so forever. Every breath, every heartbeat, every thesis, every book, every friend puts me another degree deeper in debt to grace. In this I rejoice, because the Giver of such grace gets all the glory (1 Pet. 4:11).

Soli deo Gloria!

ABBREVIATIONS

AB	Anchor Bible
ABD	*Anchor Bible Dictionary*. Edited by D. N. Freedman. 6 vols. Garden City, New York: Doubleday, 1992.
ABR	*Australian Biblical Review*
ACR	*Australasian Catholic Record*
AJBI	*Annual of the Japanese Biblical Institute*
AnBib	Analecta biblica
ANF	*Ante-Nicene Fathers*
ANTC	Abingdon New Testament Commentaries
AsSeign	*Assemblées du Seigneur*
AUSS	*Andrews University Seminary Studies*
BBR	*Bulletin for Biblical Research*
BDAG	W. Bauer, F. W. Danker, W. F. Arndt, and F. W. Gingrich, *Greek–English Lexicon of the New Testament and other Early Christian Literature*. 3rd edn. Chicago: University of Chicago Press, 2000.
BDB	F. Brown, S. R. Driver, and C. A. Briggs, *The Brown–Driver–Briggs Hebrew and English Lexicon*. Peabody: Hendrickson, 2004.
BDF	F. Blass, A. Debrunner, and R. W. Funk, *A Greek Grammar of the New Testament and Other Early Christian Literature*. Chicago: University of Chicago Press, 1961.
BECNT	Baker Exegetical Commentary on the New Testament
BETL	Bibliotheca ephemeridum theologicarum lovaniensium
BGU	*Aegyptische Urkunden aus den Königlichen Staatlichen Museen zu Berlin, Griechische Urkunden*. 15 vols. Berlin, 1895–1983.
BHR	Bibliotheca humanistica et reformatorica
Bib	*Biblica*
BibLeb	*Bibel und leben*

BJRL	*Bulletin of the John Rylands University Library of Manchester*
BJS	Brown Judaic Studies
BL	*Bibel und Liturgie*
BNTC	Black's New Testament Commentary
BSac	*Bibliotheca sacra*
BSNTS	*Bulletin of the Society for New Testament Studies*
BTB	*Biblical Theology Bulletin*
BZ	*Biblische Zeitschrift*
CBQ	*Catholic Biblical Quarterly*
CBR	*Currents in Biblical Research*
CD	Karl Barth, *Church Dogmatics*. 13 vols. Edinburgh: T&T Clark, 1956–75.
ConJ	*Concordia Journal*
CT	*Christianity Today*
CTJ	*Calvin Theological Journal*
CTM	*Concordia Theological Monthly*
DJG	*Dictionary of Jesus and the Gospels*. Edited by Joel B. Green, Scott McKnight, and I. Howard Marshall. Downers Grove: IVP, 1992.
DLNT	*Dictionary of the Later New Testament and its Developments*. Edited by Ralph P. Martin and Peter H. Davids. Downers Grove: IVP, 1997.
DPL	*Dictionary of Paul and his Letters*. Edited by Gerald F. Hawthorne, Ralph P. Martin, and Daniel G. Reid. Downers Grove: IVP, 1993.
DTIB	*Dictionary for Theological Interpretation of the Bible*. Edited by K. J. Vanhoozer, C. G. Bartholomew, D. J. Treier, and N. T. Wright. Grand Rapids: Baker, 2005.
EDNT	*Exegetical Dictionary of the New Testament*. Edited by H. Balz and G. Schneider. 3 vols. Grand Rapids: Eerdmans, 1990–93.
EKKNT	Evangelisch-katholischer Kommentar zum Neuen Testament
EstBib	*Estudios biblicos*
ESV	English Standard Version
EuroJT	*European Journal of Theology*
EvQ	*Evangelical Quarterly*
ExAud	*Ex auditu*
Exp	*Expositor*
ExpTim	*Expository Times*

Gramcord	Windows software program that performs sophisticated searches on a morphologically tagged Greek New Testament (UBS⁴) as well as Greek Old Testament (*Septuaginta* [Rahlfs]) and Hebrew Old Testament (*BHS*). Marketed by the Gramcord Institute, Battle Ground, Wash., and programmed by Paul Miller.
GTJ	*Grace Theological Journal*
HBT	*Horizons in Biblical Theology*
HNT	Handbuch zum Neuen Testament
HTKNT	Herders theologischer Kommentar zum Neuen Testament
ICC	International Critical Commentary
IDB	*Interpreter's Dictionary of the* Bible. Edited by G. A. Buttrick. 4 vols. Nashville: Abingdon Press, 1962.
ISBE	*The International Standard Bible Encyclopedia.* Edited by G. W. Bromiley. 4 vols. Rev. edn. Grand Rapids: Eerdmans, 1979–86.
JBL	*Journal of Biblical Literature*
JETS	*Journal of the Evangelical Theological Society*
JOTT	*Journal of Translation and Textlinguistics*
JR	*Journal of Religion*
JSNTSup	Journal for the Study of the New Testament Supplement Series
JSOT	*Journal for the Study of the Old Testament*
JTS	*Journal of Theological Studies*
LCL	Loeb Classical Library
LD	Lectio divina
LEH	J. Lust, E. Eynikel, and K. Hauspie (eds.), *Greek English Lexicon of the Septuagint.* Rev. edn. Stuttgart: Deutsche Bibelgesellschaft, 2003.
L&N	J. P. Louw and E. A. Nida, *A Greek–English Lexicon of the New Testament based on Semantic Domains.* 2 vols. New York: United Bible Societies, 1988.
LS	C. T. Lewis and C. Short, *A Latin Dictionary.* Oxford: Clarendon Press, 1996 [1879].
LSJ	H. G. Liddell, R. Scott, and H. S. Jones, *A Greek–English Lexicon.* 9th edn. with revised supplement. Oxford: Oxford University Press, 1996.
LXX	Septuagint (Greek Old Testament)
LW	*Luther's Works.* Edited by J. Pelikan. 55 vols. St. Louis: Concordia, 1955–86.

MM	J. H. Moulton and G. Milligan, *Vocabulary of the Greek Testament*. London: Hodder & Stoughton, 1930. Reprint, Peabody: Hendrickson, 1997.
MSJ	*Master's Seminary Journal*
MVAG	Mitteilungen der Vorderasiatisch-ägyptischen Gesellschaft.
NAC	New American Commentary
NCB	New Century Bible
NDBT	*New Dictionary of Biblical Theology*. Edited by T. D. Alexander and B. S. Rosner. Downers Grove: IVP, 2000.
Neot	*Neotestamentica*
NETS	*New English Translation of the Septuagint*. Edited by A. Pietersma and B. G. Wright. Oxford: Oxford University Press, 2007.
NICNT	New International Commentary on the New Testament
NICOT	New International Commentary on the Old Testament
NIDCC	*The New International Dictionary of the Christian Church*. Edited by J. D. Douglas. Grand Rapids: Zondervan, 1978.
NIDNTT	*The New International Dictionary of New Testament Theology*. Edited by Colin Brown. 4 vols. Exeter: Paternoster Press, 1978.
NIGTC	New International Greek Testament Commentary
NLH	*New Literary History*
NovT	*Novum Testamentum*
NovTSup	Novum Testamentum Supplements
NPNF	*A Select Library of Nicene and Post-Nicene Fathers of the Christian Church*. 1st series. 14 vols. Edited by P. Schaff. Edinburgh: T & T Clark; Grand Rapids: Eerdmans, 1983–98.
NRSV	New Revised Standard Version
NRTh	*La nouvelle revue théologique*
NSBT	New Studies in Biblical Theology
NTAbh	Neutestamentliche Abhandlungen
NTD	Das Neue Testament Deutsch
NTF	Neutestamentliche Forschungen
NTS	*New Testament Studies*
NTSR	New Testament for Spiritual Reading
OGIS	*Orientis graeci inscriptiones selectae*. Edited by W. Dittenberger. 2 vols. Leipzig, 1903–5.

OTP	*Old Testament Pseudepigrapha.* Edited by J. H. Charlesworth. 2 vols. New York: Doubleday, 1983.
PMLA	*Published by the Modern Language Association*
ProEccl	*Pro ecclesia*
RCT	*Revista catalana de teología*
RevExp	*Review and Expositor*
ResQ	*Restoration Quarterly*
RTL	*Revue théologique de Louvain*
SB	Sources bibliques
SBET	*Scottish Bulletin of Evangelical Theology*
SBFLA	*Studii biblici Franciscani liber annus*
SBT	Studies in Biblical Theology
SCHNT	Studia ad corpus hellenisticum Novi Testamenti
SJLA	Studies in Judaism in Late Antiquity
SJT	*Scottish Journal of Theology*
SP	Sacra pagina
ST	*Studia theologica*
StPB	Studia post-biblica
Str-B	H. L. Strack and P. Billerbeck, *Kommentar zum Neuen Testament aus Talmud und Midrash.* Munich: C. H. Beck, 1961.
StudM	*Studia missionalia*
SwJT	*Southwestern Journal of Theology*
TBT	*The Bible Today*
TD	*Theology Digest*
TDNT	*Theological Dictionary of the New Testament.* Edited by G. Kittel and G. Friedrich. Translated by G. W. Bromiley. 10 vols. Grand Rapids: Eerdmans, 1964–76.
TE	*The Theological Educator*
THKNT	Theologischer Handkommentar zum Neuen Testament
TNTC	Tyndale New Testament Commentaries
TrinJ	*Trinity Journal*
TTZ	*Trierer theologische Zeitschrift*
TynBul	*Tyndale Bulletin*
TZ	*Theologische Zeitschrift*
UBT	Understanding Biblical Themes
USQR	*Union Seminary Quarterly Review*
WA	*D. Martin Luthers Werke.* Kritisch Gesamtausgabe. Weimar: Hermann Böhlau, 1883–.
WBC	Word Biblical Commentary
WTJ	*Westminster Theological Journal*

WUNT	Wissenschaftliche Untersuchungen zum Neuen Testament
YJS	Yale Judaic Studies
ZAW	*Zeitschrift für die alttestamentliche Wissenschaft*
ZBK	Zürcher Bibelkommentare
ZNW	*Zeitschrift für die neutestamentliche Wissenschaft und die Kunde der älteren Kirche*

INTRODUCTION

1. Salvation in 1 Peter

David Ford in his book *Theology: A Very Short Introduction*, observes that '[b]ecause of its many dimensions, salvation is a topic where most key theological issues can be seen to converge'.[1] As Ford demonstrates, a number of key issues come into focus when we address the theme of salvation: the way we think about God, creation and providence, evil and sin, the person and work of Jesus Christ, the church and sacraments, the Christian life and ethics, and the future consummation of all things.[2] *Soteriology* is thus inseparably related to *theology* (the doctrine of God), *anthropology* (the doctrine of humanity and sin), *Christology* (the doctrine of the person and work of Christ), *ecclesiology* (the doctrine of the church and sacraments), and *eschatology* (the doctrine of last things). Joel Green suggests that '[i]f we take seriously that "theme" expresses "a relation of being about," that the "theme" of a text has to do with unifying the many and often distinct and sometimes discontinuous elements of a text, then there is an important sense in which we are justified in speaking of salvation as the theme of Scripture. Here is the integrating center of Scripture, just as it is the coordinating center of theology.'[3]

However, in 1995 I. H. Marshall wrote, '[a]lthough this subject [salvation] is of central importance to the Bible and is treated in standard theological dictionaries and encyclopedias, it has had remarkably little attention directed to it in theological monographs'.[4] The present situation has improved only a little since then.[5] The same, however, cannot be said

---

[1] Ford, *Theology*, 103.   [2] Ibid., 105–10.   [3] Green, *Salvation*, 2.

[4] Marshall, 'Nature of Christian Salvation', 30.

[5] Recently two monographs on salvation have been published: The edited volume of Van der Watt, *Salvation in the New Testament* and the published PhD dissertation of Wieland, *The Significance of Salvation*.

with regard to 1 Peter.[6] Commentators have long recognised the theological richness of 1 Peter in general and the importance and richness of its soteriological language in particular. However, as van Rensburg has recently observed, '[t]he soteriology of 1 Peter has, to a large extent, been neglected. No monograph on soteriology in 1 Peter could be located – only scattered and sporadic remarks in commentaries and in articles'.[7] This neglect is evidenced by a recent survey by M. Dubis, 'Research on 1 Peter: A Survey of Scholarly Literature Since 1985' in *Currents of Biblical Research* (2006), in which he lists only two recent (1987, 2002) scholarly treatments of 1 Peter's soteriology (neither of which are very substantial): one article treats redemption in 1 Peter (two and a half pages)[8] while the other addresses the issue of whether a predestination to judgment appears in 2:8 (four and a quarter pages).[9] Scholarly literature treating the topic of salvation generally consists of either a few pages set aside in the introductions of some commentaries on 1 Peter or treatments of the theme of salvation in 1 Peter as part of broader surveys. The theme of salvation does not fare much better in doctoral dissertations. A number of dissertations on 1 Peter have appeared in recent years treating such themes as the doctrine of God, Christology, baptism, hope, suffering, obedience, the Christian life, ethics, even the atonement, the new birth, and election, however there has been no similar study carried out on the theme of salvation. The importance of such a study becomes immediately apparent, for, as we noted above, the theme of salvation is inseparably related to our understanding of God and the person and work of Christ, and is foundational for our understanding of the Christian life, baptism, obedience, ethics, suffering, and hope.

The present study is an investigation of the understanding of salvation in the first letter of Peter, asking (1) what is the content of the concept of salvation expressed in it, given the propositional content, illocutionary force, and rhetorical role of those texts treating this concept in 1 Peter, and (2) given that content, what contribution can 1 Peter make to the broader theological conversation between the different theological traditions (e.g., Reformed, Neo-orthodox, Lutheran, Arminian, Pelagian, Wesleyan) and how might that conversation shape, sharpen, and safeguard our own understanding of 1 Peter's soteriology? Since my interests are

---

[6] Since the completion of this study Stephen Fagbemi has published his work: *Who are the Elect in 1 Peter? A Study in Biblical Exegesis and its Application to the Anglican Church of Nigeria.*

[7] Van Rensburg, 'Metaphors in the Soteriology in 1 Peter', 409.

[8] Kennard, 'Petrine Redemption', 399–405.

[9] Panning, 'What Has Been Determined (ἐτέθησαν) in 1 Peter 2:8?', 48–52.

both exegetical and theological, I need a methodology that will accommodate both interests. This methodology, which I have called 'theological-critical exegesis', is outlined in chapter 1 of this work. Moreover, since I am concerned with the 'concept' of salvation I am not merely concerned simply with an analysis of 'salvation language' (i.e., words that translate the Greek verb σῴζω and its derivatives), though it is no less than that.[10] The reason for this is that the concept of salvation is much larger than the language itself.[11] Thus to confine ourselves strictly to 'salvation language' would, in the words of Moisés Silva, lead to a 'distorted picture' and 'an unrefined understanding of the topic'.[12] On the one hand, then, I *will* be investigating the uses of the σῴζω word-group which is primarily concerned with (negatively) the hope of deliverance at the final judgment and (positively) the gift of coming glory. On the other hand, I will also be investigating those aspects of salvation which are expressed in other terminology (that of election, atonement, new birth, and calling).

To achieve these goals, the present work has been divided into three parts: (1) Methodology, (2) Literal Sense Exegesis, and (3) Intercatholic Conversation. In **part I**, chapter 1, entitled 'Theological-Critical Exegesis', I outline the presuppositions and approach to theological interpretation taken in this work. Basic to a theological interpretation of Scripture, we will note, is the recognition of its dual authorship as a divine and human communicative action embodied in written discourse. This means that the interpreter must be oriented primarily toward the subject matter of the biblical text and be committed to discerning the meaning placed there by the author. This is another way of saying that the theological interpreter must take seriously the literal sense of the text. To do this, I will suggest, involves three things: (1) a careful exegesis of the text itself, (2) an intercanonical conversation, and (3) an intercatholic conversation.

In **part II**, chapters 2–6, then, I conduct a careful exegesis of those passages in 1 Peter that treat the subject of salvation. This section begins, in chapter 2, in eternity past with God's eternal, sovereign, free, and gracious election of some to salvation (1 Pet. 1:1–2; 2:4–10) and others to damnation (2:8). The theme of election is of great significance to the author of 1 Peter (it has been referred to as a 'controlling concept' with 'thematic significance')[13] and serves to underscore the initiative

---

[10] As in the study of Wieland, *The Significance of Salvation*.
[11] See Silva, *Biblical Words*, 26–8; Barr, *Semantics of Biblical Language*, 206–96.
[12] Silva, *Biblical Words*, 27.
[13] Schrenk, 'ἐκλεκτός', *TDNT*, 4: 190.

and sovereignty of God in the believers' salvation and the unbelievers' damnation.

The divine initiative in salvation is further underscored in chapter 3 which examines those passages that deal with God's gracious provision of salvation in Jesus Christ (1 Pet. 1:18–19; 2:21–5; 3:18). This chapter brings us to the heart of the doctrine of salvation, which, for Peter, is grounded in the death, resurrection, ascension, and exaltation of Jesus Christ. More specifically, it seeks to answer the question: How is the death of Jesus actually said to 'save'?

While chapter 3 deals with the provision of salvation outside of us and apart from us, chapter 4 contains an analysis of those passages (1:3, 23) that treat the application of that salvation to us under the metaphor of the 'new birth', 'regeneration', or 'calling'. Peter once again highlights the initiative of God in the believers' salvation by reminding them that it was God 'who, according to his great mercy has caused us to be born anew' (v. 3bc).

Having explored God's eternal election to salvation (chapter 2), the historical provision of that salvation in Jesus Christ (chapter 3), and the application of that salvation in the rebirth of the believer (chapter 4), chapters 5 and 6 (1 Pet. 1:3–12 and 3:18–4:6 respectively) bring this section to a close (and a climax) with its focus on the consummation of the believer's salvation, which Peter declares is 'ready to be revealed in the last time' (1:5; cf. v. 7d).[14] Unique to Peter's presentation of eschatological salvation is his focus on God's vindication of Christ's innocent suffering through his resurrection (3:18e, 21d), ascension (vv. 19, 22b), victorious proclamation to the spirits in prison (v. 19), and exaltation to God's right hand (v. 22), as a model designed to provide suffering believers with the assurance that God will one day vindicate them also by raising them from the dead (3:18e/4:6c) and bestowing upon them praise, glory, and honour (see 1:7). I will argue that Peter's unique presentation of the believers' final salvation in terms of future vindication and victory through suffering is designed to engender hope amongst a small minority group of believers facing the onslaught of a hostile world against their faith (see '2. The situation of the addressees', below).

In **part III**, chapters 7–8, I seek to bring the results of my exegesis into dialogue with a variety of theological traditions (e.g., Reformed, Neo-orthodox, Lutheran, Arminian, Pelagian, Wesleyan) in order to allow 1 Peter to make its own distinctive contribution to the ongoing discussion

---

[14] The original thesis also dealt with the subject of baptism in 1 Pet. 3:20d–21 (pp. 465–97).

(both between the traditions and between the Bible and theology) but also to allow that dialogue to shape and sharpen my own understanding of salvation in 1 Peter. Because of the confines of space, I have limited my discussion here to the doctrine of election (chapter 7 – building on chapter 2) and the atonement (chapter 8 – building on chapter 3).[15] Part III, with its dialogue between New Testament exegesis and systematic theology, is the second area in which this work aims to make a distinctive contribution. As such it seeks to overcome the present and unfortunate segregation of biblical studies and systematic theology and hopes to further open up the way for a more fruitful dialogue between the two.

2. The situation of the addressees

The occasional nature of 1 Peter demands that we say something about the situation which Peter's addressees were facing and which called forth the need for this letter to be written to them in the first place. As Elliott has pointed out, '[t]he most prominent and repeatedly emphasised feature of the addressees' situation as portrayed in 1 Peter is the undeserved suffering that they were undergoing as a result of the disparagement and abuse to which they were subjected to by hostile nonbelievers'.[16] It is necessary, therefore, at the outset of this study to consider the nature and cause of the suffering being experienced by Peter's readers, for as Selwyn points out, '[t]he question [of Christian suffering] is ... of importance because some of the deepest teaching of the Epistle is bound up with the trials through which its readers were passing'.[17] We know from the letter that its readers were experiencing some form of hostility from outsiders on account of their faith (1:6–7; 2:18–20; 3:1, 13–17; 4:1–6, 12–19; 5:10). But what was the actual nature and cause of this hostility? Was it the result of an official policy of the Roman Empire or was it due to unofficial harassment of a more local and sporadic kind?

A number of earlier commentators sought to trace the suffering of 1 Peter to an official policy of persecution on the part of Rome. Proponents of this view have sought to link these persecutions to the reign of Nero (54–68), Vespasian (69–70), Domitian (81–96), or Trajan (98–117). The following arguments have been advanced: (1) Some commentators point to the reign of Nero from which comes the first

---

[15] The original thesis also dealt with the doctrine of regeneration (pp. 425–56).
[16] Elliott, *1 Peter*, 97–8.   [17] Selwyn, *First Epistle of St. Peter*, 53.

evidence of specific persecution against Christians. This connection has at times been made on the basis of 1 Pet. 4:12 with its reference to the 'fiery ordeal coming upon you' (τῇ ἐν ὑμῖν πυρώσει), which, according to Thurston, 'seems particularly applicable to the Neronian persecution, in which many Christians were burned to death. This reference may therefore suggest that some Christians had already been burned, or at least sentenced to such a death.'[18] (2) Others see a connection between 1 Peter's reference to persecution 'for the name [of Christ]' (ἐν ὀνόματι [Χριστοῦ]) in 4:14 and Pliny's desire to know whether Christians should be punished for the 'name itself' (*nomen ipsum*) 'albeit without crimes, or only the crimes associated therewith' (Pliny, *Ep.* 10.96). (3) The phrase ἕτοιμοι ἀεὶ πρὸς ἀπολογίαν ('always be prepared to give a defence') in 1 Pet. 3:15 has been taken, by some commentators, to imply a formal judicial interrogation (e.g., before a Roman magistrate). (4) Finally, the reference in 1 Pet. 5:9 to the 'the same sufferings [τὰ αὐτὰ τῶν παθημάτων] being experienced by your fellow Christians *throughout the world* [ἐν [τῷ] κόσμῳ]', has been interpreted by some commentators as a reference to an official empire-wide policy of persecution.

These arguments, however, are far from conclusive, and the objections to them can be stated briefly: (1) The persecution of the Christians by Nero was confined to the city of Rome itself and did not spread to Asia Minor, and, as Elliott observes, it 'resulted in no official proscription of Christianity, and set no official precedent for any policy of Rome toward the Christian movement in general'.[19] (2) As the exchange of correspondence between Pliny and Trajan demonstrates (Pliny, *Ep.* 10.96–7), there was no official Roman policy proscribing Christianity at this time, and Trajan was unwilling to establish one. Moreover, the expression 'for the name [of Christ]' (ἐν ὀνόματι [Χριστοῦ], 4:12; cf. 4:16, ὡς Χριστιανός) is linked to verbal rather than physical abuse (see 4:12–16, esp. v. 14). (3) The phrase ἕτοιμοι ἀεὶ πρὸς ἀπολογίαν ('always be prepared to give a defence', 1 Pet. 3:15) more likely denotes a reply to accusations of a more general and informal rather than a legal and formal nature, as the generalising expressions ἀεί ('always') and παντὶ τῷ αἰτοῦντι ('to everyone who asks') indicate. (4) The assumption that the phrase ἐν [τῷ] κόσμῳ ('throughout the world') points to an official policy of persecution on the part of the Roman Empire simply lacks evidence. As Davidson points out, the first systematic and empire-wide attack on Christians was not

---

[18] Thurston, 'Interpreting First Peter', 176.   [19] Elliott, *1 Peter*, 98.

launched until AD 250 during the brief reign of emperor Decius (October 249–June 251).[20] There is thus no internal nor external evidence indicating an official Roman policy of persecution against Christians that would have prompted the situation described in 1 Peter.

A more comprehensive consideration of the language of persecution in 1 Peter leads us in a different direction. The language of 1 Peter suggests that the cause of the Christians' suffering was more verbal than physical, informal than formal, social and unofficial than state-organized and official. Right from the outset of the letter we see that the believers' theological status as God's 'elect' (ἐκλεκτοῖς, 1:1b; cf. v. 2a: κατὰ πρόγνωσιν θεοῦ πατρός) and 'set apart' (ἐν ἁγιασμῷ πνεύματος, v. 2b) people has put them in tension with surrounding society. The sociological effect of their theological or sociospiritual status is that they have become 'strangers [παρεπιδήμοις] of the Diaspora of Pontus, Galatia, Cappadocia, Asia, and Bithynia' (1 Pet. 1:1). As a result, they are misunderstood (cf. 2:15) and maligned (cf. 4:4): 'Beloved, I exhort you *as aliens and strangers* [ὡς παροίκους καὶ παρεπιδήμους] to abstain from fleshly desires which wage war against the soul; having your conduct honourable *among* the Gentiles [ἐν τοῖς ἔθνεσιν] so that, when they *speak against you* [καταλαλοῦσιν ὑμῶν] as evil doers, from observing your good deeds they may glorify God on the day of visitation' (2:11–12). The verb 'speak against' translates the Greek καταλαλέω ('speak ill of, speak degradingly of, speak evil of, defame, slander'),[21] which appears again in 3:16 ('when you are slandered [καταλαλεῖσθε], those who malign [ἐπηρεάζοντες] your good conduct in Christ'), and is only one of a number of terms employed in 1 Peter to depict the hostile verbal abuse that is directed against Christians by society around them: λοιδορέω (2:23, 'revile, abuse'), λοιδορία (3:9, 'speech that is highly insulting, abuse, reproach, insulting'),[22] ἀντιλοιδορέω (2:23, 'revile in return'), βλασφημέω (4:4, 'to speak in a disrespectful way that demeans, denigrates, maligns'; [in relation to humans]: 'slander, revile, defame'),[23] ἐπηρεάζω (3:16, 'threaten, mistreat, abuse'),[24] and ὀνειδίζω ('reproach, revile, mock, heap insults on').[25] As Elliott observes, '[a]ll these related terms illustrate the kind of oppression to which the nonbelievers subjected the believers: verbal abuse, disparagement, denigration, maligning, insult, contemptuous reproach, public defamation and public shaming on the suspicion of their "doing what is wrong" [cf. 2:12]'.[26]

---

[20] Davidson, *Birth of the Church*, 322.
[21] BDAG, 519. [22] BDAG, 602. [23] BDAG, 178. [24] BDAG, 362.
[25] BDAG, 710. [26] Elliott, *1 Peter*, 467.

According to 1 Peter, because believers have distanced themselves as non-conformists from the 'way of life' (ἀναστροφή) handed down to them by their ancestors (1:18), '[i]gnorance (2:15), curiosity (3:15), suspicion of wrongdoing (2:12, 14–16) and aggressive hostility (3:13–14, 16; 4:4) were the public reactions which the Christians had encountered and under which they suffered'.[27] The situation is well illustrated in 4:3–4:

> For the time that is past was more than enough for carrying out the will of the Gentiles, having lived in sensuality, lusts, drunkenness, revelries, drinking parties, and lawless idolatries. In this they are surprised that you no longer join with them into the same flood of dissipation, and they malign you.

This verse provides us with an important key for understanding the nature of the suffering alluded to in 1 Peter. The difficulties being experienced by many of the Petrine readers, as we will note below, resulted not from an official policy of state-organised persecution, but instead involved various forms of social persecution beginning with astonishment and suspicion and leading to resentment, ostracism, verbal abuse, and perhaps in isolated cases more serious forms of persecution. And so '[i]f this precarious situation of innocent suffering was not to lead to disillusionment, despair, defection, and the ultimate demise of the movement in Asia Minor, those who suffered had to be provided with a persuasive rationale for remaining firm in their faith and resolute in their commitment to God, Jesus Christ, and one another'.[28] This 'persuasive rationale' finds embodiment in the form of a letter, the first letter of Peter. And at its heart is the message of what God has done for believers in Jesus Christ, the message of salvation: 'I have written to you briefly exhorting and witnessing that this is the true grace of God. Stand fast in it!' (1 Pet. 5:12).

---

[27] Elliott, *A Home for the Homeless*, 79.   [28] Elliott, *1 Peter*, 103.

PART I

Methodology

1

THEOLOGICAL-CRITICAL EXEGESIS

1. Introduction

This study is an exercise in what we might call 'theological-critical exegesis'[1] as opposed to (merely) 'historical-critical' or even 'historical-grammatical' exegesis (though it is no less than these). Historical criticism tends to focus on what lies *behind* the text rather than *in* the text itself. 'Historical criticism seeks to answer a basic question: to what historical circumstances does this text refer, and out of what historical circumstances did it emerge?'[2] Since the Enlightenment, most biblical scholars in the university or seminary have by and large adopted a strictly historical approach to the study of the biblical texts in order to concentrate on historical 'facts' rather than theological 'values'.[3] As a result, the text came to be viewed as 'a means to a historical end, namely, the reconstruction of what *really* happened'.[4] Theological-critical exegesis, on the other hand, does not dispense with all of the methods of historical criticism, but resists seeing them as an end in themselves. The difference between the two, then, lies not so much in methodology (though we will see some significant differences) but in the ultimate aim of interpretation. For the theological exegete, the goal of interpretation is to hear the word of God and to behold the glory of God in Scripture and to be transformed by it (personal transformation is preferred over historical reconstruction and doxology is preferred over methodology). Theological-critical exegesis, then, is to be governed by the following convictions (many of which will be enlarged upon below): (1) that the principal interest of the Bible's authors, of the text itself, and of the

---

[1] This term represents a blending of what Vanhoozer, 'Introduction', 22, calls 'theological criticism' and Childs, 'Toward Recovering Theological Exegesis', as the title indicates, labels 'theological exegesis'.
[2] Burnett, 'Historical Criticism', 290.
[3] See Vanhoozer, *Is There a Meaning?*, 284.
[4] Ibid., 285 (emphasis mine).

ongoing Christian community over time was theological: reading the Scriptures therefore meant coming to hear God's word, to know God better, and to be transformed by that knowing; (2) that the ultimate goal of biblical interpretation is beholding the glory of God in Scripture; (3) that there is a correspondence between the words of Scripture and the Word of God (the 'Scripture principle'); (4) that a proper reading of Scripture is that which attends to the whole of Scripture as canon (the 'canonical principle'); (5) that all theological interpretation is to be submitted to the biblical text (and not the interpreting community) as the ultimate authority and final arbiter on all theological matters; (6) that exegesis will be oriented towards specifically theological questions; (7) that scholarly tools and methods may be usefully employed in the theological exegesis of Scripture to the extent that they illuminate points 1–6 above; (8) that a theological interpretation of Scripture must occur 'in the Spirit'; (9) that theological interpretation will ideally be practised in community;[5] (10) that a theological interpretation of Scripture will be carried out in dialogue with other faith traditions (the 'catholic principle'); (11) that the present fragmentation of theology into a set of discrete and disconnected disciplines (i.e., Old Testament studies, New Testament studies, systematic theology, practical theology, church history, etc.) is to be resisted. While each discipline will have some inevitable division of labour, we must labour as far as possible to overcome these distinctions. Before moving on I want to say a little more about this fragmentation.

2. New Testament studies and systematic theology

In 1993 in his *Biblical Theology of the Old and New Testaments*, Brevard Childs spoke of the presence of 'an iron curtain [that] separated Bible from theology'.[6] The presence of this 'iron curtain' can be felt at many levels: the student wanting to relate one part of the university curriculum to another; the pastor seeking to bridge the gap between 'original meaning' and 'contemporary significance'; and 'the scholar trained according to accredited standards that guard the one discipline from what are typically regarded as the naïve or imperialistic efforts of the other'.[7]

One of the earliest attempts to distinguish 'biblical' theology from 'systematic' theology can be found in J. P. Spener's *Pia Desideria* (1675) in which he distinguished between *theologia biblica* (based on the original

---

[5] See Fowl and Jones, *Reading in Communion*; Vanhoozer, *Is There a Meaning?*, 410–12, 415–21, 430–1.

[6] Childs, *Biblical Theology*, xvi.   [7] Green, 'Scripture and Theology', 23.

meaning of the text) and *theologia scholastica* (the Aristotelianism of Protestant orthodoxy). In this context 'biblical theology' took on an aura of protest, of being 'more biblical' than the prevailing dogmatics.[8] At this point 'biblical theology' did not yet refer to a new or separate discipline. However, this situation was about to change under the influence of rationalism. In the seventeenth and eighteenth centuries scholars applied the tool of reason to the biblical text with the result that (1) only those parts of Scripture which passed the test of rational inquiry should be retained, and (2) there ought to be an 'insistence that the historical analysis of each biblical writing should precede any theological treatment of it'.[9] Spinoza (1632–77), for example, declared at the beginning of his *Theologico-Political Treatise*:

> I determined to examine the Bible afresh in a careful, impartial, and unfettered spirit, making no assumptions concerning it, and attributing to it no doctrine which I did not find clearly therein set down. With these precautions I constructed a method of Scriptural interpretation.[10]

For Spinoza, doctrine should have no bearing on the interpretation of a text; instead 'doctrine should be reached only after strict scrutiny and thorough comprehension of the Sacred Books ... and not be set up on the threshold, as it were, of inquiry'.[11] In the following century scholars such as Johann Salomo Semler (1725–91), Gotthilf Traugott Zachariä (1729–77), and Johann August Ernesti (1707–81) continued to teach that the study of the biblical texts must be carried out separately from and preliminary to the concerns of systematic or dogmatic theology.

The stage was then set for a highly significant statement by Johann Philipp Gabler (1753–1826),[12] in his inaugural lecture at the University of Altdorf entitled *De justo discrimine theologiae biblicae et dogmaticae regundisque recte utriusque finibus* (31 March 1787).[13] In this lecture Gabler warned against the 'inappropriate combination of the simplicity and ease of biblical theology with the subtility and difficulty of dogmatic theology'.[14] By 'biblical theology' he meant the inductive study of

---

[8] Carson, 'New Testament Theology', 796.
[9] Thielman, *Theology of the New Testament*, 22.
[10] Spinoza, *Chief Works*, 1: 8.   [11] Ibid.
[12] To borrow the words of Thielman, *Theology of the New Testament*, 23.
[13] Gabler, 'Oratio de iusto discrimine theologiae biblicae et dogmaticae regundisque recte utriusque finibus'. The English translation used here can be found in Sandys-Wunsch and Eldredge, 'Gabler'.
[14] Sandys-Wunsch and Eldredge, 'Gabler', 135.

the biblical texts,[15] and by 'dogmatic theology' he meant the changing philosophical systems of modern times.[16] As Carson observes, Gabler's 'primary appeal was not that the Bible must first be read historically … but that biblical theologians may properly go about their task without being directly bound by doctrinal aims'.[17] His proposal was soon widely adopted. For example, in the following century William Wrede composed his *Über Aufgabe und Methode der sogenannten neutestamentliche Theologie* (1897),[18] in which he attempted 'to resurrect Gabler's distinction between biblical and dogmatic theology, this time with reference specifically to New Testament theology'.[19] As the title of his work indicates ('So-Called [*sogenannten*] New Testament Theology'), Wrede claimed that 'the name New Testament theology is wrong', for '[t]he New Testament is not concerned merely with theology, but is in fact far more concerned with religion'.[20] Wrede's programmatic statement reads: 'I must state from the outset that my comments presuppose the strictly historical character of New Testament theology.'[21] Any attempt at a unified New Testament theology, let alone a synthesis with systematic theology, is a chimera.[22] As Wrede notes:

> Biblical theology has to investigate something from given documents … It tries to grasp it as objectively, correctly and sharply as possible. That is all. How the systematic theologian gets on with its results and deals with them – that is his own affair. Like every other real science, New Testament theology has its goal simply in itself, and is totally indifferent to all dogma and systematic theology. What could dogmatics offer it?[23]

Such thinking has resulted in the present drift toward the increasingly atomistic, in which biblical studies has been cut off from any obligation to systematic theology.[24]

Fortunately, a small but growing number of scholars have, in the past few years, sounded a strong challenge to the Enlightenment prejudice, whose goal, as Childs puts it, 'was to free the study of the Bible from

---

[15] See Ibid., 138–42.   [16] See Ibid., 144.
[17] Carson, 'New Testament Theology', 796.
[18] Gottingen: Vandenhoeck and Ruprecht, 1897; ET: 'The Task and Methods of "New Testament Theology"', in Morgan, *The Nature of New Testament Theology*, 68–116.
[19] Thielman, *Theology of the New Testament*, 24.
[20] Wrede, 'Task and Methods', 116.   [21] Ibid., 69.
[22] To borrow the words of Carson, 'New Testament Theology', 797.
[23] Wrede, 'Task and Methods', 69.
[24] To paraphrase Carson, 'New Testament Theology', 797.

the so-called heavy-hand of dogma',[25] and who are working toward the recovery of a theological understanding of Scripture. In this work I will be interacting with some of these scholars (the current chapter) and then applying the insights gleaned from this interaction as I seek to work out, in practice, a theological-critical study of the doctrine of salvation in 1 Peter (chapters 2–8). The aim of this study, as noted in the introduction to this book, is to seek to contribute to the overcoming of the present and unfortunate segregation of biblical studies and systematic theology and to further open up the way for a more fruitful dialogue between the two.

3.　Why do theological interpretation?

Before setting out the approach of this work (which I have called 'theological-critical exegesis'), I need to offer some justification for it. We have already considered some of the historical roots of the present divide between biblical studies and systematic theology. What reasons can we now give for wanting to bridge this divide through a consciously theological approach to biblical interpretation? A number of reasons could be put forward, but I offer what I consider to be the two most important.

It is true to the nature of Scripture.

The primary reason why Scripture should be interpreted *theo*logically is because it is ultimately the word (*logos*) of God and about God (*theos*) (which are both themselves issues of theology). Theological interpretation is ultimately the practice of God's Spirit in which both the original human authors and the ongoing community of readers participate in quite different ways.[26] As Vanhoozer points out, '[t]he Scriptures are the Spirit's work from first to last. The Spirit is involved in Scripture in the very messy historical process of producing Scripture – prompting, appropriating, and coordinating human discourse to present God's Word – as well as in the process of bringing about understanding of Scripture among present day readers.'[27] John Webster helpfully locates this whole process under the notion of sanctification which, '[i]n its broadest sense refers to the work of the Spirit of Christ through which creaturely realities are elected, shaped and preserved to undertake a role in the economy of salvation: creaturely realities are sanctified by divine use'.[28] The concept

---

[25] Childs, 'Toward Recovering Theological Exegesis', 121.
[26] See Vanhoozer, *Drama of Doctrine*, 226.　　[27] Ibid.
[28] Webster, *Holy Scripture*, 26.

of sanctification helpfully integrates both divine communicative action and the humanness of those elements which are appointed by God to the service of his self-presentation in Scripture. What makes the biblical text *Scripture*, then, is the fact that it is *these* particular texts that have been sanctified, that is, 'Spirit generated and preserved – *in* this field of action – the communicative economy of God's merciful friendship with his lost creatures'.[29] Inspiration, canonization, and interpretation, then, are all sub-themes of sanctification.[30]

Inspiration, as a sub-theme of the broader notion of revelation and sanctification, 'is a matter of the Spirit's prompting the human authors to say just what the divine playwright intended. Prompting – urging, assisting, recalling to mind, supplying the right words is the operative notion, the very thing Jesus assures the disciples the Spirit will do (John 14:26).'[31] Webster provides a helpful account of the nature of inspiration by means of a gloss on 1 Pet. 1:21 (an instance of systematic theology): 'No prophecy ever came by human will, but men and women moved by the Holy Spirit spoke from God.' He notes four things: (1) The leading theme of any doctrine of inspiration is captured by the words 'from God' (ἀπὸ θεοῦ): '[I]nspiration is not primarily a textual property but a divine movement and therefore a divine moving'.[32] (2) The operative expression 'from God' carries with it a negation: 'no prophecy ever came by human will' (οὐ θελήματι ἀνθρώπου): 'Talk of inspiration indicates that the general impulse of the biblical text is not human spontaneity … it is not a voluntary, self-originating movement, but a "being moved".'[33] (3) This 'being moved' is 'particularly appropriated to the Holy Spirit' who ensures that 'creaturely objects and causes are indeed *moved* realities'.[34] Inspiration, therefore, does not mean the elimination of creatureliness in the production of Scripture, but its right ordering so that it may 'fittingly assist in that work which is proper to God'.[35] (4) The Spirit generates language: '[T]he moving of the Spirit, the direction of the ἀπὸ θεοῦ, is to human communicative acts. Those moved by the Spirit *spoke* [ἐλάλησαν (ἀπὸ θεοῦ)].'[36] Inspiration is thus verbal: 'What is inspired is not simply the *matter* (*res*) of Scripture but its verbal *form* (*forma*).'[37]

Scripture thus represents both a divine and human communicative action. The challenge here is to affirm the realities of both the divine and human authors. Some 'high' views of inspiration, on the one hand,

---

[29] Ibid., 29 (emphasis his).   [30] See ibid., 30.
[31] Vanhoozer, *Drama of Doctrine*, 227–8.   [32] Webster, *Holy Scripture*, 36.
[33] Ibid., 37.   [34] Ibid.   [35] Ibid., 27.   [36] Ibid., 37 (emphasis his).
[37] Ibid., 38 (emphasis his).

have tended to so overemphasise divine authorship that the human authors only *appear* to be communicative agents. In John Rice's *Our God-Breathed Book*, the human author is reduced to a secretary who takes down dictation from God: 'A secretary is not ashamed to take dictation from man. Why would a prophet be ashamed to take dictation from God?'[38] Rice's theory of dictation borders on the textual equivalent of docetism (the Bible only appears to be a human book): 'The Scriptures are fundamentally the Word of God, not the word of men, except in some incidental and controlled and limited sense.'[39] The error in this theory is to 'construe the Spirit as a competing speaker who outshouts all others'.[40] In the end this theory fails to do justice to the humanity of the Scriptures (e.g., stylistic differences, diverse theological emphases, etc.).

Karl Barth, on the other hand, posits a

> fundamental discontinuity between human speech and the Word of God. Barth acknowledges that the human authors were 'inspired' in the sense that they were immediately related to the content of revelation, Jesus Christ himself, as commissioned witnesses. Inspiration has more to do with the special content of the witness rather than its verbal forms. The human witness becomes the Word of God only when the Spirit graciously appropriates the words for the purpose of self-revelation.[41]

Barth's theory, which construes Scripture as prophetic or apostolic witness, results in the textual equivalent of adoptionism. Under this view, however, it is difficult to conceive how anyone could know anything about God if there is no form of verbal communication on the part of God. As Abraham observes: 'Without his word, the alternative is not just a tentative, carefully qualified guessing at what God is doing, but a radical agnosticism.'[42] In the end, Scripture is neither a compendium of human writings employed by God in the act of communication (Barth), nor is it a collection of divinely dictated texts devoid of any real human history (Rice), it is rather the embodiment of both divine and human speech acts in written discourse.[43] Commenting on 1 Pet. 1:25, Calvin writes: '[N]o mention is made here of the Word which lies hid in the bosom of God, but that which has proceeded from his mouth, and has come to us ... God has purposed to speak to us by the apostles and prophets, and their

[38] Rice, *Our God-Breathed Book*, 287.   [39] Ibid., 141.
[40] Vanhoozer, *Drama of Doctrine*, 227.   [41] Vanhoozer, *First Theology*, 135–6.
[42] Abraham, *Divine Revelation*, 23.   [43] See Vanhoozer, *First Theology*, 131.

lips are the mouth of the one true God.'[44] The bottom line is that exegesis forfeits the right to be called *theological* when it fails to do justice to the priority of God as the ultimate author and end of Scripture.

Nevertheless, if we stop there we are in danger of isolating the divine activity simply to the production of the texts and we fail to develop a fully theological account of biblical interpretation. For the danger in relegating the Spirit's activity to the past is that interpretation in the present becomes solely a human affair (and the best method becomes historical criticism). However, as we noted in the introduction to this chapter, the principal aim of theological interpretation is to hear God's word, to know God better, and to be transformed by that knowing. Hearing, knowing, and being transformed all begin with and depend on the (prior) action of God and not humans (as my chapters on election and atonement will indicate). An account of the church's reading of Scripture, then, must be located within the broader context of the mystery of God's self-manifestation as Word. 'As Word, God is not absent or mute but present and communicative, not as it were waiting to be "made sense of" by our cognitive and interpretative activities, but accomplishing in us the knowledge of himself.'[45] As Word, affirms Webster, (1) God is self-communicative;[46] (2) that self-communication is a free and sovereign act;[47] and, as such, (3) it is therefore purposive, that is, it achieves its goal of establishing the knowledge of God in those to whom he manifests himself.[48]

The means by which God effects this knowledge and transformation is Holy Scripture. 'Holy Scripture is dogmatically explicated in terms of its role in God's self-communication, that is, the acts of Father, Son and Spirit which establish and maintain that saving fellowship with humankind in which God makes himself known to us and by us.'[49] How, then, are these two aspects of the Bible – both its humanness and its ability to mediate divine speech (the 'to us' and 'by us') – to be related? Webster proposes a *sacramental* account of the relationship between the two:

> The text is "sacramental" in that God's agency is real and effective and yet indirect – not in the sense of being pushed to the background, but in the sense that God speaks through the intelligible words of the text and acts in, with and under the acts of the church's reading of it.[50]

---

[44] Calvin, *Epistles of St. Peter*, 254.   [45] Webster, *Word and Church*, 64.
[46] Ibid.   [47] Ibid., 68.   [48] Ibid.   [49] Webster, *Holy Scripture*, 8.
[50] Webster, *Word and Church*, 74.

Thus for Webster, both word and work, speech and act coinhere. How, then, are these two aspects (speech and act) to be related to each other? According to speech act philosophers J. L. Austin and John Searle the basic unit of meaning is not simply the words of a sentence but the speech act. In uttering a sentence, says Searle, the speaker is performing at least three distinct kinds of acts: (1) *utterance acts* – the uttering of words (morphemes, sentences); (2) *propositional acts* (referring and predicating); and (3) *illocutionary acts* (stating, questioning, promising, commanding, etc.).[51] Then, to these he adds a fourth: (4) *perlocutionary acts* – the consequences or effects that speech acts have upon the feelings, thoughts, actions, etc. of hearers.[52] These distinctions enable Searle to distinguish between the *content* (words, reference and prediction, etc. [(1) and (2)]), the *force* (what we are *doing* with the content of our sentence, for example commanding, promising, etc. [(3)]), and the *effects* or *consequences* (convincing, persuading, deterring, etc. [(4)]) of what we are saying. Applied to the Word of God, speech act theory enables us to transcend the frequent (and false) dichotomy between 'God saying' (the propositional) and 'God being and acting' (the personal and performative).[53] Scripture, then, is 'neither simply the recital of the acts of God nor merely a book of inert propositions. Scripture is rather composed of divine-human speech acts that, through what they say, accomplish several authoritative cognitive, spiritual and social functions.'[54] Through Scripture the Spirit of God accomplishes, among other things, understanding (the knowledge of God), transformation (into the likeness of God), and worship (the glory of God).

We do it anyway so let's do it well.

The second reason why we should engage in theological interpretation is because we cannot avoid doing it so we need to learn to do it well. The fact is, we cannot avoid interpreting Scripture from within our own theological/ecclesial traditions and with our own agendas and philosophical presuppositions. We saw how, for Wrede, New Testament scholarship was essentially a historical enterprise that sought to free itself from the shackles of dogmatic presuppositions. However, as McGrath notes,

> the idea that biblical exegesis is a neutral or value-free enterprise is to be rejected: its methods and presuppositions are

---

[51] See Searle, *Speech Acts*, 24.   [52] See ibid., 25.
[53] See Vanhoozer, *First Theology*, 130.   [54] Ibid., 131.

seins- and *ortsgebunden.* The exegete brings to the text questions which he or she has been conditioned to ask through his or her experience, social position, political conviction, gender and so forth. The recognition that human thought – whether sociology, theology, ethics or metaphysics – arises in a specific social context is of fundamental importance to the sociology of knowledge.[55]

More recently, The Jesus Seminar has claimed that by applying certain 'critical', 'scientific', or 'scholarly' criteria they have been able to arrive at a definitive answer to the question 'What did Jesus *Really* Say?'[56] (the sub-subtitle of its 1993 publication, *The Five Gospels: The Search for the Authentic Words of Jesus*). Critical scholarship, for The Jesus Seminar, meant making 'empirical, factual evidence – evidence open to confirmation by independent, neutral observers – the controlling factor in historical judgments. Non-critical scholars are those who put dogmatic considerations first and insist that the factual evidence confirm theological premises.'[57] But as Wright, in a thorough critique of presuppositions and prejudices of The Jesus Seminar, observes,

> The idea that by historical investigation one might arrive at a position of unbiased objective certainty, of absolute unconditioned knowledge, about anything, has been shot to pieces by critiques from a variety of points of view. All knowledge is conditioned by the context and agenda of the knower; all reconstructions are somebody's reconstruction, and each 'somebody' sees the world through their own eyes and not their neighbor's. This is so widely acknowledged that one would have thought it unnecessary to state, let alone stress.[58]

Does this, then, mean that there is no such thing as genuine historical knowledge? Is it realistic to aim for an objective understanding of the text as it is or does ideology and theology so infect the relationship between text and reader that it makes such an aim unrealistic? According to Norman Holland, '[a]ll of us, as we read, use the literary

---

[55] McGrath, *Genesis of Doctrine*, 89 (see also 90).
[56] Emphasis added because that appears to be the sense in which the Seminar would have their title read, as their subtitle—*The Search for the <u>Authentic</u> Words of Jesus* (underline added)—would seem to indicate.
[57] Funk and Hoover, *The Five Gospels*, 34 (see also pp. 1, 3, 5, 7).
[58] Wright, 'Five Gospels but no Gospel', 96.

work to symbolize and finally to replicate ourselves'.[59] The authors of *The Postmodern Bible* concur:

> Biblical scholars have been slow to awaken from the dream in which positivist science occupies a space apart from interests and values, to awaken to the realization that our representations of and discourse about what the text meant and how it means are inseparable from what we *want* it to mean, from how we *will* it to mean.[60]

Is there an alternative to absolute disinterestedness ('objective knowledge') claimed by many historical critics (e.g., Wrede, The Jesus Seminar) and the absolute interestedness (subjective preference) of many postmoderns (e.g., Derrida, Fish, and the authors of the Postmodern Bible)? With Vanhoozer I opt for a 'mediating position that recognizes both the knowability of the text (e.g., a reality principle) and the partiality of the reader (e.g., a bias principle)'.[61] He refers to this mediating position as a 'moderate realism'[62] or 'critical hermeneutic realism'.[63] A critical realism insists that though our knowledge is partial, it can still be true.[64]

How can we do this? First, we need to recognise that certain presuppositions are necessary for interpreting the text (I have outlined many of these above). Bernard Lonergan has labelled presuppositionless exegesis as 'the *Principle of the Empty Head*'.[65] According to this principle, he says, 'the less one knows the better an exegete one will be'.[66] It is a principle, he suggests, that 'rests on a naïve intuitionism'.[67] He explains:

> The less that experience, the less cultivated that intelligence, the less formed that judgment, the greater the likelihood that the interpreter will impute to the author an opinion that the author never entertained. On the other hand, the wider the interpreter's experience, the deeper and fuller the development of his understanding, the better balanced his judgment, the greater likelihood that he will discover just what the author meant.[68]

[59] Cited in Bible and Culture Collective, *The Postmodern Bible*, 28 (see Holland, 'Unity Identity Text Self', *PMLA* 90 [1975]: 813–22).
[60] Bible and Culture Collective, *The Postmodern Bible*, 14.
[61] Vanhoozer, *Is There a Meaning?*, 382.
[62] Vanhoozer, *Drama of Doctrine*, 289.
[63] Vanhoozer, *Is There a Meaning?*, 300
[64] Vanhoozer, *Drama of Doctrine*, 289 (see also 291).
[65] Lonergan, *Method in Theology*, 157.
[66] Ibid.   [67] Ibid.   [68] Ibid.

The preunderstanding that informs this work is a traditionally Christian one: 'A fiduciary framework is the beginning of knowledge.'[69] More specifically, the present writer is committed to the Reformed expression of that faith. According to Moisés Silva, a 'Reformed' approach to biblical interpretation is governed by at least three presuppositions: (1) '[I]t is not feasible to separate biblical interpretation from theology';[70] (2) '[O]ur evangelical view of the unity of Scripture demands that we see the whole Bible as the context of any one part';[71] (3) '[A]n appreciation for the Calvinist or Augustinian doctrine of divine sovereignty and election'.[72] To these I would add a fourth: (4) A Reformed approach to biblical interpretation must, as I will indicate below, continually be open to being reformed. Just as *ecclesia reformata semper reformanda*, we may also say *interpretatio reformata semper reformanda*.

Second, the theological exegete must approach the text with the conviction that there is something in the text that transcends him or her, viz., 'the communicative act of another'.[73] How does the exegete do this? By acknowledging the text as 'other' and responding to what is there. In reality, this means 'acknowledging a communicative act for what it is, namely, a verbal work whereby an author says something about something to someone'.[74] Since the Bible is also a divine communicative act, its categories and content transcend the human existential condition. Thus the goal of interpretation must be to perceive the meaning resident in the text. What this means in practice will be taken up below.

Third, the interpreter needs to allow his or her own presuppositions to be modified, reshaped, or even completely altered by the text itself. Following Heidegger's formulation of the principle of the 'hermeneutical circle', Gadamer further stressed the way in which a text 'invites the correction and revision of preliminary understanding'.[75] Gadamer observes that '[i]nterpretation begins with fore-conceptions that are replaced by more suitable ones'.[76] Our 'fore-projections', he says, need to be 'constantly revised in terms of what emerges as [the interpreter] penetrates into the meaning … understanding what is there'.[77] This involves: (1) being open to the communicative act of another for what it is (see [2] above) and allowing that to confront, correct, and even change one's own preunderstanding (or what Gadamer refers to as 'being pulled

---

[69] Vanhoozer, *Drama of Doctrine*, 295.
[70] Silva, 'Case for Calvinistic Hermeneutics', 259.
[71] Ibid., 262.   [72] Ibid., 266.
[73] Vanhoozer, *Is There a Meaning?*, 394.   [74] Ibid., 395.
[75] Thiselton, *Two Horizons*, 304.   [76] Gadamer, *Truth and Method*, 269.
[77] Ibid.

up short by the text').[78] As Gadamer notes: 'A hermeneutically trained consciousness must be, from the start, sensitive to the text's alterity ... All that is being asked is that we remain open to the meaning of the *other* person or text.'[79] (2) It involves being aware of the preunderstanding that one brings to the text and how it may influence one's interpretation of it. We inevitably come to the text with our preunderstanding, however '[t]he important thing is to be aware of one's own bias, so that the text can present itself in all its otherness and thus assert its own truth against one's own fore-meanings'.[80] (3) Finally, it involves engaging in open dialogue with those outside of one's own interpretive tradition. I will say more on this below.

Preunderstanding is not a negative thing in itself, but, as Lewis points out, it helpfully calls attention to the provisional status of interpretation: 'Presuppositions carry only provisional authority until adequately tested and affirmed.'[81] As Gadamer has noted, ' "prejudice" means a judgment that is rendered before all the elements that determine a situation have been fully examined'.[82] Further examination may then either confirm or correct our preunderstanding. This is not a one-off event but the beginning of a continual process, since we are never able to separate fully our preunderstanding from subsequent understandings of the text (in this sense all interpretation remains provisional).[83] Gadamer described this process in terms of a 'hermeneutical circle', though it is probably better to speak of a 'hermeneutical spiral'. 'Instead of going round and round an endless hermeneutical circle, one can as it were "spiral in" on the truth, as one asks better questions of a text, and hears more accurate answers.'[84] As this description of the process indicates, all theological interpretation is to be submitted to the biblical text as the ultimate authority and final arbiter on all theological matters (point [5] above). The rest of this chapter will be devoted to outlining an approach to theological interpretation that respects these principles.

4.   Theological interpretation

The swing in postmodernism from author/text-centred interpretation to reader-centred interpretation is mirrored by two basic approaches to theological interpretation: a more reader-centred approach (the 'ruled

---

[78] Ibid., 270.   [79] Ibid., 271 (emphasis added).   [80] Ibid., 271–2.
[81] Lewis, 'Response to Presuppositions of Non-Evangelical Hermeneutics', 620.
[82] Gadamer, *Truth and Method*, 273.
[83] A point made by Thiselton, *Two Horizons*, 305.
[84] Carson, *Gagging of God*, 121.

reading' approach) and a more author/text centred approach (what I will call the 'literal sense' approach). I will begin by outlining the 'ruled reading' approach before moving on to the approach of this work, the literal sense approach.

'Ruled reading' approach

In his book, *Engaging Scripture*, Stephen Fowl sets out 'three different accounts of biblical interpretation'.[85] (1) The first account argues that biblical interpretation is *determinate* (the view of this work): 'The aim of this determinate interpretation is to produce, uncover, or illuminate the meaning of the biblical text.'[86] (2) The second account argues that interpretation is *indeterminate* or *anti-determinate*, since it rejects the claim that there is a single, determinate meaning in the text, in favour of the notion that '[n]obody's interpretation is better than anyone else's; everyone has the right to his/her interpretation; it is rude and not inclusive to fail to accept someone's interpretation as true for that person'.[87] (3) Fowl opts instead for what he calls 'underdetermined interpretation'.[88] According to this third account of biblical interpretation, the quest for (determinate) textual meaning is abandoned in favour of 'interpretive interests': 'The central interpretive claim here is that our discussions, debates, and arguments about texts will be better served by eliminating claims about textual meaning in favor of more precise accounts of interpretive aims, interests, and practices.'[89] But whose interests should theological interpreters of Scripture be looking to? (a) The persons responsible for producing the text (the biblical authors)? (b) The reading communities seeking to use Scripture for a certain end? or (c) God as the ultimate author of Scripture? Fowl and Jones opt for the second option: 'As a social activity [of the church], interpretation is conformed, constrained, and determined by the political constitution of those contexts in which interpretation takes place.'[90]

The result of such an approach, however, is that the aims of the biblical text, that is, the aims, interests and intentions of the divine and human biblical authors who produced it, become subordinated to the aims, interests and intentions of the particular interpretive communities. In other words, the question 'What does Scripture mean?' is supplanted by the question 'How does the church use Scripture?'[91] Thus, it is not the text

---

[85] Fowl, *Engaging Scripture*, 32.   [86] Ibid.   [87] Ibid., 40.
[88] See ibid., 33, 56–61.   [89] Ibid., 56.
[90] Fowl and Jones, *Reading in Communion*, 17.
[91] Vanhoozer, *Drama of Doctrine*, 169.

itself but the way that the text is used by the church that becomes normative. For Fowl '[l]imiting a text's meaning to the author's intention presupposes a definitive account of what the meaning of a text is (or ought to be)'.[92] The problem with this, he insists, is that 'our situation is marked by interminable debate and disagreement about just what the meaning of a text is'.[93] Thus, he concludes, 'we should eliminate talk of "meaning" in favor of other terms that will suit our interpretive interests and put a stop to futile discussions'.[94]

Further justification for the primacy of the interpretive community over that of the biblical author is supplied by Robert Wall, who appeals to the church's 'Rule of Faith' (also appealed to by Fowl). At the beginning of his essay, Wall proposes that 'Scripture's performance as a persuasive word and enriching sacrament depends upon interpretation that constrains the theological teaching of a biblical text by the church's "Rule of Faith." Simply put, the Rule of Faith is the grammar of theological agreements which Christians confess to be true and by which all of Scripture is rendered in forming a truly Christian Faith and life.'[95] The primacy of the community's Rule in rendering a truly theological interpretation of Scripture is justified on the basis that it was the Christian community which, on the basis of its 'Rule of Faith', decided which writings should be canonised in the first place: 'the church preserved and canonized certain writings, and then formed the Christian Bible with them, because (when used and used properly) these writings agree with the Rule of Faith in content and consequence'.[96] Consequently, 'a theological reading of Scripture is the primary practice of a diverse community of faithful interpreters who together apply the church's Rule of Faith to the biblical text to lead all believers toward theological understanding'.[97] Thus, concludes Wall, 'the canon that measures the legitimacy and efficacy of the Bible's interpretation is the church's Rule of Faith'.[98]

However, there are number of problems with the 'Ruled Reading' approach: First, it should be noted that interpretive communities are not always right, nor do they always agree on what is right (they are communities of saints *as well as* sinners).[99] Therefore, to what 'authority' should one appeal in order to adjudicate between competing readings of Scripture among the various interpretive communities? Scripture itself? The Rule of Faith (= tradition)? Or should we just accept as many

---

[92] Fowl, 'The Role of Authorial Intention', 78.   [93] Ibid.
[94] Ibid., 80.   [95] Wall, 'Reading the Bible', 104.   [96] Ibid.
[97] Ibid.   [98] Ibid., 96.   [99] Vanhoozer, *Is there a Meaning?* 379.

interpretations as there are interpretive communities (pluralism [Derrida, Fish, Fowl (?)])?

Second (and related to the first), as Fowl and Jones themselves admit, the 'recognition of the plurality of interpretive interests does not resolve the important question, "What interpretive interest should one pursue in any given situation?"'[100] They suggest that 'an answer will only be found within the political constitution of the various contexts in which interpretation takes place ... Hermeneutics is inevitably ... a "political" discipline.'[101] The question that then needs to be asked is: 'Why *their* interpretive interest?'[102] As Tanner notes, 'the appeal here to communal norms is only plausible if the problem of diversity in Christian practice is far less serious than it appears to be'.[103] Postliberals like Lindbeck try to get around this problem (i.e., the lack of Christian consensus) by suggesting that at least well-trained or competent Christians will so agree (and therefore those learning from them will as well).[104] However, the problem with this is that 'there is no noncircular way of specifying who the competent players are in a situation characterised by this much disagreement ... Appeal to communal norms will not guarantee, then, as postliberals want to, stability underneath the changing forms of history.'[105]

Third, if appeal is made to *the* [?] Rule of Faith then we need to ask: Which rule of faith are we talking about? And how catholic is the Rule of Faith? And is *catholicity* in itself an adequate criterion by which a particular interpretation is adjudged legitimate? The first two questions cannot be easily answered; the third is given a resounding 'No' below.

Fourth, while the Rule of Faith may be an adequate summary of 'the heart of the Christian faith',[106] it is by no means comprehensive enough to serve as a criterion for assessing the legitimacy or otherwise of one's interpretation of every part of Scripture. The 'Rule of Faith', as Fowl points out, is helpful in so far as it 'sets out the *boundaries* within which interpretation must operate if Christians are to read Scripture properly'.[107] However, it is more difficult to specify how the Rule is able to offer any positive guidance for determining, for example, who were the 'spirits' of 1 Pet. 3:19, where were they imprisoned, and what was the content of Christ's proclamation to them? Or, what is the relationship between

---

[100]   Fowl and Jones, *Reading in Communion*, 16.   [101]   Ibid.
[102]   Vanhoozer, *Drama of Doctrine*, 174.   [103]   Tanner, *Theories of Culture*, 141.
[104]   See Lindbeck, *The Nature of Doctrine*, 100.
[105]   Tanner, *Theories of Culture*, 142, 141.
[106]   Wall, 'Reading the Bible', 89.
[107]   Fowl, *Engaging Scripture*, 8 (emphasis mine).

divine sovereignty and human disobedience in 1 Pet. 2:8? And so on. As Vanhoozer notes, '[t]he Rule ... is hardly a hermeneutical panacea; one cannot solve every interpretative dispute simply by appealing to the *regula fidei*'.[108]

Fifth, Wall is wrong to ascribe primacy to the Rule of Faith on the basis that it was the Christian community which, on the basis of this Rule, decided which writings should be canonised in the first place.[109] As Vanhoozer points out, '[t]he church never was without Scripture; it had the Law and the prophets from the beginning, then later the Gospels and the epistles ... The church looked to the Old Testament from the start because it served as the crucial interpretative framework for understanding the history of Jesus.'[110] In Jn 5:39 Jesus challenged his hearers to 'search the Scriptures ... it is these that bear witness of me'. So, for example, when Peter wants to explain the significance of Jesus' passion he turns to Isa. 53 (2:21–5), or the Passover and Exodus (1:18–19), or the Old Testament sacrificial system in general (3:18).[111] 'To think of the church as the context within which Scripture becomes canon appears plausible in terms of history and sociology, but it is theologically inadequate.'[112] A theological account of the canon, as we noted above, rather views canonisation as a subset of the Spirit's sanctifying action:

> The holiness of the biblical canon is acquired, and indicates the use of the canonical texts by God as an instrument of his self-attestation. 'Sanctification' here is used to cover the entire range of processes of which the text is at the centre: processes of production (including tradition and redaction history); processes of canonization; and processes of interpretation. Sanctified in this way, the canonical texts are, then, a field of divine activity.[113]

The effect of this is, therefore, to indicate (1) that it is the canon which constitutes the church (and not vice versa), and (2) that it is the canon by which all of the speech of the church is normed.

Sixth, by making the Rule of Faith and not Scripture the 'canon that measures the legitimacy ... of the Bible's interpretation',[114] Wall, and others like him, has effectively elevated tradition above Scripture (giving it a magisterial rather than ministerial role) and the church's

---

[108] Vanhoozer, *Drama of Doctrine*, 205.
[109] Wall, 'Reading the Bible', 104.
[110] Vanhoozer, *Drama of Doctrine*, 149, 148.   [111] See Chapter 3.
[112] Vanhoozer, *Drama of Doctrine*, 149.
[113] Webster, *Word and Church*, 32.   [114] Wall, 'Reading the Bible', 96.

formulations of the truth above the truth itself. However, as Webster correctly notes:

> Creeds and confessions have no freestanding existence; they are not a replacement for, or improvement on Holy Scripture; they are not even a nonnegotiable, normative 'reading' of Scripture. Creeds and confessions are wholly a function of the Word of God, which is given in Scripture as, through the power of the Spirit, the risen Christ testifies to himself.[115]

These inadequacies lead me to propose a different (though hardly new) approach to the theological interpretation of Scripture.

'Literal sense' approach

In this section I want to outline very briefly the basic methodological approach to theological exegesis taken in this work. The approach is set out under three headings (each of which contribute to an understanding of the text's 'literal sense'): (1) 'Literal sense exegesis'; (2) Intercanonical conversation (conference table 1); (3) Intercatholic conversation (conference table 2). I mention this simply in order to indicate that in (3) I am still dealing with issues of meaning (or illocution) and have not moved on to significance (or perlocution). It will become clear that (3) is an integral part in the interpretive process. Also, it should be noted that, as my discussion on the nature of Scripture and preunderstanding has already indicated, theological reflection does not begin at (3) but is already present at (1) and is only further refined in (3).

'Literal sense exegesis'

In contrast to the ruled reading approach, I heed the call of Vanhoozer to

> recognise the ecclesial and hermeneutical priority of God, specifically, the priority of his speech agency or 'authorship' of Scripture. To interpret the Bible theologically is to interpret it as the verbal communication of God that bears witness to God's historical communicative actions in the history of Israel and of Jesus Christ. There are indeed many possible interpretive aims and interests, but the people of God must above all concern themselves with what God is saying, and doing, in and through the Scriptures.[116]

---

[115] Webster, 'Confession and Confessions', 125.
[116] Vanhoozer, *First Theology*, 290.

To do this, suggests Vanhoozer, we do not need another interpretive aim, but rather an interpretive *norm*.[117] This norm reflects not the interest of some interpretive community, but rather the divine–human communicative interest embodied in written discourse (= Scripture).[118] Theological interpretation, then, is to be oriented toward the subject matter of Scripture and committed to determining the meaning placed there (i.e., in the text) by its divine and human authors. This is another way of saying that the theological interpreter must take seriously the literal sense (or 'natural sense' or 'plain meaning') of Scripture.[119]

What is the literal sense of Scripture and how can we arrive at it? The literal sense of Scripture is related to two things: authorial intention and authorial convention. Intention relates to what an author is doing in, with, and through the text (that is to say, meaning is 'a matter of intending to perform an illocutionary … act').[120] Convention relates to the rules (shared by both author and reader) governing communicative acts (in this case semantic and generic rules). A combination of intention and convention is important for discerning a text's meaning. The author's intentions will be understood in general if the reader understands its meaning, that is, understands the semantic rules governing its elements.[121] My previous sentence represents an illocutionary act (i.e., a statement). My illocutionary act was performed by making a number of marks on the page. However, an illocutionary act, as we have already seen, cannot simply be reduced to this. What, then, is the difference between making marks on a page and performing an illocutionary act? 'One difference is that the sounds or marks one makes in the performance of an illocutionary act are characteristically said to *have meaning*, and a second related difference is that one is said to *mean something* by the utterance of those sounds or marks.'[122] What is it that gives the marks on this page meaning? The question must be answered by an appeal to both authorial *intention* and *convention*. Gilbert Ryle illustrates this well in discussing the difference between a wink and a blink (note the combination of intention and convention):

> Two boys swiftly contract the eyelids of their right eyes. In the first boy this is only an involuntary twitch; but the other

---

[117] Ibid., 291.   [118] Ibid.

[119] I have borrowed the term 'literal sense exegesis' from Wall, 'Canonical Context', 170, n. 4, who defines 'literal sense' as 'the sense an exegeted text plainly makes, given the words used and their grammatical relations, its rhetorical role within a particular composition, and the composition's role within the wider biblical canon; that is, the literal sense of a biblical text is a literary-critical and not a historical-critical construction'.

[120] Searle, *Speech Acts*, 44.   [121] To paraphrase ibid., 48–9.

[122] Ibid., 42.

is winking conspiratorially to an accomplice. At the lowest or thinnest level of description the two contractions of the eyelids may be exactly alike. From a cinematograph-film of the two faces there might be no telling which contraction, if either, was a wink, or which, if either, was a mere twitch. Yet there remains the immense but unphotographable difference between a twitch and a wink. For the wink is to try to signal to someone in particular, without the cognizance of others, a definite message [intention] according to an already understood code [convention] … We are just drawing the familiar distinction between a voluntary, intentional, and, in this case, collusive and code-governed contraction of the eyelids from an involuntary twitch.[123]

The difference between a blink and a wink, then, is that the latter represents a rule-governed form of intentional behaviour. Searle makes a similar distinction between what he calls 'brute' and 'institutional' facts.[124] For example,

[a] marriage ceremony, a baseball game, a trial, and a legislative action involve a variety of physical movements, states, and raw feels [brute facts], but a specification of one of these events only in such terms is not so far a specification of it as a marriage ceremony, baseball game, a trial, or a legislative action [institutional facts].[125]

In other words, the institutional event (e.g., baseball) may be performed by certain physical actions (e.g., swinging a piece of wood horizontally at a small sphere [a brute fact]) but cannot be reduced to them.[126] It is only given the institution of baseball that certain physical actions (such as swinging a piece of wood, hitting a small sphere, and running towards a square plate [brute facts]) constitute a homerun. The formula, then, would be: 'X counts as Y in context C'.[127] Making marks on a page, then, constitutes a brute fact; performing a speech act, on the other hand (i.e., giving a command, making a promise, stating a fact, etc.), is an institutional and, therefore, a rule-governed (convention) and intentional form (intention) of behaviour.[128] Or to put it another way, a writer intends that his or her intention(s) will be recognised by means of the

---

[123] Ryle, *Collected Papers*, 2: 480–1 (see also his example on 484).
[124] See Searle, *Speech Acts*, 50–3.   [125] Ibid., 51.
[126] See the example in Ibid., 52.   [127] Ibid.   [128] See ibid., 40, 57–61.

reader's knowledge of certain rules governing the elements of his or her communicative act.[129] As Vanhoozer notes:

> It is the *author's* use of words in communicative action that determines their particular sense. True, words have a range of verbal or conventional senses, but the way authors employ linguistic and literary conventions usually indicates which of the many conventional senses (and there may be more than one) are intended. The natural sense, in short, is the authorially *intended* sense: the sense the words bear when used in *this* context by *this* author.[130]

Understanding those linguistic and literary conventions (which needs to be done in light of the linguistic/cultural world within which they were originally performed) is necessary for understanding the author's intention = the literal sense (the literal sense is thus the literary sense). Thus, in this work I employ a number of the tools of historical, grammatical, and literary criticism in order to arrive at the author's intended meaning.

Intercanonical conversation (conference table 1)

At this point we need to take into account the criticism of Stephen Fowl against authorial intention since it impinges on 1 Peter's extensive use of the Old Testament, especially his Christological reading of Isaiah 53 in 2:22–5. Fowl contends that authorial intention is insufficient to explain 'christological readings of various OT texts. A single meaning determined by authorial intention will either force Christians into rather implausible arguments about the communicative intention of Isaiah, for example, or lead them to reduce the christological aspect of those passages into a subsidiary or parasitic role.'[131] But is this really the case? Here the theological interpreter must employ a further tool, this time from the toolbox of canonical criticism. Canonical criticism, as I am employing it here, does not refer to the final form of a particular biblical book (though it is no less than that), but rather the theological role that book plays within the completed canon of Scripture. How does this relate to literal sense exegesis and authorial intention? Vanhoozer suggests that

> [t]he task of literal interpretation is to say what authors have done with their words. If one takes divine authorship of Scripture

---

[129] To paraphrase Searle's own analysis (*Speech Acts*, 49–50).
[130] Vanhoozer, *First Theology*, 292.
[131] Fowl, 'The Role of Authorial Intention', 81.

seriously, then literal interpretation must have recourse to the canonical context, for the meaning of the parts is related to the whole of Scripture. The literal sense of Scripture as intended by God is the sense of the canonical act (the communicative act when seen in the context of the canon).[132]

In the case of 1 Peter's Christological interpretation of Isaiah 53, does this mean that, at a canonical level, the divinely intended meaning of Isaiah 53 in 1 Pet. 2:22–5 has gone beyond or even contravened the human author's (the author of Isaiah 53) originally intended meaning? Or did the author of Isaiah 53 actually *intend* a Christological fulfilment for this passage? According to 1 Pet. 1:10–12, the prophet Isaiah was aware that his prophecy was not for his time but awaited a future Christological fulfilment:

> Concerning this salvation, the prophets who prophesied concerning the grace that has come to you, searched and inquired, inquiring as to what or what kind of time the spirit of Christ in them was indicating, when he predicted the sufferings [destined] for Christ and the glories after these sufferings. *It was revealed to [the prophets]* that they were serving not themselves but rather you in these things, which now have been announced to you by those who proclaimed the good news to you by the Holy Spirit sent from heaven, into which things angels long to look.

In this passage Peter makes the following claims pertinent to the present study: (1) That Old Testament prophets were 'actively seeking enlightenment on the issue of the Messianic times and the grace which would extend to the Gentiles';[133] (2) that the Spirit informing the Old Testament prophets, the Spirit of Christ, was the same Spirit at work in those who proclaimed the gospel to the Gentile Christians;[134] and (3) most importantly for us, '[h]e claims not only that the OT prophets were ministering ultimately to believers in the eschaton, but that the prophets *knew* it by revelation'.[135] Thus, according to 1 Pet. 1:10–12, Isaiah *intended* to announce in advance the death and resurrection of Christ ('the sufferings [destined] for Christ and the glories after these sufferings') even though the exact details of these events were beyond

---

[132] Vanhoozer, *First Theology*, 292.
[133] McCartney, 'The Use of the Old Testament', 40.
[134] See ibid., 41.   [135] Ibid. (emphasis his).

his immediate comprehension. E. D. Hirsh, whose work on intentionality is well known, offers the following helpful illustration from the history of science:

> Joseph Priestley has been credited with having isolated oxygen, because he observed that combustion required a certain kind of gas, which he successfully isolated. But because he mistakenly adhered to the phlogiston theory, Priestley called his combustion-inducing gas *dephlogisticated air*. Despite that peculiar and, in the event, wrong description, historians of science rightly allegorize dephlogisticated air as *oxygen*. Why is the allegory legitimate? Because in saying *dephlogisticated air* Priestley referred to and **intended** to refer to a gas we currently understand to be oxygen.[136]

In the same way we can say that Isaiah intended to prophesy of Christ's death and resurrection (as 1 Pet. 1:10–12 indicates) even though his comprehension of these events was greatly limited. Thus we could say that a Christological fulfilment was in accord with authorial intention but went beyond authorial comprehension (thus while there is no contradiction between divine and human intention here there is a gap between divine and human comprehension). As Vanhoozer notes:

> The canon is a complete and completed communicative act structured by a divine authorial intention. *The divine intention does not contravene the intention of the human author but rather supervenes on it.* In the same way, the canon does not change or contradict the meaning of Isaiah 53 but supervenes on it and specifies its referent. In speaking of the Suffering Servant, Isaiah was referring to Christ (viz., God's gracious provision for Israel and the world), just as Priestley, speaking of dephlogisticated air, was referring to oxygen.[137]

Thus, as he goes on to note, the dual authorship of Scripture qualifies, but does not overthrow, the notion of meaning as intentional communicative action.[138] In the end this is not an appeal to the *sensus plenior* of a biblical text (a notion that is rejected here),[139] but rather, as Carson puts it, 'it

---

[136] Hirsch, 'Transhistorical Intentions', 562–3 (emphasis his; bold mine).
[137] Vanhoozer, *Is there a Meaning?*, 265 (emphasis his).   [138] See ibid.
[139] See Moo, 'The Problem of *Sensus Plenior*', 179–211.

is an acknowledgement that with greater numbers of pieces of the jigsaw puzzle provided, the individual pieces and clusters of pieces are seen in new relationships not visible before'.[140] (It should be noted at this point that 1 Peter's use of the Old Testament extends beyond just prophecy and fulfilment, but also includes such methods as 'midrash' and 'pesher' [e.g., 1 Pet. 2:4–10],[141] as well as typology [1 Pet. 1:19; 1 Pet. 3:19–22], none of which violate authorial intention.)[142]

Using a different analogy, G. B. Caird in his *New Testament Theology* speaks of what he has termed the 'conference table approach':

> The presupposition of our study is simply stated: to write a New Testament theology is to preside at a conference of faith and order. Around the table sit the authors of the New Testament, and it is the presider's task to engage them in a colloquium about theological matters which they themselves have placed on the agenda'.[143]

In a similar way, Vanhoozer speaks of the canonical 'SBL':

> [W]e may speak of the 'society' of biblical literature, where the focus is on the voices in Scripture itself, together with their typical communicative practices ... Understanding these texts is less a matter of being socialized into a scholarly society than of being textualized (so to speak) into the company of the canon.[144]

As these images suggest, a canonical approach to interpretation is concerned with the distinctive witness of each writer as well as the distinctive contribution each makes to the overall canonical witness (and vice versa). Thus the canonical interpreter seeks 'to relate the different ideas of particular biblical writers and canonical units together in contrapuntal yet complementary ways, to expose the self-correcting ... and mutually-informing ... whole of New Testament theology'.[145] In this way the rule or norm for the theological interpreter is canonical and not catholic (in the sense that it is the former that norms the latter and not vice versa). While this is not a strong focus in this work (understanding Peter on his own merits and bringing that understanding into

---

[140] Carson, 'Unity and Diversity', 91.
[141] See Bauckham, 'James, 1 and 2 Peter, Jude', 310–12.
[142] See Klein, Blomberg and Hubbard, *Biblical Interpretation*, 183–5.
[143] Caird, *New Testament Theology*, 18.
[144] Vanhoozer, *Drama of Doctrine*, 212.   [145] Wall, 'Canonical Context', 179.

conversation with systematic theology is), where appropriate I seek to bring 1 Peter into conversation with the other biblical authors in order both to highlight Peter's distinctive witness and also to offer a 'thicker description'[146] of what I believe is Peter's witness.

Intercatholic conversation (conference table 2)

Because our knowledge is only partial, suggests Osborne, we need an ' "interpretive realism" that is in constant dialogue with the various communities of faith in order to refine and reformulate theories on the basis of further evidence or more coherent models'.[147] *Fallibilism*, suggests Vanhoozer, is a matter of a person's willingness to submit their beliefs to critical testing. Basically, it means submitting one's beliefs to two tests in particular: '(1) the canonical: Does the interpretation do justice to the parts and to the whole of Scripture? (2) the catholic: Does the interpretation accord with the Christian tradition?'[148] The former has priority over the latter (and hence I have dealt with them in that order) in that 'the claim to be "canonical" (viz., "according to the Scriptures") should be tempered by the claim to be "catholic" ("according to tradition")'.[149] However, it is also to say that the 'canon is properly realized only by a plurality of interpretative traditions [the catholic]'.[150] This, then, is our second 'conference table' and it involves a conversation between 1 Peter and the different faith/theological traditions (e.g., Reformed, Neo-orthodox, Lutheran, Arminian, Pelagian, Wesleyan, etc.). This happens at two levels in this book. First, and most obviously, it takes place at a more exegetical level through conversation with the various commentaries (including monographs and articles) on the text of 1 Peter written from within a variety of theological traditions. Second, and most distinctively for this work, it involves bringing the results of my exegetical study of those texts in 1 Peter relating to salvation into dialogue with the writings of systematic theologians – dealing with the same topics – from various theological traditions (see chapters 7–8 below).

What then is the proper place for systematic theology in biblical interpretation? For many scholars interpretation should be carried out

---

[146] See Vanhoozer, *Is there a Meaning?* 313–14.
[147] Osborne, *Hermeneutical Spiral*, 413.
[148] Vanhoozer, *Drama of Doctrine*, 303.
[149] Ibid. [150] Ibid., 422.

exclusively in the following direction (in agreement with Spinoza, Gabler, Wrede, and others):[151]

Exegesis ⟶ Biblical Theology ⟶ [Historical Theology] ⟶ Systematic Theology

However, not only is such a paradigm naïve, it is undesirable. As we have already noted above, '[n]o exegesis is ever done in a vacuum. If every theist is in some sense a systematician, then he is a systematician *before* he begins his exegesis.'[152] Carson then proposes a better model:

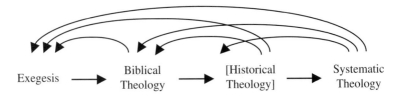

Exegesis ⟶ Biblical Theology ⟶ [Historical Theology] ⟶ Systematic Theology

In this diagram there are feedback lines as well as lines going forward. The lines going forward are important in so far as they recognise that the norm for any theological statements we make is canonical Scripture. Nevertheless, the feedback lines remind us that our theology is, at the very same time, shaping our exegesis. Packer writes:

> The maxim that exegesis and biblical interpretation are for the sake of an adequate theology is true; yet if one stops there one has told only half the story. The other half, the complementary truth which alone can ward off the baleful misunderstanding that a particular rational orthodoxy is all that matters, is that the main reason for seeking an adequate systematic theology is for the sake of better and more profound biblical interpretation.[153]

In the end, biblical exegesis cannot be separated from the concerns of systematic theology. In effect, this means that '[systematic] theology operates best when it is a kind of gloss on Scripture – a discursive

---

[151] The diagram is from Carson, 'Unity and Diversity', 91.
[152] Ibid.   [153] Packer, 'Preaching as Biblical Interpretation', 188.

reiteration or indication of the truth of the Christian gospel as it is encountered in the gospel'.[154] Defined in this way we would be hard pressed to separate the two disciplines quite as neatly as modern scholarship has done. In the end the process might better be diagrammed like this:

**Hermeneutical situation:
The presence of the living Christ**

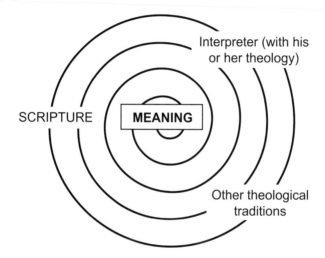

SCRIPTURE

MEANING

Interpreter (with his or her theology)

Other theological traditions

As this diagram indicates, the theological exegete of Scripture (along with all of his or her theological baggage) enters the hermeneutical spiral with the aim of discerning the communicative intentions of Scripture's divine and human authors in order to hear God's word and as a result to know God better. The Christian reader enters the spiral, as we have already noted, not on the basis of his or her own initiative but on the basis of God's initiative-taking freedom and sovereignty in making himself known to him or her. The reader therefore 'does not enter the hermeneutical spiral from the outside, or escape from it by transcendent theory; she does not occupy a position of superiority or neutrality, from which the situation can be surveyed at a distance and judgments can be made about it … For it is a situation in which we are addressed by the God and

---

[154] Webster, *Holy Scripture*, 130.

Father of our Lord Jesus Christ.'[155] Therefore the 'situation' in which hermeneutics takes place, as noted in the diagram, is 'the presence of the living Christ' by whose Spirit God's speech is encountered in the very act of reading. Moreover, as the diagram again indicates, this act is ultimately a communal and not an individual event: 'The Spirit's leading readers into all truth is a matter of nurturing a Pentecostal conversation about the correct interpretation of the Word's past meaning *and* present significance.'[156] We spiral closer to the meaning of the text as we carry out our interpretation prayerfully (in the presence of Christ), humbly (in submission to the Spirit), and dialogically (in conversation with the community it [i.e., the text] has brought into being).

This second dialogue or conversation does a number of things: First, it provides a secondary set of checks and balances for my own exegetical work. Since my exegesis of 1 Peter is carried out by a fallible interpreter operating within a certain spatio-temporal context, it is necessary, therefore, in order to balance out my own parochialism, to submit my exegesis not only to a canonical but also a catholic test.[157] Second,

the[se] checks and balances are reimagined as interecclesial conversations that continue to guide the whole church in its various ecumenical conversation ... Informed readings of biblical texts and ecclesial contexts can be more easily linked together, particular communions with particular NT writers, in order to define the normative checks and balances of a complementary conversation that maintains and legitimizes traditional distinctives, on the one hand, with the prospect of correcting a tendency toward triumphal sectarianism on the other.[158]

Third, it allows 1 Peter to provide its own checks and balances for the work of systematic theology. This is important, for ultimate authority must be accorded to the canonical over the catholic, the textual over the traditional, the scriptural over the communal. Fourth, it shapes and sharpens my own understanding of 1 Peter's doctrine of salvation. As we noted above, the task of biblical interpretation relates not only to the literal and canonical, but also to the theological and interecclesial (and beyond that to the practical and doxological). Fifth, it recognises, on the one hand, that texts have determinate meaning, but, on the other, that no

---

[155] Webster, *Word and Church*, 64.
[156] Vanhoozer, *Is there a Meaning?*, 421.
[157] See also Vanhoozer, *Drama of Doctrine*, 322; Wolterstorff, *Divine Discourse*, 238.
[158] Wall, 'Canonical Context', 182.

one person or tradition can lay absolute claim to having discovered all there is to that meaning. Thus, approximately 20 percent of this book is devoted to this intercatholic theological conversation or dialogue.

5.　　Conclusion

The theological interpretation of Scripture, it has been suggested, rests on the presupposition of Scripture's dual authorship as a divine–human communicative action enacted in written discourse. This means that theological interpretation is to be oriented toward the subject matter of Scripture and committed to determining the meaning placed there (in the text) by the divine and human authors. I suggested that this is another way of saying that the theological interpreter must take seriously the literal sense (= the literary sense = the authorially intended meaning) of Scripture. While the theological interpreter invariably and necessarily comes to the text with his or her theological convictions (or presuppositions), I also maintained that 'the form and content of a communicative act – what it is and what it is about – can be known with relative adequacy'.[159] We then noted that this is best achieved through what I have called the 'literal sense' approach. This approach is comprised of three components: (1) 'Literal sense exegesis': discerning the sense an exegeted text plainly makes given its propositional content, illocutionary force, and rhetorical role within a particular composition. (2) 'Intercanonical conversation': the willingness to submit our interpretive results to the canonical witness: 'Does the interpretation do justice to the parts and to the whole of Scripture?'[160] (3) 'Intercatholic conversation': the willingness to submit our interpretive results to the catholic witness: 'Does the interpretation accord with the Christian tradition?'[161] All of this, I said, takes place in the presence of Christ by whose Spirit God's speech is encountered in the very act of interpretation. For this work, this will involve bringing the results of our exegetical study (chapters 2–6) into dialogue with the various theological traditions (Reformed, Lutheran, Pelagian, Wesleyan, etc.) (chapters 7–8). Together, these three components will enable a theologically 'thicker' description of the text while at the same time providing a series of checks and balances for the interpretive enterprise.

---

[159] Vanhoozer, *Is there a Meaning?*, 367.
[160] Vanhoozer, *Drama of Doctrine*, 303.　　[161] Ibid.

PART II

Literal Sense Exegesis

2

CHOSEN FOR SALVATION
Election in 1 Peter

1.   1 Peter 1:1–2: chosen by God: the basis, means, and purpose of election

It is appropriate that we begin our discussion of salvation in 1 Peter with an exegesis of those passages that treat the subject of election, since it is chronologically the beginning of God's personal dealing with believers in grace. As such, election represents the first step in God's sovereign and gracious plan in bringing salvation to believers. Our discussion of Petrine soteriology thus begins in eternity past with God's sovereign and eternal election of some to salvation (1:1–2; 2:4–10) and of others to damnation (2:8).

The significance that Peter attaches to the concept of election is signalled from the very outset of the letter by this declaration of his readers' status as 'elect' (by God) cast in a proto-Trinitarian framework 'that presupposes the divine actions that generate the elect community of believers: God's choice, the Spirit's sanctifying acts, and Christ's giving his life's blood'.[1] This carefully structured elaboration of the believer's election along with the emphatic position occupied by the word ἐκλεκτός signals Peter's concern with theological identity rather than geographical locality. The term 'elect' itself identifies believers in terms of their relationship to God, the community of believers, the historic community of Israel, and society around them. As such, the note of election struck at the beginning echoes right throughout the letter. As Schrenk observes, '1 Peter is the only NT work in which ἐκλεκτός has from the very outset thematic significance. Here everything is worked out in terms of this controlling concept.'[2]

Context

This initial declaration of the believer's elect status and its elaboration is situated within the epistolary prescript of the letter (vv. 1–2). The

---

[1] Boring, *1 Peter*, 53.   [2] G. Schrenk, 'ἐκλεκτός', *TDNT*, 4: 190.

epistolary greeting shares the formal characteristics of typical Hellenistic letter openings with its ὁ δεῖνα τῷ δεῖνα χαίρειν ('A to B, greetings'). Thus vv. 1–2 indicate: (1) the writer's name (*superscriptio*), (2) the addressees (*adscriptio*), and (3) a salutation (*salutatio*). The identification of the writer and the addressees is followed by expanded descriptions of both, which indicate their status in relation to God in Christ. Peter identifies himself as ἀπόστολος Ἰησοῦ Χριστοῦ ('an apostle of Jesus Christ'), while the addressees are called 'elect' (ἐκλεκτοῖς) followed by a threefold description of their election in terms of the work of the Father, Spirit, and Son. The usual Hellenistic greeting, χαίρειν ('greeting'), has been replaced by the words χάρις ὑμῖν καὶ εἰρήνη πληθυνθείη ('grace to you and peace be multiplied'). These words function as both 'an affirmation regarding the grace and peace of God in which they already participate, and a prayer that they may appreciate and experience these blessings more fully'.[3]

Structure

The following diagram of 1:1–2c indicates some of the major grammatical decisions made in this section:

Πέτρος = ἀπόστολος

       Ἰησοῦ Χριστοῦ   (χαιρείν)

  παρεπιδήμοις   =   ἐκλεκτοῖς

    διασπορᾶς   ↑κατὰ   πρόγνωσιν

      ↑Πόντου,   θεοῦ πατρὸς

       Γαλατίας,   ἐν   ἁγιασμῷ

       Καππαδοκίας,   πνεύματος

       Ἀσίας καὶ   εἰς ὑπακοὴν

       Βιθυνίας,   καὶ

                       ῥαντισμὸν

                       αἵματος

                     Ἰησοῦ Χριστοῦ,

---

[3] P. T. O'Brien, 'Letters, Letter Forms', *DPL*, 551.

Content

The believers' status as 'elect' (1:1)

The verbal adjective ἐκλεκτός ('choice, selected, picked out', here as the masc. pl. dat. ἐκλεκτοῖς), which was sometimes used absolutely, denoted the person or thing that has been chosen or selected. It was used by Thucydides for a 'chosen [ἐκλεκτούς] body of the light armed troops' (6.100; the word ἐκλογή ['choice, selection'] is also used in a military context in Polybius 5.63.1; 9.13.9). The technical term *iudices selecti (OGIS*, 499.3; second century AD; cf. *OGIS*, 567.10, ἐπιλεκτον κριτήν) is paralleled in Plato by the phrases τοὺς δικαστὰς τοὺς ἐκλεκτοὺς ('the select judges', *Leg*. 956d), τοὺς ἐκλεκτοὺς δικαστάς ('select judges', *Leg*. 946d), and τῷ τῶν ἐκλεκτῶν δικαστηρίῳ ('of select judges', *Leg*. 938b). In the papyri and inscriptions, ἐκλεκτός often has the sense of 'choice' or 'select' of things of best quality (e.g., P.Rein. 43; P.Oxy. 14:1631; P.Fay. 102; *BGU* 2.603). The closest parallel to Peter's use of ἐκλεκτός (in terms of its presence in a letter greeting) comes from the final greeting contained in a fourth-century Christian letter preserved on papyrus: πάντες οἱ ἐνθάδε ἀδελφοὶ πρ[οσ]αγορεύσιν ὑμᾶς. ἀσπάσαι κα[ὶ] τοὺς σὺν σοὶ πάντας ἀδελφοὺς ἐκλέκτου[ς] τε καὶ [κα]τηχουμένους (P.Oxy. 31:2603).

The word ἐκλεκτός occurs 100 times (in 95 verses) in the LXX rendering, where there is a Hebrew original, the verb בָּחַר ('choose, select') and its derivatives (44×), and the nouns מִבְחָר ('choicest, best'), מִבְחוֹר ('choice', 2 Kgs 3:19 v.l.; 19:23), as well as a number of other phrases (including the words חֶמְדָּה ['desire', 4×; cf. LXX Jer. 3:19 (γῆν ἐκλεκτὴν) and Hag. 2:7 (τὰ ἐκλεκτὰ)] and חֵפֶץ ['delight, pleasure'; cf. LXX Isa. 54:12, λίθους ἐκλεκτοὺς]). As in the papyri it often has the sense of 'choice' with reference to things of best quality (e.g., LXX Exod. 14:7; Ps. 140(141):4; Jer. 3:19; Ezek. 27:24), value (Hag. 2:7) or condition (Gen. 23:6; 2 Esd. 15:18; Ps. 77[78]:31; Song 5:15; Jer. 31:15). It is also used to denote young men (4 Kgdms [2 Kgs] 8:12; Lam. 1:15; Isa. 40:30) or chosen or picked fighters (Judg. 20:15; 1 Kgdms [1 Sam.] 24:3[2]; 1 Chron. 7:40; Jdt. 2:15; 1 Macc. 4:1).

Of importance for our study is the use of ἐκλεκτός to denote the people of God as 'chosen'. In LXX Ps. 105[106]:23 Moses is referred to as ὁ ἐκλεκτὸς αὐτοῦ ('his [God's] chosen [one]'). Repeatedly Israel is spoken of as 'Israel my [God's] chosen ('Ισραηλ τοῦ ἐκλεκτοῦ μου, Isa. 45:4); 'my chosen race' (τὸ γένος μου τὸ ἐκλεκτόν, Isa. 43:20); 'my chosen [ones]' (οἱ ἐκλεκτοί μου, Isa. 65:15; τοῖς ἐκλεκτοῖς μου,

65:15), 'your chosen [ones]' (οἱ ἐκλεκτοί σου, Tob. 8: 15); 'his elect' (τοῖς ἐκλεκτοῖς αὐτοῦ, Wis. 3:9; cf. 4:15; Sir. 46:1; 47:22, ἐκλεκτῶν αὐτου). While the word ἐκλεκτός denotes, in some contexts, that which is of best quality, best of its kind, valuable, worthy, and so on, it is interesting to note that in the Old Testament these are not conditions for God's election of Israel. In Deut. 7:6 we have the classical formulation of the concept of election: 'For you are a people holy to the Lord your God; the Lord your God has chosen you out of all the peoples on earth to be his people, his treasured possession.' This statement is immediately followed by the words: 'It was not because you were more numerous than any other people that the Lord set his heart on you and chose you – for you were the fewest of all peoples' (v. 7). In the case of Israel, then, the notion of election drew attention not to the importance or value of Israel, but rather to the sovereignty of 'God's free acts of grace which indeed runs counter to all human concepts of merit'.[4]

In the New Testament, the word ἐκλεκτός occurs much less frequently (22×) than in the LXX. We may group the different occurrences as follows (allowing for some overlap): (1) being considered the best in the course of a selection, 'choice, excellent' (1 Pet. 2:4, 6); (2) being especially distinguished, 'elect' (perhaps Lk. 23:35; Jn 1:34 v.l.); (3) being selected, 'elect, chosen': (a) of Jesus as elect (1 Pet. 2:4, 6; Lk. 23:35 [cf. 9:35, ὁ υἱός μου ὁ ἐκλελεγμένος]; Jn 1:34 v.l.); (b) of angels as elect (1 Tim. 5:21); (c) of people as chosen by God (for salvation; Mt. 22:14; 24:22 [= Mk 13:20], 24 [= Mk 13:22], 31 [= Mk 13:27]; Lk. 18:7; Rom. 8:33; 16:13; Col. 3:12; 2 Tim. 2:10; Tit. 1:2; 1 Pet. 1:1; 2:9; 2 Jn 1:1, 13; Rev. 17:14).

Moreover, God's election of people may be conceived of in personal (e.g., Rom. 16:13 ᾿Ροῦφον τὸν ἐκλεκτὸν ἐν κυρίῳ ['Rufus, chosen in the Lord']) or corporate terms (e.g., Col. 3:12, ἐκλεκτοὶ τοῦ θεοῦ ['God's chosen ones']; 1 Pet. 2:9, γένος ἐκλεκτόν ['a chosen race']). The word itself appears five times in 1 Peter (including the compound συνεκλεκτός, 5:13 [only here in the NT]), twice with reference to Christ (2:4, 6) and three times with reference to believers (1:1; 2:9; 5:13). As such, despite being smaller than most New Testament writings, Peter uses the term ἐκλεκτός (including συνεκλεκτός) more than any other New Testament document. Moreover, the motif of election provides a thematic inclusion for the letter as a whole with believers being described as 'elect' at both the opening (1:1, ἐκλεκτοῖς) and close (5:13,

---

[4] L. Coenen, 'ἐκλέγομαι, κτλ.', *NIDNTT*, 1: 538.

συνεκλεκτή, 'also chosen', 'co-elect') of the letter, further suggesting its importance for our author.

It is difficult to decide whether ἐκλεκτοῖς in 1:1 is functioning as an adjective (modifying παρεπιδήμοις [i.e., 'elect strangers']) or a substantive. Elliott prefers to regard '*eklektos* as an adjective modifying *strangers* rather than as a substantive joined to *stranger*'.[5] However, it is probably better construed as a substantive with παρεπιδήμοις in apposition to it (i.e., 'to the chosen who are also strangers').[6] The fact that ἐκλεκτός elsewhere in the New Testament functions as an important designation for the church suggests a certain priority for it here as well (which would not be the case if it is simply modifying παρεπιδή-μοις as the head substantive).[7] Moreover, because ἐκλεκτοῖς is a word that points directly to the action of God, it (and not the entire phrase ἐκλεκτοῖς παρεπιδήμοις διασπορᾶς κτλ.) is best understood as the antecedent of the three prepositional phrases of v. 2: Peter's readers are 'chosen' (and consequently 'strangers') according to God's foreknowledge, by means of the Spirit's consecrating action, and for the purpose of obedience and the sprinkling of Christ's blood. Other commentators, however, have taken the three prepositional phrases of v. 2 as qualifying ἀπόστολος or even the entire thought of v. 1. Yet, as Jobes remarks,

> [S]uch a view diffuses the focus of these phrases as the basis on which the addressees are to place their hope and be encouraged. Peter does not dwell on a defense of his apostleship or on the geographical situation of his recipients ... Therefore, it is exegetically preferable to understand these phrases as modifying the term that fundamentally defines who these Christians are: the *eklektoi*, the chosen.[8]

Construing παρεπιδήμοις as a substantive in apposition to ἐκλεκτοῖς ('to God's elect, strangers ...'), then, emphasises 'both the vertical and the horizontal dimensions of their identity as Christians. On the one hand, they are chosen with respect to God (the vertical dimension), but at the same time, they are foreigners with respect to their sociopolitical world (the horizontal dimension).'[9] As a result, our examination of the believers' election in these verses will take into account, first, the horizontal (or 'negative') side of the believers' election (in terms of their estrangement

---

[5] Elliott, *1 Peter*, 315 (emphasis his).
[6] See Achtemeier, *1 Peter*, 81; Jobes, *1 Peter*, 67.
[7] See Michaels, *1 Peter*, 7.   [8] Jobes, *1 Peter*, 67–8.   [9] Ibid., 67.

from society around them, v. 1b), and second, the vertical (or 'positive') side to their election (as delineated in v. 2a-c).

The term παρεπίδημος ('a person who for a period of time lives in a place which is not his normal residence, "alien, stranger, temporary resident"',[10] 'stranger, sojourner, resident alien'[11]) is rare in the classical writers,[12] the papyri,[13] LXX (2×),[14] and New Testament (3×; only once outside of 1 Peter).[15] It particularly denotes 'the *transient stranger* visiting *temporarily* in a given foreign locale'.[16] For example, Aristophanes of Byzantium (*c.* 257–180 BC) notes that

> [A] metic [μέτοικος] is someone from a foreign city [ξένης ἐλθών ἐνοικῇ τῇ πόλει], paying a tax according to certain established needs of the city. For a certain number of days [ποσῶν ἡμερῶν], such a person is called **a transient foreigner [παρεπίδημος]** and is not taxed [ἀτελής]; if he exceeds the fixed period, he then becomes a metic and is taxed.[17]

In LXX Gen. 23:4 Abraham refers to himself as a παρεπίδημος ('visiting stranger') and πάροικος ('resident alien') among the Hittites. These same terms are associated in the *parallelismus membrorum* of Ps. 38[39]:12: πάροικος ἐγώ εἰμι παρὰ σοὶ καὶ παρεπίδημος καθὼς πάντες οἱ πατέρες μου ('I am a resident alien with you, a visiting stranger, like all my fathers'). In Heb. 11:13 παρεπίδημος is joined with ξένος ('stranger, alien')[18] in a saying that evokes Abraham's confession in Gen. 23:4: 'All of these died in faith without having received the promises, but from a distance they saw and greeted them. They confessed that they were strangers and foreigners on the earth [ξένοι καὶ παρεπίδημοί εἰσιν ἐπὶ τῆς γῆς].'[19] In 1 Pet. 2:11 παρεπίδημος is again coupled with πάροικος when Peter exhorts his readers 'as resident aliens and visiting strangers [ὡς παροίκους καὶ παρεπιδήμους]'. While the term πάροικος generally bore more political and legal overtones than παρεπίδημος in Greek literature, it is clear from these quotations that the biblical writers are using them interchangeably to denote simply residence in a foreign place.[20]

---

[10] L&N, 11.77.   [11] BDAG, 775.
[12] Polybius, 32.6.4; Athenaeus, *Deipnosophistae* 5.196a.
[13] P.Petr. 1.19 (225 BC); 3.7 (238–7 BC).   [14] Gen. 23:4; Ps. 38:13.
[15] Heb. 11:13; 1 Pet. 1:1; 2:11.   [16] Elliott, *1 Peter*, 312 (emphasis his).
[17] Fragment 38 in Nauck, *Aristophanis Byzantii Grammatici Alexandrini Fragmenta*, 193 (emphasis added).
[18] BDAG, 684.   [19] NRSV. See Lane, *Hebrews*, 2: 357.
[20] See Chin, 'Heavenly Home for the Homeless', 96–112.

What does Peter mean when he refers to his readers as 'visiting stran-gers' (παρεπιδήμοις)? Grudem suggests that 'they are "sojourners" [παρεπιδήμοις], not in the earthly sense (for many no doubt had lived in one city their whole lives), but spiritually: their true homeland is heaven and any earthly residence therefore temporary'.[21] Elliott, on the other hand, contends that the terms παρεπίδημος and πάροικος indicate not the spiritual, but the actual sociopolitical situation of the address-ees as 'resident aliens' and 'visiting strangers' prior to their conversion to Christ, a conversion that only further exacerbated their already pre-carious situation vis-à-vis surrounding society.[22] Thus he maintains that '*some* of these addressees had already been resident aliens and strangers in a *literal* sense prior to their conversion'.[23] However, Elliott's admis-sion that only *some* were literal resident aliens and strangers would seem to imply that the rest were only so in a metaphorical sense, that is, as a direct result of their conversion to Christianity (a view that Elliott else-where denies,[24] though see below). The question is, how is the modern reader able to discern when in fact Peter is applying these terms literally and when he is applying them metaphorically?[25] Elliott explains that it is not an either/or scenario, since the terms παρεπίδημος and πάροικος can describe *both* the social *and* religious situation of the addressees.[26] Thus he concedes that while they may describe the sociopolitical situa-tion of *some* of Peter's readers, they do in fact function as a metaphorical description of *all* Christians as a result of their conversion to Christ:

> The experience of *many* as actual strangers and resident aliens
> provided an existential basis for the depiction of *all* believers
> as strangers and resident aliens in a *metaphorical sense*. The
> discrimination and suspicion, which many encountered prior to
> their conversion as actual strangers and resident aliens, even-
> tually became the experience *of all who pledged an exclusive
> loyalty to a strange God and rejected Christ*.[27]

The same conclusion is reached by Jobes, who also begins with a socio-political interpretation of the terms παρεπίδημος and πάροικος. She

[21] Grudem, *First Epistle of Peter*, 48–9.
[22] See Elliott, *A Home for the Homeless*, 37–49, 67–8, 131–2.
[23] Elliott, *1 Peter*, 481 (emphasis his).
[24] See ibid., 313.
[25] Seland, 'πάροικος καὶ παρεπίδημος', 257, in fact, questions whether even the author had enough information about his addressees to accurately apply any one label to them.
[26] See Elliott, *A Home for the Homeless*, 42.
[27] Elliott, *1 Peter*, 482 (emphasis mine).

contends that Peter's readers originally comprised those who had been deported from Rome and resettled in Claudius' newly established colonies in Asia Minor.[28] However, Jobes' sociopolitical interpretation very quickly gives way to a sociospiritual one, and I am left pondering the relevance of the former for her study:

> Once the letter circulated away from its original historical destination, the *figurative sense* naturally emerged as the *predominant understanding*. Although Peter's readers may in fact have been resident aliens and strangers in Asia Minor, the cause of their deeper alienation from society is their faith in Christ … Because they are citizens of the kingdom of God, they are to understand themselves as resident aliens and foreigners wherever they may be residing.[29]

The problem, however, as Volf correctly sees it, is that 'Elliott [and Jobes I would add] seem to assume … that if the terms "aliens" and "sojourners" are not meant metaphorically, they must describe the social situation of Christians before conversion. But there is no reason why they could not describe their social situation *after* conversion.'[30] As passages such as 1 Pet. 4:2–4 indicate, believers had in fact not been marginalised prior to their conversion but were thoroughly integrated among their unbelieving contemporaries, and their status as παρεπίδημοι and πάροικοι is a direct result of their conversion (vv. 2–4):

> For the time that is past was more than enough for carrying out the will of the Gentiles, having lived in sensuality, lusts, drunkenness revelries, drinking parties, and lawless idolatries. In this they are surprised that *you no longer join with them* into the same flood of dissipation, and they malign you.

That believers no longer participate in the same practices as their unbelieving neighbours is a direct result of their conversion (1:2d), a conversion which Peter traces back to the Son's atoning work (v. 2d), the Spirit's consecrating and regenerating action (v. 2c), and the Father's electing initiative (1:1, 2a). As God's elect (v. 1b, 2a) believers have been set apart from (v. 2b) and in tension with (cf. 4:2–3) their social neighbours. The readers' 'alien status' is thus a result not of their sociopolitical status, but of their sociospiritual status as God's elect and set-apart people, which leads to a sociological effect (as the juxtaposition of the

---

[28] See Jobes, *1 Peter*, 38–41.   [29] Ibid., 38 (emphasis mine).
[30] Volf, 'Soft Difference', 28, n. 14 (emphasis original).

two terms ἐκλεκτός and παρεπίδημος in v. 1 suggests). As Goppelt observes:

> The sociological effect of being a foreigner is in view: Christians distance themselves as nonconformists from handed-down life-styles (1:17f.); therefore, those around them are 'estranged' regarding them (4:3f.). In both Christians and those around them the effects of this foreignness can or should be felt – the letter speaks of this in the parenesis – but the foreignness is established by election.[31]

Even though the sociological interpretations advanced by Elliott and Jobes are unpersuasive in the end, they rightly highlight the sociological implications of being elect and set apart by God.

The final term applied to these churches, διασπορά ('diaspora, dispersion, scattering';[32] related linguistically to the verb διασπείρω, 'to scatter' [LXX, 69x, NT 3x]), further indicates the metaphorical nature of these descriptions. Like the word ἐκλεκτός, διασπορά is drawn from Jewish tradition, where it denoted the 'dispersion' of the Jewish people among the Gentiles beyond the borders of the Holy Land (cf. Deut. 28:25; 30:4; Jer. 15:7; 41:17).[33] Because of this fact, Calvin concluded that the letter must have been written to Jews.[34] However, since, as the majority of commentators now rightly believe, Peter is most probably writing to a mixed audience of Jews and Gentiles, it is better to take this term as a metaphorical designation for all Christians, who, like the dispersed Jews, lived as strangers in their surrounding society. Goppelt writes:

> 1 Peter and other early Christian uses of 'diaspora' appropriate essentially only the sociological components: Christians are diaspora as a people living in small communal organisations scattered among the peoples and awaiting expectantly for its ingathering in the eschaton. The scattering, however, is not the product of judgment, but of an election that separates and estranges them from global society.[35]

As Goppelt goes on to note,

> the ingathering is not described as a reuniting around Jerusalem or a return to the heavenly commonwealth (Phil. 3:20), but as a future gathering around the Lord, when faith becomes vision (1

---

[31] Goppelt, *1 Peter*, 67–8.   [32] See BDAG, 236.
[33] See K. L. Schmidt, 'διασπορά', *TDNT*, 2: 98–101.
[34] See Calvin, *Epistles of St. Peter*, 230.   [35] Goppelt, *1 Peter*, 65–6.

Pet. 1:8). The diaspora situation is an expression of the eschato-logical already-and-not-yet, an expression of being elected and being a foreigner.[36]

Thus, while it is important that Peter's readers identify themselves with Israel (as this dispersed and exiled people of God), it is even more important that they 'grasp that the narrative of Israel is itself determined by the story of Jesus and by the soteriological journey and eschatological hope it engenders'.[37]

The basis, means, and purpose of election (1:2)

In v. 2, three prepositional phrases (beginning with κατά, ἐν, and εἰς) cast in a proto-Trinitarian framework (θεοῦ πατρός [v. 2a], πνεύματος [v. 2b], Ἰησοῦ Χριστοῦ [v. 2c]) and qualifying ἐκλεκτοῖς (v. 1), describe the *basis* (v. 2a), *instrumentality* (v. 2b), and *goal* (v. 2c) of the believers' election (by God).

The basis *of the believer's election (1:2a):* κατὰ πρόγνωσιν θεοῦ πατρός

The preposition κατά (with the accusative, 'according to, in accordance with, in conformity with'; 10× in 1 Peter),[38] functioning here as a 'marker of norm of similarity or homogeneity',[39] indicates the criterion in light of which God's electing action is performed, namely, his foreknowledge (πρόγνωσιν).[40] What does Peter mean when he says that the believers' election has been carried out in conformity with God's foreknowledge? In classical Greek to 'foreknow' (προγινώσκω, πρόγνωσις) usually meant to 'know, perceive, learn, or understand beforehand'[41] as far as human foresight, cleverness, or ability made it possible (e.g., Euripides, *Hipp.* 1072; Plato, *Theag.* 203d; *Resp.* 4.426c; Thucydides 2.64.6; Hippocrates, *Prog.* 1), 'though any real foreknowledge of destiny is concealed from man (Homer, *Hymn. Cer.* 256f.)'.[42] The noun πρόγνωσις ('foreknowl-edge') occurs only twice in the LXX (Jdt. 9:6; 11:19; the related verb, προγινώσκω ['foresee, make known in advance'] occurs only 3×), in both cases without a Hebrew equivalent. In Jdt. 9:6 it denotes God's foreknowledge, which decreed the fall of the Egyptians, and in 11:19

---

[36] Ibid., 66.   [37] Green, 'Faithful Witness in the Diaspora', 288.
[38] BDAG, 512 (s.v., 5).   [39] BDAG, 512 (s.v., 5).
[40] See Harris, 'Prepositions and Theology', 1200.
[41] See LSJ, 1473.   [42] R. Bultmann, 'προγινώσκω, πρόγνωσις', *TDNT*, 1: 715.

it refers to foreknowledge that is made available through prophecy. The notion of God's predetermining knowledge (cf. Jdt. 9:6) is expressed with a number of other related terms in Jer. 1:5 (ἐπίσταμαι, 'to know, to be acquainted with'), Amos 3:2 (γινώσκω, 'to know, come to know, perceive'), and Hos. 5:3 (γινώσκω). In Amos 3:3 the verb 'know' refers to God's election of Israel: 'Only you have I known [ἔγνων] of all the tribes of the earth.' Then in a passage with some similarity to ours, the Lord says to Jeremiah (1:5): 'Before I formed you in the belly I knew you [ἐπίσταμαί σε], and before you came forth from the womb I had consecrated you [ἡγίακά σε; cf. 1 Pet. 1:2a,b, κατὰ πρόγνωσιν/ἐν ἁγιασμῷ].'[43] Hebrew parallelism may suggest that the second phrase is a more specific restatement of the first, indicating that God's knowledge of Jeremiah was more than just an intellectual knowing; it was a predetermining, consecrating knowing.

In the New Testament the noun πρόγνωσις ('foreknowledge, predetermination') is found twice (Acts 2:23; 1 Pet. 1:2), while the related verb προγινώσκω ('have foreknowledge, choose beforehand') occurs five times (Acts 26:5; Rom. 8:29; 11:2; 1 Pet. 1:20; 2 Pet. 3:17). In Acts 2:23 πρόγνωσις is linked (by means of one governing article and the word καί) with the words τῇ ὡρισμένῃ βουλῇ ('the definite plan'; cf. Lk. 22:22, κατὰ τὸ ὡρισμένον, 'in accordance with the [divine] decree'): 'This [Jesus], handed over to you according to the definite plan and foreknowledge of God [τῇ ὡρισμένῃ βουλῇ καὶ προγνώσει τοῦ θεοῦ], you crucified and killed by the hands of those outside the law.' Barrett comments: 'What appeared to be a free concerted action by Jews and Gentiles was in fact done because God foreknew it, decided it, and planned it.'[44] The concept of divine foreknowledge is again Christologically oriented in 1 Pet. 1:20 where the verbal form is used: προεγνωσμένου πρὸ καταβολῆς κόσμου ('he [= Christ, v. 19] was destined [lit. 'foreknown'] before the foundation of the world'). It is unlikely that Peter is saying that God *merely* foresaw the coming of Christ; the idea is that the coming of Christ took place in accord with God's sovereign and eternal plan and intention (cf. Lk. 22:22; Acts 2:23; 4:27–8; 13:32–3; Rom. 1:1–4; 1 Cor. 15:34; cf. Mk 8:31; 2 Tim. 1:9–10).[45] Divine foreknowledge and predetermination are again linked in Rom. 8:29–30:

> For those whom he foreknew [προέγνω] he also predestined [προώρισεν] to be conformed to the image of his Son ... And those whom he predestined [προώρισεν] he also called

---

[43] NETS.   [44] Barrett, *Acts of the Apostles*, 1: 142.
[45] See Spicq, *Les Épîtres de Saint Pierre*, 69; Schreiner, *1 Peter*, 53–4.

[ἐκάλεσεν; cf. 1 Pet. 1:25; 2:9, 21; 3:9; 5:10]; and those whom he called [ἐκάλεσεν] he also justified; and those whom he justified he also glorified.

As Dunn notes, 'προγινώσκω obviously means more than simply foreknowledge, knowledge before the event ... It has in view the Hebraic understanding of "knowing" as involving a relationship experienced and acknowledged.'[46] As Schreiner indicates, the background of this term is to be located in the Old Testament 'where for God "to know" (יָדַע, *yāda*) refers to his covenantal love in which he sets his affection on those whom he has chosen (cf. Gen. 18:19; Exod. 33:17; 1 Sam. 2:12; Ps. 18:43; Prov. 9:10; Jer. 1:5; Hos. 13:5; Amos 3:2)'.[47] Divine election and foreknowledge are again linked in 1 Pet. 1:2.

Thus, when Peter says that believers are 'elect ... according to the foreknowledge of God the Father' (ἐκλεκτοῖς ... κατὰ πρόγνωσιν θεοῦ πατρός), his point is that the 'Father' (note the use of this very personal appellation) has chosen for salvation those upon whom he has set his eternal covenantal affection.[48] The salvation of believers is not something that God merely 'saw beforehand' as he looked down through the corridors of time, but is instead a direct *consequence* of God's eternal foreknowledge and saving purposes. Thus the words 'according to' (κατά) may also indicate 'cause' or 'result': the believers' election to salvation is *because of* or a direct *result of* God's sovereign and saving initiative in salvation.

The means *of the believer's election (1:2b):* ἐν ἁγιασμῷ πνεύματος

The second qualification of the word ἐκλεκτός is introduced with the preposition ἐν: ἐν ἁγιασμῷ πνεύματος. Three choices need to be made here: (1) Should the preposition ἐν be construed as locative or instrumental? (2) Is πνεύματος a reference to the human spirit or to God's Holy Spirit? (3) Should ἁγιασμῷ be understood as the progressive transformation of character, or a setting apart or consecrating to God in terms of regeneration and conversion? Once these three questions have been answered, the meaning of the expression ἐν ἁγιασμῷ πνεύματος will become clear.

Selwyn argues that although the preposition 'ἐν might be instrumental here, as often in Hellenistic Greek, "in virtue of"' it is simplest to take it

---

[46] Dunn, *Romans*, 1: 482.   [47] Schreiner, *Romans*, 452.
[48] Schreiner, *1 Peter*, 53–4.

as a slight extension of the ordinary local sense, meaning 'in the sphere of'.[49] Selwyn takes the sphere or location to be the inner person where 'the inward part of the sacrament of baptism' occurs.[50] Thus the phrase ἐν ἁγιασμῷ πνεύματος denotes the sanctifying work of the Spirit which takes place in the sphere of the inner person.[51] Grudem also construes ἐν as locative; however, he takes the sphere to be not the inner person but the sanctifying work of the Spirit: 'Peter is saying that his readers' *whole existence* as "chosen sojourners of the Dispersion ..." is being lived "in" [ἐν] **the realm of** the sanctifying work of the Spirit.'[52] In the end there seems to be little difference between the idea of being chosen into the realm of the sanctifying work of the Spirit whereby one is sanctified (by the Spirit; locative interpretation), and being chosen by the sanctifying work of the Spirit (instrumental interpretation). According to both interpretations, the believer's election is effected, in time, through the sanctifying action of the Spirit (whether we say it occurs in that 'realm' or not). In the end it is probably best, with the majority of commentators, to simply construe ἐν ἁγιασμῷ as an instrumental dative.[53] Thus the formulation ἐν ἁγιασμῷ πνεύματος denotes the means by which the believers' election has been effected in time: it is through the sanctification (ἐν ἁγιασμῷ) accomplished by the Spirit (πνεύματος). As Bénétreau notes, 'le deuxième élément, *par la sanctification de l'Esprit*, ne considère plus l'élection comme mystère caché en Dieu mais dans sa manifestation historique (la "vocation" chez Paul et dans 1 Pet. 1:15 et 5:10) appelée *hagiasmos*, sanctification'.[54] Since this statement stands in parallel with two other prepositional phrases referring to God the Father (θεοῦ πατρός, v. 2a) and Jesus Christ (Ἰησοῦ Χριστοῦ, v. 2c), πνεύματος here is almost certainly to be understood as the Holy Spirit (= subjective genitive) and not the human spirit (= objective genitive).[55] Together, all three prepositional phrases indicate the divine initiative of the Godhead in the believers' election.

What does Peter actually mean when he says that believers are 'elect ... according to the sanctification of the Spirit'? Grudem argues that 'the sanctifying work of the Spirit, the work whereby he gradually works in Christians to free them more and more from remaining sin and to make them increasingly like Christ in holiness, faith, and love, is in view in the phrase *and sanctified by the Spirit*'.[56] While the term

---

[49] Selwyn, *First Epistle of St. Peter*, 119.   [50] Ibid.   [51] Ibid., 119–20.
[52] Grudem, *First Epistle of Peter*, 52 (emphasis his; bold added).
[53] See Spicq, *Les Épîtres de Saint Pierre*, 42; Feldmeier, *Brief des Petrus*, 37.
[54] Bénétreau, *Première épître de Pierre*, 79.
[55] See Feldmeier, *Brief des Petrus*, 37.
[56] Grudem, *First Epistle of Peter*, 51 (italics his).

ἁγιασμός often does refer to the believer's progressive growth in holiness (e.g., 1 Thess. 4:3, 4; 1 Tim. 2:15; Heb. 12:14), that does not seem to be the meaning here. In this context the focus is Christian conversion. As the words ἐκλεκτοῖς ... ἐν ἁγιασμῷ πνεύματος indicate, Peter is explaining the means (ἐν ἁγιασμῷ πνεύματος) by which believers came to be a part of God's elect people (ἐκλεκτοῖς).[57] It is thus a divine act of consecration by which believers have been gathered into the community of the elect. Through the consecrating action of the Spirit (ἁγιασμῷ as a noun of action), believers have been set apart from society around them (and are thus παρεπιδήμοις διασπορᾶς, v. 1) and set apart for God and service to him. As Michaels points out, this consecration probably took place when they first responded to the good news that was effectively proclaimed to them in the power of the Holy Spirit (v. 12).[58]

A number of commentators point out the affinities between 1 Pet. 1:1–2 and 2 Thess. 2:13, a verse which contains a similar complex of ideas:

> But we must always give thanks to God for you, brothers and sisters beloved by the Lord, because God chose you [εἵλατο ὑμᾶς] as the first fruits [other ancient authorities read 'from the beginning' (ἀπαρχήν)] for salvation [εἰς σωτηρίαν] through sanctification by the Spirit [ἐν ἁγιασμῷ πνεύματος] and through belief in the truth [πίστει ἀληθείας] (cf. 1 Cor. 6:11).

In a similar way, Peter points to his readers' belief – an immediate fruit of the Spirit's consecrating action – as evidence that they have been chosen according to the foreknowledge of God the Father. As Jobes notes,

> The electing purpose of God is made real by the faith of believers, but that faith is itself a completely gratuitous act of the Holy Spirit. It is the Spirit who first stirs in the heart a reaching toward God, quickening one's understanding of the gospel, convicts of sin, reassures of pardon, and transforms the character by his fruit of virtues.[59]

The purpose *of the believer's election (1:2c):* εἰς ὑπακοὴν καὶ ῥαντισμὸν αἵματος Ἰησοῦ Χριστοῦ

This third and final qualification of the word ἐκλεκτός is introduced with the preposition εἰς: εἰς ὑπακοὴν καὶ ῥαντισμὸν αἵματος Ἰησοῦ

Χριστοῦ. There are a number of choices that need to be made here also: (1) Should the preposition εἰς be construed as denoting cause or purpose (or even result)? (2) What is the sense of the genitive αἵματος 'Ιησοῦ Χριστοῦ ('of the blood of Jesus Christ') and its relationship to ὑπακοήν and ῥαντισμόν ? (3) What is the relationship of ὑπακοήν ('obedience') to ῥαντισμόν ('sprinkling')?

Elliott construes the εἰς as causal ('because of') contending that this final prepositional phrase 'roots the *cause* of Christian election in Jesus Christ's obedience to the Father's will and his suffering and death'.[60] He thus translates v. 2c as '*because of* the obedience and the sprinkling of the blood of Jesus Christ'.[61] This case has also been carefully argued by Agnew, who, however, is forced to admit that such a construal would be highly unusual in 1 Peter.[62] As Agnew admits, 'the preposition εἰς appears 42 times in 1 Peter, nowhere else in a way that might be construed as causal'.[63] In fact, as Harris has demonstrated, 'such a sense for *eis* seems unlikely in any one of the [NT] passages sometimes adduced'.[64] On the other hand, εἰς frequently has the value of purpose elsewhere in 1 Peter (1:3, 4, 5, 7, 22; 2:5, 7, 8, 9, 14, 21; 3:7, 9; 4:2, 7), and it should be construed as such in 1:2c. As Achtemeier observes, 'in the immediately following verses 3–5, εἰς is used three times with its normal telic force, indicating the likelihood that the author also meant it to have that force in this phrase'.[65] Thus, with the majority of commentators, it is best to construe εἰς as telic in force, yielding the sense that believers have been chosen for the *purpose* of 'obedience and sprinkling' (ὑπακοὴν καὶ ῥαντισμόν).[66]

A number of commentators read 'Ιησοῦ Χριστοῦ as an objective genitive and construe it with ὑπακοήν, thus rendering the construction, 'for obedience to Jesus Christ'.[67] However, there are two potential difficulties with this interpretation: (1) It would either demand that we also construe 'Ιησοῦ Χριστοῦ as an objective genitive with respect to the second noun ῥαντισμόν ('sprinkling') resulting in the unusual notion of 'the sprinkling of the blood [whose object is] Christ', or (2) that we take 'Ιησοῦ Χριστοῦ as an objective genitive with ὑπακοήν ('obedience to Jesus Christ') but as a subjective genitive with ῥαντισμὸν αἵματος ('sprinkling of the blood of Jesus Christ' [= the blood Jesus

---

[60] Elliott, *1 Peter*, 319 (emphasis his). [61] Ibid., 307, 319 (emphasis mine).

[62] Agnew, '1 Peter 1:2: An Alternative Translation', 70.

[63] Ibid. [64] Harris, 'Prepositions and Theology', 1187.

[65] Achtemeier, *1 Peter*, 87.

[66] See, e.g., Wohlenberg, *Petrusbriefe*, 33; Spicq, *Les Épîtres de Saint Pierre*, 42.

[67] See Grudem, *First Epistle of Peter*, 52; Hart, 'First General Epistle of Peter', 41.

sprinkles]). Yet, as Achtemeier points out, 'that demands that the same genitive ʼΙησοῦ Χριστοῦ function two different ways in the same sentence, something of a grammatical monstrosity and surely confusing to the reader/listener'.[68] Such a 'grammatical monstrosity' can be avoided if we take ὑπακοήν to be functioning absolutely ('for obedience') and construe the genitive ʼΙησοῦ Χριστοῦ exclusively with ῥαντισμὸν αἵματος: 'for obedience, and [for] the sprinkling of the blood of Jesus Christ'.[69] What does Peter mean when he says that believers have been 'chosen ... for obedience and the sprinkling of the blood of Jesus Christ'?

Grudem contends that ὑπακοή ('obedience') here denotes 'the daily obedience of believers' and not the 'initial (saving) obedience to the gospel'.[70] In fact, maintains Grudem, 'no clear examples of *hypakoē* meaning "initial saving response to the gospel" are found [in the NT]'.[71] Michaels, on the other hand, argues that ὑπακοή here 'refers to conversion from paganism to Christianity' and as such is being used 'absolutely in the sense of willing acceptance of the gospel'.[72] A number of considerations tip the balance in favour of this second interpretation: (1) First, Grudem is mistaken in his claim that ὑπακοή never refers to conversion. For example, in Rom. 1:5 Paul speaks of his calling to 'bring about the obedience of faith [ὑπακοὴν πίστεως] among all the Gentiles for the sake of his name'.[73] Then in 15:18 he speaks of 'what Christ has accomplished through me to win obedience from the Gentiles [ὑπακοὴν ἐθνῶν] ... so that from Jerusalem and as far around as Illyricum I have fully proclaimed the good news of Christ [τὸ εὐαγγέλιον τοῦ Χριστοῦ]'. However, says Paul a little earlier, 'not all have obeyed the good news' (οὐ πάντες ὑπήκουσαν τῷ εὐαγγελίῳ, 10:16). In these texts the 'obedience of faith' (ὑπακοὴν πίστεως), the 'obedience of the Gentiles' (ὑπακοὴν ἐθνῶν), and obedience 'to the gospel' (ὑπήκουσαν τῷ εὐαγγελίῳ) most naturally refer to conversion.

(2) Second, this seems to be the most likely sense of the word (ὑπακοή) as used elsewhere in 1 Peter. In 1:14 the expression ὡς τέκνα ὑπακοῆς ('as obedient children') presupposes a conversion experience that forms the basis for the ethical injunction that follows: μὴ συσχηματιζόμενοι ταῖς πρότερον ἐν τῇ ἀγνοίᾳ ὑμῶν ἐπιθυμίαις. Then in 1:22 'obedience' (ὑπακοή) is further qualified as 'obedience to the truth' (τῇ ὑπακοῇ τῆς ἀληθείας): that is, acceptance of the truth embodied in the

---

[68] Achtemeier, *1 Peter*, 87.
[69] See, e.g., Bénétreau, *Première épître de Pierre*, 79.
[70] Grudem, *First Epistle of Peter*, 53.   [71] Ibid., 52.
[72] Michaels, *1 Peter*, 11, 12.
[73] See Dunn, *Romans 1–8*, 17; Moo, *Romans*, 52–53.

proclamation of the gospel (cf. v. 25). Negative constructions similar to Rom. 10:16 and 2 Thess. 1:8 also appear in 1 Peter (using the verb ἀπειθέω, 'disobey, be disobedient').[74] Peter speaks of those who 'disobey the word' (τῷ λόγῳ ἀπειθοῦντες, 2:18; cf. 3:1, 'even if some of them do not obey the word [ἀπειθοῦσιν τῷ λόγῳ], they may be won over without a word') and 'those who disobey the gospel of God' (τῶν ἀπειθούντων τῷ τοῦ θεοῦ εὐαγγελίῳ, 4:17). In these texts, 'obedience' indicates obedient response in faith to the gospel, while 'disobedience' denotes rejection of it.

(3) That conversion is intended in 1:2c is confirmed by the parallel expression ῥαντισμὸν αἵματος Ἰησοῦ Χριστοῦ ('sprinkling of the blood of Jesus Christ'). As Michaels observes, 'such an understanding helps explain why obedience precedes rather than follows "sprinkling of the blood of Jesus Christ." The latter phrase gives concreteness and vividness to Peter's brief glance at Christian conversion.'[75] The most probable background to this passage is Exod. 24:3–8, where the establishment of the first covenant was inaugurated with animal sacrifice (v. 5) and the sprinkling of the blood of the animal on the altar (v. 6), then the people (v. 8). Preceding the sprinkling of the blood on the people, the people pledged their obedience to the God of the covenant (vv. 3, 7). In v. 3 we read: 'And Moyses [Moses] went in and recounted to the people all God's words and statutes. And all the people answered with one voice saying, "All the words which the Lord has spoken we will do and heed"'. Then again in v. 7: 'And taking the book of the covenant, he read in the ears of the people and they said, "All that the Lord has said we will do and heed"'. At that point we read: 'Then Moyses [Moses], taking the blood, sprinkled the people [λαβὼν τὸ αἷμα κατεσκέδασεν τοῦ λαοῦ]' (v. 8a). This blood, we are then told, is 'the blood of the covenant [τὸ αἷμα τῆς διαθήκης (Heb., דַּם־הַבְּרִית)] which the Lord has made with you concerning all these words' (v. 8b). Thus the sprinkling of blood ratified the covenant between the two covenant partners, Yahweh and Israel.

In 1 Pet. 1:2c the blood is specifically said to be αἵματος Ἰησοῦ Χριστοῦ ('the blood of Jesus Christ'). If I am right in suggesting Exod. 24:3–8 as the most probable background, then it would appear that Peter is thinking of Christ's death as a covenant sacrifice. Just as the blood of the animal sealed the first covenant (Exod. 24:8), so the 'sprinkling of Christ's blood' (a metaphorical expression for

---

[74] BDAG, 99.   [75] Michaels, *1 Peter*, 12.

his sacrificial death) represents the inauguration and ratification of the new covenant. The force of εἰς ὑπακοὴν καὶ ῥαντισμὸν αἵματος᾽Ιησοῦ Χριστοῦ in 1 Pet. 1:2c, then, is that believers have been 'chosen and destined' by God (ἐκλεκτοῖς ... κατὰ πρόγνωσιν θεοῦ πατρός) for the purpose (εἰς) of ὑπακοὴν καὶ ῥαντισμὸν αἵματος᾽Ιησοῦ Χριστοῦ, that is, for admission into the new covenant. The juxtaposition of the two nouns ὑπακοήν and ῥαντισμόν joined by καί and governed by the preposition εἰς suggests they are to be considered coordinate.[76] Jobes suggests that they (ὑπακοήν and ῥαντισμόν) serve as a hendiadys (i.e., expressing a single thought by two words) to refer to 'God's covenant relationship with people'.[77] The divine side of the (new) covenant is represented by the word 'blood' (αἷμα) while the human side is represented by the word 'obedience' (ὑπακοή). As Spicq notes, 'dans la nouvelle Alliance, chaque chrétien faisant profession de foi bénéficie de l'efficacité du sacrifice de Jésus qui scelle la *diathéké* avec Dieu'.[78]

Summary

Peter's readers were facing difficult times. Their Christian faith had put them at odds with contemporary society. As a result of their allegiance to Jesus Christ, they encountered discrimination and marginalisation, suspicion and slander (cf. 2:11–12; 4:2–3). The precariousness of their situation is signalled right from the outset of the letter by Peter's description of them as 'strangers of the Diaspora' (1:1; cf. 1:17; 2:11). To prevent this situation of suffering from leading to disillusionment, discouragement, or even defection, Peter wrote to these believers in order to provide them with a 'persuasive rationale for remaining firm in their faith and resolute in their commitment to God, Jesus Christ, and one another'.[79] This 'persuasive rationale', embodied in the form of a letter, is founded on the insight in these opening verses that 'becoming a foreigner with respect to society is a consequence of being chosen to participate in the new covenant in Christ'.[80] Far from being a sociological or sociopolitical accident, the believers' present experience of alienation and marginalisation is a direct result of their eternal election by God. And despite the precariousness of their situation vis-à-vis society, their election could not be more sure for it is founded on the immutable and eternal purpose of

---

[76] See Olson, 'The Atonement in 1 Peter', 269.   [77] Jobes, *1 Peter*, 72.
[78] Spicq, *Les Épîtres de Saint Pierre*, 43.   [79] Elliott, *1 Peter*, 103.
[80] Jobes, *1 Peter*, 74.

the triune God. It is based on the eternal, loving, predetermining knowledge of God the Father (v. 2a), which is effected in time by means of the Spirit's consecrating action in setting apart a people (v. 2b) for the purpose of covenantal relationship with God established by the blood of Christ (v. 2c).

2. 1 Peter 2:4–10: election and rejection: Christ, believers, and unbelievers

According to the opening lines of his letter, Peter addressed his readers as 'elect ... according to the foreknowledge of God the Father, by [means of] the consecration of the Spirit ...' (1:1–2). The theme of election encountered in these opening verses now receives further elaboration in 2:4–10, where God's election of believers (2:5, 9–10) is seen to depend on God's prior election of Christ (2:4, 6; cf. 1:20). In addition to that, honorific appellations used previously only to describe ancient Israel as the elect people of God are now applied to the Christians of Asia Minor. Thus the major thrust of this passage is the elect character of the new covenant community of believers.

Context

Verses 4–10 are linked to the immediately preceding context by the conjunctive participial phrase πρὸς ὃν προσερχόμενοι (lit., 'to whom coming'). The relative pronoun (masc. sing. acc.) ὃν ('whom') has as its antecedent the words ὁ κύριος (i.e., Jesus Christ; cf. 2:5) in v. 3. It is possible that the words πρὸς ὃν προσερχόμενοι have been inspired by the language of LXX Ps. 33:6 (προσέλθατε πρὸς αὐτόν), since v. 9 of the same psalm is cited in the previous verse (2:3) and vv. 13–17a are cited in 3:10–12. The appropriateness of Ps. 33:6 in this context can also be seen in two other expressions which are echoed in 2:4–10: 'Come to him [προσέλθατε πρὸς αὐτόν], and be enlightened [φωτίσθητε corresponds to the thought of 2:9e, εἰς τὸ θαυμαστὸν αὐτοῦ φῶς]; and your faces shall never be put to shame [οὐ μὴ καταισχυνθῇ corresponds to final words of the quotation of Isa. 28:16 in 2:6c: οὐ μὴ καταισχυνθῇ]' (Ps. 33:6).[81] Thus for Peter, the exhortation to 'come to him' (= God) in LXX Ps. 33:6, is being fulfilled in the lives of his readers as they come to Jesus Christ in faith (2:4a) and are 'built as living stones into God's grand building project of redemption'.[82]

---

[81] NETS. [82] Jobes, *1 Peter*, 145.

Content

In this unit (2:4–10) the election of Christ and his honouring by God is presented as the basis for the believers' own election and honour, which is in turn contrasted with the rejection of unbelievers and their shame (which is also contrasted with the election of Christ in vv. 6b and 8c). Reference to the believers' election in both vv. 5 and 9 is followed by two purpose statements indicating the goal of the believers' election (vv. 5e and 9e). The unit as a whole then concludes with a number of Old Testament allusions indicating the result of the believers' election and conversion (v. 10).

Jesus the Elect-Rejected Stone (vv. 4, 6–8a)

In v. 4 the 'Lord' (the ὅν ['him'] at the beginning of v. 4 refers back to the words ὁ κύριος ['the Lord'] at the end of v. 3) to whom believers come (πρὸς ὃν προσερχόμενοι) in faith is depicted by the metaphor of a λίθον ζῶντα ('living stone'). The word λίθος ('stone') occurs frequently in the LXX (301×)[83] usually translating the Hebrew. אֶבֶן ('stone'). It can denote a 'stone' in general (Gen. 28:11; 31:46; 1 Sam. 17:40) or a special kind of stone such as those used in a building (1 Kgs 6:7), of gods (made of stone, Deut. 4:28; Ezek. 20:32), a large stone used to seal a well (Gen. 29:2, 3, 8), precious stones (1 Kgs 10:2), a potter's wheel (Jer. 18:3), and so on. More important, however, are those occurrences of λίθος in theologically pregnant passages which were later taken up in the New Testament and applied to the Messiah (e.g., Isa. 8:14; 28:16; Ps. 117[118]:22; Dan. 2:23f.). We will return to these in a moment.

In the New Testament λίθος appears 59 times (Mt. [11×], Mk [8×], Lk–Acts [16×], Jn [7×], Pauline corpus [4×], 1 Pet. [5×], Rev. [8×])[84] and denotes a stone in general (Mt. 3:9; 4:3; Mk 5:5; Lk. 3:8; 4:3, 11), stones used in building (Mt. 24:2; Mk 13:1; Lk. 19:44; 21:6), precious stones (usually with τίμιος, Rev. 18:12, 16; 21:11, 19), large stones used to seal graves (Mt. 27:60; Mk 15:46; Lk. 24:2; Jn 11:38), stone images (of gods, Acts 17:29), and a millstone (λίθος μυλικός, Lk. 17:2). However, a distinctive and theologically significant use in the New Testament is the figurative use of λίθος in connection with Old Testament citations which are given a messianic interpretation (Mt. 21:42; Mk 12:10; Lk. 20:17; Acts 4:11; 1 Pet. 2:7 [= Ps. 117[118]:22]; cf. Eph. 2:20; Mt. 21:44; Lk.

---

[83] Gramcord.   [84] Gramcord.

20:18 [= Isa. 8:14; Dan. 2:34]; Rom. 9:32–33; 1 Pet. 2:8 [= Isa. 8:14]; 1 Pet. 2:6 [= Isa. 28:16]).

The adjective ζῶντα ('living'), an attributive participle modifying λίθος, however, is not derived from any of these Old Testament 'stone' texts but is instead a distinctive feature of Petrine vocabulary. Interestingly, elsewhere in the New Testament, λίθος is depicted as a lifeless thing and is contrasted with God (Acts 17:29), Abraham's children (Mt. 3:9 = Lk. 3:8), or humans who praise God (Lk. 19:40). The expression 'living stone' (λίθον ζῶντα) is thus something of a paradox, as Bénétreau notes: '[L]a formule pierre vivant ait été retenue en raison de son caractère paradoxal. Une pierre est symbole d'inertie et de mort; une pierre vivant est une contradiction dans les termes, un contraste absolu.'[85] In early Latin works (e.g., Ovid, *Heroides* 6.88; *Metam.* 5.317; Virgil, *Aen.* 1.167; 3.688), the expression 'living stone' (*vivi lapides* and *vivum saxum*; cf. Vulg. 1 Pet. 2:4, *lapidem vivum* [λίθον ζῶντα]; 2:5, *lapides vivi* [λίθοι ζῶντες]) often denoted a stone 'in its natural untouched condition: it is fresh and unaffected by exterior agencies, appearing to live still with the breath given it by nature'.[86] In this context, an appropriate synonym for *vivo* might be *naturalis* ('natural').[87] Peter, however, refers not to a stone in its natural state, but one that has been hewn and dressed, ready for its use in construction (as the adjective ἀκρογωνιαῖον suggests). Instead, the word 'living' is most probably a reference to Christ's resurrection from the dead (by virtue of which he is now 'living'), as Vanhoye notes: 'L'Apôtre évoque la résurrection du Christ: depuis Pâques, le Christ est désormais "le vivant", celui qui a définitivement triomphé de la mort humaine ... c'est par sa résurrection que le Christ est devenue pierre vivante.'[88] As 'living' (ζῶντα, 2:4b), he mediates life to all who come to him (πρὸς ὃν προσερχόμενοι, v. 4a), who have been reborn for a 'living' (ζῶσαν) hope (1:3) and who, as 'living stones' (λίθοι ζῶντες, 2:5a) themselves, both 'live' (ζήσωμεν) for doing what is right now (2:24) and look forward to a time in the future when they also, like Christ (cf. 3:18) will 'live' (ζῶσι) in the spirit (4:6c).

The final part of v. 4 contains a couplet of antithetical phrases modifying λίθος:

ὑπὸ	ἀνθρώπων	μὲν	ἀποδεδοκιμασμένον	
παρὰ	δὲ θεῷ		ἐκλεκτὸν	ἔντιμον

---

[85] Bénétreau, *Première épître de Pierre*, 119–20.
[86] Plumpe, 'Vivum saxum, vivi lapides', 6.   [87] See ibid., 1.
[88] Vanhoye, 'La maison spirituelle', 20.

The adversative particles μέν and δέ underline the contrast of the two clauses and most probably have a concessive sense: 'though rejected by humans, [he is] elect, honoured in the sight of God'.[89] The μέν clause is subordinate and preliminary to the positive conclusion, 'elect, honoured in the sight of God', thus making the election and honouring of Christ the focal point and climax of the passage.[90] The language in this contrasting pair of phrases derives from LXX Ps. 117[118] and Isa. 28, both of which are cited in vv. 6–7. The terms λίθον ('stone') and ἀποδεδοκιμασμένον ('rejected') in 2:4 derive from LXX Ps. 117[118]:22, which is quoted by Peter in v. 7cd (λίθον ὃν ἀπεδοκίμασαν οἱ οἰκοδομοῦντες, Ps. 118:22a). This psalm is also quoted in Mk 12:10 (= Mt. 21:24; Lk. 20:17), Acts 4:11 and *Barn.* 6:2–4, indicating that from a very early point, Jesus was identified with 'the stone' of Ps. 118:22–3.[91] Such an identification probably goes back to Jesus himself. At the end of the parable of the vineyard (Mk 12:1–12 = Mt. 21:33–46 = Lk. 20:9–18), Jesus applied this psalm to himself (λίθον ['the stone']) to describe his rejection (ἀπεδοκίμασαν) by the Jewish leaders (οἱ οἰκοδομοῦντες ['the builders']; Mt. 21:42, 45 = Mk 12:10, 12 = Lk. 20:17, 19). The Targum on Ps. 118:22 interprets the 'stone' messianically: הות בנשי וזכה לאמנאה למליך ושולטן טליא שביקו ארדיכליא. Evans suggests that '[t]he substitution of טליא *talyā* for אבן *eben* grows out of the Hebrew בן/אבן *eben/bēn* wordplay'.[92] It is possible that Jesus' own quotation of this psalm reflects this wordplay between the words 'son' (בן *bēn*/ υἱός in Mk 12:6) and 'stone' (אבן *eben*/λίθος in Mk 12:10).[93] As Evans notes, it is 'plausible to view this as fragments of an agenda generated by Jesus, inspired by certain Scriptures, frequently interpreted in light of their understanding in the Aramaic-speaking synagogue, and passed on by his disciples'.[94] Then in Acts 4 in his speech before the Sanhedrin in Jerusalem (Acts 4:8–12), Peter identified Jesus Christ as the rejected stone of Ps. 117[118]:22 when he applied the text directly to him (in a modified form): 'This [οὗτός =ʼΙησοῦ Χριστοῦ of v. 10] stone [ὁ λίθος] that was rejected by you, the builders, which has become the cornerstone' (v. 11).

In 1 Pet. 2:4c the words οἱ οἰκοδομοῦντες ('the builders', Ps. 118:22a) have been replaced by the word ἀνθρώπων ('humans') suggesting that

---

[89] Michaels, *1 Peter*, 99.   [90] Ibid.

[91] Trebilco, 'When Did the Early "Christians" First Call Themselves "the Believers"?', 18.

[92] Evans, *Mark 8:27–16:20*, 229.

[93] See Snodgrass, *Parable of the Wicked Tenants*, 63–4, 113–18; Evans, *Mark 8:27–16:20*, 229

[94] Evans, *Mark 8:27–16:20*, 229.

the focus has now shifted from the Jews and their religious leaders in particular (as in Mk 10:12 = Mt. 21:42 = Lk. 20:17; Acts 4:11) to all non-believers who reject Jesus Christ. Mention of Jesus' rejection by non-believers is probably also intended as an encouragement to those (also identified 'as living stones' [ὡς λίθοι ζῶντες] in 2:5a) who also experience rejection because of their allegiance to Christ. As Jobes observes, 'Peter reintroduces the theme of election (cf. 1 Pet. 1:1–2) and associates the rejection of the Living Stone with the rejection of those who come to him. The parity of Jesus' experience with the experience of Peter's readers is a conceptual structure throughout the book.'[95]

The second member of the contrast, introduced by the adversative δέ, emphasises the positive assessment of the 'stone' by God (παρὰ θεῷ) in contrast to the negative rejection by humans.[96] The preposition παρά followed by the dative (here the masc. sing. dat. θεῷ) functions as a 'marker of one whose viewpoint is relevant' and as such denotes 'in the sight or judgment of somebody'.[97] In contrast to all human judgment, Christ is 'elect, honoured, in the sight of God' (v. 4d). The words 'elect' (ἐκλεκτόν) and 'honoured' (ἔντιμον) derive from Isa. 28:16, which is quoted in 2:6 (indicating that Peter anticipated this citation in v. 4): 'For it stands in Scripture: "Behold I am placing in Zion a stone, a corner stone, elect, honoured."' The adjective 'elect' (ἐκλεκτός) here (2:6 quoting Isa. 26:16 referring to the Messiah) supplied the ἐκλεκτός of v. 4d (referring to Jesus Christ) and anticipates the third occurrence of ἐκλεκτός in v. 9a (referring to believers as a γένος ἐκλεκτόν ['elect race']). Thus the theme of election pervades and gives unity to the entire pericope. Christ's election was also referred to earlier in 1 Peter by the related term προγινώσκω (1:20): '[Christ] was foreknown [προεγνωσμένου] before the foundation of the world'.

The context of Isa. 28 is a message of judgment on Ephraim (v. 3 [but also Jerusalem and Judah, cf. vv. 14–22]) who, instead of trusting God, has 'made a covenant with death' (28:15 [possibly a reference to an alliance with Egypt]). As such they have allied themselves with a lie ('we have made falsehood our refuge and we have concealed ourselves with deception', v. 15), the idea that human power is to be trusted rather than God's.[98] God's response appears in vv. 16–19. It is possible that the stone here (MT אֶבֶן; LXX λίθος) could refer to the Davidic monarchy (cf. Zech. 3:9; see also Pss. 2:6; 110:2), or to the Lord himself (Isa. 8:14).

[95] Jobes, *1 Peter*, 146.   [96] Elliott, *1 Peter*, 410.   [97] BDAG, 757.
[98] Oswalt, *Isaiah*, 319.

This possibility is raised by the LXX of Isa. 28:16 which includes the prepositional phrase ἐπ' αὐτῷ ('in him'):

> διὰ τοῦτο οὕτως λέγει κύριος ἰδοὺ ἐγὼ ἐμβαλῶ εἰς τὰ θεμέλια Σιων λίθον πολυτελῆ ἐκλεκτὸν ἀκρογωνιαῖον ἔντιμον εἰς τὰ θεμέλια αὐτῆς καὶ ὁ πιστεύων **ἐπ' αὐτῷ** [MT: יָחִישׁ לֹא הַמַּאֲמִין] οὐ μὴ καταισχυνθῇ.

While the masc. sing. αὐτῷ may simply have been added to agree with the masc. sing. acc. λίθον ('stone') and thereby be understood impersonally ('it'), it can however, as Jobes points out, 'in collocation with the verb *pisteuō* ... also be taken as personal (as the NETS translator [n. 60] apparently took it) and possibly as a reference to the Messiah'.[99] Though the words ἐπ' αὐτῷ are omitted in some manuscripts,[100] Snodgrass has argued persuasively that their inclusion in the LXX is not the result of a later Christian interpolation.[101] He suggests that '[t]he translators for the LXX had difficulty with the statement in Isa. viii. 14 that Yahweh would be a sanctuary and a stone of stumbling and a rock of offense so the verse was prefaced with the protasis of a conditional sentence and the statements about destruction were negated'.[102] Following Ziegler,[103] he suggests that this restructuring was dependent on Isa. 28:16 with the protasis καὶ ἐὰν ἐπ' αὐτῷ πεποιθὼς ᾖς (8:14) being derived from the words καὶ ὁ πιστεύων ἐπ' αὐτῷ in 28:16.[104] Thus, he concludes, 'if the protasis of vii. 14 was derived from xxviii. 16, the appearance of ἐπ' αὐτῷ in the NT quotations of Isa. xxviii. 16 and in some manuscripts of the LXX is not the result of a Christian interpolation. It too was accomplished in the Jewish tradition'.[105] This is confirmed by the interpretation of אֶבֶן ('stone', Isa. 28:16) as a 'strong and mighty king' in the Targum of Isa. 28:16 (the innovative wording of the Targum is in italics): 'Therefore thus says the Lord God, "Behold I am *appointing* in Zion a *king*, a *strong*, *mighty* and *terrible king*. *I will strengthen him and harden him*", says the prophet, *"and the righteous* who believe *in these things* will not be *shaken when distress comes.*"'[106] This pre-Christian interpretive tradition paved the way for associating the 'stone' of Isa. 28:16 with Jesus as the Messiah. Thus, as Jobes remarks, 'when Peter describes the

---

[99] Jobes, *1 Peter*, 147.

[100] It is omitted by 393, 535 Syh^txt Or.III 196.197, and is accompanied in 88 by an obelus (see Ziegler, *Isaias*, 218). Nevertheless, Joseph Ziegler considers this the original Greek reading (218). See also Jobes and Silva, *Invitation*, 190.

[101] Snodgrass, '1 Peter II.1–10', 99.   [102] Ibid.   [103] See Ziegler, *Isaias*, 95.

[104] Snodgrass, '1 Peter II.1–10', 99.   [105] Ibid.

[106] Chilton, *The Isaiah Targum*, 56 (Chilton has put the innovative wording of the Targum into italics).

Lord to whom his readers are coming as the Living Stone, it is likely a metaphor that would have been understood – at least by Jewish readers – as the resurrected Messiah'.[107]

Perhaps the most interesting variation from that of the LXX, for our purposes, is the substitution of the verb τίθημι ('lay, put', 'appoint assign', 'make, consign')[108] in the Petrine version for the LXX's ἐμβάλλω ('to lay, set'; Heb.יָסַד, 'establish, found, fix', 'lay [a foundation]').[109] This use of τίθημι (2:6) where the LXX Isa. 26:16 has ἐμβάλλω possibly stems from Peter's selection of an alternative text form known also to Paul (Rom. 9:33) and the author of *Barn.* 6:2–3. τίθημι was already used in classical Greek for the laying of a foundation (θεμείλια; e.g., Homer, *Il.* 12.28f.), and in LXX Exod. 40 (vv. 3, 5, 6, 22, 24, 26, 29), which recounts the erection of the tabernacle; it alternates with such words as ἐμβαλλω (v. 20; cf. Isa. 28:16), ἵστημι (vv. 2, 17, 18, 33), and εἰσφέρω (vv. 4, 21). But, as Bauckham notes,

> the author of 1 Peter has *selected* it for *his* purpose, because it can also mean 'appoint', and so again stresses the theme of election at the outset of his series of texts. The use of the same verb in this sense at the end of verse 8 (ἐτέθησαν) forms an *inclusio* with τίθημι in v 6, and so marks the theme of election as the overarching theme of [vv 6–8].[110]

To this issue we now turn our focus.

Unbelievers as 'elect' (v. 8bc)

While those who trust in the cornerstone that God has placed in Zion are promised a share in the honour that God has bestowed upon it (1 Pet. 2:6b, 7a), those who reject the stone in unbelief will suffer the shame of judgment by God (v. 8b; cf. v. 6c), 'the one who ultimately arbitrates honour and shame'.[111] Peter employs these 'stone' texts (Isa. 28:16; Ps. 118:22; Isa. 8:14) in order to show that Christ himself is the touchstone of one's ultimate destiny,[112] as Beare himself notes, 'Christ is now seen as the key to all human destiny and the touchstone of all endeavour; faith in him leads to honour, unbelief to disaster'.[113] There is no neutral ground. Either one comes to him in faith and so is incorporated into

---

[107] Jobes, *1 Peter*, 147–8.   [108] BDAG, 1003–4.   [109] BDB, 413–14.
[110] Bauckham, 'James, 1 and 2 Peter, Jude', 311 (emphasis his).
[111] Jobes, *1 Peter*, 152–3.   [112] Ibid., 153.
[113] Beare, *First Epistle of Peter*, 99.

God's redemptive building project,[114] or one rejects him in unbelief and comes to eternal ruin.

Peter then explains the reason why they stumble over the cornerstone: οἳ προσκόπτουσιν τῷ λόγῳ ἀπειθοῦντες. The relative pronoun οἵ (masc. pl. nom. of ὅς) refers back to the ἀπιστοῦσιν ('unbelieving ones') of v. 7b and is to be construed with προσκόπτουσιν rather than ἀπειθοῦντες. The present active participle ἀπειθοῦντες is causal explaining the reason why they stumble, that is, '*because* they disobey'. The object of their disobedience is τῷ λόγῳ ('the word'), elsewhere defined as λόγου ζῶντος θεοῦ καὶ μένοντος ('the living and enduring word of God', 1:23), ῥῆμα κυρίου ('the word of the Lord', 1:25a), τὸ ῥῆμα τὸ εὐαγγελισθὲν εἰς ὑμᾶς ('the word that was proclaimed to you', 1:25b), and τῷ τοῦ θεοῦ εὐαγγελίῳ ('the gospel of God', 4:17). Thus the reference to 'disobeying the word' (τῷ λόγῳ ἀπειθοῦντες) in 2:8b should be understood as rejection of and unbelief toward the gospel proclamation. The word ἀπειθέω ('disobey, be disobedient'), a term used to designate unbelievers elsewhere in Scripture (Jn 3:36; Acts 14:2; 19:9; Rom. 15:31), is complementary to the participle ἀπιστοῦσιν ('unbelieving') in v. 7b and designates all who fail to trust Christ and submit to his Lordship.

The use of the verb ἀπειθέω ('disobey') emphasises that such stumbling is not accidental; it is an instance of human sin and rebellion. However, such disobedience is not outside the purview of God's sovereignty. Peter goes on to add the provocative comment: εἰς ὃ καὶ ἐτέθησαν ('to which also they were appointed', 2:8c). As we noted above, the verb τίθημι repeats the same verb used in v. 6b to denote God's 'placing/appointing' (τίθημι, v. 6b) of a stone in Zion. The aorist passive ἐτέθησαν is a divine passive indicating God as subject. The word τίθημι occurs frequently in the LXX (554 times) with various meanings (e.g., 'to set, put, place, lay', 'make, construct', 'establish, institute', 'make a decree, ordain', 'appoint', etc.). Of interest to our study are those instances in which God is the subject of the verb (as in the case of 2:6b and 8c). According to Maurer, over one quarter of the occurrences of the verb τίθημι in the LXX have God as its subject variously denoting his creative, saving, and judging action:[115] he sets the stars in the sky (Gen. 1:17); he gathers the waters of the deep and puts them in storehouses (Ps. 32:7); he sets a boundary for the seas (Ps. 103:9; Job 38:10); he turns rivers into deserts (Ps. 106:33) and deserts into pools of water (v.

---

[114] To borrow the words of Jobes, *1 Peter*, 144.
[115] C. Maurer, 'τίθημι', *TDNT*, 8: 154.

35). He is the God who made Abraham the father of many nations (Gen. 17:5f.), who made the offspring of Jacob as the sand of the sea (Gen. 32:13), who caused his name to dwell in the house of the Lord (1 Kgs 9:3), who appointed Jeremiah a prophet to the nations (Jer. 1:5), who made David the first born, the highest of the kings of the earth (Ps. 88:28) and established his throne forever (v. 30), who makes his priest-king's enemies a footstool under his feet (Ps. 109:1). As a judge he punishes sin (Ps. 89:8); he makes his enemies like a fiery furnace and consumes them (Ps. 20:10); and he makes idols an annihilation (Mic. 1:7). He also brings salvation to his people (Ps. 11:6; Isa. 26:1) granting them life and mercy (Job 10:12). He who once appointed a place for Israel (1 Chron. 17:9) and set her in the centre of the nations (Ezek. 5:5), will again place her in her own land (Ezek. 37:14).

The verb τίθημι occurs 100 times in the New Testament. In about a quarter of these occurrences God is the subject and 'the thought of God settling what shall be by sovereign decision runs through all these passages':[116] he has appointed the Son heir of all things (Heb. 1:2); he has made Abraham a father of many nations (Rom. 4:17 quoting Gen. 17:5); he has set Paul and Barnabas to be a light for the Gentiles (Acts 13:46 quoting Isa. 49:6); he has '[made] your enemies your footstool' (Mk 12:36; Mt. 12:44; Lk. 20:43; Acts 2:25; 1 Cor. 15:25; Heb. 1:13; 10:13 quoting Ps. 109:1); he has '[placed] in Zion a stone' (Rom. 9:33; 1 Pet. 2:6 quoting Isa. 28:16); he sets the times and seasons 'by his own authority' (Acts 1:7); he arranges the members in the body (1 Cor. 12:18); he appoints apostles, prophets, teachers, overseers, and so forth for the church (1 Cor. 12:28; Acts 20:28); he appointed Paul to service (1 Tim. 1:12), as a herald and apostle and teacher (1 Tim. 2:7; 2 Tim. 1:11), entrusting to him the message of reconciliation (2 Cor. 5:19). The use of the construction τίθημι + εἰς (or εἰς + τίθημι) to describe God's appointing or ordaining occurs six times in the New Testament (Acts 13:47; 1 Thess. 5:9; 1 Tim. 1:12; 2:7; 2 Tim. 1:11; 1 Pet. 2:8).[117] For example, in 1 Thess. 5:9 Paul writes: 'For God has destined [ἔθετο] us not for [εἰς] wrath but for [εἰς] obtaining salvation through our Lord Jesus Christ.' As Spicq observes, 'le verbe *tithémi* ... fait partie du vocabulaire primitive pour exprimer la vocation d'un être, le rôle que Dieu lui destine ... Il correspond donc à la prescience ou prédestination divine.'[118]

---

[116] J. I. Packer, 'τίθημι', *NIDNTT*, 1: 477.   [117] Gramcord.
[118] Spicq, *Les Épîtres de Saint Pierre*, 89.

The question that now arises is: What has been appointed or destined (ἐτέθησαν) by God? Another way of asking this question is: What is the antecedent of the relative pronoun in the prepositional phrase εἰς ὅ ('to which [they were appointed]')? Rendel Harris suggests that these words 'refer to Christ and not to the disobedient or unbelievers, and that the text should be corrected from εἰς ὃ ἐτέθησαν to εἰς ὃ ἐτέθη' (which he renders, 'for which cause also the stone was laid').[119] However, such a proposed textual emendation lacks any kind of support in the manuscripts. Hillyer, on the other hand, suggests that the words '"they were appointed" may perhaps mean not that individuals are predestined to stumble but that the stumbling of many against the rock is foretold in Scripture'.[120] This interpretation is not persuasive either as the text emphasises the destiny appointed for people and not the fulfilment of Scripture.

A more widely held view is that the words εἰς ὅ refer back to the finite verb προσκόπτουσιν ('they stumble') rather than the modifying participle ἀπειθοῦντες ('because they disobey').[121] Panning contends:

> The Scriptures make it very plain that there is an inseparable connection between unbelief and the punishment for unbelief. In the case of unbelievers there invariably is a 'stumbling' and a 'falling' that leads to eternal death. However, what has been determined is not that some should be unbelievers, but that their unbelief will be punished.[122]

Thus 2:8c could be translated something like: 'they who do not believe, stumble; they who stumble are also appointed for stumbling',[123] or 'they must fall in judgment because they don't obey the word'.[124] Abernathy puts forward the following grammatical arguments:

> However, there are some grammatical clues within the text that incline us to associate the verb ἐτέθησαν 'they were appointed' with προσκόπτουσιν 'they stumble' instead of with the participle ἀπειθοῦντες 'not obeying' (or 'not believing'). While ἐτέθησαν is in closer proximity to ἀπειθοῦντες, the fact that προσκόπτουσιν is the finite verb makes it the main thought of

[119] Harris, *Testimonies*, 1: 31.
[120] Hillyer, '"Rock-Stone" Imagery in 1 Peter', 63.
[121] Panning, 'What has been Determined?', 48–52; Calloud-Genuyt, *La Première épître de Pierre*, 129; Spörri, *Der Gemeindegedanke*, 163–5.
[122] Panning, 'What has been Determined?', 51.
[123] Bengel, *Gnomon*, 5: 55.   [124] Abernathy, 'Exegetical Considerations', 38.

the clause, and the explanatory function of ἐτέθησαν would be more likely to be associated with the main verb than with the participle (Best [*1 Peter*, p.] 106). A second clue would be the causal force of the participle: they stumble *because* [italics original] they disobey. If disobedience is given as the cause of the stumbling, then καὶ ἐτέθησαν adds an additional explanatory note: they stumble, and they were appointed to do so *also* [italics added: see comment below] because they disobey.[125]

However, there is a basic problem with each of Abernathy's grammatical arguments. First, in Greek, the neuter singular relative pronoun (ὅ) normally refers back to a general concept which can be deduced from what precedes rather than one single idea or word (whether it be προσκόπτουσιν or ἀπειθοῦντες).[126] This is, of course, also true of the construction εἰς ὅ which we have here (εἰς ὃ καὶ ἐτέθησαν; cf. Col. 1:29; 2 Thess. 1:11; 1 Tim. 2:7; 2 Tim. 1:11; incidentally, if Peter was intending to refer back to only one idea, we might rather have expected either εἰς τοῦτο ['for this'] or εἰς αὐτό τοῦτο ['for this very reason/thing']). Since the neuter relative pronoun here (ὅ) is without qualification and without a specific neuter noun which it could claim as an antecedent, it should be understood as referring to the entire preceding thought, namely, believers stumble over the stone because of their disobedience.[127] The desire to emphasise one idea over the other (either the 'stumbling' or the 'disobedience') reflects more one's theological presuppositions than good Greek grammar.

Abernathy's second 'grammatical clue' is also problematic: 'If disobedience is given as the cause of the stumbling, then καὶ ἐτέθησαν adds an additional explanatory note: they stumble, and they were appointed to do so *also* because they disobey.'[128] However, the καί is probably not functioning conjunctively but adverbially. As adverbial, ὃ καί is intensive, meaning 'even', 'indeed', 'certainly', and so on: 'to *which* **indeed** they were appointed' (εἰς ὃ **καὶ** ἐτέθησαν). This construction, in which καί is followed by the neuter accurative relative pronoun (ὅ), occurs in ten other places (in addition to 1 Peter) in the New Testament, and in every instance it functions as an intensive (and not a conjunction).[129] The force

---

[125] Ibid., 31.
[126] See Boyer, 'Relative Clauses', 247; Robertson, *Grammar*, 714.
[127] See Achtemeier, *1 Peter*, 162–3; ' Spicq, *Les Épîtres de Saint Pierre*, 89.
[128] Abernathy, 'Exegetical Considerations', 31 (emphasis mine).
[129] See Acts 11:30; 26:10; 1 Cor. 11:23; 15:1, 3; Gal. 2:10; Col. 1:29; 4:3; 2 Thess. 1:11; 2:14.

of this text, then, is that those who stumble over Christ the stone because of their disobedience to the word were indeed appointed by God to such.

Believers the elect people of God (vv. 5, 9–10)

In these texts the motif of election is paramount. In vv. 5, 9–10 Peter (1) relates the election of believers both to that of Christ (v. 4) and God's covenant people, the Israelites (v. 9), (2) indicates the purpose of their election in terms of their witness to the 'mighty acts' of the one who has chosen them for salvation (vv. 5e, 9e), and (3) concludes with the results of their election: they are now a people who have been shown mercy (v. 10).

The nature of the believers' election (vv. 5, 9a-d)

In contrast (δέ) to those who have been appointed to stumbling over the stone through disobedience, believers (ὑμεῖς), on the other hand, says Peter, are an 'elect race' (γένος ἐκλεκτόν, 2:9a). Peter's description of believers as an 'elect race' in v. 9a is paralleled by his description of Jesus Christ as an 'elect stone' (λίθον ... ἐκλεκτόν) in v. 4d. This parallelism (Christ the elect stone/believers an elect race) coincides with another in vv. 4–5 in which the divine election of Christ as λίθον ζῶντα ('a living stone', v. 4) is linked (καὶ αὐτοί ['yourselves also'], v. 5a) with that of believers who are 'also' (καί) described ὡς λίθοι ζῶντες ('as living stones', v. 5a). Furthermore, the honour that is conferred upon Christ as elect (παρὰ δὲ θεῷ ἐκλεκτὸν ἔντιμον, v. 4d) parallels the honour conferred upon believers as elect (as the titles in v. 5 suggest; cf. v. 7a, ὑμῖν οὖν ἡ τιμὴ τοῖς πιστεύουσιν; v. 6c, ὁ πιστεύων ἐπ' αὐτῷ οὐ μὴ καταισχυνθῇ). One further, important link between Christ and believers that Peter will go on to develop is the experience of suffering and rejection that is shared by both as God's elect (e.g., 2:18–25; 2:13–22; 4:1–6, 12–16; 5:1). In v. 4, Christ's election by God (as we noted above) is coupled with his rejection by humans (ὑπὸ ἀνθρώπων μὲν ἀποδεδοκιμασμένον παρὰ δὲ θεῷ ἐκλεκτὸν ἔντιμον), a rejection which led directly to his redemptive death for believers. Peter's reformulation of the 'traditional crucifixion/resurrection kerygma' in terms of rejection/election-honour here in vv. 4–7 enables him to 'emphasise the election and honour (2:4cd, 7a) that bind the rejected, suffering, and yet elect Christ with his rejected, suffering, and elect followers, as further explicated in vv 5–10'.[130] Similarly, the theme of the believers' election

130 Elliott, *1 Peter*, 411.

by God and rejection by society was sounded right from the outset of the letter (1:1–2): 'to [the] elect [ἐκλεκτοῖς], strangers of the Diaspora [διασπορᾶς] ... [elect] according to the foreknowledge of God [πρόγν-ωσιν θεοῦ]'. Thus the suffering, rejection, and election of believers corresponds to the suffering, rejection, and election of Christ. The correspondence, of course, is not accidental, for as God's elect instrument of salvation (cf. 1:20), Jesus Christ is the one through whom the believing community constitute an 'elect race' (γένος ἐκλεκτόν in v. 9). The notion of election is then reinforced in v. 9 where Peter appropriates and applies to the community of believers several honorific epithets that once designated the elect people of Israel. As Elliott observes, '[t]he prestigious predicates are derived from Isa. 43 and Exod. 19 and are arranged so as to give precedence and prominence to the concept of *election*'.[131] The first phrase γένος ἐκλεκτόν ('an elect race', v. 9a), drawn from Isa. 43:20 (τὸ γένος μου τὸ ἐκλε-κτόν), stands at the front of this list of honorific descriptions resuming Peter's focus on the believing community as God's elect (in contrast to the divine shaming of nonbelievers in the previous verses [vv. 7b-8]). The Greek word γένος ('descendant', 'family', 'nation, people')[132] denotes a group of people with a common ancestry, in the case of Isa. 43 (from which this phrase was taken), the descendants of Abraham. However, in contrast to Isa. 43, it is not biological bloodline that determines one's inclusion in the 'elect race' of God, but rather election (1:1–3; 2:5, 9; 5:13), new birth (1:3, 23), and faith (1:5, 7, 9, 21; 2:6, 7). While a γένος ἐκλεκτόν in the sight of God, in the eyes of Pagan society they were a *genus hominum superstitionis novae ac maleficae* ('a class of men given to a new and maleficent superstition', Suetonius, *Nero* 16.2).[133] Once again, it was precisely their election (ἐκλεκτός) by God constituting them a new race (γένος) that gave rise to this perception among the believers' pagan contemporaries (cf. 1:1, ἐκλεκτοῖς παρεπιδήμοις).

The second and third pair of honorific epithets (βασίλειον ἱεράτευμα, ἔθνος ἅγιον) derive from the covenantal formulation of LXX Exod. 19:6, and apply identifications to the new covenant people in Christ that originally described ancient Israel as God's elect, covenant people: ὑμεῖς δὲ ἔσεσθέ μοι βασίλειον ἱεράτευμα [Heb. כֹּהֲנִים מַמְלֶכֶת] καὶ ἔθνος ἅγιον ('And you shall be for me a royal priesthood and a holy nation'). It is difficult to know whether βασίλειον should be

---

[131] Ibid., 435 (emphasis his).   [132] BDAG, 194 (3).
[133] See Elliott, *1 Peter*, 435; Jobes, *1 Peter*, 159.

construed as an adjective ('a *royal* priesthood' [as the NETS translator construes it]) or a substantive ('a *kingdom*, a priesthood').[134] In favour of construing it substantively is the fact that it frequently has nominal force in the LXX,[135] a number of other Old Testament versions,[136] Philo,[137] *Jubilees*,[138] and Targumic versions of Exod. 19:6.[139] However, that our author understood in an adjectival sense is suggested by the fact that this phrase (βασίλειον ἱεράτευμα) stands as one of four phrases in which the other three involve a noun that is modified by another word(s) (i.e., γένος ἐκλεκτόν ['an *elect* race', v. 9a], ἔθνος ἅγιον ['a *holy* nation', v. 9c], λαὸς εἰς περιποίησιν ['a people *for [God's] special posses-sion*', v. 9d]). While it is true that the other modifiers follow the words they modify, the word order here is to be accounted for by our author's reliance on the LXX, which, as Achtemeier notes, has dictated the present order (cf. LXX Exod. 19:6 [*βασίλειον ἱεράτευμα, ἔθνος ἅγιον*]; Isa. 43:20 [*τὸ γένος τὸ ἐκλεκτόν*]).[140] As most commentators recognise, ἱεράτευμα functions in a collective or corporate sense denoting the entire Christian community (though this does not necessarily deny a priestly function to individuals within the community, as Best points out).[141] Together these two words (βασίλειον ἱεράτευμα) refer to 'the Christian community as a body of priests in the service of God their "king" to whom they now owe their allegiance as his people'.[142]

A third couplet, also drawn from the covenant formula of LXX Exod. 19:6, stands in apposition to 'a royal priesthood': ἔθνος ἅγιον ('a holy nation'). In the context of both Exodus and 1 Peter, the term ἅγιος points to the covenant community's separation from all that (and who) is unholy, and separation unto God who is holy (cf. 1:14–16). The pairing of the two ideas of election and holiness here (ἐκλεκτόν [v. 9a], ἅγιον [v. 9c]) recalls 1:1–2, where Peter addresses the believers in Asia Minor as ἐκ-λεκτοῖς … κατὰ πρόγνωσιν θεοῦ πατρὸς ἐν ἁγιασμῷ πνεύματος. A similar pairing of ideas occurs in 1 Pet. 1:15: κατὰ τὸν καλέσαντα ὑμᾶς ἅγιον καὶ αὐτοὶ ἅγιοι ἐν πάσῃ ἀναστροφῇ γενήθητε.

In the fourth and final descriptor Peter refers to the community of believers as λαὸς εἰς περιποίησιν ('a people for God's special pos-session'). The noun περιποίησις can have the idea of 'keeping safe,

---

[134] See Elliott, *The Elect and the Holy*, 149–54; Brox, *Petrusbrief*, 94.
[135] 2 Sam. 1:10; 1 Chron. 28:4; 2 Chron. 23:11; Prov. 18:19; Dan. 4:34.
[136] See Elliott, *The Elect and the Holy*, 78, n. 1.
[137] Philo, *Sobr*. 66; *Abr*. 56.   [138] *Jub*. 16:18.
[139] See Elliott, *The Elect and the Holy*, 76–7.
[140] See Achtemeier, *1 Peter*, 164.   [141] See Best, '1 Peter 2:4–10', 287.
[142] Achtemeier, *1 Peter*, 165.

preservation' (e.g., Plato, *Def.* 415c.7) and the verb περιποιέω (περιποι-έομαι in the NT) similarly means 'keep safe, preserve' (e.g., Herodotus 3.36; Thucydides 2.25.2). Moreover, and more importantly for our purposes, the noun can also mean 'gaining possession of, acquisition',[143] and similarly the verb, 'acquire, gain possession of'.[144] The noun is used three times in the LXX, once with the idea of 'preservation' (LXX 2 Chron. 14:13), and twice of 'possession' (Hag. 2:9; Mal. 3:17). It is this latter meaning (i.e., 'acquire, obtain, possess') that predominates in the papyri with regard to both the verb (e.g., P.Oxy. 22.2349; P.Brem. 22; P.Lond. 1915; P.Mich. 87; P.Tor. 2.8; P.Amh. 2.34) and the less common noun (P.Tebt. 2.317; P.Rein. 52; *SB* 10537). In the New Testament it means (excluding the present passage) 'preserving' or 'saving' on one occasion (Heb. 10:39), otherwise it carries the idea of 'acquisition, possession' (Eph. 1:14; 1 Thess. 5:9; 2 Thess. 2:14). In the Thessalonian correspondence believers are said to have been destined εἰς περιποίησιν σωτηρίας (i.e., 'for the possessing of salvation', 1 Thess. 5:9) or εἰς περιποίησιν δόξης ('for the possessing of glory', 2 Thess. 2:14). In these two cases the noun has the more active sense of 'possessing, acquiring'.

However, in 1 Pet. 2:9 περιποίησις is clearly being used with the passive sense of 'having been acquired, possessed', with God as the implied subject (cf. Eph. 1:14). Thus the expression λαὸς εἰς περιποίησιν ('a people for God's special possession'), has affinities with Exod. 19:5, Isa. 43:21 (both of which have already been cited in this verse), and possibly Mal. 3:17 'where it refers to an OT concept that the redeemed people of God are God's possession'.[145] Exodus 19:5–6 reads, 'you shall be to me a special people (λαὸς περιούσιος, translating the Heb. סְגֻלָּה ['possession, property,' 'valued property, particular treasure'])[146] above all nations. For all the earth is mine. And you shall be for me a royal priesthood and a holy nation.'[147] Although the whole earth belonged to God, ancient Israel was to be his special possession, chosen from among the nations.

The expression 'special people' is then further defined by the words 'a royal priesthood and a holy nation'. While Exod. 19:5 clearly sits at the background, Peter's wording (along with the purpose clause that follows) is actually closer to that of Isa. 43:21, λαόν μου ὃν περιεποιησάμην τὰς ἀρετάς μου διηγεῖσθαι ('my people whom I have acquired to set forth my excellencies').[148] Peter makes the same point in 2:9 (though with some changes in syntax and lexis): λαὸς εἰς περιποίησιν ὅπως

---

[143] LSJ, 1384; BDAG, 804 (2). [144] LSJ, 1384.
[145] Hoehner, *Ephesians*, 244. [146] BDB, 688. [147] NETS. [148] NETS.

τὰς ἀρετὰς ἐξαγγείλητε ('a people for God's special possession, that you might proclaim the mighty acts …'). The prepositional phrase εἰς περιποίησιν is identical to that of LXX Mal. 3:17 (note also the language of election): 'And they shall be mine [καὶ ἔσονταί μοι], says the Lord Almighty, in the day when I make them **my possession** [ἐγὼ ποιῶ εἰς περιποίησιν], and I will choose them as a person who chooses his son who serves him.'[149] While Mal. 3:17 begins with the future middle of εἰμί (ἔσονταί; cf. the future middle ἔσεσθέ in Exod. 19:5), 1 Pet. 2:9 begins with an implied present: ἐστέ ('are'; the words ὑμεῖς δέ involve an ellipsis with an implied ἐστέ: 'but you [are]'). The εἰς ('for') here, as Elliott rightly points out, denotes purpose, that is, God has acquired a people *for the purpose that* they be his special possession. It does not, however, as Michaels contends, have a future reference.[150] If, as we have just noted, a present ἐστέ is understood, then all of the predicates of ὑμεῖς ('you') must have a present reference, that is, 'but you [**are**] an elect race … a people for God's special possession'. This is further confirmed by the double use of νῦν ('now') in v. 10: 'You who once were no people, but **now** [νῦν] you are the people of God; once you were not shown mercy, but **now** [νῦν] have been shown mercy.' Thus the εἰς denotes present purpose, that is, you have been acquired by God for the purpose of being his special possession (which indeed is what you now are).

The purpose *of the believers' election (vv. 5e, 9e).*

Our passage contains two purpose clauses which indicate the purpose of the believers' election. The first of these is found in v. 5e where we are told that God has constituted believers as 'a spiritual house [οἶκος πνευματικός] for a holy priesthood, **to offer** [ἀνενέγκαι] spiritual sacrifices [πνευματικὰς θυσίας] acceptable to God through Jesus Christ'. The infinitive ἀνενέγκαι ('to offer') here indicates the purpose of the ἱεράτευμα ἅγιον ('holy priesthood'), which is to offer up (ἀναφέρω, 'take, lead, bring up', in this context, 'to offer as a sacrifice, offer up')[151] πνευματικὰς θυσίας ('spiritual sacrifices'). The expression ἀνενέγκαι … θυσίας ('to offer sacrifices') recalls the Old Testament sacrificial system (cf. Lev. 17:5; Isa. 57:6; 1 Esd. 5:49; 2 Macc. 1:18; Heb. 7:27). However, since such animal sacrifices are passé for our author, how is the expression πνευματικὰς θυσίας to be understood within the context of 1 Peter? The adjective πνευματικάς ('spiritual') which modifies θυσίας

---

[149] NETS.   [150] See Michaels, *1 Peter*, 109.   [151] BDAG, 75.

indicates that these sacrifices are prompted or inspired by the Spirit.[152] As Elliott notes, 'the connection between πνευματικαί θυσίαι [v. 5e] and οἶκος πνευματικός [v. 5c] becomes obvious. The Divine Spirit Who dwells in the house is the same Spirit Who controls the sacrifices, thereby making them acceptable to God.'[153]

What is the nature of these Spirit-inspired sacrifices (θυσίαι)? In the New Testament the noun θυσία (28 times) also refers to (1) the offering of oneself (Rom. 12:1; Phil. 2:17), (2) doing good deeds and sharing (Heb. 13:16), (3) monetary gifts (Phil. 4:8), and (4) praise to God (Heb. 13:15). Any one of these examples (or, for that matter, any combination of them) are possible for the connotation of θυσίας here in v. 5. Is it possible to be more specific? We have already noted that vv. 4–5 introduce themes in vv. 6–10. There we noted that the themes of election, holiness, and priesthood in vv. 9–10 are already anticipated in v. 5. Thus it is also probable that the purpose clause of v. 5e anticipates the purpose clause of v. 9e (introduced by the conjunction ὅπως) and should be interpreted in light of it: 'you are an elect race, a royal priesthood ... **that [ὅπως]** you might proclaim the mighty acts of the one who called you out of darkness into his marvellous light'.

Peter is probably again alluding to Isa. 43:21, where God refers to his people as [v. 20] τὸ γένος μου τὸ ἐκλεκτόν [v. 21] λαόν μου ὃν περιεποιησάμην **τὰς ἀρετάς μου διηγεῖσθαι** ('[v. 20] my chosen race, [v. 21] my people who I have acquired **to set forth my excellencies**').[154] Peter substitutes the aorist active subjunctive ἐξαγγείλητε (under the influence of Ps. 9:15? Isa. 42:12?) for the infinitive (present middle) διηγεῖσθαι but retains the plural τὰς ἀρετάς. This is the only occurrence of the verb ἐξαγγέλλω ('proclaim, report, publish abroad')[155] in the New Testament. However, it occurs twelve times in the LXX (with the meaning 'to tell out, to proclaim, to make known') where it is used primarily for public declarations of God's praise.[156]

The content of that proclamation is then indicated as **τὰς ἀρετὰς** ἐξαγγείλητε τοῦ ἐκ σκότους ὑμᾶς καλέσαντος εἰς τὸ θαυμαστὸν αὐτοῦ φῶς ('**the mighty acts** of the one who called you out of darkness into his marvellous light'). The noun ἀρετή (here in the acc. pl. ἀρετάς) can denote: (1) the 'quality of moral excellence, "outstanding goodness, virtue"'[157] (e.g., Xenophon, *Mem.* 2.1.21; Plato, *Resp.* 500d; *Leg.* 963a;

---

[152] See Schreiner, *1 Peter*, 107.
[153] Elliott, *The Elect and the Holy*, 175 (capitals original).
[154] NETS. [155] BDAG, 343; J. Schniewind, ἐξαγγέλλω', *TDNT*, 1: 69.
[156] LEH, 209. [157] L&N, 88.11.

Aristotle, *Eth. nic.* 1102a6; *Pol.* 1295a37), (2) a 'manifestation of power characterized by excellence, "wonderful act, powerful deed, wonderful deed"'[158] (e.g., *SIG* 1172; Strabo, *Geogr.* 17.1.17), or (3) the 'reward' (i.e., 'fortune', 'fame', 'success'; in relation to God, 'praise' or 'glory'; see, e.g., Sophocles, *Phil.* 1420; Plato, *Symp.* 208d; Hesiod, *Op.* 313; Homer, *Od.* 13.45) that such virtues or deeds elicit on the part of the beneficiaries or witnesses. The meaning that best fits the present context is the second of these ('powerful' or 'mighty deed') since, as the text goes on to note, the one whose ἀρεταί are to be proclaimed is τοῦ ἐκ σκότους ὑμᾶς καλέσαντος εἰς τὸ θαυμαστὸν αὐτοῦ φῶς ('the one who called you out of darkness into his marvellous light').

God's calling of his people is a prominent theme in both the book of Isaiah[159] as well as in the New Testament.[160] This 'calling' (καλέω), as we have noted elsewhere, implies not merely an invitation, but God's sovereign, electing, effectual calling of believers (cf. 1:15; 2:9; 5:10), through the proclamation of the gospel (cf. 1:12, 25), to conversion (2:9), holiness (1:15), and final salvation (3:9; 5:10). The notion of being called from darkness into light serves, for our author, as a vivid picture of Christian conversion. The believers' conversion is depicted here in language that recalls Isaiah's portrayal of Israel's deliverance from the darkness of Egyptian and then Babylonian captivity (Isa. 42:16; 58:10). For example, we read in Isa. 9:2, 'O you people who walk in darkness, see a great light! O you who live in the country and in the shadow of death, light will shine on you!'[161] As symbols, darkness was often associated with ignorance, sin, death, and the forces of evil,[162] while light, on the other hand, symbolised the presence and glory of God, and functioned as an image of salvation and deliverance.[163] Thus, as Elliott points out, 'the phrase *from darkness to light* ... in the Petrine context ... serves as a metaphor for sharing in the glory of God and as an image of salvation, transition, and transformation'.[164] This salvation, transition, and transformation receives further emphasis in the final verse of this pericope.

---

[158] L&N, 76.14.

[159] Isa. 49:1; 42:6; 43:1, 22; 48:12, 15; 49:6; 51:2; 54:6; 65:12; 66:4.

[160] See Mt. 20:16; Rom. 8:30; 1 Cor. 1:1, 9; Gal. 1:15; Eph. 4:1, 4; Col. 3:15; 1 Thess. 2:12; 4:7; 2 Pet. 1:3.

[161] NETS.

[162] See Exod. 10:22; Prov. 2:12; Ps. 91:5–6; 104:22–3; Acts 26:18; Rom. 1:21; 2 Cor. 4:4, 6; Eph. 5:8; Col. 1:13.

[163] See Feldmeier, *Brief des Petrus*, 93; Achtemeier, *1 Peter*, 166–7.

[164] Elliott, *1 Peter*, 441 (emphasis his).

The result *of the believers' election (v. 10)*

Finally, the result of the believer's divine election and calling is now stated in a pair of antithetical phrases which reflect the language found in Hos. 2:23 and serve to further underline the identity of believers as the elect people of God:

οἵ ποτε οὐ λαός (10a)
νῦν δὲ λαὸς θεοῦ, (10b)
οἱ οὐκ ἠλεημένοι (10c)
νῦν δὲ ἐλεηθέντες (10d)

The plural relative pronoun οἵ (lit., 'those who', v. 10a) has the plural ὑμεῖς ('you' = believers, 2:9a) as its antecedent. The pairing of the enclitic particle ποτέ ('once', v.10a [assumed in v.10c]) with νῦν δέ ('but now', v. 10bd) further underscores the contrast between the believers' pre- and post-conversion states. The negative phrases οὐ λαός (lit. 'not-people', v. 10a) and οὐκ ἠλεημένοι (lit., 'not-shown-mercy', v. 10c) recall, respectively, the LXX's Οὐ-λαός-μου ('Not My People', 1:9; 2:1 [1:10]; 2:25; Heb. לֹא־עַמִּי [the name of Hosea's third child]) and Οὐκ-ἠλεημένη ('Not Pitied', 1:6, 8; 2:25; Heb. לֹא־רֻחָמָה [the name of Hosea's second child]) and signify that God would no longer have mercy on Israel nor regard them as his people. Nevertheless, Hosea looks to a time in the future when God will again show mercy on his people and reclaim them as his own. At that time the daughter Οὐκ-ἠλεημένη will be renamed Ἠλεημένη ('Pitied', 2:3[1]; Heb. רֻחָמָה) and the son Οὐ-λαός-μου will be called Λαός-μου ('My People', 2:3[1]; 2:25[23]; Heb. עַמִּי). While Hosea focused exclusively on the ancient people of Israel, Peter uses these names to describe the conversion experience of both Gentile and Jewish Christians who have now experienced God's lavish mercy as the reborn children of God (cf. 1:3).

Summary

First Peter 2:1–10 presents the divine election and honouring of Christ as the basis for the believers' own election and honour which is in turn contrasted with the divine rejection and shaming of nonbelievers. Though rejected by humans (as Peter's readers also find themselves in relation to society), Christ is 'elect, honoured, in the sight of God' (v. 4). As living stones, believers share in the election and honour of the Living Stone 'that the builders rejected' (v. 7). The significance and purpose of the Christian community as God's elect and honoured people is underscored by the application of several honorific appellations that were used previously only to describe ancient Israel as the elect people of God: 'you are an elect race, a royal priesthood, a holy nation, a people for God's special possession, that you might proclaim the mighty acts of the one who called you out of darkness into his marvellous light' (v. 9). Finally, turning to the rich theology of Hosea to conclude his exposition of believers as the elect people of God, Peter describes the great transformation that they have experienced as a result of their election and conversion: 'once estranged from God, they are now God's elect people; once without mercy, they now enjoy mercy in its fullness'.[165] As Elliott concludes,

> Stress on the idea of election thus permeates this unit from start to finish, frames the unit as an inclusion, and represents an integrating theme, according to which the different traditions employed here have been united. The election of both Jesus and believers identified them as demarcated and dignified, elite and exalted in God's sight. The elect status once claimed by Israel as a concomitant of its exclusive covenant with God is now claimed by those in union with God and God's elect one.[166]

[165] Ibid., 449.   [166] Ibid., 411.

3

THE PROVISION OF SALVATION
The atonement in 1 Peter

1.   1 Peter 1:18–19: 'Christ's suffering as redemptive'

In this chapter we are brought to the heart of the doctrine of salvation as we examine those passages that deal with God's gracious provision of salvation in Jesus Christ (1 Pet. 1:18–19; 2:21–5; 3:18). As McGrath notes, '[f]irst, salvation – however that is subsequently defined – is understood to be linked with the life, death, and resurrection of Jesus Christ'.[1] More specifically, we are preoccupied with the question: How is the death of Jesus actually said to 'save'? We will see that, for Peter, Jesus' death saves because it (1) ransoms believers from bondage to a futile, empty, and aimless past (1:18–19), (2) bears the penal consequences which their sins merited (2:21–5), and (3) reconciles believers to God as a substitutionary sacrifice (3:18).

Context

Verses 18–19 are linked to v. 17 by means of the participle εἰδότες ('knowing') and the link word ἀναστροφή. The participle εἰδότες is causal, supplying the reason for the preceding imperative: ἐν φόβῳ ἀναστράφητε ('conduct yourselves with fear', v. 17). The verb ἀναστρέφω ('act, behave, conduct oneself, live', v. 17)[2] and its cognate noun ἀναστροφή ('way of life, conduct, behaviour', v. 18),[3] contrast the believer's 'way of life' before and after their conversion: the empty and futile way of life they formerly lived (τῆς ματαίας ὑμῶν ἀναστροφῆς, v. 18) and the life of reverence toward God in which they now live (ἀναστροφὴ ἐν φόβῳ, v. 17). Verses 17–19, in turn, belong to a larger unit of thought (1:13–21) which consists of a series of aorist imperatives and associated nominal plural participles: ἐλπίσατε with ἀναζωσάμενοι and νήφοντες (v. 13); γενήθητε with συσχηματιζόμενοι (vv. 14–16);

---

[1] McGrath, *Christian Theology*, 407.   [2] BDAG, 73.   [3] BDAG, 73.

ἀναστράφητε with εἰδότες (vv. 17–18); ἀγαπήσατε with ἡγνικότες and ἀναγεγεννημένοι (vv. 22–3). The noun ἐλπίδα (v. 21c) and the imperative ἐλπίσατε (v. 13) form an inclusion bracketing the entire unit of vv. 13–21. Here, as elsewhere, Christ's suffering and death (vv. 18–19) are presented as a motivation for and the basis of Christian behaviour (vv. 13–17; cf. 2:18–20/21–5; 3:13–17/18–22). However, as our passage indicates, Peter does not *merely* present Christ's redemptive suffering as a *motivation* for holy living, but as the very *basis* for it when he tells his readers that 'you were ransomed from the futile way of life inherited from your ancestors' (v. 18b). This chapter focuses on the latter of these two issues.

Content

Verses 18–21 can be divided into two parts: **(1) The *Nature* of Christ's Redemptive Work**. Verses 18–19 discuss the redemptive nature of Christ's death by means of an οὐ … ἀλλά contrast: they have been ransomed (ἐλυτρώθητε) not (οὐ) with money (ἀργυρίῳ ἢ χρυσίῳ), as would normally be the case, but (ἀλλά) with the precious blood of Christ (τιμίῳ αἵματι Χριστοῦ). **(2) The *Effect* of Christ's Redemptive Work** is stated in v. 18b where Peter says that believers have been ransomed (ἐλυτρώθητε) 'from [ἐκ] the futile way of life inherited from [their] ancestors' (v. 18b).

The nature of Christ's redemptive work (vv. 18–19)

The participial expression εἰδότες ὅτι ('knowing that') is used frequently in the New Testament to introduce a reason or reasons for a preceding imperative (1 Cor. 15:58; Eph. 6:8–9; Col. 3:24; 4:1; Jas 3:1; cf. 2 Tim. 2:23; 3:14; Tit. 3:11). Hort suggests that it represents 'an appeal to an elementary Christian belief'[4] (or, as Kelly puts it, 'an excerpt from standardised teaching').[5] The elementary Christian belief presumed by the author is the redemption (ἐλυτρώθητε) of Christians by the death of Christ (αἵματι … Χριστοῦ). The implication is that this basic information was communicated to the Petrine readers 'by those who proclaimed the good news to you' (ἀνηγγέλη ὑμῖν διὰ τῶν εὐαγγελισαμένων ὑμᾶς, 1:12).

---

[4] Hort, *First Epistle of Saint Peter*, 75.   [5] Kelly, *The Epistles of Peter*, 72.

ἐλυτρώθητε τιμίῳ αἵματι Χριστοῦ

The Greek word rendered 'redeemed', ἐλυτρώθητε (aorist passive indicative of λυτρόω), in the above translation was used in the Greco-Roman world to denote (in the active) 'release on receipt of a ransom, hold to ransom (for such a sum as is agreed on)', (and in the middle voice) 'release by payment of a ransom, redeem'.[6] Its cognate noun, λύτρον, denoted the 'price of release, ransom' (cf. also ἀπολύτρωσις, ἀπολύω, λύτρωσις, λυτρωτής; cf. also ἀγοράζω, ἐξαγοράζω). The word is derived from the verb λύω which has the general meaning 'to loose'.[7] Among its varied uses, when applied to people it could denote 'release, deliver, esp[ecially] from bonds or prison, and so, generally, from difficulty of danger' (cf. Homer, *Il.* 15.22; *Od.* 8.245; 12.53). More specifically, when applied to the freeing of prisoners in general or prisoners of war in particular it could denote 'release on receipt of a ransom, admit to ransom, release' (active, Homer, *Il.* 1.29; 24.137, 55; *Od.* 10.298) or 'release by payment of a ransom, get a person released, redeem' (middle, cf. Homer, *Il.* 1.13, 24; 24.118; *Od.* 10. 284, 385; Plato, *Menex.* 243c). In order to give this expression more precision, the suffix -τρον (a contraction of τήριον) was added to the root λυ- to give the noun λύτρον.[8] The suffix -τρον denoted the means by which the action of the verb (λύω) was carried out (thus λύτρον signified the 'means of releasing'), and then the payment which accomplished the action of the verb (i.e., 'price of releasing, ransom price'). Hill notes that

> throughout the whole history of profane Greek literature this verb seems to have maintained unbrokenly the sense 'to ransom'. In the active voice it means 'to release on receipt of a ransom' ... in the middle voice, the sense is 'to release by payment of a ransom', and in the passive, 'to be ransomed'. The suggestion that in this verb and especially in the middle voice the λύτρον-idea may be neglected and the meaning regarded merely as 'to deliver' cannot be validated from classical Greek sources.[9]

For example, Plutarch talks about 'the friends and kinsmen of the captives [who] came down and ransomed every one of them at a great price [ἐλυτροῦντο μεγάλων χρημάτων ἕκαστον]' (*Cim.* 9.4). Aristotle, in his

---

[6] LSJ, 1067.   [7] See LSJ, 1067; O. Procksch, 'λύω, κτλ.', *TDNT*, 4: 329.
[8] See Hill, *Greek Words*, 49; Moulton, *Grammar*, 2: 368–9.
[9] Hill, *Greek Words*, 50.

Ethica nichomachea, asks: ἴσω᾽ δ᾽ οὐδε τοῦτ᾽ ἀεί, οἷον λυτρωθέντι παρὰ ληστῶν πότερα τὸν λυσάμενον ἀντιλυτρωτέον, κἂν ὁστισοῦν ᾖ μὴ ἑαλωκότι ἀπαιτοῦντι δὲ ἀποδοτέον, ἢ τὸν πατέρα λυτρωτέον; δόξειε γὰρ ἂν καὶ ἑαυτοῦ μᾶλλον τὸν πατέρα (*Eth. nic.* 1164b33–65a2). Finally we may note a passage from Demosthenes, which again mentions the payment of a ransom price in the exchange:

> Let me now tell you how many of the captives I ransomed myself [ἐλυσάμην τῶν αἰχμαλώτων] ... some of the prisoners ... told me that they were willing to provide for their own ransom [λύσασθαι] ... and offered to borrow their ransom-money [τὰ λύτρα], three minas, five minas, or as the case might be. So when Philip agreed to get the release of the rest, I called together these men, to whom I had lent the money as a friendly loan, reminded them of the transaction, and made them a free gift of their ransom-money [ἔδωκα δωρεὰν τὰ λύτρα], lest they should ... have been ransomed [λελυτρῶσθαι], though poor men, at their own expense.[10]

The same notion (i.e., of a price paid in exchange) is also conveyed by the related verb ἀπολυτρόω (e.g., Demosthenes 12.3; Polybius 2.6.6; Plutarch, *Pompey* 24.4) and the cognate noun λύτρον (e.g., P.Oxy. 1:48, 49, 50; 4.722, 784; 38.2843; 43.3117).

Josephus uses the verb λυτρόω to denote 'ransom' (for a price paid in exchange; *B.J.* 1.274; *A.J.* 14.371) and the noun for the 'amount required for someone's redemption, redemption money' (*B.J.* 1.274, 325, 384; *A.J.* 12.28, 33, 46). Philo's use of the verb λυτρόω is wholly reliant on and in the context of discussion on LXX Exod. 13:11–13, Lev. 25:13–34, and 27:16–21. His use of the noun λύτρον to denote the ransom price (paid in exchange) is in keeping with those authors surveyed above. In *Her.* 44 it denotes 'the price of their redemption' (τὰ λύτρα)'. In *Ios.* 193 it refers to 'the delivery of the prisoner with a considerable ransom [λύτρα]' (cf. *Flacc.* 60). In *Spec.* 2.122 we are told that '[m]asters are to ... give [their purchased slaves] secure access to liberty on the spot if they can provide their ransom [λύτρα]'. Finally, we may note its use in *Conf.* 93 to refer to those who 'cry aloud to God the only Saviour to ... provide a price [λύτρα] of the soul's salvation to redeem it into liberty' (cf. *Sacr.* 121; *Her.* 124; *Spec.* 1.77).

---

[10] Demosthenes, *Fals. leg.* 19.170; see also Polybius, 18.16.1; P.Oxy. 1.114; 3.530; 6.936; P.Tebt. 3.1091.

From this brief survey it can be seen that this word-group was readily employed before, during, and after the time of the New Testament to denote release from some form of captivity by the payment of a ransom price.[11] In fact Deissmann can go as far to say that 'when anybody heard the Greek word λύτρον, "ransom", in the first century, it was natural for him to think of the purchase money for manumitting slaves'.[12] Taking into account the fact that a number of Peter's readers were Greek-speaking slaves (cf. 2:18–20), it is difficult to see how else they would have understood Peter's language in these verses (1:18–19).

The verb (λυτρόω) occurs 109 times in the LXX, the majority of the time rendering, where there is a Hebrew original, the words פָּדָה ('ransom', 42×) and גָּאַל ('redeem, act as a kinsman', 45×). It can refer to the redemption (by a redeemer, i.e., kinsman) of land and/or houses by a monetary payment (Lev. 25:8–34; cf. Jer. 32:6–15; Ruth 2:20; 3:12–13; 4:1–9), or the redemption of a fellow Israelite who had sold him/herself into indentured servitude (again by a monetary payment, Lev. 25:35–55). In this context it is also worth noting one example in which the noun (λύτρον) and not the verb (λυτρόω) is used. In the instance where a person's ox is in the habit of goring and it kills someone, the owner, as well as the ox, is to be put to death (Exod. 21:29). However, 'if a ransom [λύτρα] is imposed upon him, he shall pay a ransom [λύτρα] for his life' (v. 30, i.e., he can redeem himself from the death penalty by the payment of a ransom price). The verb was also used in cultic settings. A cultic offering could be 'redeemed' (λυτρόω) by a monetary payment. The offering of an unclean animal (Lev. 27:9–13), a house (vv. 14–15), a field (vv. 16–25), or a tithe from the land (vv. 30–1) could all be redeemed (λυτρόω, 11× in this passage) by the owner through the payment of their full value plus 20 per cent. Another aspect of cultic redemption is the sanctifying of first-born males (both animals and humans):

> But when Pharao[h] grew hard to send us away, he killed every first born in the land, Egypt, from the first born of human beings to the first born of animals. Therefore I am sacrificing to the Lord everything opening the womb, the males, and I will redeem [λυτρώσομαι] every first born of my sons (Exod. 13:15).

---

[11] Deissmann, *Light From the Ancient East*, §58 (326), finds a background in the process of sacral manumission (see also Lyonnet and Sabourin, *Sin, Redemption, and Sacrifice*, 105–10). But see Harris, *Slave of Christ*, 121–2; Bartchy, *Mallon Chrēsai*, 121–5; Bömer, *Untersuchungen über die Religion der Sklaven*, 2: 133–41). Byron, *Slavery Metaphors*, 204, notes that 'comparisons of Sacral Manumission practices to NT slavery images have, for the most part, been abandoned'.

[12] Deissmann, *Light From the Ancient East*, 331–2.

However, if the first-born animal was unclean the owner could redeem it (λυτρόω) by a monetary payment (of its value plus 20 per cent, Lev. 27:26–7) or a sheep (Exod. 13:13; 34:20; Num. 18:15). The redemption price (τὰ λύτρα, Num. 3:46, 48, 49, 51) for all first-born male Israelites was five shekels (Num. 3:46–51). Thus the idea of exchange or substitution is closely tied up with the idea of ransom.

However, when God is the subject of the verb, the primary image is that of God as redeemer and the resulting deliverance effected by him, and the emphasis is not on a price that God paid. In fact, on one occasion we are told specifically that God did not pay anything (Isa. 52:3): 'Because this is what the Lord says: You were sold for nothing, and not with money you shall be redeemed [οὐ μετὰ ἀργυρίου λυτρωθήσεσθε]' (NETS; though such a statement tacitly recognises that λυτρόω normally includes the notion of a ransom price). Instead, God's redemption of his people is said to take place by means of his 'raised arm and mighty judgment' (ἐν βραχίονι ὑψηλῷ καὶ κρίσει μεγάλῃ, Exod. 6:6; cf. Deut. 9:26) or 'great power and strong hand' (ἐν δυνάμει τῇ μεγάλῃ καὶ ἐν τῇ χειρί τῇ κραταιᾷ, 2 Esd. 11:10). The archetypical act of divine redemption was God's saving of his people from bondage to the Egyptians (Exod. 6:6): 'I am the Lord and I will bring you out from the domination of the Egyptians and I will deliver you [ῥύσομαι ὑμᾶς] from slavery and I will redeem [λυτρώσομαι ὑμᾶς] you with a raised arm and great judgment'. Here the word λυτρόω parallels ῥύομαι ('rescue, save, deliver') suggesting that, in this context, they are being used synonymously. Elsewhere in the LXX λυτρόω is coupled with such terms as ἐξάγω ('bring out', LXX Exod. 6:6; Deut. 7:6; 9:26; 13:6; also ἀνάγω ['to bring up']), ἐξαιρέω ('take away, set free, deliver, rescue', Jer. 38:11), σῴζω ('save, preserve', 1 Macc. 4:11; Ps. 105:10; Isa. 63:9), κτάομαι ('get, acquire, gain', Ps. 73:2), and ῥύομαι (Ps. 68:19; Hos. 13:14; Mic. 4:10). Specifically, redemption may be from slavery (Exod. 6:6; Deut. 7:8; 13:6; 15:15; 24:18; Ps. 33:23; Mic. 6:4), adversity and trouble (2 Kgs 7:23; 1 Sam. 1:29; Ps. 24:22; 106:2), death (Pss. 48:16; 102:4; Hos. 13:14), enemies/oppressors (Pss. 43:27; 68:19; 77:42; 106:2; 118:134; 135:24; Sir. 50:24; Jer. 15:21), the wicked (Ps. 26:11), and sin/punishment for sin (Ps. 129:7–8; Isa. 44:22). In all of these examples it is the thought of deliverance or rescue that comes to the fore rather than the payment of a ransom price.

Morris, however, contends that even though 'the idea of the price paid tends to fade when Yahweh is the subject of the verb ... nevertheless, it does not disappear. There is reference to a price in the insistence that

Yahweh's redemption is at the cost of the exertion of his mighty power.'[13] Though Marshall suggests that we should probably distinguish 'cost' and 'price', reserving the use of 'the term "price" for those cases where some *payment* or exchange is *received* by the person from whom the captive is delivered, and to use the term "cost" for whatever *expenditure* of money, life, and effort is *demanded* on the part of the redeemer'.[14] However, there is a danger here (more so in Morris than in Marshall) of an 'unwarranted adoption of an expanded semantic field',[15] or as it is sometimes called, 'illegitimate totality transfer',[16] a phrase intended to stress the fact that 'any one instance of a word will not bear all the meanings possible for that word'.[17] For example, it would be wrong to overload Isa. 52:3 with all the senses in which λυτρόω is used in Scripture; some of the senses – e.g., liberation by the payment of a ransom price – would be contradictory in this verse (since God specifically says that 'you shall be redeemed without money'). In the end, context must be the determining factor.

The word λυτρόω appears in only two other places in the New Testament (Lk. 24:21; Tit. 2:14). In Lk. 24:21, the disciples 'are clearly using "redeem" in the typically Jewish manner of the long awaited intervention by Almighty God, when his power would free his people from all their enemies and bring in a period of blessing and prosperity'.[18] Titus 2:14, on the other hand, contains a specifically Christian use of the verb λυτρόω: 'who gave himself [ἔδωκεν ἑαυτόν] for us [ὑπὲρ ἡμῶν] in order that [ἵνα] **he might redeem** [λυτρώσηται] us from all lawlessness'. This verse emphasises the ransom price (ἔδωκεν ἑαυτὸν [the verb δίδωμι indicates what he 'gave' as a ransom – ἑαυτὸν, 'himself']), its substitutionary nature (ὑπὲρ ἡμῶν), and the effect of this ransoming (ἀπὸ πάσης ἀνομίας καὶ καθαρίσῃ ἑαυτῷ λαὸν περιούσιον).[19] It is in 1 Pet. 1:18–19, however, that the idea of being ransomed by the payment of a price (as represented by the verb λυτρόω) is made explicit. While Isaiah's (52:2) point was that it is 'not with money you shall be redeemed' (οὐ μετὰ ἀργυρίου λυτρωθήσεσθε), Peter explicitly states that the believer's redemption came at a much higher cost than money: 'not with perishable [things] [such as] silver or gold, were you redeemed ... but

[13] Morris, *Apostolic Preaching*, 26.
[14] Marshall, 'Redemption in the New Testament', 154, n. 4 (emphasis original).
[15] Carson, *Exegetical Fallacies*, 60.
[16] Barr, *Semantics of Biblical Language*, 218.
[17] Silva, *Biblical Words and their Meaning*, 25.
[18] Morris, *Apostolic Preaching*, 38.
[19] See Mounce, *Pastoral Epistles*, 431; Towner, *1–2 Timothy and Titus*, 249.

with the precious blood of Christ' (οὐ φθαρτοῖς, ἀργυρίῳ ἢ χρυσίῳ, ἐλυτρώθητε ... ἀλλὰ τιμίῳ αἵματι Χριστοῦ).

The notion of ransom price, however, has been challenged by Beare, who contends that '[Peter] does not use for this the genitive of price, which would be the normal way of indicating the amount of the ransom, but the dative, which is not used at all of price (at least, not without a preposition), and it seems therefore better taken as *instrumental*'.[20] However, we may note the following in response: (1) Moule notes that 'a distinguishable extension of the instrumental use is that of *price*: Rev. 5:9 ἠγόρασας ... ἐν τῷ αἵματί σου (which also illustrates, again, the overlap with the simple dative, for 1 Pet. 1:18–19 has ἐλυτρώθητε ... τιμίῳ αἵματι)'.[21] (2) The contrast (οὐ ... ἀλλά ['not ... but']) here is between **what was not** (οὐ ἀργυρίῳ ἢ χρυσίῳ) and **what was** (ἀλλὰ τιμίῳ αἵματι Χριστοῦ) the price of the believer's redemption (ἐλυτρώθητε). Believers have not been bought with the τιμή ('price, value') of silver and gold but, in what might be an implied play on words, with the τίμιος ('costly, precious, of great worth/value') blood of Christ.[22] As Bénétreau notes, 'l'idée de rançon comme prix payé est bien présente ici, comme le prouve la comparaison avec l'argent et l'or, moyens habituels de paiement'.[23] This contrast may be more easily perceived if we set the text out in the following way:

> | οὐ   φθαρτοῖς, <u>ἀργυρίῳ ἢ χρυσίῳ,</u>
>
> ἐλυτρώθητε
> |
> | ἐκ τῆς ματαίας ὑμῶν ἀναστροφῆς
> |
> | πατροπαραδότου
> |
> | ἀλλὰ   τιμίῳ   <u>αἵματι Χριστοῦ</u>
>
>   ὡς ἀμνοῦ
>
>   ἀμώμου καὶ ἀσπίλου

(3) The οὐ ... ἀλλά structure suggests that Peter has chosen the dative ἀργυρίῳ ἢ χρυσίῳ (v. 18) in order to make explicit the contrast with

---

[20] Beare, *First Epistle of Peter*, 78.   [21] Moule, *Idiom Book*, 77 (emphasis his).
[22] Jobes, *1 Peter*, 117.   [23] Bénétreau, *Première épître de Pierre*, 105.

the dative αἵματι (v. 19). The dative αἵματι, in turn, probably reflects Peter's use of Old Testament sacrificial language, e.g., καὶ πρωτότοκον ὑποζυγίου λυτρώσῃ **προβάτῳ** (neuter singular dative) ('and you shall redeem the first born of a draft animal **with a sheep**'; cf. Exod. 13:13); ἀλλ᾽ ἢ **λύτροις** [neuter plural dative] λυτρωθήσεται τὰ πρωτότοκα τῶν ἀνθρώπων ('but the first born of people shall be redeemed **with a ransom**', Num. 18:15). Thus the contrast between what was (the blood of Christ) and what was not the ransom price (money – as suggested by the words ἀργυρίῳ ἢ χρυσίῳ) suggests that Peter intends for us to understand the former (αἵματι Χριστοῦ) in terms of a ransom price paid for the believer's redemption (ἐλυτρώθητε). What does Peter mean when he speaks of the blood of Christ?

αἵματι Χριστοῦ

The Greek word αἷμα ('blood') appears 397 times in the LXX rendering, where there is a Hebrew original, the word דָּם.[24] We may group the different occurrences as follows: (1) death by some kind of violence (e.g., LXX Gen. 9:6; Num. 35:19; Deut. 32:42; 1 Chron. 22:8; Ps. 9:13; 2 Macc. 12:16; Wis. 12:5), (2) connecting life with blood (Gen. 9:4; Lev. 17:11, 14; Deut. 12:23), (3) eating meat with blood (Lev. 3:17; 1 Sam. 14:32), (4) sacrificial blood (Exod. 23:18; 30:10; 34:25; 2 Kgs 16:15; Passover: Exod. 12:7, 13, 22, 23), (5) a variety of other uses (e.g., turning the Nile into blood [Exod. 7:17, 19, 20, 21], processes of birth [4 Macc. 3:19; Wis. 7:2], bleeding [1 Kgs 18:28; 22:35; 2 Macc. 14:45; 4 Macc. 6:6], colour [2 Kgs 3:22], of grapes [Gen. 49:11, Deut. 32:14]; metaphorical [2 Sam. 23:17; 1 Chron. 11:19]). The most common usage of αἷμα in the LXX is to denote death, usually by violence.

In the New Testament αἷμα ('blood') occurs a total of 98 times with the following distribution: (1) violent death (25×, e.g., Mt. 23:20, 35; 27:24, 25; Lk. 11:50, 51; 13:1; Acts 22:20; Rom. 3:15; Rev. 14:20; 16:6; 17:6; 18:24), (2) the blood of Christ which, on at least 25 occasions, is linked with the saving significance of his death (e.g., Mt. 26:28; Acts 20:28; Rom. 3:25; 5:9; Heb. 9:12; Rev. 1:5; 5:9), (3) the phrase 'flesh and blood' (5×, Mt. 16:17; 1 Cor. 15:50; Gal. 1:16; Eph. 6:12; Heb. 2:14), (4) the blood of animals in general (Acts 15:20; 21:25) and the blood of sacrificial animals in particular (12×, Heb. 9:7, 12, 13, 18, 19, 20, 22 [2×], 25; 10:4; 11:28; 13:11), (5) as an apocalyptic sign (e.g., Acts 2:19, 20; Rev. 8:7, 8; 16:3, 4), as well as a number of miscellaneous uses.

---

[24] See BDB, 196–7.

The challenge in understanding the word αἷμα relates to discerning its symbolic significance: does it refer to 'life' or to 'death'? A number of scholars contend that the phrase 'the blood of Christ' stands not for his death, but for his life released through death (with the accent on life). Thus Beare writes:

> [I]n the Levitical law, it is repeated again and again that the blood of the sacrifice is the means of atonement; the thought is not at all that the offering of the victim, or its death, is in itself efficacious, but that by the sacrifice the blood is released, as it were, and made effective for the purpose (e.g., Lev. 17:11 ...). The blood, then, is the channel or medium of living and divine power, which is made effective ... for atonement, for the imparting of new life, or for deliverance from an alien (demonic) power, only when it is shed in sacrifice.[25]

Similarly, Margot contends that 'dans la Nouveau Testament, l'expression "le sang du Christ" symbolise de don librement consenti de sa *vie*'.[26] This interpretation is based on Lev. 17:11–14: 'For the life [נֶפֶשׁ] of the flesh is in the blood; and I have given it to you for making atonement [כָּפַר] for your lives on the altar; for, as life, it is the blood that makes atonement ... For the life of every creature – its blood is its life' (cf. Gen. 9:4; Deut. 12:23). However, as we have argued elsewhere, because blood symbolises life, its shedding in sacrificial slaughter must symbolise death.[27] Lev. 17:11 does not say that 'life is in the blood' but that 'life of the *flesh* [הַבָּשָׂר] is in the blood' suggesting that if the blood is spilled then life 'in the flesh' will cease. As Bigg notes, 'the blood-soul of the victim was destroyed in sacrifice. What made atonement for the worshipper was not the abiding life, but the innocent death and unmerited suffering of the victim'.[28] In the end, Christ's death is atoning because '[i]n his death [he] paid the ransom price of his life as a substitutionary payment in the place of others'.[29]

ὡς ἀμνοῦ ἀμώμου καὶ ἀσπίλου

The reference to Christ 'as a Lamb flawless and faultless' (ὡς ἀμνοῦ ἀμώμου καὶ ἀσπίλου) clearly reflects sacrificial language. The most probable background is the Passover lamb and exodus from Egypt, though Peter may also be making allusion to the Old Testament sacrificial system in general through which atonement was made. The description

[25] Beare, *First Epistle of Peter*, 78–9.
[26] Margot, *Les Épîtres de Pierre*, 30 (emphasis his).
[27] See the discussion in Chapter 8.   [28] Bigg, *Epistles of St. Peter*, 95.
[29] Jeffery, Ovey, and Sach, *Pierced for our Transgressions*, 67.

of Christ ὡς ἀμνοῦ ἀμώμου καὶ ἀσπίλου reflects the requirement that all Passover lambs are to be τέλειος ('perfect, entire, without spot *or* blemish [of sacrificial victims]',[30] Exod. 12:5: 'You shall have a perfect sheep' [NETS]; 'Your lamb shall be without blemish' [NRSV]; πρόβατον τέλειον [LXX]; שֶׂה תָמִים [MT]). More generally, the language of 1 Pet. 1:19 may also reflect the sacrificial cult practised by Israel. The adjective ἄμωμος ('pert[aining] to being without defect or blemish, *unblemished* of the absence of defects in sacrificial animals')[31] occurs 83 times in the LXX with 58 of these occurrences (Exod. [2×], Lev. [23×], Num. [22×], and Ezek. [11×]) used with reference to a sacrificial cult in which all sacrificial animals were to be perfect. The addition of the term ἄσπιλος ('pure, spotless, without defect *or* fault', not found in the LXX, and only four occurrences in the New Testament) further reinforces the notion of cultic purity.

While it might be tempting to limit Peter's source to the Old Testament sacrificial cult alone, the language of redemption (λυτρόω) in the previous verse (v. 18) does not allow such a narrow identification. It is more probable that we have a conflation of at least two sources here, the Passover/ exodus and the sacrificial cult, with the emphasis falling on the former. Spicq, however, doubts that the terminology here reflects the Passover at all, contending that 'le sang de la victime rôtie au feu d'Ex 12 a une value apotropaïque, préservant du Destructeur, et nullement rédemptrice'.[32] Achtemeier concurs: 'Israel was not redeemed from Egypt by the blood of the paschal lamb; rather it was by the power of God. The blood of the lamb has apotropaic rather than redemptive value.'[33] These arguments, however, are not decisive. Peter's blending of sacrificial *and* redemption language in 1 Pet. 1:18–19 would in fact seem to suggest otherwise.

First, as Schreiner observes, 'a false dichotomy between blood and God's power is introduced since God's power in salvation is bestowed on those who applied blood on their homes. It is quite possible that the Israelites viewed the blood on the door as that which ransomed them.'[34] While recognising that the original purpose of the Passover victim was apotropaic and not redemptive, Kelly also suggests that 'in later Jewish thought and practice this was submerged in its general role in the deliverance from Egypt'.[35] This can be seen in later celebrations of this event, for while the Passover was primarily a commemoration of Israel's redemption from Egypt, it was also spoken of as 'the Lord's offering' (τὸ

[30] LEH, 608.   [31] BDAG, 56 (emphasis original).
[32] Spicq, *Les épîtres de Saint Pierre*, 68.   [33] Achtemeier, *1 Peter*, 128.
[34] Schreiner, *1 Peter*, 87.   [35] Kelly, *The Epistles of Peter*, 75.

δῶρον κυρίῳ [LXX]; אֶת־קָרְבַּן יְהוָה [MT], Num. 9:7, 13), 'the Passover sacrifice' (θυσία τὸ πασχα [LXX]; זֶבַח־פֶּסַח [MT], Exod. 12:27), and 'the sacrifice of the festival of Passover' (θύματα τῆς ἑορτῆς τοῦ πασχα [LXX]; דַּם־זִבְחִי [MT], Exod. 24:25). Furthermore, the verb 'to sacrifice' (Gk, θύω; Heb., זָבַח) appears four times (vv. 2, 4, 5, 6) in a brief passage in Deuteronomy (16:1–8) outlining the regulations for the celebration of the Passover. The Passover sacrifice, as v. 6 indicates, was offered in commemoration of Israel's redemption from Egypt: 'you [shall] offer the Passover sacrifice, in the evening at sunset, the time of day when you departed from Egypt'. Morris concludes: 'There is no real reason for doubting that the Passover was seen as a genuine sacrifice, all the more so since in due course the slaughter of the lamb or kid took place at the temple with the priest handling the blood.'[36] Thus there is a clear association of the blood of the sacrificial animal with the redemption of Israel from Egypt.

Second, as we have noted elsewhere, in the Old Testament the salvation of the righteous is often accompanied or accomplished by judgment upon their enemies.[37] In the Exodus narrative it is the Passover which provides the most immediate and important backdrop for Israel's redemption from Egypt. In Exod. 6:6 God says: 'I will redeem you with a raised arm and great judgment' (NETS; λυτρώσομαι ὑμᾶς ἐν βραχίονι ὑψηλῷ καὶ κρίσει μεγάλῃ [LXX]; נָטוּיָה בִּזְרוֹעַ אֶתְכֶם וְגָאַלְתִּי גְּדֹלִים וּבִשְׁפָטִים [MT]). The judgment plagues are then narrated in chs. 7–12 culminating in the final plague – the death of every firstborn – and the institution of the Passover. The effect of this final judgment plague was immediate:

> Then [Pharaoh] summoned Moses and Aaron in the night, and said, 'Rise up, go away from my people, both you and the Israelites! … Take your flocks and your herds … and be gone' … The Egyptians urged the people to hasten their departure from the land, for they said, 'We shall all be dead' (Exod. 12:31–3; NRSV).

Thus Israel's redemption is clearly associated with the events of the Passover, central to which was the sacrifice of a lamb or kid and the placing of the blood.

Third, in the New Testament Jesus' death is at times linked with the Passover. In all three Synoptic Gospels the Last Supper is called a Passover meal (Mt. 26:17–18; Mk 14:14–16; Lk. 22:11–15). More

---

[36] Morris, *The Atonement*, 92.   [37] See Chapter 5.

significant is the fact that John located the death of Jesus at the time when the Passover victims were being sacrificed in the temple (see Jn 19:14ff.). Morris remarks:

> In as theological a writer as John it is difficult to escape the impression that the truth that is being conveyed is that in his death Jesus fulfilled all that the Jews looked for, but did not find, in the Passover. Jesus' death gave what the Passover pointed to but could not give. The Passover foreshadowed the great deliverance that God would bring about and for which his deliverance in ancient times formed the model. In Jesus, and specifically in his death, that great deliverance was accomplished.[38]

It is possible that Jn 1:29 is also a reference to the Passover lamb: 'The next day he [John the Baptist] saw Jesus coming to him, and said, "Behold, the Lamb of God who takes away the sin of the world!" '[39] Then in 1 Cor. 5:7 Paul specifically identifies Christ's sacrificial death with the sacrificing of the Passover lambs when he writes, γὰρ τὸ πάσχα ἡμῶν ἐτύθη Χριστός ('for Christ our Passover [lamb] has been sacrificed'). Jeremias suggests that '[t]he casual way in which Paul says: τὸ πάσχα ἡμῶν ἐτύθη Χριστός, 1 Cor. 5:7, suggests that this comparison was already familiar to the Corinthian church'.[40] In all of these references there is an implied link between the sacrificial death of the Passover lamb (or kid) and Israel's redemption from Egypt. At the very least, there is a bringing together of these two ideas and an applying of them to the sacrificial and redemptive death of Christ. Thus we should not be surprised to find a conflation of these two ideas in 1 Pet. 1:18–19. It is very probable that Peter has used them as background for his understanding of Christ's death as both sacrificial and redemptive, but extended the reference to include the idea of ransoming with a price (an idea that was already inherent in the nature of the language [λυτρόω] he was using).

The effect *of Christ's redemptive work (v. 18b)*

While Israel had been redeemed from Egyptian bondage, Peter indicates that his readers had been redeemed ἐκ τῆς ματαίας ὑμῶν ἀναστροφῆς πατροπαραδότου ('from the futile way of life inherited from your ancestors', 1:18b). The believers' past ἀναστροφή

---

[38] Morris, *The Atonement*, 102.
[39] See Carson, *The Gospel According to John*, 150–1.
[40] J. Jeremias, 'πάσχα', *TDNT*, 5: 900.

('conduct expressed according to certain principles, *way of life, conduct, behaviour*';[41] a favourite word of Peter's, 1:15, 18; 2:12, 3:1, 2, 16) is described by two different adjectives, μάταιος and πατροπαράδοτος. The term ἀναστροφή itself 'implies not merely behaviour but also the values, norms, and commitments that constitute an entire "way of life"'.[42] Peter had previously described this 'way of life' as their 'former ignorance' (πρότερον ἐν τῇ ἀγνοίᾳ, 1:14). Now here in v. 18b he describes it as μάταιος ('useless, futile, empty'; cf. also ματαιότης, ματαίωμα and ματαιόω).[43] This adjective appears 75 times in the LXX translating a variety of Hebrew words but mostly הֶבֶל ('vapour, breath', fig., 'vanity'),[44] שָׁוְא ('emptiness, vanity'),[45] כָּזָב ('lie, falsehood, deception'),[46] תֹּהוּ ('formlessness, confusion, unreality, emptiness, worthlessness'),[47] חִנָּם ('in vain'),[48] and אָוֶן ('trouble, sorrow, wickedness'; also used for 'idolatry, idols').[49] Tiedtke suggests that 'these words all denote the various ways in which man can resist the reality of God in his revelation and claims on him'.[50] The adjective μάταιος occurs in the Old Testament chiefly in three main contexts: (1) for the lying and deceptive words of false prophets (e.g., Ezek. 13:6–19; Zech. 10:2; Lam. 2:24), (2) in condemnation of the idols of the other nations (Lev. 17:7; 2 Chron. 11:15; Isa. 2:20; Jer. 2:5; 8:19; 10:15; Jon. 2:9), and (3) in statements about the futility and vanity of human life (LXX Ps. 61:10 [62:9]; Isa. 49:4; cf. the use of ματαιότης ['emptiness, vanity'] in Ecclesiastes [39×, each time rendering הֶבֶל]).

In the New Testament μάταιος occurs in only five places outside of 1 Peter (Acts 14:15; 1 Cor. 3:20; 15:17; Tit. 3:9; Jas 1:26). In Acts 14:15 the phrase τούτων τῶν ματαίων ('these vain things') refers to the practice of idolatry (cf. vv. 11–14). In 1 Cor. 3:20 Paul quotes from LXX Ps. 93[94]:11 in order to provide biblical support for his assertion that '[v. 19] the wisdom of this world is foolishness before God. [v. 20] For it is written, [γέγραπται γάρ] ... "The Lord knows the thoughts of the wise, that they are futile [μάταιοι]"'. Then in 15:17 μάταιος emphasises the utter futility of a faith that denies the resurrection of Christ: 'If Christ has not been raised, your faith is ματαίας' ('futile' [NRSV, ESV, NIV], 'worthless' [NASB], 'useless' [CEV]). Titus 3:19 warns that 'foolish controversies and genealogies and strife and disputes about the law' are μάταιοι (3:9). Finally, James warns that '[i]f any think they are religious,

---

[41] BDAG, 73.   [42] Elliott, *1 Peter*, 370.   [43] L&N, 65.37.
[44] BDB, 210.   [45] BDB, 996.   [46] BDB, 469.   [47] BDB, 1062.
[48] BDB, 336; E. Tiedtke, 'μάταιος', *NIDNTT*, 1: 550.
[49] BDB, 19–20.   [50] Tiedtke, 'μάταιος', *NIDNTT*, 1: 550.

and do not bridle their tongues but deceive their hearts, their religion is μάταιος' (1:26). Goppelt explains this adjective as describing

> what a world of mere appearances erects against reality, what therefore is deceptive, pointless, and senseless. Greek tragedy, like the LXX and NT, speaks of a form of human conduct that strides senselessly into the void ... According to the New Testament all are futile who in point of fact deny God, Christians included (1 Cor. 15:17; Tit. 3:9; Jas 1:26). Those who do not draw their life from God lose themselves in their world to unrelatedness, since they understand neither themselves nor those with whom they come in contact in terms of their origin and destiny.[51]

The second adjective, πατροπαράδοτος (lit., 'handed down from the fathers')[52] is a *hapax legomenon* in the New Testament and does not appear at all in the LXX. In Greco-Roman literature and inscriptions it designates 'the positive sense of values, traditions, and customs that are rooted in the past and transmitted by the fathers as a worthy heritage'.[53] The earliest known text (5 October 135 BC) containing the word πατροπαράδοτος is a letter written by King Attalus III [reigned 138–133 BC] to the council and people of Pergamum informing his subjects that his mother Stratonice was πρὸς ἄπαντας μὲν τοὺς θεοὺς εὐσεβῶς προσηνέχθη, μάλιστα δὲ πρὸς τὸν Δία τὸν Σαβάζιον πατροπαράδοτον αὐτὸν κομίσασα εἰς τὴν πατρίδα ἡμῶν (*Perg.* 248.49). This word is also used on a number of occasions by Diodorus of Sicily (active between 60 and 30 BC). He provides one interesting example when explaining how Alexander dealt with the many problems that 'beset his kingdom on every side' (*Hist.* 17.3.6). Diodorus explains:

> First he dealt with the Thessalians, reminding them of his ancient relationship to them through Heracles [ὑπομνήσας τῇ ἀρχαίας ἀφ᾽ Ηρακλέους συγγενείας] and raising their hope by kindly words and by rich promises as well, and prevailed upon them by formal vote of the Thessalian League to recognise as his the leadership of Greece which he had inherited from his father [τὴν πατροπαράδοτον ἡγεμονίαν]. (17.4.1)

Thus in the hope of winning the good will of the Thessalian people Alexander appeals to what is πατροπαράδοτον. Another very interesting

---

[51] Goppelt, *1 Peter*, 117.   [52] Elliott, *1 Peter*, 370.   [53] Ibid.

example of this usage can be found in his *Hist.* 4.8.5 where Diodorus speaks of the lack of gratitude and veneration shown Heracles for his great accomplishments:

> And strange it would be indeed that Heracles, while yet among mortal men, should by his own labours have brought under cultivation the inhabited world, and that human beings should nevertheless forget the benefactions which he rendered them generally and slander the commendation he received for the noblest deeds, and strange that our ancestors should have unanimously accorded immortality to him because of his exceedingly great attainments, and that we should nevertheless fail to cherish and maintain for the god the pious devotion which has been handed down to us from our fathers [τὴν πατροπαράδοτον].

Van Unnik remarks: 'In all these texts πατροπαράδοτος has a favourable meaning. What is called so, recommends itself thereby.'[54] The ancients placed a high value on the ancestral character of life and so to live 'in conformity with the ancestral customs and conventional wisdom of the past was the mark of a wise and moral person'.[55] Porphyry (*c.* 232–303), for example, writes: 'The greatest fruit of piety is to worship the gods according to the traditions of our ancestors' (*Marc.* 14; cf. the citation from *Perg.* 248.49 above).[56] Neglect of one's ancestral roots, religion, and tradition, on the other hand, 'were signs of gross disrespect and "impiety" and cause for social disdain and alienation (Cicero, *Leg.* 2.7.19–27; Plutarch, *Am. Prol.* 756; Dio Cassius 52.36)'.[57] Nevertheless, Peter labels it all as 'futile' and 'empty' (μάταιος) and something from which Christ, at a great personal cost (τιμίῳ αἵματι Χριστου), has liberated believers (ἐλυτρώθητε ἐκ). Bauernfeind remarks: '[T]he fact that, with no special emphasis, μάταιος is quite naturally set alongside a word like πατροπαράδοτος, is quite shattering for the man who for his part thinks that he may use this word with thankfulness'.[58] Moreover, as Elliott points out, this liberation was accomplished by one already 'foreknown/predestined before the foundation of the world' (προεγνωσμένου μὲν πρὸ καταβολῆς κόσμου, 1:20a) and as a result of a more ancient and superior pedigree than any human ancestral custom. In sum, the effect or result of Christ's redeeming, sacrificial death was that

---

54 Van Unnik, 'The Critique of Paganism in 1 Peter 1:18', 135.
55 Elliott, *1 Peter*, 371.   56 Cited in Elliott, *1 Peter*, 371.
57 Ibid.   58 O. Bauernfeind, 'μάταιος', *TDNT*, 4: 522.

believers have been liberated from the futile, empty, and inherited ways of their past.

Summary

In this passage (1:18–19), Peter provides his readers with a Christological basis for the preceding imperative to conduct their lives 'with reverence [toward God]' (v. 17, ἐν φόβῳ … ἀναστράφητε, [v. 18] εἰδότες ὅτι …). In doing so, Peter does not *merely* present Christ's redemptive suffering as a *motivation* for conducting their lives in an attitude of holy reverence toward God but as the very *basis* for it. The basis for such reverent 'conduct' (ἀναστράφητε, v. 17) lies in the fact that they have been 'ransomed' (ἐλυτρώθητε) from a 'way of life' (ἀναστροφή, v. 18b) governed, not by the fear of God, but by the dictates of pagan custom and religion inherited from their ancestors (πατροπαραδότου). Redemption, our author asserts, entails a divine liberation from bondage to these futile, empty, and aimless (ματαίας) ways of the past (v. 18). In a creative blending of elements pertaining to Israel's historic redemption from Egypt and the ransoming of slaves, Peter describes the liberation achieved by Christ as coming at the extraordinarily high price of his own blood shed in sacrificial slaughter on the cross (οὐ φθαρτοῖς, ἀργυρίῳ ἢ χρυσίῳ … ἀλλὰ τιμίῳ αἵματι ὡς ἀμνοῦ ἀμώμου καὶ ἀσπίλου Χριστοῦ, v. 19). Moreover, the death of Christ ransoms because it is substitutionary, that is, he 'pays the price' (= death) that believers should have paid for the futile and foolish way of life they formerly practised (ἀναστροφὴ ματαία, v. 18) in contrast to the life of reverence (toward God, ἀναστροφὴ ἐν φόβῳ [v. 17]) demanded by God (the imperative of v. 17).

2. 1 Peter 2:21–25: 'Christ's suffering as sin-bearing'

This passage represents the heart of 1 Peter's Christology, bringing together ethics and theology in a profound and creative manner. It is particularly notable for its creative and original fusing of early Israelite, Hellenistic, and primitive Christian traditions to produce a unique three-fold portrayal of Jesus Christ (1) as a personal paradigm for suffering believers, (2) as the suffering servant of God through whose substitutionary death believers have been freed from the consequences of sin, spiritually healed, and enabled to live a life of righteousness, and (3) as the shepherd and overseer to whom his followers have been returned. As the heart of Peter's Christology, 2:21–5 represents a creative blending of Old Testament material and elements of Christ's passion resulting in a unique and powerful interpretation of the death of Christ as to its nature (vv. 21b, 24a), purpose (vv. 21d, 24b), and results (vv. 24d, 25b). Hence Morris is justified in his assessment of vv. 21–5 as 'perhaps the most significant passage in the Epistle for an understanding of the atonement'.[59]

Context

This passage is situated within a *Haustafel* (2:11–3:12) developed by means of a structural transition (2:11–12), followed by a general exhortation concerning subordinate conduct to civil authorities (2:13–17), particular exhortations to Christian wives (3:1–6) and husbands (3:7), and then a concluding exhortation to all believers (3:8–12). The entire section concerns the appropriate conduct of believers living as a minority group (or 'aliens and strangers', 2:11) in a pagan society that is suspicious of and hostile to them. The goal of such conduct is spelled out in 2:12: 'Having your conduct honourable among the Gentiles so that ... they may glorify God in the day of visitation' (cf. 4:11). The motivation for that conduct is set forth in 2:19–20 (God's eschatological approval) and 2:21–5 (Christ's own exemplary and redemptive suffering). Verses 21–5 are joined syntactically with the previous section (vv. 18–20) by means of the introductory conjunction γάρ ('for') and the words εἰς τοῦτο ἐκλήθητε ('to this you have been called'), καί ('also'), and ὑπο-γραμμός ('[leaving you an] example').

Content

Verses 21–5 can be divided into two parts with (1) vv. 21–3 dealing with the nature (v. 21a-c) and purpose (vv. 21d–23) of Jesus' suffering as exemplary and (2) vv. 24–5 dealing with the nature (v. 24a), purpose (v. 24b-c), and result (vv. 24d–25) of Jesus' suffering as a substitutionary bearing of the believers' sins.

Christ's suffering as exemplary (vv. 21–3)

Its nature (v. 21a-c)

The explanatory γάρ ('for') at the beginning of v. 21 explains why believers suffer unjustly. The answer is: εἰς τοῦτο ἐκλήθητε (lit. 'to this you have been called'). The telic phrase εἰς τοῦτο ('to this'), indicating the goal of the believer's calling, points back to the believer's patient

---

[59] Morris, *The Cross in the New Testament*, 322.

endurance in suffering for doing what is right (as such it picks up on the previous two occurrences of τοῦτο ['this'] in vv. 19 and 20 which also refer to doing what is right despite unjust suffering). The verb ἐκλήθητε ('called', aorist passive of καλέω, 'choose for receipt of a special benefit or experience, *call*')[60] is a passive implying God as the subject and hence the one who has called them. In 1 Peter the notion of the believers' calling (cf. 1:15 [τὸν καλέσαντα ὑμᾶς]; 2:9 [τοῦ ὑμᾶς καλέσαντος]; 3:9 [ἐκλήθητε]; 5:10 [ὁ θεὸς … ὁ καλέσας ὑμᾶς]) is linked closely with the idea of their election (2:9; 5:10) and denotes the sovereign, electing, and effectual calling of believers by God (cf. 1:15; 2:9; 5:10), through the proclamation of the gospel (cf. 1:12, 25), to conversion (2:9), holiness (1:15), and final salvation (3:9; 5:10).

The ὅτι that follows is causal ('because') supplying the reason why believers have been called to suffer for doing what is right: **ὅτι** καὶ Χριστὸς ἔπαθεν ὑπὲρ ὑμῶν ὑμῖν ὑπολιμπάνων ὑπογραμμόν. The phrase ὅτι καὶ Χριστὸς ἔπαθεν ('because Christ also suffered') recurs in 3:18 where it once again introduces an extended reflection on the passion of Christ in order to provide a Christological basis for doing what is right despite suffering (3:13–17/18–22; cf. 2:18–20/21–5). The words καὶ ἔπαθεν ('also suffered') here in 2:21 point back to the πάσχοντες ('suffering') of v. 20, making explicit the relationship between the suffering of Christ and that of believers. Here Christ's innocent suffering (ὃς ἁμαρτίαν οὐκ ἐποίησεν ['who committed no sin'], v. 21a) is held up as an 'example' (ὑπογραμμος, v. 21c) for the unjust suffering of Christian slaves (and by implication all believers) (2:19–20).

It is possible that the words Χριστὸς ἔπαθεν ὑπὲρ ὑμῶν ('Christ suffered for you') denote, in anticipation of the ensuing discussion (v. 24), Christ's substitutionary suffering (which includes his death) in the place of believers (ὑπὲρ ὑμῶν). While this undoubtedly reflects an accurate understanding of the formulation Χριστὸς ἔπαθεν ὑπὲρ ὑμῶν, the significance attached to it by the author in this context, however, is to be found in the phrase that immediately follows it: ὑμῖν ὑπολιμπάνων ὑπογραμμόν. The present participle ὑπολιμπάνων (lit. 'leaving behind', only here in biblical Greek) should probably be construed as an adverbial participle of result denoting the outcome or result of Christ's suffering (as denoted by the main verb ἔπαθεν).[61] As such the words Χριστὸς ἔπαθεν ὑπὲρ ὑμῶν ὑμῖν ὑπολιμπάνων ὑπογραμμόν should be translated something like: 'Christ suffered for you *with the result of*

---

[60] BDAG, 503 (s.v. 4).   [61] See Wallace, *Greek Grammar*, 637.

leaving you an example'. Thus the focus here is on the exemplary nature of Christ's suffering.

The Greek word translated 'example', ὑπογραμμός (lit., 'model, pattern, outline, writing-copy'),[62] occurs only here in the New Testament and once in the LXX where it refers to the main 'outlines' of a story (ὑπογραμμοῖς τῆς ἐπιτομῆς, 2 Macc. 2:28). Much later Clement of Alexandria used it to refer to a 'copy head' or 'writing-copy for children' (ὑπογραμμός παιδικός, *Strom.* 5.8.49.1) containing all of the letters of the alphabet over which children learning to write would trace. The more common cognate verb, ὑπογράφω ('write under, i.e., trace letters for children to write over'), is used by Plato who speaks of 'writing-masters [who] first draw letters in faint outline with the pen for their less advanced pupils [οἱ γραμματισταί τοῖς μήπω δεινοῖς τῶν παίδων ὑπογράψαντες γραμμάς τῇ γραφίδι], and then give them the copy-book and make them write according to the guidance of their lines [οὕτω τὸ γραμματεῖον διδόασι καὶ ἀναγκάζουσι γράφειν κατὰ τὴν ὑφήγησιν τῶν γραμμῶν]'.[63] Origen uses the verb in a more figurative sense when he speaks of the Lord's Prayer as a 'model' or 'example' to followed (τὴν ὑπογραφεῖσαν ὑπὸ τοῦ κυρίου προσευχήν, *Or.* 18.1).

Along similar lines is the figurative use of ὑπογραμμός in early Christian literature to denote a 'model' or 'example' in the moral sense. The noun appears three times in *1 Clement*, twice with reference to Christ (as an example [ὁ ὑπογραμμός] of humility, 16.17[64] [note the use of Isa. 53 in this context], and as a model [τὸν ὑπογραμμόν] of doing good works [= doing God's will], 33.8) and once of the apostle Paul (whom Clement refers to as 'the greatest example of endurance' [ὑπομενῆς γενόμενος μέγιστος ὑπογραμμός], 5.7). In a passage (Polycarp, *Phil.* 8.1–2) with many affinities to our own (2:21–4), Polycarp calls his readers to 'be imitators [μιμηταὶ γενώμεθα] of [Christ's] endurance … for he set this example [τὸν ὑπογραμμόν] for us through what he did' (8.2). In this context in 1 Peter (v. 21), the result of Christ's suffering was that he left his followers with an example to follow. As Jobes puts it, 'he is *the* paradigm by which Christians write large the letters of his gospel in their lives. If Christians are to live as servants of God (2:16), the essence of that identity is a willingness to suffer unjustly as Jesus did, exemplifying in suffering the same attitude and behaviour he did.'[65]

---

[62] LSJ, 1877.   [63] Plato, *Prot.* 326D (Elliott, *1 Peter*, 526, wrongly has 362D).
[64] *1 Clem.* 16.17 (Elliott, *1 Peter*, 526, wrongly has 16.7).
[65] Jobes, *1 Peter*, 195 (emphasis hers).

Its purpose (vv. 21d–23). The purpose of this example is indicated by the ἵνα ('that, in order that') clause (v. 21d): ἵνα ἐπακολουθήσ
ητε τοῖς ἴχνεσιν αὐτο. The ἵνα plus the subjunctive (here ἐπακολουθήσητε [aorist active subjunctive]) frequently denotes purpose/result in the
New Testament.[66] The verb ἐπακολουθέω ('follow, follow after') occurs
only sixteen times in the LXX (e.g., of 'following' God [Num. 14:24;
Josh. 14:9, 14], idols [Lev. 19:4], mediums [Lev. 19:31; 20:6], the ways
of the other nations [Deut. 12:30], and of pursuit in battle [Jdt. 14:4])
and four times in the New Testament (Mk 16:20 [v.l.], διὰ τῶν ἐπα-
κολουθούντων [following as a result] σημείω; 1 Tim. 5:10, ['to devote
oneself']; 5:24 ['to follow after (of sins)']). This verb, however, is related
to the more common ἀκολουθέω ('be a disciple, follow', 'come after',
'accompany', 90× in the New Testament).[67] It is most commonly used by
the Gospel writers (70×) to refer either to those who followed Jesus in
the physical sense, whether as his disciples or interested others (60×), or
in the more figurative sense of participating in his suffering (Mt. 10:38;
16:24; Mk 8:34; Lk. 9:23; 4:27; Jn 13:36; 21:19). In 1 Pet. 2:21, the verb
ἐπακολουθέω is used in this latter figurative sense.

The word ἴχνος ('footprint') occurs thirty-one times in the LXX and
variously denotes the 'sole' (of the foot [9×], e.g., Deut. 11:24, 28:35;
Jdt. 6:4]), 'feet' (of a person, 2 Kgs 9:35; even the 'foot' of God, Ezek.
43:7), 'hoofs' (of cattle, Ezek. 32:17), 'tracks' (of an eagle, Prov. 30:19),
'trace' (of a ship, Wis. 5:10), 'footsteps' (LXX Ps. 17[18]:37), 'steps'
(as a mode of behaviour, Prov. 5:5; Sir. 21:6; cf. Philo, *Opif.* 144). It
may also be used either for 'an individual impression on the ground [i.e.,
"footprint"] or a continuous line of such impressions, i.e., a trail'.[68] In
the New Testament ἴχνος is used in only two other places (Rom. 4:12;
2 Cor. 12:18) and always with a figurative sense. In Rom. 4:12 it refers
to following (τοῖς στοιχοῦσιν) the 'example' (lit. 'footsteps', τοῖς
ἴχνεσιν) of the faith that Abraham had. In 2 Cor. 12:18 Paul assures
the Corinthians that he and his co-worker Titus walk (περιεπατήσαμεν)
'in the same footsteps' (τοῖς αὐτοῖς ἴχνεσιν) and 'in the same spirit'
(τῷ αὐτῷ πνεύματι). Closer to the setting of 1 Pet. 2:21 are two later
passages which use ἴχνος in the context of martyrdom. In his *Epistle to
the Ephesians* (12.2) Ignatius speaks of wanting to 'be found in [Paul's]
footsteps when I attain to God' (ὑπὸ τὰ ἴχνη εὑρεθῆναι, ὅταν θεοῦ
ἐπιτύχω). In the second text the author of the *Martyrdom of Polycarp*
speaks of 'the blessed Polycarp [who] bore witness unto death' and then

---

[66] See Wallace, *Greek Grammar*, 473–4.   [67] Gramcord.
[68] A. Stumpff, 'ἴχνος', *TDNT*, 3: 402.

concludes with the words: 'May we be found to have followed in his footsteps [τὰ ἴχνη εὑρεθῆναι] in the kingdom of Jesus Christ' (22.1).

In 1 Pet. 2:21 the expression ἐπακολουθήσητε τοῖς ἴχνεσιν αὐτοῦ is also being used figuratively. But in what sense are the readers to follow Christ? Bigg suggests that 'Christ is spoken of as the pattern which we are to reproduce in every stroke of every letter, till our writing is a facsimile of the Master's'.[69] Kelly, on the other hand, rightly notes that Peter did not intend to convey the idea that his readers should attempt 'to reproduce all the particular details of Christ's passion which he is recapitulating ... Rather it is that they should expect to suffer, and to suffer without in anyway having earned it, and that they should be ready to exhibit the same uncomplaining acceptance.'[70] The words τοῖς ἴχνεσιν ('in his steps') are to be construed as a dative of rule specifying 'the rule or code a person follows or the standard of conduct to which he or she conforms'.[71] As the immediate context indicates, the 'standard of conduct' consists in Christ's example of innocent behaviour (v. 22ab), refusal to retaliate when suffering (v. 23ab), and commitment of his cause to God (v. 23c). The call (ἐκλήθητε) to follow (ἐπακολουθήσητε) in the footsteps (τοῖς ἴχνεσιν) of Christ, then, consists more in discipleship than imitation, direction than details; it is a track to be followed rather than a track to be imitated. Jobes concludes:

> Jesus left us a pattern over which we are to trace our lives, in order that we might follow in his footsteps. This is a strong image associating the Christian's life with the life of Christ. For one cannot step into the footsteps of Jesus and head off in any other direction than the direction he took, and his footsteps lead to the cross, through the grave, and onward to glory.[72]

Christ's suffering as substitutionary (vv. 24–5)

Coming to v. 24 it is immediately apparent to the reader that Peter is presenting Christ's suffering as far more than just an example. In a very brief but theologically pregnant statement, Peter unfolds for us the significance of Christ's suffering ὑπὲρ ὑμῶν ('for you', v. 21b). Morris, as we noted above, considers this statement to be 'the most significant

---

[69] Bigg, *Epistles of St. Peter*, 146.   [70] Kelly, *The Epistles of Peter*, 120.
[71] Wallace, *Greek Grammar*, 157.   [72] Jobes, *1 Peter*, 195.

passage in the epistle for an understanding of the atonement'.[73] Denny
puts it well:

> It is as though the apostle could not turn his eyes to the cross
> for a moment without being fascinated and held by it. He saw
> more in it habitually, and he saw far more in it now than was
> needed to point his exhortation to the wronged slaves. It is not
> *their* interest in it, as the supreme example of suffering inno-
> cence and patience, but the interest of all sinners in it as the only
> source of redemption by which he is ultimately inspired.[74]

Its nature (v. 24a)

The opening statement of v. 24a expands on v. 21b explaining in what
sense Christ suffered ὑπὲρ ὑμῶν ('for you'). In this first clause it is possible that Peter is actually alluding to three different verses in Isa. 53:

Isa. 53:4	οὗτος	τὰς	ἁμαρτίας	ἡμῶν		φέρει
Isa. 53:11		τὰς	ἁμαρτίας	αὐτῶν αὐτὸς		ἀνοίσει
Isa. 53:12	αὐτὸς		ἁμαρτίας	πολλῶν		ἀνήνεγκεν
1 Pet. 2:24	**ὃς**	**τὰς**	**ἁμαρτίας**	**ἡμῶν αὐτος**		**ἀνήνεγκεν**

The verb ἀναφέρω ('take, lead, bring up', 'offer up';[75] in this context
'to bear'[76]) can have the meaning of 'to offer [a sacrifice]' (as in 2:5,
ἀνενέγκαι πνευματικὰς θυσίας ['to offer spiritual sacrifices']; cf. Heb.
7:27; 9:28; 13:15; Jas 2:21). Weiss notes that it is used as a technical
term in the LXX, in a few cases for the bringing of offerings but more
generally for the sacrifice itself.[77] It is used in the LXX to render a variety of Hebrew words, though the hiphil of עָלָה ('offer [sacrifice]')[78]
and קְטַר ('make sacrifices smoke, offer them by burning')[79] are the most
common. Bigg suggests that in light of the fact that 'ἀναφερεῖν is commonly used in the LXX of bringing a sacrifice and laying it on the altar',
the entire phrase of v. 24a, therefore, must '[represent] Christ as not only
the sin-offering ... but as the priest who took the sins, or the sin-offering
and laid the sacrifice on the altar of the cross'.[80] While not wanting to
completely reject any notion of sacrifice here, it should however be noted
that (1) nowhere in the New Testament is the cross ever depicted as an

---

[73] Morris, *The Cross in the New Testament*, 322.
[74] Denny, *The Death of Christ*, 57 (emphasis his).
[75] BDAG, 75. [76] J. Kremer, 'ἀναφέρω', *EDNT*, 1: 94.
[77] K. Weiss, 'φέρω', *TDNT*, 9: 60. [78] BDB, 750.
[79] BDB, 883. [80] Bigg, *Epistles of St. Peter*, 147.

altar, and (2) the idea that God could accept our sins as an acceptable sacrifice is, as Michaels notes, 'intolerable in any known Jewish or early Christian context (contrast, e.g., the faultless and flawless lamb whose blood is shed for redemption according to 1:19)'.[81] While Schelkle also agrees that 2:24 depicts the cross as an altar, he is quick to point out that is not 'our sins' (τὰς ἁμαρτίας ἡμῶν) that were offered up on it, but Christ's body: '[D]as Opfer, das der Erlöser auf diesen Altar hinauftrug, ist natürlich nicht die Sünde, sondern es ist sein Leib.'[82] The problem with this view, however, is that τὰς ἁμαρτίας ἡμῶν ('our sins') and not τῷ σώματι αὐτοῦ ('[in] his body') is the object of the verb ἀνήνεγκεν. Nor is it certain that ἀνήνεγκεν means 'offered up [a sacrifice]' here.

Deissmann, on the other hand, completely rejects any notion of sacrifice, contending that ἐπί with the accusative 'at once introduces the meaning *to carry up to*'.[83] Thus v. 24a should be rendered, 'he himself carried our sins in his body up to the cross'.[84] Deissmann remarks:

> The simplest explanation is this: when Christ *bears up to* the cross the sins of men, then men have their sins no more; the *bearing up* is a *taking away*. The expression thus signifies quite generally that Christ took away our sins by his death: there is no suggestion whatever of the special ideas of substitution or sacrifice.[85]

This understanding of ἐπί suggests to a number of commentators that Christ is being likened to the scapegoat upon which the sins of the people were placed and then carried away into the wilderness (Lev. 16:20–2).[86] A few comments need to be made in response: (1) First, as Beare notes, Deissmann's insistence on rendering the words ἀνήνεγκεν ἐπὶ τὸ ξύ-λον as 'bear up *to* the cross' is dependent upon the 'erroneous supposition that ἐπί with the accusative can only mean "up to", not "upon"'.[87] But, as Beare goes on to explain, 'the accusative at this period is invading the territory of the other cases and is well on the way to the victory which it has won in modern Greek and ἐπί with the accusative frequently does mean "upon"'.[88] According to Harris, ἐπί 'basically denote[s] position *on* something which forms a support or foundation'.[89] He goes on to note that 'in this primary sense of "on", "upon", *epi* is followed by the acc.,

---

[81] Michaels, *1 Peter*, 148.   [82] Schelkle, *Petrusbriefe*, 85.
[83] Deissmann, *Bible Studies*, 89.   [84] Ibid., 89–90.
[85] Ibid., 90 (emphasis his).
[86] See Brox, *Petrusbrief*, 138; Goldstein, 'Die Kirche', 33–4, n. 27.
[87] Beare, *First Epistle of Peter*, 123.   [88] Ibid., 123–4.
[89] Harris, 'Prepositions and Theology', 1193.

the gen., or the dat., often without distinction in meaning'.[90] In the New Testament, ἐπί is most commonly used with the accusative (464×; genitive, 216×; dative, 176×), and as BDF points out, it 'is used not only in response to the question "whither?" [i.e., "*to* the cross"] … but often also in response to the question "where"? [i.e., "*on* the cross"]'.[91] Thus, the rendition '*to* the cross' is not demanded by the preposition ἐπί with the accusative. (2) It is doubtful that we have here a reference to the scapegoat ritual in which the sins of the people were symbolically transferred to the goat and then carried away (Lev. 16). (i) First, it is not certain that Isa. 53, which serves as the source of Peter's words here, involves any evident allusions to the scapegoat ritual (though there are some formal similarities). (ii) Second, as Olson observes, 'the scapegoat was not slain in sacrifice but was driven away into the wilderness' (though there was perhaps the expectation that it would die).[92] (iii) In the end, the explanation that simply says that Christ carried the believers' sins *to* or *up to* the cross fails to explain adequately how this action actually atoned for those sins. Something more needs to be said.

A third and more probable translation of ἀναφέρω is 'to bear' with ἐπὶ τὸ ξύλον carrying the sense of 'on/upon the cross'. Thus the phrase ὃς τὰς ἁμαρτίας αὐτὸς ἡμῶν ἀνήνεγκεν ἐπὶ τὸ ξύλον is best rendered 'he himself bore our sins upon the cross'. The notion of bearing sins is a familiar one in the Old Testament, where it generally carries the sense of 'to bear the consequences (or punishment) of those sins' (e.g., Exod. 28:38, 43; Lev. 5:1, 17; 7:18; 19:8; 20:19, 20; 22:9; 24:15; Num. 5:31; 9:13; 14:33–5; 18:1, 22; Ezek. 18:20). This is probably the meaning the expression has here in 1 Pet. 2:24a. As Cranfield remarks, 'the bearing of our sins means suffering the punishment of them in our place'.[93]

At least three arguments can be put forward in support of this interpretation. First, this meaning of 'bearing sins' is well attested in the Old Testament, where the same (and similar – נָשָׂא is translated by both ἀναφέρω and λαμβάνω) Greek and Hebrew words appear.[94] For example, we are told in Num. 14:33–5 that Israel 'bore her sins' *by* wandering in the wilderness for forty years until they perished:

> But your sons shall be feeding in the wilderness for forty years; and they shall bear [Gk, ἀναφέρω; Heb., נָשָׂא] your fornication [τὴν πορνείαν ὑμῶν] until your limbs are wasted in the

---

[90] Ibid.   [91] BDF, §233 (1).   [92] Olson, 'The Atonement in 1 Peter', 338.

[93] Cranfield, *First Epistle of Peter*, 67–8.

[94] See Denny, *The Death of Christ*, 59; Morris, *The Cross in the New Testament*, 324.

wilderness. According to the number of the days, as many as you spied out the land – forty days, a day per year – you shall bear [Gk, λαμβάνω; Heb., נָשָׂא] your sins [τὰς ἁμαρτίας ὑμῶν] for forty years, and you shall know the wrath of my anger. I the Lord have spoken; surely I will do thus to this evil congregation that has banded together against me. In this wilderness they shall be utterly consumed, and there they shall die.[95]

Similarly, in Ezek. 18:20 we read that each person will bear the responsibility for their own sins: 'The person who sins will die. The son will not bear [Gk, λαμβάνω; Heb., נָשָׂא] the punishment for the father's iniquity [Gk, ἀδικία; Heb.,עָוֺן] nor will the father bear [Gk, λαμβάνω; Heb., נָשָׂא] the punishment for the son's iniquity [Gk, ἀδικία; Heb.,עָוֺן]; the righteousness of the righteous will be upon himself, and the wickedness of the wicked will be upon himself.' Thus 'bearing sins' is equivalent to 'bearing the consequences of sins'.

Second, Isa. 53, which, as we have already noted, serves as the source of Peter's words, also suggests a clear relationship between 'bearing sins' and 'bearing the punishment for sins'. Beginning with the phrase οὗτος τὰς ἁμαρτίας ἡμῶν φέρει ('this one bears our sins', LXX Isa. 53:4a [quoted in 1 Pet. 2:24]) we read (vv. 4–5):

> This one bears our sins
> and suffers pain for us;
> and we accounted him to be in trouble
> and calamity and ill-treatment.
> But he was wounded for our transgressions,
> and has been weakened because of our sins;
> upon him was the discipline of our peace,
>   by his bruise we are healed.[96]

The writer begins with the parallel expressions οὗτος τὰς ἁμαρτίας ἡμῶν φέρει καὶ περὶ ἡμῶν ὀδυνᾶται ('This one bears our sins and suffers pain for us', v. 4). The Greek φέρω ('to bear') translates the Hebrew נָשָׂא ('bear, carry'; cf. v. 12, וְהוּא חֵטְא־רַבִּים נָשָׂא, 'he himself bore the sins of many'), which, in this context, suggests BDB, carries the sense of to 'bear guilt or punishment'.[97] Then in v. 11 the Hebrew סָבַל ('bear', cf. v. 4b; translated by the Gk ἀναφέρω ['to take upon oneself, to bear']) is used in conjunction with עָוֺן ('iniquity, guilt, or punishment of iniquity';[98] Gk ἁμαρτίας ['sins']). Thus the expression

---

[95] NETS.   [96] NETS.   [97] BDB, 671.   [98] BDB, 731.

הוּא וַעֲוֹנֹתָם לָרַבִּים עַבְדִּי (v. 11, τὰς ἁμαρτίας αὐτῶν αὐτὸς ἀνοίσει)
can be rendered, 'the consequences of their iniquities he shall bear'.[99]
But is this interpretation supported by the context? According to v. 5
the servant 'was wounded for our transgressions, and has been weak-
ened because of our sins; upon him was the discipline of our peace, by
his bruise we are healed'. The 'wounding' (τραυματίζω, 'to wound';
חָלַל, 'pierce, wound'), 'weakening' (μαλακίζομαι, 'to be weakly, to
be sick';[100] דָּכָא, 'crush', cf. 53:10), 'disciplining' (παιδεία, 'discipline, correction, chastisement';[101] מוּסָר, 'chastisement'), and 'bruising' (μώλωψ, 'stripe, bruise'; חַבּוּרָה, 'blow, stripe [inflicted upon the
servant]'[102]) of the servant all denote the punishments he bore, not for
his own sins (cf. v. 9b, ἀνομίαν οὐκ ἐποίησεν οὐδὲ εὑρέθη δόλος ἐν
τῷ στόματι αὐτου [quoted in 1 Pet. 2:22] but 'for our transgressions'
(διὰ τὰς ἀνομίας ἡμῶν) and 'because of our sins' (διὰ τὰς ἁμαρτίας
ἡμῶν). The contrast between third person singlar ([οὗτος = 'he' (lit.,
'this one)], αὐτὸν, v. 4; αὐτός, αὐτοῦ, v. 5) and first person plural
(ἡμῶν [2×], ἡμεῖς, v. 4; ἡμῶν [3×], ἡμεῖς, v. 5) pronouns 'serves to
underline the simple fact that the servant, who is distinct from God's
people, suffered in their place, as their substitute'.[103] Thus 'bearing
sins' in this context signifies 'bearing the consequences *or* punishment
for sins'.

Third, the very fact that Christ bore our sins 'on the cross' (ἐπὶ τὸ
ξύλον) – an instrument of punishment – suggests that 'bearing sins'
here signifies 'bearing the punishment for sins'. The Greek word rendered 'cross' here is ξύλον ('wood, tree, cross')[104] and not, as we might
have expected, σταυρός ('cross'; related to σταυρόω, 'to crucify').[105]
The noun ξύλον was used in the Greco-Roman world to denote wood
(dead or alive) or timber, a building material, and just about anything
made out of wood: that is, utensils, cultic objects, weapons, and instruments of punishment. As an instrument of punishment, ξύλον could
denote a heavy wooden collar which was put on the neck of the prisoner (Aristophanes, *Nub.* 592; *Lys.* 680) or stocks into which the feet
were fastened (Herodotus, *Hist.* 9.3.7; Aristophanes, *Eq.* 367, 394, 705).
ξύλον could also denote the 'stake' upon which criminals were impaled
(Alexander, *De Figuris* 222.10). As Schneider observes: 'Already, then,
in secular Gk. the word ξύλον took on the sense of something disgraceful

---

[99] This is the rendering given by BDB, 731.   [100] LEH, 382.
[101] LEH, 455–6.   [102] BDB, 289.
[103] Jeffery, Ovey, and Sach, *Pierced for our Transgressions*, 54.
[104] BDAG, 685.   [105] BDAG, 941.

or shameful. From this, by way of the LXX, it is but a step to the New Testament sense of "cross." '[106]

In the LXX ξύλον is used more commonly in the sense of 'living wood' (i.e., a tree; e.g., Gen. 1:11; 2:9; Isa. 14:8; Ps. 1:3). It is also mentioned as a fuel (Gen. 22:3), building material (Gen. 6:14; Exod. 25:10; 1 Kgs 6:15), and as an instrument of punishment ('stocks', Job 33:11; 'gallows', Gen. 40:19; Esth. 2:23; 5:14). In Deut. 21:22–3 ξύλον is used to refer to the 'tree' or 'stake' upon which the body of an executed criminal was hung and exposed to public view and shame: 'Now if there is in someone sin punishable by death and he died, and you hang him on a tree [ἐπὶ ξύλου], his body shall not be left to hang all night upon the tree [ἐπὶ τοῦ ξύλου]; but with burial you shall bury him that same day, for anyone hanging on a tree [ἐπὶ ξύλου] is cursed by God' (cf. Josh. 10:26).[107]

The word ξύλον appears twenty times in the New Testament and denotes a building material (1 Cor. 3:12; Rev. 18:12), a weapon ('clubs', Mt. 26:47, 55; Mk 14:43, 48; Lk. 22:51; 22:52), an instrument of punishment ('stocks', Acts 16:24), and the 'tree of life' (τὸ ξύλον τῆ' ζωῆ, Rev. 2:7; 22:2, 14, 19). However, a distinctive and theologically significant use in the New Testament is the use of ξύλον as a synonym for σταυρός, a cross employed for the purpose of crucifixion and in particular the cross upon which Jesus was crucified (Acts 5:30; 10:39; 13:29; Gal. 3:13; *Barn.* 5:13; 8:5; 12:11; Polycarp, *Phil.* 8:1). In Acts 5:30 Peter accused the Jewish leaders of killing Jesus 'by hanging him on a tree' (κρεμάσαντες ἐπὶ ξύλου; cf. 10:39; 13:29). Siede suggests that 'the expression is reminiscent of Deut. 21:23, and stresses the shame of crucifixion. For as someone hanged on a tree, Jesus stood under the curse of God'.[108] This is in fact the very inference drawn by Paul in Gal. 3:13: 'Christ redeemed us from the curse of the law by becoming a curse for us – for it is written, "Cursed is everyone who hangs on a tree" [ἐπικατάρατος πᾶς ὁ κρεμάμενος ἐπὶ ξύλου].' The use of the word 'tree' to denote the 'cross' of crucifixion is also found in *The Temple Scroll*, where crucifixion is prescribed for those Israelites who are guilty of capital crimes, who curse their own people and betray them to foreign nations (11QT19 LXIV 7–12 [note the concluding allusion to Deut. 21:22–3]). Thus the notion of Jesus hanging upon a 'tree' carries with it the connotations of punishment, shame, and even accursedness of God.

However, it is the notion of punishment that appears to come to the fore in this expression in 1 Peter. Peter notes that Christ not only bore

---

[106] J. Schneider, 'ξύλον', *TDNT*, 5: 37.   [107] NETS.
[108] B. Siede, 'ξύλον', *NIDNTT*, 1: 390.

our sins 'on the tree' (ἐπὶ τὸ ξύλον) but that he bore them 'in his body' (ἐν τῷ σώματι αὐτοῦ). As Elliott notes, the phrase ἐν τῷ σώματι αὐτοῦ places stress 'on the bodily aspect of Christ's suffering and death' and as such 'recalls the earlier references to his shed blood (1:2, 19)'.[109] Thus when Peter says that Christ bore our sins 'in his body', he means Christ bore our sins by 'suffering the punishment of the cross in his body'. This focus on Christ's bodily suffering receives further emphasis from the final phrase of v. 24: οὗ τῷ μώλωπι ἰάθητε (discussed in depth below). The reference to Christ's wound(s) (τῷ μώλωπι) as a means of healing indicates that the punishment borne by Christ (as denoted by the phrase τῷ μώλωπι) was the means of the believers' salvation (as denoted by ἰάθητε [again, see below]). Thus the words ἐν τῷ σώματι ... ἐπὶ τὸ ξύλον ... οὗ τῷ μώλωπι ('in his body ... on the cross ... by his wounds') indicate an explicit link between the physical punishment borne by Christ and the salvation experienced by believers.[110] The implied teaching is that Christ's sufferings and death were vicarious; as our substitute (and representative?, see below) he suffered the penalty and bore the judgment which our sins merited. Selwyn asks: 'In what sense, may we ask, did Christ "bear" our sins? In the sense that he took the blame for them; suffered the curse of them (cf. Deut. 21:23, quoted in Gal. 3:13), which is separation from God; and endured their penal consequences.'[111] Having established that Christ's death represents a vicarious or substitutionary bearing of the punishment due for our sins, is there anything we can say about its representative significance? To that topic we now turn.

Its purpose (v. 24b-c)

The ἵνα ('so that') plus the subjunctive ζήσωμεν (aorist active subjunctive; cf. 1:7; 2:21d; 3:18c)[112] states the intended purpose and result of Christ's vicarious suffering and bearing of the punishment due for our sins: **ἵνα** ταῖς ἁμαρτίαις ἀπογενόμενοι τῇ δικαιοσύνῃ **ζήσωμεν**. The verb ἀπογίνομαι (only here in the New Testament) literally means 'to be away from, have no part in',[113] or 'to cease, to stop' in the sense of 'a complete and abrupt change'.[114] The verb can also be used figuratively with the sense of 'to depart (from life)', that is, 'to die' (e.g., P.Grenf. 2.69[10], τῷ ἀπογεγονότι πατρὶ αὐ[τ]οῦ, 'his departed father'). Many

---

[109] Elliott, *1 Peter*, 534.
[110] Though at the same time I do not wish to imply that Christ's sufferings were merely physical (see Cranfield, *First Epistle of Peter*, 68).
[111] Selwyn, *First Epistle of St. Peter*, 180.
[112] See Wallace, *Greek Grammar*, 473–4.   [113] LSJ, 194.   [114] L&N, 68.37.

commentators opt for the latter option based on two principal observations: (1) ἀπογενόμενοι is parallel to ζήσωμεν ('might live') suggesting the translation 'having died'.[115] (2) ἀπογίνομαι is used here with a dative of reference (ταῖς ἁμαρτίαις) rather than the genitive of separation (BDF, §180) as we might have expected if Peter were referring to separation *from* sins (e.g., Thucydides 1.39.3, τῶν ἁμαρτημάτων ἀπογενόμενοι; cf. Josephus, *Ant.* 19.178 and also the following phrase in 1 Pet. 2:11, ἀπέχεσθαι τῶν σαρκικῶν ἐπιθυμιῶν). Thus most translations render v. 24bc something like, 'that we might die to sin and live to righteousness' (ESV).

The thought here, remarks Hooker, 'is very close to that which Paul expresses in Rom. 6:1, where Christ's death and resurrection mean that believers die to sin and live to righteousness'.[116] Thus for Hooker, the key idea that ties New Testament Christology to soteriology is that of solidarity or *representation*.[117] What do we mean by 'representation'? Dunn explains, 'To adapt the words of Irenaeus, *Jesus became one with man in order to put an end to sinful man in order that a new man might come into being. He became what man is in order that by his death and resurrection man might become what he is.*'[118] In his death Christ represents all those who die, while in his resurrection he represents those who identify with him in his life from death (i.e., believers). Thus in dying to sins, remarks Miguéns, 'les chrétiens étaient tous récapitulés dans le Christ lors de sa mort; le baptême, qui les incorpore à la mort du Christ, leur en fait prendre conscience; par conséquent, le chrétien est déjà mort à tout ce que signifie la péché; il ne lui reste plus, logiquement, qu'à vivre selon la volonté de Dieu, ce qui équivaut à la justice'.[119] While this may adequately represent the theology of Paul (as found in such passages as Rom. 5:12–21; Rom. 6:1–11; 1 Cor. 15:20ff.; 2 Cor. 5:14), there is some question as to whether the language of 1 Pet. 2:24bc can be similarly understood.

First, when Paul speaks of 'dying' to sin he uses the verb ἀποθνῄσκω ('die, be about to die, face death',[120] Rom. 6:2, 7, 10; cf. Rom. 6:8, 9; 1 Cor. 15:22, 31; 2 Cor. 5:14), but never once does he employ the verb ἀπογίνομαι. Peter, on the other hand, never uses ἀποθνῄσκω. However, when he does want to make a contrast between death and life he uses θανατόω ('put to death', 3:18), otherwise he uses the verb πάσχω

---

[115] See BDAG, 109.   [116] Hooker, *Not Ashamed of the Gospel*, 128.
[117] See Hooker, 'Interchange and Atonement', 462–80; 'Interchange in Christ', 349–61.
[118] Dunn, *The Christ and the Spirit*, 192 (emphasis his).
[119] Miguéns, 'La "passion" du Christ total', 30–1.   [120] BDAG, 111.

('suffer, endure', 'suffer death, be killed',[121] 2:21; 3:18; 4:1). Not only that, in choosing ἀπογίνομαι he has specifically chosen a very rare verb (only here in the New Testament, not at all in the LXX) over the much more common ἀποθνῄσκω (111× in the New Testament; 259× in the LXX). This needs to be accounted for.

Second, Peter uses the plural ἁμαρτίαις ('sins') while Paul always uses the singular (cf. Rom. 6:2 [ἀπεθάνομεν τῇ ἁμαρτίᾳ]; 6:7 [ὁ ἀποθανὼν δεδικαίωται ἀπὸ τῆς ἁμαρτία]; 6:10 [τῇ ἁμαρτίᾳ ἀπέθανεν]). As Michaels notes, 'the plural is concrete where Paul's singular is abstract'.[122] Peter consistently uses the word ἁμαρτία to denote concrete acts of sin (cf. 2:22, 24; 3:18; 4:8) and not, as in Paul, a power that controls humans. Even in 2:22a where he does employ the singular (ἁμαρτίαν), its use in conjunction with ποιέω ('to do') in the phrase ὃς ἁμαρτίαν οὐκ ἐποίησεν (lit., 'who did no sin') indicates that Peter is still thinking in terms of concrete acts of wrongdoing. This is confirmed by the verses which immediately follow and explain the expression 'he did no sin': no deceit was found in his mouth (v. 22b), he did not revile (v. 23a), and he did not threaten (v. 23b). It is also probable that Peter has substituted Isaiah's ἀνομίαν (ἀνομίαν οὐκ ἐποίησεν, 53:9 [note the use of ποιέω]) for ἁμαρτίαν in order to link this thought back to v. 20b and the verb ἁμαρτάνοντες ('do what is wrong').[123] Thus Peter's use of the plural ἁμαρτίαις in conjunction with ἀπογίνομαι suggests that he is not talking about death to sin as a power (as in, for example, Rom. 6:2) but, as we will note below, separation from sinful conduct (typified by concrete acts of sin).

Third, the expression ζάω τῇ δικαιοσύνῃ does not occur in Paul, nor in the rest of the New Testament. Furthermore, as most commentators recognise, 'righteousness' (δικαιοσύνη) in this context refers to 'just, upright behaviour', 'righteous living', 'doing what is right'.[124] Thus Peter diverges substantially from the Pauline notion of the 'righteousness of God' or the righteousness bestowed by God. As Schrenk observes, 'in 1 Peter δικαιοσύνη is always the doing of right as acceptable conduct'.[125] The noun δικαιοσύνη appears again in 1 Pet. 3:14 where it functions as a synonym for ἀγαθοποιέω ('to do good, do what is right', 3:17; cf. 2:15, 20; 3:6, 11, 17; 4:19; cf. 3:11–12 where δικαίους [v. 12] is synonymous with ποιησάτω ἀγαθόν [v. 11]). The expression πάσχοιτε διὰ δικαιοσύνην ('suffer because of righteousness' or 'because of

[121] BDAG, 785 (s.v. πάσχω, 3.a. α).   [122] Michaels, *1 Peter*, 149.
[123] Elliott, *1 Peter*, 528.   [124] Ibid., 535.
[125] G. Schrenk, 'δικαιοσύνη', *TDNT*, 2: 199.

upright behaviour') in 3:14 is equivalent to κρεῖττον ἀγαθοποιοῦντας ('to suffer for doing good' or 'for what is right') in 3:17. Once again δικαιοσύνη denotes 'upright behaviour' or 'doing what is right'. Thus the expression τῇ δικαιοσύνῃ ζήσωμεν should be translated with the sense of 'we might live for doing what is right'.

In light of the foregoing discussion, it is difficult to detect in this verse any notion of representation as set out by Dunn with respect to Paul and argued for by Hooker and others. The focus of this passage, as we have seen, is not on dying and rising with Christ (representation), but on ceasing from wrongdoing/sins and living for doing what is right (ethics). The Pauline theology of mystical union and death with Christ in baptism in Rom. 6 is clearly absent from 1 Peter. Instead, as my examination of the expression ταῖς ἁμαρτίαις ἀπογενόμενοι τῇ δικαιοσύνῃ ζήσωμεν has indicated, some form of separation or break from sinful conduct and a commitment to 'just, upright behaviour' or 'righteous living' is intended. Thus the effect of Christ's bearing 'our sins' (v. 24a) is that 'believers' ('we') might be delivered from the control of and compulsion to wrongdoing/sin and be committed to doing what is right/righteousness. As such we can paraphrase v. 24 as follows: '[Christ] bore [the punishment due] our sins with the result that we, having abandoned wrongdoing, might live for doing what is right'.

Its result (vv. 24d–25). You have been healed (v. 24d)

The fourth and final relative clause in this passage turns the focus onto the result of Christ's vicarious suffering in the experience of those who have become believers: οὗ τῷ μώλωπι ἰάθητε ('by whose wounds you have been healed', v. 24d). Here Peter is alluding to Isa. 53:5:

1 Pet. 2:24d		οὗ	τῷ	μώλωπι			ἰάθητε
Isa. 53:5	ἐπ'	αὐτόν	τῷ	μώλωπι	αὐτοῦ	ἡμεῖς	ἰάθημεν

Peter indicates that it is by Christ's wounds (τῷ μώλωπι) that believers have been healed (ἰάθητε). The Greek word μώλωψ ('welt, wale, bruise, wound')[126] was common among the physicians of the Greco-Roman world for 'weal' or 'welt' (e.g., Hyperides, *Poll. onom.* 3.79; Aristotle, *Probl.* 9.1.889b.10), 'swelling' (resembling a mosquito bite) resulting from a sting (Herodotus, *Med. Aet. Amid.* 5.129), or a blood-clot (Paulus Aegineta 6.8). The related verb μωλωπίζω ('beat and bruise severely') and adjective μωλωπικός ('suitable for weals') do not occur in the LXX

---

[126] BDAG, 663.

or New Testament. The noun μώλωψ occurs eight times in the LXX rendering, where there is a Hebrew original, חַבּוּרָה ('stripe, blow, stroke',
Gen. 4:23; Exod. 21:25; Ps. 37:6; Isa. 1:6)[127] or חָלַל (po'al, 'pierced,
wounded', Isa. 53:5).[128] It is used of wounding a person in return (*lex
talionis*, Gen. 4:23; Exod. 21:25), beating a slave (Sir. 23:10), the
result of being whipped ('welt', Sir. 28:17), the wounding of the servant of Yahweh (Isa. 53:5), and figuratively in Ps. 37:6 and Jdt. 9:13. It
appears only in 1 Pet. 2:24 in the New Testament. Its use in the context
of 2:18–25 with its exhortation to 'slaves' (οἰκέται; cf. Sir. 23:10, 'a
servant [οἰκέτης] who is constantly under scrutiny will not lack bruises
[μώλωπος]') who risk being beaten (κολαφίζω, 2:20) by harsh masters
(τοῖς δεσπόταις τοῖς σκολιοῖς, 2:18) suggests the meaning 'bruise'
or 'welt' caused by blows or a whip. It is possible that this bruising
(denoted by μώλωψ) is meant to recall the scourging Jesus received in
conjunction with his crucifixion (Mt. 20:19; 27:26; Mk 15:15; Jn 19:1).
However, the fact that this 'bruise' effects the healing of believers suggests that μώλωψ, like πάσχω elsewhere in 1 Peter (2:21; 3:18), is a
'metonymy for Christ's entire ordeal of suffering and effects the healing
of the servants/slaves that their suffering could not. Along with 2:21a and
24 it further underlines the substitutionary nature and power of Christ's
suffering and death.'[129]

The word ἰάομαι ('heal, cure, restore') denotes the result of Christ's
wounding, 'you have been healed'. It is used frequently in the LXX (67
times) to denote healing in both the literal (bodily sickness, e.g., Gen.
20:17; Lev. 14:3, 48; Deut. 28:27; 2 Sam. 20:5) and figurative sense (spiritual sickness [see below]). While there were many physicians in Old
Testament times, it was important for the people of God to remember that
Yahweh alone was the source of all healing (ἐγὼ εἰμι κύριος ὁ ἰώμενος
σε ['I am the Lord who heals you'], Exod. 15:27; cf. 2 Kgs 5:7). Since
bodily sickness was closely connected with sin in Old Testament thinking, healing becomes a vivid picture of God's forgiveness and mercy.
Thus in a number of Old Testament passages, healing is closely associated with the forgiveness of sins (e.g., Deut. 30:3; 2 Chron. 7:14; Pss.
6:2 [LXX 6:3]; 30:2 [29:3]; 41:4 [40:5]; 103:3 [102:3]; Isa. 6:10; 53:5).
In Ps. 41:4 [LXX 40:5] David pleads with the Lord to 'heal my soul for
I have sinned against you' (ἴασαι τὴν ψυχήν μου ὅτι ἥμαρτόν σοι). In
Ps. 103:3 [102:3] 'the one who forgives all your iniquities' (τὸν εὐιλα-
τεύοντα πάσαις ταῖς ἀνομίαις σου) is 'the one who heals all your dis-
eases' (τὸν ἰώμενον πάσας τὰς νόσους σου). In Isa. 53:5 (which is the

---

[127] BDB, 289. [128] BDB, 319. [129] Elliott, *1 Peter*, 536–7.

source of 1 Pet. 2:24d) the statement τῷ μώλωπι αὐτοῦ ἡμεῖς ἰάθημεν ('by his bruise we are healed') comes in the context of the servant's vicarious suffering 'for our transgressions' (διὰ τὰς ἀνομίας) and 'because of our sins' (διὰ τὰς ἁμαρτίας ἡμῶν) suggesting the believers' healing includes the forgiveness of sins. I say 'includes' because the notion of healing here is probably broader than just the forgiveness of sins. Of interest is the parallelism between lines three and four of v. 53:

παιδεία εἰρήνης ἡμῶν ἐπ᾽ αὐτόν
τῷ μώλωπι αὐτοῦ ἡμεῖς ἰάθημεν

Here the Greek word εἰρήνη ('peace') translates the Hebrew שָׁלוֹם ('completeness, soundness, welfare, peace').[130] The parallel ideas of 'peace' (Gk εἰρήνη; Heb. שָׁלוֹם) and 'healing' (Gk ἰάομαι; Heb. רָפָא) suggests that

> the use of ἰάομαι in 1 Pet. 2:24[d] probably reflects the Old Testament in its holistic view of man rather than the Greek view of soul and body. This wholeness or healing affects a man in all aspects of his being. Therefore the term here indicates that as a result of Christ's sufferings sinful men are healed. They are restored to health, though primarily in a spiritual sense, in all aspects of their existence.[131]

Thus healing here includes the forgiveness of sins, but also embraces the restoration of fellowship with God, and all of the benefits that derive from that fellowship.

You have been returned (v. 25)

The statement in 1 Pet. 1:25 expresses a further result of Christ's vicarious suffering on the cross: ἦτε γὰρ ὡς πρόβατα πλανώμενοι, ἀλλὰ ἐπεστράφητε νῦν ἐπὶ τὸν ποιμένα καὶ ἐπίσκοπον τῶν ψυχῶν ὑμῶν ('for you were straying like sheep, but now you have been returned to the Shepherd and Overseer of your lives'). The explanatory conjunction γάρ ('for') connecting v. 25 to v. 24 indicates that v. 25 functions as an explanation for what he has just said in the previous clause. Thus healing (v. 24d) now takes the form of turning to Christ (v. 25). Similarly, in the Old Testament there exists a close connection between 'returning' (ἐπιστρέφω) to God and being 'healed' (ἰάομαι) by God: καὶ **ἐπιστρέψωσιν** καὶ **ἰάσομαι** αὐτούς ('and **turn** – and **I would heal** them', Isa. 6:10; cf. Mk 4:12; Mt. 13:15; Jn 12:40; Acts 28:27); καὶ

---

[130] BDB, 1022.   [131] Olson, 'The Atonement in 1 Peter', 370.

ἐπιστραφήσονται προς κύριον ... καὶ ἰάσεται αὐτούς ('and **they will return** to the Lord ... and **he will heal** them', Isa. 19:22); ἐπιστράφητε υἱοὶ ἐπιστρέφοντες καὶ ἰάσομαι τὰ συντρίμματα ὑμῶν ('**Return**, O sons who are given to turning, and **I will heal** your fractures', Jer. 3:22).

The image of straying as sheep derives from Isa. 53:6:

Isa. 53:6a	πάντες	ὡς	πρόβατα	ἐπλανήθημεν
1 Pet. 2:25a	ἦτε γὰρ	ὡς	πρόβατα	πλανώμενοι

Once again (cf. v. 24d and my comments there) a first person plural verb (ἐπλανήθημεν) has been replaced with a second person plural construction (ἦτε πλανώμενοι). The imperfect periphrastic ἦτε πλανώμενοι ('you were going astray') describes the lives of those addressed prior to their conversion. It is probable that the periphrastic, in this context, is intended to emphasise a continuing action or state in the past.[132] Thus the point is not that the readers had been with the Shepherd and then at some point had wandered away (and then had subsequently returned [see below]), but that their pre-conversion experience was characterised by straying, that is, by sin and alienation from God. Michaels notes that while 'Isaiah (and Jewish tradition in general) saw the straying sheep as the Jewish people alienated from their God (e.g., Ezek. 34:5–6; cf. Mt. 9:36; 10:6; 15:24, where they are the "lost sheep of the house of Israel"), Peter sees them as Gentiles'.[133]

The contrastive conjunction ἀλλά ('but') that follows indicates the decisive change that has 'now' (νῦν) taken place. The νῦν underlines the contrast between their past state of wandering and alienation from God and their present state of having been returned to him. The verb ἐπιστρέφω ('turn, turn around, return') is used frequently in the LXX (545×), rendering a variety of Hebrew words but predominantly שׁוב ('turn back, return', 408×). In the LXX ἐπιστρέφω can mean 'turning to or from', 'turning away', or 'returning', or can be used religiously of 'apostasy' or 'conversion'.[134] Turning or conversion is described in the LXX as a turning from evil (Jer. 18:8), idols (Isa. 31:6–7; cf. Acts 14:15; 1 Thess. 1:9), and sin (Ps. 50[51]:15; Hos. 14:2[1]; Sir. 17:25), and a turning to God (e.g., Deut. 4:30; 30:2; Hos. 3:5; 6:1; Joel 2:12; Isa. 19:22; 31:6; 45:22; 55:7, etc.).

In the New Testament ἐπιστρέφω occurs thirty-six times (along with another three occurrences in variant readings [Lk. 10:6 (D); Acts 15:16 (D); 2 Pet. 2:21 (TR)]). In half of these instances (18×) ἐπιστρέφω

---

[132] See Robertson, *Grammar*, 887–8.   [133] Michaels, *1 Peter*, 150.
[134] G. Bertram, 'στρέφω', *TDNT*, 7: 723.

retains its secular or spatial meaning and denotes the physical movement of turning, returning, turning away, and so forth (e.g., Mt. 10:13;
12:44; Mk 13:6; Lk. 2:20; 2 Pet. 2:22). Otherwise ἐπιστρέφω occurs
(18×) with its theological meaning of conversion (e.g., Lk. 1:16, 17; Acts
3:19; 9:35; 11:21; 14:15; 15:19; 26:18; 26:20; 2 Cor. 3:16; 1 Thess. 1:9).
The related noun ἐπιστροφή appears in the New Testament only in Acts
15:3, where it denotes 'a change of one's way of thinking or believing'
and is rendered 'conversion'.[135] Twice ἐπιστρέφω is used in conjunction with μετανοέω ('change one's mind', 'repent, be converted') (Acts
3:19; 26:18–20).[136] Perhaps the most significance use of the verb is with
reference to turning to God or Christ (12×, Lk. 1:16, 17; Acts 3:19; 9:35;
11:21; 14:15; 15:19; 26:18, 20; 2 Cor. 3:16; 1 Thess. 1:9; 1 Pet. 2:25).
Thus in 1 Pet. 2:25 our author indicates that 'now you have been returned
[ἐπεστράφητε] to [ἐπί] the Shepherd and Overseer of your lives'.

The passive ἐπεστράφητε is most probably a 'divine passive' implying God is the agent of their turning ('you have been returned [by God]';
cf. Ezek. 34:16, τὸ πλανώμενον ἐπιστρέψω ['I will bring back the
strayed']). As Laubach observes, 'it is God [who] gives the impulse to
conversion; God first moves man (Jer. 31:18; Lam. 5:21). Even when
man returns, it is because he has first received (Jer. 24:7).'[137] Thus the
sense here is that it is God who has returned those who are now believers
to Christ, 'the Shepherd and Overseer of your lives' (τὸν ποιμένα καὶ
ἐπίσκοπον τῶν ψυχῶν ὑμῶν). Elliott remarks:

> The straying, scattering, and return of God's sheep eventually
> became one of several metaphors for the final gathering and
> salvation of God's scattered people. In this Petrine construction,
> 'straying' does not imply Christian defection *after* conversion
> but, rather, estrangement from God *prior* to baptism and rebirth.
> The return of those who have strayed is a composite metaphor
> for salvation as such.[138]

This 'return' of those who are now believers portrays another aspect of
their 'healing': reconciliation and fellowship with Christ.

Summary

In this section (2:21–5) Peter provides his readers with a Christological
model (ὑπογραμμόν, v. 21c) for doing what is right despite suffering

---

[135] BDAG, 382.   [136] BDAG, 640.
[137] F. Laubach, 'ἐπιστρέφω', *NIDNTT*, 1: 354.
[138] Elliott, *1 Peter*, 538 (emphasis his).

(2:20). The purpose (ἵνα) of Christ's exemplary suffering was 'that you should follow in his footsteps' (v. 21d). However, once again Peter goes beyond the exemplary nature of Christ's innocent suffering to focus on its unique redemptive character: 'he himself bore our sins in his body on the tree' (v. 24). The implied teaching is that Christ's sufferings and death were vicarious; as our substitute he bore the judgment which our sins merited. The purpose (ἵνα) of Christ's substitutionary bearing of the judgment for sin has ethical implications: 'so that we, having abandoned wrongdoing, might live for doing what is right' (v. 24b). Finally, the atoning work of Christ has resulted in the conversion, forgiveness, and spiritual health and wholeness of those who 'have been healed' (v. 24d) and 'returned [by God] to the Shepherd and Overseer of [their] souls' (v. 25b).

3. 1 Peter 3:18a-c: 'Christ's suffering as sacrificial'

Context

Verse 18a-c belongs to a larger unit of thought (3:18–22) which recounts the innocent and vicarious nature of Christ's suffering (v. 18ab) and death (v. 18d) as well as God's vindication of his suffering and death through his resurrection (vv. 18e, 21d), ascension (vv. 19, 22), and exaltation to God's right hand (v. 22). 1 Peter 3:18–22 is joined syntactically and thematically with both the previous (3:13–17) as well as the following section (4:1–6). 1 Peter 3:18 is linked to 3:13–17 by means of the causal conjunction ὅτι ('because, for'), the connective καί ('also'), as well as the words Χριστός ('Christ', 3:15, 16, 18a), πάσχω ('suffer', 3:14, 17, 18a), and δικαιοσύνη/δίκαιος ('righteousness'/'righteous', 3:14/18b). The ὅτι at the beginning of v. 18 provides a Christological basis for the foregoing exposition (3:13–17) for doing what is right despite suffering (πάσχοιτε διὰ δικαιοσύνην, 3:14). Christ's innocent suffering (v. 18ab) is presented as both a model for innocent suffering as well as the basis for present and future salvation (v. 18bc). 1 Peter 3:18[–22] is also linked to 4:1[–6] by the inferential conjunction οὖν ('therefore', 4:1) and also by the words Χριστός ('Christ', 3:18a; 4:1a), πάσχω ('suffer', 3:18a; 4:1ac), and σάρξ (3:18d; 4:1ac). The inference drawn from 3:18 is stated in 4:1ab: 'Therefore since Christ suffered in the flesh you also [must] arm yourselves with the same way of thinking.' Once again Christ's suffering and death are presented as a model (4:1ab; cf. 4:6b/3:18d) for innocent suffering (cf. 4:1–4). At the same time, Peter goes beyond the exemplary nature of Christ's innocent suffering to focus on its unique redemptive character. As Spicq remarks, 'l'objet le plus fondamental de la foi est que la mort du Christ fut salutaire, expiatoire de péchés, parce que ce fut le sacrifice d'une victime s'offrant en propitiation, *péri amartias*'.[139]

Content

The nature of Christ's redemptive suffering (3:18ab)

The opening words of this verse (3:18ab) provide us with 'an affirmation of a fundamental NT doctrine about the redemptive and atoning power of the death of Christ'.[140] Peter's exposition of the nature of Christ's redemptive suffering is contained in three succinct but significant sayings: (a) Χριστὸς ἅπαξ ... ἔπαθεν ('Christ suffered once for all'); (b) περὶ ἁμαρτιῶν ('for sins'); (c) δίκαιος ὑπὲρ ἀδίκων ('a righteous one for unrighteous ones'). We will examine each of these expressions in turn.

Χριστὸς ἅπαξ ... ἔπαθεν

While a great majority of texts read that Christ 'died' (ἀπέθανεν) rather than 'suffered' (ἔπαθεν), the latter is in agreement with both the immediate context (πάσχοιτε [3:14]; πάσχειν [3:17]; παθόντος, παθὼν [4:1]) as well as the overall thematic emphasis on suffering that pervades the letter, and so is to be preferred.[141] In any case, this reference to his suffering also includes reference to his death (as v. 18d indicates [θανατωθεὶς μὲν σαρκί]). This is in keeping with the use of πάσχω in other parts of the New Testament, where it can also be used as a metonym for 'to die' or 'to be crucified' (see, e.g., Mt. 17:12; Lk. 22:15; 24:46; Acts 1:3; 3:18; 27:3; Heb. 9:26; 13:12; 1 Pet. 2:21; cf. Acts 26:23 [παθητός]). For example, in Heb. 13:12 we are told that Jesus' suffering (ἔπαθεν) took place ἔξω τῆς πύλης ('outside the gate'), indicating that this is a reference to his death and not simply the preceding events that took place within the city itself. A good example of this use of πάσχω can be found in Ignatius' letter *To the Smyrneans* where he writes: 'For he suffered [ἔπαθεν] all these things for our sake [δι' ἡμᾶς], that we might be saved [ἵνα σωθῶμεν]; and he truly suffered [ἀληθῶς ἔπαθεν], just as he also truly raised himself [ὡς καὶ ἀληθῶς ἀνέστησεν ἑαυτόν] – not as some unbelievers say, that he suffered only in appearance

---

[139] Spicq, *Les Épîtres de Saint Pierre*, 135.
[140] Senior, *1 Peter*, 99.
[141] See Metzger, *Textual Commentary*, 692–3.

[τὸ δοκεῖν πεπονθέναι]' (Ignatius, *Smyrn.* 2). Peter's choice of the verb πάσχω, then, ably fulfils the double duty of, on the one hand, creating a correspondence between the suffering of Christ (3:18; 4:1a) and that of believers (3:14, 17; 4:1c), and on the other, functioning (in conjunction with the expressions περὶ ἁμαρτιῶν and δίκαιος ὑπὲρ ἀδίκων) as a reference to the vicarious death of Christ. As Elliott remarks, '[t]he thought thus reflects early Christian affirmation of the vicarious death of Christ, which the Petrine author has modified here and in 2:21 by replacing "died" with "suffered" in accord with his thematic emphasis upon the innocent *suffering* that unites Christ and his followers'.[142]

The decisive and comprehensive aspect of Christ's suffering is then indicated by the adverbial modifier ἅπαξ ('pert[aining] to a single occurrence and decisively unique, *once and for all*').[143] The word ἅπαξ may be used 'as a numer[ical] term pert[aining] to a single occurrence' and so be rendered 'once' (e.g., 2 Cor. 11:25; 1 Thess. 2:18).[144] When used with reference to the uniqueness of Christ's atoning sacrifice for sins, ἅπαξ expresses 'the singular, comprehensive, and conclusive aspect of Christ suffering',[145] and should be rendered something like 'once for all', 'once and for all', or 'once for all time'. It is used in this way in Heb. 9:26 where the once-for-all (ἅπαξ) offering of Christ as a sacrifice (διὰ τῆς θυσίας αὐτοῦ) at the end of the age (ἐπὶ συντελείᾳ τῶν αἰώνων) to remove sin (εἰς ἀθέτησιν [τῆς] ἁμαρτίας) is contrasted with the annual visit of the high priest into the Holy Place with the blood of animals (v. 25; cf. also vv. 27–8). The related term ἐφάπαξ (5× in the NT), which means 'once for all, once and never again',[146] is a 'technical term for the definitiveness and therefore uniqueness or singularity of the death of Christ and the redemption thereby accomplished'.[147] In Rom. 6:10 it refers to Christ's death to sin 'once for all' (ἐφάπαξ). In Heb. 7:27 the writer refers to Christ's sacrifice as being 'once for all' (ἐφάπαξ) when he offered himself up for the sins of the people (ἁμαρτιῶν θυσίας ἀναφέρειν; cf. also Heb. 9:12). In conjunction with the phrases περὶ ἁμαρτιῶν and ὑπὲρ ἀδίκων, the expression ἅπαξ ἔπαθεν, then, moves beyond the exemplary nature of Christ's suffering to the uniqueness of Christ's atoning suffering in contrast to the suffering of believers.

---

[142] Elliott, *1 Peter*, 640 (emphasis his). [143] BDAG, 97 (s.v. 2).
[144] BDAG, 97; G. Stählin, 'ἅπαξ, ἐφάπαξ', *TDNT*, 5: 381.
[145] Elliott, *1 Peter*, 641. [146] BDAG, 417.
[147] G. Stählin, 'ἅπαξ, ἐφάπαξ', *TDNT*, 5: 383.

περὶ ἁμαρτιῶν

While the expression περὶ ἁμαρτιῶν ἔπαθεν ('suffered for sins') is only found here in the New Testament, it echoes a number of other formulations in both the Old and New Testaments. Some commentators see a rather general reference to sin here, so that the phrase means something like 'in respect of sins',[148] 'for our sins',[149] 'concerning sins',[150] or 'to deal with sin'.[151] But given general Old Testament usage (on which see below), the rendering 'as a sacrifice for sins' may be more appropriate in this context. The phrase περὶ ἁμαρτιῶν is used elsewhere in the New Testament for a sacrifice for sins (Heb. 5:1, 3; 7:27; 10:18, 26; 1 Jn 2:2; 4:10; cf. Heb. 5:1; 7:27; 10:12 where the parallel phrase ὑπὲρ ἁμαρτιῶν is used), as is the related phrase περὶ ἁμαρτίας (Heb. 10:6, 8 [citing LXX Ps. 39(40):7], 18; 13:11; cf. Rom. 8:3). The background for these phrases is the Old Testament sacrificial system. Wright has shown that of the fifty-four occurrences of the phrase περὶ ἁμαρτίας in the Old Testament, no fewer than forty-four refer to a sin-offering.[152] This phrase (along with the less common τὰ περὶ τῆς ἁμαρτίας [Lev. 6:23] and τὸ περὶ τῆς ἁμαρτίας [Lev. 14:19]) generally renders the Hebrew חַטָּאת ('sin-offering') or חַטָּאת ('sin, sin-offering'). Wright concludes that 'whereas περὶ τῆς ἁμαρτίας usually means "for sin", and τὸ περὶ τῆς ἁμαρτίας means "*the* sin-offering", περὶ ἁμαρτίας should usually be translated either "sin-offering" or "as a sin-offering"'.[153] Of the remaining ten (out of fifty-four) occurrences, Isa. 53:9–11 is the most relevant for our study (there the phrase περὶ ἁμαρτίας [v. 10] renders the Hebrew אָשָׁם ['offence, guilt', 'trespass-offering']).[154] Isaiah 53, which has already provided much of the language for 2:21–5 (a passage with many similarities to this one), may well stand behind this passage as well, as the following comparisons demonstrate. The primary thought pattern of 3:18a-c is as follows (with reference to Christ):

a.   who had done no wrong (δίκαιος),
b.   was made a sin-offering for us (περὶ ἁμαρτιῶν ἔπαθεν δίκαιος ὑπὲρ ἀδίκων),
c.   that we might be brought to God (ἵνα ὑμᾶς προσαγάγῃ τῷ θεῷ).

---

[148] Selwyn, *First Epistle of St. Peter*, 196.
[149] Grudem, *First Epistle of Peter*, 156.
[150] Robertson, *Word Pictures*, 115.   [151] Margot, *Les Épîtres de Pierre*, 60.
[152] Wright, 'περὶ ἁμαρτίας in Romans 8.3', 454.
[153] Ibid.   [154] BDB, 79.

The same is said of the suffering servant (Isa. 53:9–11):

v. 9   he has done no wrong (ἀνομίαν οὐκ ἐποίησεν οὐδὲ εὑρέθη
       δόλος ἐν τῷ στόματι αὐτοῦ [v. 9]; δίκαιον [v. 11])

v. 10 he gave his life as a sin-offering (ὅτι ἐὰν δῶτε περὶ ἁμαρτίας
       [אָשָׁם] ἡ ψυχὴ ὑμῶν)

v. 11 through his suffering he will justify many (δικαιῶσαι δίκαιον
       εὖ δουλεύοντα πολλοῖς)

Here the suffering servant is described as the righteous one (δίκαιον
[v. 11]) who will give his life as an offering 'for sin' (περὶ ἁμαρτίας).
Against the background of Isa. 53 we can suggests that the phrase περὶ
ἁμαρτιῶν in 1 Pet. 3:18 should be understood to refer to 'the sacrifice
of Christ for the redemption of his people'.[155] The redemptive and vicarious nature of Christ's suffering, as we will see, was the means by which
the barrier of sin was removed and access to God was made possible
(ἵνα ὑμᾶς προσαγάγῃ τῷ θεῷ): '[D]ie Hinführung zu Gott bedeutet die
Eröffnung des bis dahin blockierten "Zugangs" zu Gott durch Christi
Leben und Sterben'.[156]

δίκαιος ὑπὲρ ἀδίκων

This phrase picks up on a theme I began to develop in the previous section. The formulation δίκαιος ὑπὲρ ἀδίκων both parallels and further
expands on the phrase Χριστὸς ἅπαξ περὶ ἁμαρτιῶν ἔπαθεν in its
description of Christ as the one who not only suffers innocently but
also vicariously and redemptively. The substantive δίκαιος ('righteous one', 'upright one', or 'just one') denotes the one 'qui accomplit
la volonté de Dieu'.[157] In the LXX δίκαιος most commonly represents
צַדִּיק ('just, righteous')[158] or יָשָׁר ('straightforward, just, upright').[159] In
the background is the use of this term to refer to God as δίκαιος thus
'prepar[ing] the ground for the crucial religious importance of the term
in the NT'.[160] As a predicate of the Messiah, Schrenk notes that the term
δίκαιος 'is common both in the Synagogue and in Apocalyptic'.[161] He
points out that the Synagogue was fond of the designation 'the Messiah
our righteousness' (see, e.g., *Pesiq. Rab.* 36 [162a]).[162] The rabbis spoke
of the 'righteous Messiah' on the basis of such texts as Jer. 23:5, 6, 33:5,
and the description found in Zech. 9:9. In Wisdom literature, δίκαιος

---

[155] H. Riesenfeld, 'περί', *TDNT*, 6: 55.   [156] Brox, *Petrusbrief*, 167–8.
[157] Spicq, *Lexicon*, 126.   [158] BDB, 843.   [159] BDB, 449.
[160] G. Schrenk, 'δίκαιος', *TDNT*, 2: 185.   [161] Ibid., 186.
[162] Ibid., 186–87.

appears to function as a name for the Messiah (Wis. 2:18 [ὁ δίκαιος υἱὸς θεοῦ]; Ps. Sol. 17:32 [καὶ αὐτὸς βασιλεὺς δίκαιος]; cf. also Ps. Sol. 17:25, 28, 31, 42; 18:8f.), as does the expression 'the righteous one' (ὁ δίκαιος) in *1 Enoch* (*1 En.* 38:2, 3 ['the Righteous One']; 53:6 ['the Righteous and Elect One']). Longenecker, however, doubts that the expression '"the righteous one" was definitely a pre-Christian messianic title in the Jewish world'.[163] He suggests instead that 'whatever be thought of its pre-Christian titular appearance, the eventual employment of "the Righteous One" as a messianic appellation was undoubtedly based in large measure on the common messianic predicates "righteous" and "righteousness" in later Judaism' (noted above).[164]

This background of usage is important for understanding the way in which the New Testament writers employ δίκαιος not only as an attribute of Jesus (Mt. 27:19; 1 Jn 1:9; 2:29), but also as a Christological title (Acts 3:14; 7:52; 22:14; Jas 5:6; 1 Jn 2:1, 29; 3:7; *Diog.* 9:2; Justin Martyr, *Dial.* 17; Melito, *Peri Pasch.* 94; *Mart. Pol.* 17.2). In 1 Pet. 3:18 δίκαιος is used in this substantival sense. It is possible that Peter's language in this verse is also reliant on the Old Testament image of the Suffering Servant (see especially Isa. 53:11): 'the righteous one (LXX δίκαιος [MT צַדִּיק]; cf. 1 Pet. 3:18b) my servant, shall make many righteous (δικαιῶσαι), and he shall bear their iniquities (τὰς ἁμαρτίας αὐτῶν ἀνοίσει; cf 1 Pet. 3:18a)'. The phrase δίκαιος ὑπὲρ ἀδίκων (1 Pet. 3:18b) recalls the contrast between the righteous servant (Isa. 53:11) and the sinfulness of those on whose behalf he suffered (53:5, 6, 11, 12). Earlier in 2:21–5 Peter had already anchored his exhortations about enduring unjust suffering in an appeal to the example of Christ in language drawn from Isaiah's portrait of the Suffering Servant (adding further weight to the suggestion of Isa. 53 as a background for 3:18): 'He committed no sin, neither was deceit found in his mouth. When he was reviled, he did not revile in return; when he suffered he did not threaten ... he himself bore our sins in his body on the tree' (vv. 22–4). Dalton comments: 'The phrase of 3:18, "the righteous on behalf of the unrighteous", sums up the earlier expression of 2:24: "He himself bore our sins in his body on the tree", and recalls the contrast between the righteousness of the servant and the sinfulness of those for whom he suffered (Is 53:5, 6, 11, 12).'[165]

The formulation ὑπὲρ ἀδίκων, in conjunction with the previous phrase περὶ ἁμαρτιῶν [ἔπαθεν], emphasises further the substitutionary and redemptive nature of the sacrificial death of Christ. The most

---

[163] Longenecker, *Christology of Early Jewish Christianity*, 46.
[164] Ibid.   [165] Dalton, *Christ's Proclamation*, 133.

common meaning that the preposition ὑπέρ bears (i.e., 'for, on behalf of')[166] appears to have developed from 'the image of one person standing or bending *over* another in order to protect or shield him, or of a shield lifted *over* the head which suffers the blow instead of the person'.[167] With the genitive ὑπέρ may express one of three basic ideas: (1) representation or advantage: *on behalf of, for the sake of*; (2) reference or respect: *concerning, with reference to*; (3) substitution: *in place of, instead of*.[168] There is, however, some overlap between some of these categories since to act *on behalf of* someone (representation [1]) often involves acting *in their place* (substitution [3]).[169] As Turner notes, 'the boundary between ἀντί and ὑπέρ c. gen. is very narrow (substitution), necessarily so because what is done *on behalf of one* is often done *in one's stead*'.[170] As a result, ὑπέρ not infrequently carries the sense of ἀντί ('instead of, in place of').[171] The substitutionary sense of ὑπέρ is evident in classical Greek,[172] the LXX,[173] the papyri,[174] the New Testament,[175] and the early church writers.[176] In light of the well-established usage of ὑπέρ to denote substitution in Hellenistic Greek, there seems to be no reason not to adopt this nuance as part of the Petrine doctrine of the atonement. At a minimum, there is here the idea of substitution (we have discussed elsewhere whether Peter attributes representative significance to the death of Christ). This interpretation of the ὑπέρ saying in 3:18 also fits best with the sacrificial language of the previous phrase, περὶ ἁμαρτιῶν (which I have translated as 'a sacrifice for sins'). As Morris notes, 'when a sacrifice was offered we should see it as a killing of the animal *in place of* the worshipper and the manipulation of the blood as the ritual presentation to God of the evidence that a death has taken place to atone for sin'.[177] The death of Christ is substitutionary because he is dying the death of the unrighteous (that is, the death the unrighteous should die because of their unrighteousness). While substitution does not say all there is to

---

[166] Robertson, *Grammar*, 630.

[167] Harris, 'Prepositions and Theology', 1196 (emphasis his).

[168] Wallace, *Greek Grammar*, 383.

[169] See Harris, 'Prepositions and Theology', 1196.

[170] Turner, *Syntax*, 271.

[171] See Harris, 'Prepositions and Theology', 1196.

[172] See, for example, Plato, *Republic* 590a; Xenophon, *Anabasis* 7.4.9–10.

[173] See, for example, Deut. 24:16; Isa. 43:3–4; Jdt. 8:12; 1 Macc. 16:3.

[174] See Wallace, *Greek Grammar*, 385, n. 82, for examples.

[175] Wallace, *Greek Grammar*, 383, suggests that ὑπέρ carries a substitutionary sense in the following 'soteriologically significant' texts: Jn 11:50; 2 Cor. 5:14; Gal. 3:13; 1 Tim. 2:6. To these I would also add: Rom. 5:6, 7, 8; 14:15; 1 Thess. 5:10.

[176] Note, for example, the *Letter to Diognetus* 9:2–3; *Mart. Pol.* 17.2.

[177] Morris, *The Atonement*, 62 (emphasis mine).

say about the atonement, it is an important reminder of the fact that in his death Jesus 'did something for us which we needed to do but could not'.[178] Robertson summarises it well for us when he writes:

> [N]o one of the theories of the atonement states all the truth nor, indeed, do all of them together. The bottom of this ocean of truth has never been sounded by any man's plumb-line. There is more in the death of Christ for all of us than any of us has been able to fathom ... However, one must say that substitution is an essential element in any real atonement.[179]

In summary, the phrase δίκαιος ὑπὲρ ἀδίκων, in conjunction with the earlier formulation περὶ ἁμαρτιῶν ἔπαθεν, provides us with a succinct description of the atoning work of Christ as a vicarious atoning sacrifice 'in place of' or 'instead of' the unrighteous.

The purpose of Christ's redemptive suffering: ἵνα ὑμᾶς προσαγάγῃ τῷ θεῷ

Having outlined the nature of Christ's death as an atoning sacrifice offered in the place of the unrighteous, Peter now goes on to express the saving effect of that redemptive work: access to and hence reconciliation with God. The ἵνα ('so that') plus the subjunctive προσαγάγῃ (aorist active subjunctive) gives a clear and concise statement of the ultimate redemptive purpose of Christ's vicarious suffering in the place of the unjust: that he might bring (προσαγάγῃ) them (ἀδίκων = ὑμᾶς = the readers in their unconverted state) to God (τῷ θεῷ). The verb προσαγάγῃ (the aorist subjunctive of προσάγω) in the transitive means 'bring' and has the sense of to 'bring into someone's presence'.[180] This verb is used in only three other places in the New Testament and only in Luke–Acts (Lk. 9:41; Acts 16:20; 27:27). In Acts 16:20 προσάγω appears to be used as a legal term echoing Classical Greek (Xenophon, *Cyr.* 7.5.45; Philostratus, *Vit. soph.* 2.32), the LXX (Exod. 21:6; Num. 25:67; 27:5), and the papyri (P.Hal. 8. 5; P.Ryl. 2.75³). προσάγω was also used in Classical Greek (Herodotus, *Hist.* 3.24; Lucian, *Jupp. conf.* 5) and the LXX (Exod. 29:10; Lev. 1:2) as a 't[echnical] t[erm]' of sacrificial procedure'[181] in the sense of 'bring' (perhaps also with the sense of 'offer') sacrifice before God. Appealing to the cultic use of προσάγω in the LXX

---

[178] Packer, 'What Did the Cross Achieve?', 19.
[179] Robertson, *The Minister and his Greek New Testament*, 40–1.
[180] BDAG, 875.   [181] BDAG, 875.

to denote 'the consecration of persons to the ritual service of God',[182] and Peter's earlier reference to Christians as 'a holy priesthood, to offer spiritual sacrifices to God through Jesus Christ' (2:5), Dalton suggests that 'in the προσαγάγη of 3:18 we have an implicit reference to the consecration of the Christian priesthood'.[183] Yet, as Elliott rightly notes, the 'thrust of this verse and its context, however, is soteriological rather than ecclesiological'.[184] Significantly, one of the Old Testament passages that Peter does allude to in ch. 2 is Exod. 19:3–6. Here the verb προσάγω appears in a very significant soteriological statement that resembles our passage: 'You yourselves have seen what I did to the Egyptians and how I bore you on eagle's wings and brought you to myself' (καὶ προσηγα-γόμην ὑμᾶς πρὸς ἐμαυτόν, Exod. 19:4). This expression describes the saving activity of God on behalf of his people when he brought them out of Egypt and made them a people unto himself. In both passages (1 Pet. 3:18; Exod. 19:4) προσάγω denotes the saving intention of God: to bring people to himself.

In the New Testament the related noun προσαγωγή expresses the idea that one has 'access' to God (Rom. 5:2; Eph. 2:18; 3:12; cf. Exod. 19:4; 29:4; 20:12; Lev. 8:24; 16:1; Num. 8:9). It is this latter sense which is to be preferred here in 3:18. As Selwyn avers, 'as so often, the simplest is the most profound: Christ's atoning sacrifice brings us to God'.[185] This Petrine formulation, then, indicates that the ultimate redemptive purpose of Christ's vicarious suffering was to bring believers into God's presence.[186] As Schmidt points out, the use of προσάγω here in 3:18 may indicate more than simply 'to bring to'. It must also include the idea of reconciliation with God which is brought about by the atoning work of Christ on the cross.[187] In this sense the word προσάγω is approaching the meaning that it conveys in the middle (προσάγεσθαι): 'negotiate peace, reconcile' (cf. Justin, *Dial.* 2.1; Josephus, *Ant.* 14.272). As Hiebert remarks, 'the compound verb "might bring" (προσαγάγη) in the aorist indicates that the purpose was to bring the estranged into an actual intimate relationship with God'.[188] The expression ἵνα ὑμᾶς προσαγάγη τῷ θεῷ, then, expresses the intended result of Christ's atoning sacrifice in terms of both 'access to' and 'reconciliation with' God as the ultimate goal of salvation. The focus here then is on conversion. Those who were

---

[182] Dalton, *Christ's Proclamation*, 135, n. 46, cites Exod. 29:4, 8; 40:12; Lev. 8:24; Num. 8:9–10.
[183] Dalton, *Christ's Proclamation*, 135.   [184] Elliott, *1 Peter*, 643.
[185] Selwyn, *First Epistle of St. Peter*, 196.
[186] Elliott, *1 Peter*, 642–3.   [187] K. L. Schmidt, 'προσάγω', *TDNT*, 1: 133.
[188] Hiebert, 'The Suffering and Triumphant Christ', 148.

formerly prevented from entering the presence of God because of their unrighteousness have now been granted spiritual access to God through the sacrifice of Jesus. It is possible that Peter may also be thinking of the access that believers will one day enjoy when, at the second coming, Christ will usher them into the very presence of God. As Michaels notes, 'if the immediate benefit of Christ's sacrificial death is religious conversion, its ultimate benefit is eschatological salvation'.[189]

Summary

In this section Peter provides his readers with a Christological basis for doing what is right despite suffering (πάσχοιτε διὰ δικαιοσύνην, 3:14; Χριστὸς... ἔπαθεν, δίκαιος ὑπὲρ ἀδίκων, 3:18). At the same time he goes beyond the exemplary nature of Christ's innocent suffering to focus on its unique redemptive character. In doing so Peter points out at least four important characteristics of Christ's suffering: it is singular (ἅπαξ, v. 18a), sacrificial (περὶ ἁμαρτιῶν, v. 18a), substitutionary (δίκαιος ὑπὲρ ἀδίκων, v. 18b), and therefore salvific (ἵνα ὑμᾶς προσαγάγῃ τῷ θεῷ, v. 18c). As such we can paraphrase v. 18abc as follows: 'Christ also suffered as a unique, once-for-all sacrifice for sins, a righteous man in the place of unrighteous people, for the express purpose that he might bring you reconciled to God.'

[189] Michaels, *1 Peter*, 203.

4

REBIRTHED UNTO SALVATION

The new birth in 1 Peter

1. 1 Peter 1:3: 'God has caused you to be born anew': the nature, basis, and goal of the new birth

Closely related to the themes of election (chapter 2) and atonement (chapter 3) is the concept of rebirth or regeneration (this chapter). While chapters 2 and 3 dealt with those aspects of salvation that occurred outside of us and apart from us (God's eternal election of believers to salvation and his consequent decision to provide atonement for them in the historic death and resurrection of Jesus), this chapter contains an analysis of those passages that treat the application of that salvation to us under the metaphor of the 'new birth' or 'regeneration' (1:3, 23). Regeneration, as we will see below, effects in time what God has ordained from all eternity; it denotes the decisive transformation by which believers have come to be a part of God's elect, holy, and set apart people. Peter once again highlights the initiative of God in the believers' salvation by reminding them that it was God 'who, according to his great mercy has caused us to be born anew' (1:3).

Context

This opening ascription of praise to God (εὐλογητὸς ὁ θεὸς) is located in the first subunit (vv. 3–5) of the first main division of the letter (vv. 3–12). In the majority of the Pauline letters the epistolary opening is traditionally followed either by a thanksgiving (with εὐχαριστέω) or a blessing formula (with εὐλογητός). Theologically, this opening blessing of God for his act of rebirthing believers (ὁ ... ἀναγεννήσας ἡμᾶς) continues the theme of the opening salutation (vv. 1–2) which highlights God's sovereign and saving initiative in the lives of the elect. The blessing is then connected to what follows by the twofold repetition of the preposition εἰς (telic 'for') indicating the goal of this divine rebirthing: εἰς ἐλπίδα ζῶσαν (v. 3d, 'for a living hope') and εἰς κληρονομίαν (v. 4a, 'for an inheritance'). Finally, mention of the believers' 'rebirthing' here also anticipates v. 23 where the same verb (ἀναγεννάω; only here and in v. 3 in the NT) is used to describe the believers' rebirth 'through the living and enduring word of God'.

Content

The nature of the new birth

The one to whom blessing (εὐλογητός) is directed is identified as ὁ θεὸς καὶ πατὴρ τοῦ κυρίου ἡμῶν ᾽Ιησοῦ Χριστοῦ ('the God and Father of our Lord Jesus Christ'). The God who made himself known to Israel is now to be understood no longer simply as the Father of Israel, but more clearly as the Father of Jesus Christ and all those whom he has 'caused to be born anew [ὁ … ἀναγεννήσας] … through the resurrection of Jesus Christ' (v. 3; cf. 1:2, 14, 17, 2:2). The verb ἀναγεννάω ('beget again, cause to be born again')[1] appears only here and in v. 23 in the New Testament, not at all in the LXX (cf. the related adjective ἀρτιγέν-νητα, 'newborn', in 2:2), and only three times in secular Greek literature (Josephus, *B.J.* 4.484; Sallustius, *De deis* 4; Hesychius, *Hesychii Alexandrini Lexicon* 3:260). It is used by Josephus in the first century AD (its only occurrence before the second century AD) of the reproduction of fruit in his description of God's judgment on Sodom: ἔτι δὲ κἂν τοῖς καρποῖς σποδιὰν ἀναγεννωμένην ('still, too, one may see ashes reproduced [ἀναγεννωμένην] in the fruits, which from their outward appearance would be thought edible').[2] During the same period the substantival form of ἀναγεννάω (viz., ἀναγέννησις) appears in Philo (also see below) in his description of the Stoic notion of the future rebirth of the cosmos (πάλιν ἀναγέννησιν κόσμου).[3] Then from the fourth century AD the verb (ἀναγεννάω) is found in Sallustius' description of the Taurobolium initiates who are 'fed on milk as though being reborn' (ἐπὶ τούτοις γάλακτος τροφὴ ὥσπερ ἀναγεννωμένων, *De deis* 4).[4] Finally, in the fifth century AD, the lexicographer Hesychius defined παλιγγενε-σία as τὸ ἐκ δευτέρου ἀναγεννηθῆναι, ἢ ἀνακαινισθῆναι.[5] Otherwise the verb and the noun appear in the writings of the early church fathers to describe the Christian experience of new birth.[6]

---

[1] BDAG, 59.   [2] Josephus, *B.J.* 4.484. Cf. *A.J.* 4.319.
[3] Philo, *Aet.* 8.   [4] Sallustius, *Concerning the Gods and the Universe*, 8.
[5] Hesychius, *Hesychii Alexandrini Lexicon*, 3: 260 (s.v. 199th entry under 'π'; Hesychius does not define ἀναγεννάω or ἀνακαινίζω).
[6] E.g., Justin Martyr (*c.* 100–165), *Apol.* 1.61.2.

Related words and concepts can also be found in Hellenistic writers leading a number of scholars to posit either a Hellenistic context in general[7] or a background in the mystery religions in particular.[8] Plato spoke of the 'soul of man' (τὴν ψυχὴν τοῦ ἀνθρώπου) as being 'born again' (πάλιν γίγνεσθαι).[9] However, this rebirth does not effect a complete or eternal rebirth since 'the soul is immortal and has been born many times' (ἡ ψυχὴ ἀθάνατός τε οὖσα καὶ πολλάκις γεγονυῖα).[10] Thus, rebirth, for Plato, does not refer to the appropriation of new life in the present (as in 1 Peter – see below), but to its future acquisition in successive reincarnations.

The more common term, however, was παλιγγενεσία ('rebirth, regeneration'; found in the NT only in Mt. 19:28; Tit. 3:5).[11] In Stoic thought the word παλιγγενεσία was used to describe the process of cosmic renewal. The Stoics understood the cosmos as being involved in a 'repeated cycle of periodic dissolution into and restoration from the primitive fire [πῦρ τεχνοκόν]'.[12] The restoration of the cosmos from its conflagration (ἐκπύρωσις) was sometimes spoken of in terms of a rebirth (παλιγγενεσία). Plutarch uses the word παλιγγενεσία in his description of the myths of Dionysus and Osiris (*Is. Os.* 364F; *E. Delph.* 389A; cf. *De esu* 996C), and in both a cosmic (*Def. orac.* 438D) as well as in an individual sense (of souls; *De esu* 996C; 998C; *Mor.* 567E). The concept of rebirth also occupied an important place in the mystery religions (cf. the reference to Sallustius above). However, it is difficult to know what role words like ἀναγέννησις (and the verb ἀναγεννάω) and παλιγγενεσία played since the use of such language is not only rare but also unattested in the first century. Parsons, who allows for some Hellenistic influence on the language of rebirth in 1 Peter, concludes that

> it becomes hazardous to speak of the meaning of rebirth in the Hellenistic Mystery Religions in any unqualified manner. Evidence as to the existence and understanding of this experience in these cults is relatively late and uneven. References to a rebirth are found in the 2nd century and later in the source material available; at most, they point to the fact that the initiate could experience a rebirth as he entered the Mysteries, but they do not indicate what this meant.[13]

---

[7] See, e.g., Kümmel, *Theology of the New Testament*, 309; White, *The Biblical Doctrine of Initiation*, 252.

[8] See, e.g., Perdelwitz, *Die Mysterienreligion*, 16ff.; Shimada, 'Formulary Material', 176.

[9] Plato, *Meno* 81B.   [10] Plato, *Meno* 81C.   [11] LSJ, 1291.

[12] Parsons, 'We Have Been Born Anew', 47.   [13] Ibid., 71.

Perhaps the earliest sense of being begotten by God in Hellenistic literature is to be found in the work of Philo with respect to God's creative activity.[14] For Philo, God is ποιητὴς καὶ γεννητης τῶν ὅλων καὶ προνοητικὸς ὧν ἐγέννησε· σωτήρ τε καὶ εὐεργέτης ('the maker and begetter of the universe and his providence is over what he has begotten; He is a saviour and a benefactor').[15] As Creator, God has also begotten the Logos,[16] humans,[17] and plants and animals.[18] However, individual rebirth as a personal experience, for Philo, occurs only at death:

> Whence came the soul, whither will it go ... what of it after death? But then, we who are here joined to the body, creatures of composition and quality, shall be no more [ἀλλ᾽ οὐκ ἐσόμεθα οἱ μετὰ σωμάτων σύγκριτοι ποιοί], but shall go forward to our rebirth, to be with the unbodied, without composition and without quality [ἀλλ᾽ εἰς παλιγγενεσίαν ὁρμήσομεν ἃ μετὰ ἀσωμάτων ἀσύγκριτοι ἄποιοί].[19]

For Philo, then, personal 'rebirth' refers to the survival of the soul after death and its transition to another, disembodied, life. Thus the term '"rebirth" [παλιγγενεσία] was not used to define the present appropriation of new life, but rather its future acquisition'.[20] In 1 Peter, however, the new birth, as we will see below, is a present experience that is eschatologically oriented (toward 'a living hope' [v. 3] and 'an inheritance ... kept in heaven' [v. 4]). Thus, in light of the very different understanding of rebirth in Hellenistic religion (whether as the rejuvenation of the world after the ἐκπύρωσις, or the deification, divinisation, reincarnation, transmigration, or the transition of the soul to another life after death)[21] and the late attestation of many of the documents available to us, we should not seek a background for the Petrine (nor the NT for that matter) understanding of regeneration here.

Other authors suggest a background in Jewish tradition.[22] Goppelt suggests that 'the statement about new birth in 1 Pet. 1:3 can be traced ... to a context of motifs emerging from the self-understanding of the Qumran

---

[14] See, e.g., Stobaeus, *Ecl.* 1.1.12; Epictetus, *Diatr.* 4.10.16; Plutarch, *Quaest. plat.* Q.2.1–2; Marcus Aurelius, 10.1.

[15] Philo, *Spec.* 1.209.   [16] E.g., Philo, *Conf.* 63.

[17] E.g., Philo, *Her.* 200; *Virt.* 204–5; *Opif.* 84, 144.

[18] E.g., Philo, *Mut.* 63.   [19] Philo, *Cher.* 114–15.

[20] Parsons, 'We Have Been Born Anew', 54.

[21] See Kelly, *The Epistles of Peter*, 49, 50.

[22] Manns, 'La théologie de la nouvelle naissance', 125–6, points to the early Jewish work *Joseph and Asenath* 8:10–11; 15:4.

community'.[23] For example, in 1 QSa II 11–12 we find reference to God's begetting of the Messiah: 'This is the assembly of famous men, [those summoned to] the gathering of the community council, when [God] begets the Messiah with them.'[24] Other passages which use birth imagery are 1QH III 6–18 and possibly 1QS III 19. We may also note that those who belong to the community are called 'the sons of light',[25] 'sons of truth',[26] 'sons of righteousness',[27] 'sons of grace',[28] and 'the sons of heaven',[29] while those outside the community are referred to as 'the sons of darkness',[30] 'sons of deceit',[31] or 'the sons of belial'.[32] However, as Parsons cautions, 'this father/son relationship is spiritual not physical. It is based on divine election to the eschatological community of Qumran and on correct adhesion and obedience to its way of life, rather than on any conviction of divine generation'.[33] Thus we are not surprised to find that it is entrance into the community which constitutes one as a new creation.[34] However, there is no suggestion that this 'new creation' would come about by a new birth. Instead, the mode of expression in the Qumran community was that of 'renewal' and not 'new birth'. Thus, the concept and vocabulary of 'new birth' or 'regeneration' that we find in 1 Peter is quite absent from the writings of Qumran.

Elliott, on the other hand, looks to the rabbinic tradition for the Jewish background of Peter's metaphor of rebirth.[35] At a first glance the evidence here looks a bit more promising. In the Palestinian rabbinic tradition converts to Judaism who had undergone proselyte baptism could be compared with a newborn child. According to R. Jose (c. 150 BC), 'One who has become a proselyte is like a child newly born' (cf. 1 Pet. 2:2, ὡς ἀρτιγέννητα βρέφη, 'as new born babes').[36] Similarly, a midrash on the Song of Songs (8:2) compares Israel to a newborn child born at Sinai: '"I would bring thee into my mother's house": this is Sinai. R. Berekiah said: Why is Sinai called "My mother's house"? Because there Israel became like a new-born child.'[37] Deliverance from sin was sometimes connected to this new birth at Sinai,[38] a connection that is not all that surprising since it was held that the Torah had power to deliver from

---

[23] Goppelt, *1 Peter*, 83.   [24] IQSa [1Q28a] II 11–12.
[25] 1QS I 9; II 16; III 13, 24, 25; 1QM I 1, 3, 9, 11, 13.
[26] 1QS IV 5f.; XI 16; 1QM XVII 8; 1QH VI 29; VII 29–30; IX 35; X 27; XI 11; XVI 18.
[27] 1QS III 20, 22; IX 14.   [28] 1QH VII 20.   [29] 1QH III 22.
[30] 1QS I 10; 1QM I 1, 7, 10, 16; III 6, 9; XIII 16; XIV 17; XVI 11.
[31] 1QS III 21.   [32] 4Q174 [4QFlor] I 8.
[33] Parsons, 'We Have Been Born Anew', 78.
[34] E.g., 1 QH III 20–1.   [35] See Elliott, *1 Peter*, 332–3.
[36] *b. Yebam.* 48b. See also *b. Yebam.* 22a; 62a; 97b. See also Str-B, 2: 422f.
[37] *Song Rab.* 8:2 §1.   [38] See, e.g., *b. Šabb.* 145b-146a; *Song Rab.* 8:2, §1.

sin.[39] Of interest here also is the notion that if a person converts another to Judaism, it is as if he or she had created them: 'You learn from this that if a man brings one creature under the wings of the Shechinah, it is accounted to him as if he had created him and formed him and moulded him.'[40] Nevertheless, it should be noted that (1) these sources postdate the composition of 1 Peter (though the influence of earlier oral tradition, as Elliott points out, may still be a factor),[41] and (2) the phrase 'newly born child' is purely a descriptive comparison (note the use of the words 'like' and 'became like') describing 'a new legal status rather than an ontological transformation'.[42]

The difficulty that faces us here should now be quite apparent: the concept of a 'new birth' or being 'newly born' was a rather ubiquitous religious symbol and thus could be used to describe a variety of religious experiences which involved a new beginning of some sort. And while the terminology sounds quite similar in each case, the substance, as we have seen, is often very different. So where then can we turn? Those commentators who see a background not in Qumran or the rabbinic tradition but in the Old Testament and early Christian tradition beginning with Jesus are probably on much firmer ground. The following dialogue between Jesus and Nicodemus recorded in John's Gospel indicates that we should probably seek a background in the former (OT) but also hints at the latter (itself being a part of Christian tradition):

> Jesus answered him, 'Very truly, I tell you, no one can see the kingdom of God without being born from above ["born again", ESV; Gk: γεννηθῇ ἄνωθεν]'. Nicodemus said to him, 'How can anyone be born after having grown old? Can one enter a second time [δεύτερον] into the mother's womb and be born?' Jesus answered, 'Very truly, I tell you, no one can enter the kingdom of God without being born of water and Spirit ... Nicodemus said to him, 'How can these things be?' Jesus answered him, 'Are you a teacher of Israel, and yet you do not understand these things?'[43]

Jesus' astonishment arises from the fact that he is speaking of things that Nicodemus, as ὁ διδάσκαλος τοῦ Ἰσραήλ (lit., '*the* teacher of Israel')

---

[39] *Sipre Deut.* 45.1.2; *'Abot R. Nat.* 16A; *b. B. Bat.* 16a; *b. Sukkah* 52b; *Pesiq. Rab Kah.* 4:6; *Lev. Rab.* 35:5; *Pesiq. Rab.* 41:4.

[40] *Song Rab.* 1:3 §3. See also *'Abot R. Nat.* 26, §54B; *Sipre Deut.* 32.2.1; *b. Sanh.* 19b, 99b.

[41] See Elliott, *1 Peter*, 333; Keener, *Gospel of John*, 1: 542–53.

[42] Keener, *Gospel of John*, 1: 543.   [43] Jn 3:3–5, 9–10 (NRSV).

should have known about. Carson remarks: 'Jesus berates Nicodemus for not understanding these things in his role as "Israel's teacher" (v. 10), a senior "professor" of the Scriptures, and this in turn suggests that we must turn to what Christians call the Old Testament to begin to discern what Jesus had in mind.'[44] The expression 'born of water and Spirit' (ἐξ ὕδατος καὶ πνεύματος) further explains what it means to be 'born again/ from above'. Since this phrase consists of two anarthrous nouns connected by καί and governed by the one preposition, we should probably view it grammatically as a conceptual unity. Perhaps the most important background for this expression is Ezek. 36:25–7 where water and spirit come together with the first signifying cleansing from impurity and the second an inner transformation effected by the Spirit (cf. Jn 7:38–9). In short, the expression 'born of water and spirit' signals 'a new begetting, a new birth that cleanses and renews, the eschatological cleansing and renewal promised by the Old Testament prophets'.[45]

This promise of eschatological cleansing and renewal is found elsewhere in the Old Testament (Ezek. 11:19–20; Isa. 44:3; 59:21; Jer. 31:29–34; Ps. 51:10; cf. Wis. 9:16–18; *Jub.* 1:22–5; 1QS III 13–IV 26). Since people are not capable of effecting such a change in themselves (cf. Gen. 6:5; 8:21; Jer. 13:23), God, as its author, must be sought in prayer: 'Create in me a clean heart, O God, and renew a right spirit within me' (Ps. 41:10). In addition, the Old Testament frequently speaks of God as the 'Father' of his chosen people (e.g., Deut. 32:6; Jer. 3:4, 19; 31:9; cf. Ps. 68:6; Sir. 4:10; 23:1, 4; 51:10; Wis. 2:13, 16, 18; 5:5; Tob. 13:4), or more specially as the Father of his chosen king (see 2 Sam. 7:14; Pss. 2:7; 89:26–7; cf. 1 Chron. 17:13–14; 22:10; 28:6). Thus we are not surprised to find that elsewhere he is depicted figuratively as the 'God who bore you [Israel]' (θεὸν τὸν γεννήσαντά σε, Deut. 32:18; cf. Num. 11:12; Isa. 45:10; 49:21 Jer. 2:27ff.; Ezek. 23:4), who has 'begotten' (γεγέννηκά) David as adopted king (Ps. 2:7; later applied to the Messiah in Acts 13:33; Heb. 1:5; 5:5; cf. 1QSa II 11; also see *Midr. Pss.* 2 §9 on Ps. 2:7; cf. Ps. 110:3), and who 'brought forth' (NRSV; γεννᾷ, LXX) Wisdom (Prov. 8:25). Likewise, in the New Testament the verb γεννάω ('beget, bear') is used figuratively of believers who have been 'born of God' (ἐκ θεοῦ ἐγεννήθησαν, Jn 1:13; 1 Jn 2:29; 3:9 [2x]; 4:7; 5:1, 4, 18 [2x]) and 'born from above/again' (γεννηθῇ ἄνωθεν, Jn 3:3). The verb παλιγγενεσία ('renewal', 'rebirth', 'regeneration') appears twice, once as an eschatological term denoting the renewal of the world (Mt. 19:28)

[44] Carson, *The Gospel According to John*, 194.
[45] Ibid., 195.

and once to denote the rebirth of the individual by God (Tit. 3:5). Thus, rather than assuming some specific background to the term ἀναγεννάω, it is better to see a more general background in the concept of rebirth in early Christianity originating in the teachings of Jesus (though not necessarily directly dependent on it), which has in turn been influenced by the eschatological language of renewal in the Old Testament and perhaps (though a much more remote possibility) that of rabbinic oral tradition.

In the context of 1 Peter, the image of rebirth/regeneration (ἀναγεννάω) in 1:3 implies not only a new beginning but also the appropriation of new life because it connects believers, through baptism (cf. 3:21), with their risen, ever-living, Lord. As Büchsel notes,

> the thought of regeneration was adopted as an expression of … hope … For Christians the resurrection was not merely an object of hope. After the resurrection of Jesus it was a present reality. In the resurrection it was revealed that the Messianic age, the αἰὼν μέλλων ['age to come'], had begun. Believers were now linked with the risen Lord by his Spirit. They had tasted of the powers of the αἰὼν μέλλων (Heb. 6:5). The new birth for which the Jews hoped was for them in some way a present reality.[46]

Thus we are not surprised to read in 1:3 that 'God … has caused us to be born anew for a living hope *through the resurrection of Jesus Christ from the dead*'. The Old Testament prophetic promises of eschatological renewal are now being realised (in part) in the latter-day new creation of believers (1:3c) through the resurrection of Jesus Christ from the dead (1:3e). The resurrection of Jesus signals the beginning of the 'last of the times' (ἐσχάτου τῶν χρόνων, 1:20) which will be consummated at 'the revelation of Jesus Christ' (1:7) when the 'salvation ready to be revealed in the last time' (1:5) is finally unveiled.

We see again in 2:4–10 that it is by virtue of their contact with the resurrected Christ that believers enjoy new life in the present. It is in coming (through the new birth by faith) to Christ, the 'living stone' (λίθον ζῶντα; 'living' by virtue of his resurrection from the dead), and sharing in his life, that believers themselves also (καὶ αὐτοί) constitute 'living stones' (λίθοι ζῶντες). As 'living stones' believers have been 'rebirthed' (ἀναγεννήσᾳ) into a 'living hope' (ἐλπίδα ζῶσαν) through the resurrection of Jesus Christ (1:3), by virtue of which they 'live [ζήσωμεν] for doing what is right' now (2:24) and, as 'co-heirs of the grace of life'

---

[46] H. M. F. Büchsel, 'ἀναγεννάω', *TDNT*, 1: 674–5.

(συγκληρονόμοις χάριτος ζωῆς, 3:7), look forward to a time in the future when they also, like Christ (cf. 3:18), will 'live' (ζῶσι) in the spirit (i.e., enjoy resurrection life, 4:6c). Thus, as Büchsel notes above, there is an eschatological element to this 'rebirth'. The future life or 'living hope' into which (εἰς) believers have been rebirthed enters their present experience through this new birth, the fullness of which still awaits a future unveiling (cf. 1:7).

A second thing that could be mentioned is that Peter's understanding of this rebirth/new birth also 'includes … entrance into a new order of existence, but combines with it that of Divine parentage: men enter the new life as children of its Author'.[47] In the context of 1 Peter, the new birth serves as a dramatic metaphor for the radical transformation that takes place in terms of the believers' relation to God and, as a consequence, his or her relationship to one another and society.[48] God is Father not by virtue of his role as Creator but 'rather because of his distinctive role in the new birth of those whom he has chosen to be set apart for the new covenant in Christ'.[49] Thus the imagery of being 'rebirthed' by God in v. 3 corresponds to the idea of being 'chosen' by God the Father in vv. 1–2.[50] In each case the imagery points (1) to the totally new and unique *origin* of the believers' conversion, and (2) to the divine *initiative* and *action* by which God became the Father of believers. Boring writes: 'The imagery of "rebirth" corresponds to that of "election", in each case affirming that Christian identity is a result of God's initiative and act, not our decision. God's choice constitutes the elect community; whether or not we are born is not an issue on which we get to vote.'[51] This idea is also communicated by the prepositional phrase that follows denoting the basis of the believers' rebirth/new birth/regeneration.

The basis *of the new birth*

The begetting again of believers is then described as being ὁ κατὰ τὸ πολὺ αὐτοῦ ἔλεος ('according to his great mercy', 1:3). The preposition κατά (with the accusative, 'according to') denotes the reason/cause[52] or basis[53] for the believers' new life. Believers deserved judgment and wrath, but God, on the basis of/because of his mercy alone, has bestowed new life upon those who were formerly alienated from him.[54] In v. 2

---

[47] Hort, *First Epistle of Saint Peter*, 33.   [48] Elliott, *1 Peter*, 333.
[49] Jobes, *1 Peter*, 83.   [50] Boring, *1 Peter*, 61 (quoted below).
[51] Ibid.   [52] See BDAG, 512–13 (5aδ); Robertson, *Grammar*, 609.
[53] See Harris, 'Prepositions and Theology', 1201.   [54] Schreiner, *1 Peter*, 61.

God's foreknowledge (πρόγνωσιν θεοῦ, that is, his foreordaining covenantal affection) provided the basis (κατά) of the believers' election. Now here in v. 3 Peter identifies a second aspect of God's character – his great mercy – as the basis (κατά) of the believers' new birth. This stress on divine mercy appears again in 2:10 where believers are described as those who 'once were not shown mercy, but now have been shown mercy'. Thus the theme of mercy serves as an inclusion framing this, the first major section of the letter (1:3–2:10).

The noun ἔλεος ('pity, mercy, compassion') appears frequently in the LXX (352×) mostly translating (172×),[55] where there is a Hebrew original (253×), the word חֶסֶד whose basic meaning is 'goodness, kindness, lovingkindness'.[56] In the LXX, ἔλεος denotes both a religious virtue[57] and, more importantly, a divine attribute.[58] As a divine attribute ἔλεος refers to God's faithful and merciful help, steadfast kindness, and covenant love. In Exod. 20:5–6 (par. Deut. 5:9–10) God vows to visit punishment on those who break the second commandment but promises to show 'mercy [Gk ἔλεος; Heb. חֶסֶד] unto thousands, for those who love me and who keep my decrees' (NETS). However, Israel violated the covenant when it broke this commandment by worshipping the golden calf (Exod. 32). Nevertheless, God revealed himself to Moses in Exod. 34 with the words: 'The Lord, the Lord God is compassionate and merciful [ἐλεήμων], patient and very merciful [Gk πολυέλεος; Heb. רַב־חֶסֶד] and truthful, and preserving righteousness and producing mercy [ποιῶν ἔλεος] for thousands' (v. 6 [NETS]). Because God remained faithful to the covenant despite Israel's unfaithfulness, his 'mercy' is understood as a gracious gift. This truth is graphically portrayed in the book of Hosea (alluded to in 1 Pet. 2:10) in which 'mercy' is seen as an 'expression of the intimate [covenant] relationship between God and Israel symbolized by fidelity and family'.[59] The addition of the adjective πολύ ('great') in the formulation κατὰ τὸ πολὺ αὐτοῦ ἔλεος ('according to his great mercy'), an expression that is unique in the New Testament but frequent in the LXX,[60] further stresses the magnitude of this divine generosity and grace which has resulted in the believers' new birth (1:3; cf. 1:23) and incorporation into the family of God (see 2:4–10).

---

[55] Gramcord.   [56] BDB, 338, 339.

[57] See, e.g., Gen. 19:19; Num. 11:15; Deut. 28:40; Job 19:21; Isa. 13:18; Jer. 50:42; Lam. 4:16; Hos. 6:6; Mic. 6:8.

[58] See, e.g., Exod. 20:6; Num. 14:19; Deut. 5:10; Pss. 26:6; 88:1–2; Isa. 54:8; Jer. 3:12; Lam. 3:22.

[59] Elliott, *1 Peter*, 331.

[60] See, e.g., Num. 14:19; Ps. 50:3[51:1]; Isa. 63:7; Lam. 3:32; Dan. 3:42.

The goal *of the new birth*

The blessing of this new status (as God's newly born [ἀρτιγέννητος, cf. 2:2]) is then further defined by two prepositional phrases (each beginning with εἰς [1:3d, 4]) indicating the goal (telic use of εἰς) of this new origin: εἰς ἐλπίδα ζῶσαν ('for a living hope', v. 3d) and εἰς κληρονομίαν ... τετηρημένην ἐν οὐρανοῖς ('for an inheritance ... kept in heaven', v. 4). Thus, as we noted earlier, while the new birth of believers is a present experience, it is one that is oriented toward the future.

SUMMARY

The first major section of the letter (1:3–2:10) opened (1:3–12) on a worshipful note of blessing and praise to God for his great mercy and regenerating action (v. 3). The rebirth or regeneration of believers is beyond human achievement. It is totally God's work ('Blessed be the God ... who has caused us to be born anew'), due to his great mercy ('according to his great mercy'), and effected through the decisive act of raising Christ from the dead ('through the resurrection of Jesus Christ from the dead'). Boring writes:

> The readers did not become Christians by accepting a new theory, by committing themselves to certain ideas and principles, or by joining another worthy cause. Just as God's act in raising Jesus was the divine overturning of all human possibilities, so begetting and birth is an apt metaphor for the conversion process: none of us decides to be born, the initiative is prior to and apart from us, we simply find ourselves having been given life.[61]

From the divine perspective, salvation had already been achieved through Christ's redemptive act, but for the recipients it involves a distinct point of change associated with the generating of new life by the Father (1:3) and coming to faith in God (cf. 2:4) in response to 'the good news that was proclaimed to you' (1:25; cf. 1:12). The effect of God's sovereign, regenerative action is the qualifying of its recipients for a living hope (v. 3), an incorruptible inheritance (v. 4), and a salvation ready to be revealed in the last time (v. 5).

[61] Boring, *1 Peter*, 62.

2.   1 Peter 1:23–25: 'You have been born anew': the role of the word of God in the new birth

Context

Verse 23 is linked to the immediately preceding context by the perfect passive participle ἀναγεγεννημένοι (lit., 'having been born anew'). This participle, parallel to the previous participle (ἡγνικότες, 'having purified', v. 22), is subordinate to and modifies the main verb of v. 22 ([ἀλλήλους] ἀγαπήσατε, 'love [one another]') explaining how it is possible for the love command (ἀγαπήσατε, aorist active imperative) to be carried out. Verses 22–5, in turn, belong to a larger unit of thought (1:13–25), which consists of a series of aorist imperatives and associated nominal plural participles: ἐλπίσατε with ἀναζωσάμενοι and νήφοντες (v. 13), γενή-θητε with συσχηματιζόμενοι (vv. 14–16), ἀναστράφητε with εἰδότες (vv. 17–21), and ἀγαπήσατε with ἡγνικότες and ἀναγεγεννημένοι (here in vv. 22–3). Verses 24–5 mark the end of the subunit with its reference to the 'good news' (εὐαγγελισθὲν, v. 25) and a concluding Old Testament quotation (cf. 1:16; 2:3; 2:4–10; 2:17; 3:10–12; 5:5).

Content

The command to 'love one another' (ἀλλήλους ἀγαπήσατε) in v. 22 is modified by two causal participles (ἡγνικότες and ἀναγεγεννημένοι), denoting the grounds of the action of the main verb 'love' (ἀγαπήσατε). Both participles are in the perfect tense suggesting that they describe a past action from which a present state has emerged.[62] While the verb ἀγνίζω ('to cause to be morally pure, purify')[63] normally denotes ceremonial purification in the LXX[64] and New Testament,[65] the following reference to 'obedience' (ὑπακοή) suggests that moral purification is in view here. The preposition phrase ἐν τῇ ὑπακοῇ τῆς ἀληθείας indicates the means (ἐν) by which this purification is achieved. While the genitive τῆς ἀληθείας could be construed as adjectival (i.e., '*true* obedience'),[66] it is more likely objective ('obedience *to the truth*')[67] and denotes 'the truth of the gospel'.[68] Thus, 'obedience to the truth' here signifies the

---

[62] See Bénétreau, *Première épître de Pierre*, 111; Piper, 'Hope as the Motivation of Love', 214.

[63] BDAG, 12 (s.v. 2).

[64] See, e.g., Exod. 19:10; Num. 6:3; 8:21; 19:12; 31:23; 2 Chron. 31:18.

[65] See, e.g., Jn 11:55; Acts 21:24, 26; 24:18.

[66] See Schwank, Stöger, and Thüsing, *The Epistles of St. Peter*, 29.

[67] Schreiner, *1 Peter*, 92; Achtemeier, *1 Peter*, 137.

[68] See Achtemeier, *1 Peter*, 136; A. C. Thiselton, 'ἀλήθεια', *NIDNTT*, 3: 888.

believers' 'acceptance of the truth embodied in the proclaimed message of the gospel',[69] 'submission to the gospel',[70] 'acceptance of ... the
Christian faith',[71] or conversion (cf. 1:2). The goal (telic use of εἰς) of
their conversion is φιλαδελφίαν ('love of brother/sister'; 'mutual love').
This first participle (ἡγνικότες) and its modifiers (ἐν τῇ ὑπακοῇ τῆς
ἀληθείας), then, describe the means (conversion) by which believers
have been incorporated into the family of God and are thus able to love
one another as members of the same family.

Does this mean, then, that both the believers' incorporation into the
family of God and love for members of that family rest on a human work
(i.e., faith/obedience)? The immediate and broader context suggests this
is not the case. First, as we have already seen in v. 2, the believers' conversion (referred to as 'obedience' [ὑπακοήν]) is ultimately a result of
their election by God and consecration (or 'setting-apart') by the Spirit
(with the εἰς in the phrase εἰς ὑπακοήν denoting the purpose/result of
this divine election and consecration). There is thus no suggestion there
that believers are the agents of their own conversion. Second (and this
will be the focus for the remainder of this section), the imperative to
'love another' in v. 22 is modified by a second subordinate perfect participle in v. 23, ἀναγεγεννημένοι (lit., 'having been born anew'), indicating that the command to love is ultimately rooted in God's prior saving
work in causing believers to be born anew. The use of the verb ἀναγεγεννημένοι here recalls that of v. 3 (ἀναγεννήσας), where we saw that
the idea of rebirth or regeneration emphasises the initiative and action
of God in conferring new life on believers. Hence, as Achtemeier notes,
'the fact that the kind of love commanded in v 22 is possible only on the
basis of the prior act of God in rebegetting Christians through the proclamation of the gospel makes apparent enough that the command in v 22
remains a matter of divine rebirth, and hence falls outside the purview
of what is normally meant by "works"'.[72] Thus, with these two participles (ἡγνικότες and ἀναγεγεννημένοι) Peter indicates two important
aspects of Christian conversion: regeneration and saving faith, both of
which are rooted in God's sovereign and saving initiative.

Peter is adamant that it was God as a Father who has conferred new life
on those whom he has chosen, brought into covenant relationship with
himself, and made his own people (1 Pet. 1:1–2; 2:9–10). He has incorporated them into a new family (2:17), whose distinctiveness is revealed
in their brotherly/sisterly love for one another (1:22) and their calling

---

[69] Michaels, *1 Peter*, 75.   [70] Schreiner, *1 Peter*, 92.
[71] Achtemeier, *1 Peter*, 137.   [72] Ibid., 140–1.

upon God as their 'Father' (1:17). Unlike the mystery religions which we surveyed earlier, 'this was not a divine action which unfolded in the mystery of some secret rite and thereby effected their dehistoricization and immortalization. Rather, it was brought about in the context of their human experience and human lives by means of or through (διά) the preaching of the word of God which they received in faith (1:23–25)'[73] and by which they continue to live as 'children of obedience' (1:14). What, then, is the role of the 'word of God' (λόγου θεοῦ) in effecting the rebirth of believers?

The participle ἀναγεγεννημένοι ('having been born anew') is qualified by two prepositional phrases which indicate the *means* (ἐκ and διά) of this rebirth:

[οὐκ]	ἐκ	σπορᾶς [φθαρτῆς ἀλλὰ] ἀφθάρτου
not	from	[perishable] seed [but of] imperishable
	διά	λόγου ζῶντος θεοῦ καὶ μένοντος
	through	the living and enduring word of God

LaVerdiere suggests that 'the difference between the prepositions *ek* and *dia* [is] highly significant. The term *spora* refers to an intrinsic incorruptible (*aphthartou*) source of regenerated life. The word *logos*, on the other hand, refers to an extrinsic principle or instrument of regeneration.'[74] However, it is more likely that the second phrase represents an explanation of the first (i.e., 'seed' = 'word [of God]') with both indicating the *means* (ἐκ σπορᾶς, διὰ λόγου) of regeneration (and God [λόγου θεοῦ] as Father [cf. v. 3] as its source). Michaels, however, suggests that 'the change of preposition from ἐκ to διά is explained by the fact that σπορά refers to the process of sowing rather than the seed that is sown'.[75] While it is true that σπορά can mean either 'the activity of sowing' or 'that which is sown, seed' (see below), it is most likely the latter which is represented in this context. First, the translation of Michaels, 'not from the *planting of* perishable *seed* but from imperishable',[76] says more than the Greek text itself actually says. Second, it seems much more natural to speak of a seed as being imperishable rather than an action. Third, the obvious parallels between σπορά as 'imperishable' (ἀφθάρτου) and the 'word of God' (λόγου θεοῦ) as 'living and enduring' (ζῶντος καὶ μένοντος) with both as the means (ἐκ and διά) of the believers' regeneration suggests that 'seed' is a better translation here since, as I will argue

---

[73] Parsons, 'We Have Been Born Anew', 204.
[74] LaVerdiere, 'Grammatical Ambiguity', 92.
[75] Michaels, *1 Peter*, 76.   [76] Ibid.

below, λόγου θεοῦ refers to the 'good news' or 'gospel' (v. 25a) and not simply the act of proclaiming (or 'sowing') it. Thus the difference between ἐκ and διά here is more formal than substantial.[77]

The feminine noun [ἡ] σπορά (only here in the New Testament) denotes 'the activity of sowing'[78] (and figuratively 'procreation', 'begetting', 'generation', or 'birth')[79] and, by metonymy, 'that which is sown',[80] and hence 'seed' (and by extension human seed or 'offspring', also 'progeny', 'race').[81] It is a cognate of the masculine [ὁ] σπόρος which can mean 'the process of sowing, sowing',[82] 'the kernel part of fruit, seed',[83] the fruit itself,[84] or human seed or 'offspring'.[85] Both nouns are related to the verb σπείρω ('sow seed',[86] 'scatter, disperse',[87] 'engender, beget [offspring]'[88]) and the nouns σπέρμα ('seed', 'posterity, descendants')[89] and διασπορά ('dispersion, diaspora').[90] The word σπορά is also attested in the papyri where it most commonly denotes the action of 'sowing',[91] though also, on occasion, it can denote that which is sown, namely, the 'seed'.[92] In each case, the meaning of the noun must be determined by the immediate context.

The word σπορά is found in Josephus and Philo, both in its original-literal sense of 'sowing',[93] but also in its transferred sense, indicating that which is sown, that is, the 'seed' or the 'offspring' of the sower.[94] Philo can also extend this usage to the action of God who is able 'to open the wombs of souls, and to sow virtues in them [σπείρειν ἐν αὐταῖς ἀρετάς], and to make them pregnant with noble things, and to give birth to them. Take note of Leah your sister, and you will find her receiving seed and offspring [λαμβάνουσαν σποράν καὶ τὴν γονήν] out of no created being but by God's own gift.'[95] Elsewhere he writes of Leah:

> But from the Ruler of all she was awarded such acceptance that her womb which he opened received the seed of divine

---

[77] See Harris, 'Prepositions and Theology', 1189.

[78] 4 Kdgms [2 Kgs] 19:29.

[79] Aeschylus, *Prom.* 870; Plato, *Leg.* 729v, 783a; Plutarch, *Mor.* 2.320b; Ptolemaeus, *Tetr.* 103, 105.

[80] BDAG, 939. [81] Sophocles, *Aj.* 1298; Aeschylus, *Prom.* 871.

[82] BDAG, 939 (1). [83] BDAG, 939 (2). [84] LEH, 564.

[85] See LEH, 564. [86] BDAG, 936 (1). [87] BDAG, 936 (2).

[88] LSJ, 1625–26 (I.2). [89] BDAG, 937. [90] BDAG, 236.

[91] P.Oxy. 6.913; P.Tebt. 2.375; P.Ryl. 2.168; P.Grenf. 2.57; *BGU* 2.586.

[92] P.Leid. W.11.50; cf. P.Oxy. 33.76 (for the same meaning with σπόρος).

[93] Josephus, *A.J.* 2.90; *B.J.* 2.200; Philo, *Opif.* 41; *Decal.* 119; *Spec.* 1.326; *Virt.* 199; *Her.* 171; *Aet.* 65.

[94] Josephus, *A.J.* 306; *C.Ap.* 2.202; *Leg.* 1.10; *Mut.* 96; *Abr.* 46; *Ios.* 43; 260; *Decal.* 129; *Aet.* 97.

[95] Philo, *Leg.* 3.180.

impregnation [τὴν μήτρα ὑπ᾽ αὐτοῦ διοιχθεῖσαν σπορὰν θείας γονῆς παραδέξασθαι], whence should come the birth of noble practices and deeds [τὴν τῶν καλῶν ἐπιτηδευμάτων καὶ πράξεων γένεσιν].[96]

Thus, as Parsons observes, 'even prior to the date of composition of the First Epistle of St. Peter this term "seed" (σπορά) had acquired a metaphorical sense of something which God could "sow" within the soul or mind of man, and which could serve to guide or direct his life'.[97]

Since the word σπορά can refer to human seed and human procreation as well as to plant seed and its sowing, it is possible that the language of rebirth (already introduced in v. 3) has promoted Peter's use of this metaphor here. Whatever the case may have been, beginning with the imagery of rebirth (ἀναγεγεννημένοι), Peter highlights the means by which this supernatural birth took place through two corresponding statements in which he parallels the action of human seed on the natural level with God's special seed – the word of God (λόγου θεοῦ) – on a supernatural level (already in the Gospel tradition a parallel had been made between the seed of a plant and the word of God).[98] Schelkle writes:

> Wie jede natürliche Geburt aus Samen geschieht, so geschah die Wiedergeburt aus ihrem Samen. Die Aussage ist sehr realistisch. Der Same der Geburt aus Gott ist unvergänglich im Gegensatz zum vergänglichen menschlichen Samen (der Gegensatz ebenso Joh 1, 12f). Der Same ist hier das lebende und bleibende Wort Gottes.[99]

As Schelkle notes, the new birth generates new spiritual life from 'imperishable' (ἀφθάρτου) seed (the word of God) as opposed to (οὐκ ἐκ ... ἀλλά) 'perishable' (φθαρτῆς) seed (human procreation). Soon (vv. 24–5) Peter will contrast this 'imperishable seed' with the transitory nature of the created world portrayed in a quotation from Isa. 40:6–8.

What is this sowing by means of which believers have been reborn? According to Peter it is the proclamation of the word of God (σπορᾶς = λόγου θεοῦ [v. 23] = τοῦτο δέ ἐστιν τὸ ῥῆμα τὸ εὐαγγελισθὲν εἰς ὑμᾶς [v. 25]). The phrase διὰ λόγου ζῶντος θεοῦ καὶ μένοντος (1:23c) that follows identifies the σπορᾶς ἀφθάρτου ('imperishable seed') through which believers have been regenerated. The word λόγος

---

[96] Philo, *Mut.* 255. See also *Praem.* 10; *Corp. herm.* 13:1, 2.
[97] Parsons, 'We Have Been Born Anew', 229.
[98] Mk 4:3–9, 14–20; Mt. 13:3–9, 18–23; Lk. 8:5–8, 11–15.
[99] Schelkle, *Petrusbrief*, 53.

('a communication whereby the mind finds expression, word'),[100] a verbal noun of λέγω ('utter in words, say, tell, give expression to,[101] speak report', etc.)[102] appears frequently in the LXX (1232×)[103] predominantly translating, where there is a Hebrew original, the word דָּבָר ('speech word'),[104] and less frequently, the words אָמַר, אִמְרָה, and מִלָּה ('utterance, speech, word').[105] In his analysis of the term דָּבָר, Kittel makes a distinction between what he calls its dianoetic and dynamic elements. As *dianoetic* it contained content or thought (νοῦς), and as *dynamic* it is 'filled with power which can be manifested in the most diverse energies, … it is present … in the objective effects which the word has in history'.[106] Thus, in its dynamic sense, the word 'possessed a power to effect what it signified'.[107] This, however, is not to suggest that דָּבָר in itself contains this dual sense, but that the alternation or the coming together of these two senses can be discerned in certain contexts. As we will see, the inner potency which gives the word its efficacy derives not from the 'word' itself but 'entirely from the shattering majesty of the one who utters it'.[108] Moreover, as speech act philosophy has taught us (see chapter 2), speaking (or speech acts) is comprised of three basic aspects or acts: (1) utterance acts, (2) propositional acts, and (3) illocutionary acts. 'The key notion is that of illocution, which has to do not simply with locuting or uttering words [utterance and propositional acts] but with what we do *in* uttering words [illocutionary acts].'[109] As a divine communicative act, it is both informative (it has propositional content) and transformative (it has illocutionary force) and therefore has perlocutionary effect (the believed is transformed or reborn).

In the Ancient Near East a 'word' not only communicated meaningful content (its noetic or propositional aspect), but, in some contexts, possessed a power which was efficacious in incantations, magic spells, blessings and curses (its dynamic or illocutionary aspect).[110] This is particularly true of the gods in Sumerian, Akkadian and Babylonian texts whose word was believed to possess this power in a dynamic and pre-eminent way, in the creation, preservation, and direction of the world.[111] According to an inscription found in Memphis, the Memphite god Ptah conceived the gods and the cosmos through the thought of his heart and

---

[100] BDAG, 599–600. [101] BDAG, 588 (1). [102] BDAG, 590 (3).
[103] Gramcord. [104] BDB, 182.
[105] BDB, (respectively) 56–7, 57, 576. [106] G. Kittel, 'λέγω κτλ.' *TDNT*, 4: 92.
[107] Parsons, 'We Have Been Born Anew', 205.
[108] Eichrodt, *Theology of the Old Testament*, 2: 72.
[109] Vanhoozer, *First Theology*, 118. [110] See Moriarty, 'Word as Power', 345–6.
[111] See Dürr, *Die Wertung des göttlichen Wortes*, 25.

the word of his mouth.[112] In Mesopotamia the divine power of the creative word received praise in the Marduk-Ellil hymns: 'His word, which passes by like a storm ... The word which rends the heavens above; the word which shakes the earth below ... His word is a storm which annihilates everything ... When his word proceeds gently along, it destroys the land.'[113] Moreover, the word of a god was regarded not only as the active agent in creation, but also the directive agent in the course of human events. The evidence thus suggests that, in some contexts, the word of a god was both dianoetic and dynamic, significative and effective, informative and performative. Do we find the same trend in the writings of the Old Testament?

In the Old Testament the term 'word of Yahweh' (Heb. דְּבַר־יְהוָה; Gk ῥῆμα/λόγος κυρίου) occurs 242 times (the plural דִּבְרֵי יְהוָה] ['words of the Lord'] occurs 18×).[114] In the majority of its occurrences (221×, 93 percent) it denotes a prophetic word of God. In exilic and post-exilic times, the expression דְּבַר־יְהוָה could, in some contexts, also 'act as a periphrasis for the creatively efficacious activity of God in creation (Gen. 1) and nature (Pss. 29 and 33). The prophetic word of promise which shapes history, the directive word of the covenant which takes possession of men and the creative word of God which determines nature and its order combine to describe the revelation of God in the OT.'[115] Thus, creation is described as resulting from the dynamic power of God's creative word (Gen. 1:1–2:4). The creation narrative begins with the words: 'In the beginning when God created the heavens and the earth, the earth was a formless void and darkness covered the face of the deep ... Then God said, "Let there be light"; and there was light' (Gen. 1:1–3). In Ps. 34[33]:6, 9 we read: 'By the word of the LORD [Heb. דְּבַר־יְהוָה; Gk ὁ λόγος τοῦ κυρίου] the heavens were made, and all their host by the breath of his mouth ... For he spoke, and it came to be; he commanded, and it stood firm.' Not only was the word of God regarded as the active agent in creation, it was also seen as the dynamic instrument of salvation: 'He sent out his word [Heb. דְּבָרוֹ; Gk τὸν λόγον αὐτοῦ] and healed them, and delivered them from destruction' (Ps. 107:20). In Ps. 119:81 we read: 'My soul languishes for your salvation [Heb. תְּשׁוּעָה; Gk σωτήριον]; I hope in your word [Heb. דָּבָר; Gk λόγος]' (cf. Ps. 119:81; cf. 119:49, 74, 114, 147; 130:5). Thus the 'word of God' was not simply

---

[112] The so-called 'Shabaka Stone', no. 498, in the British Museum. The inscription has been published by Sharpe, *Egyptian Inscriptions*, plates 36–8.

[113] Cited in B. Klappert, 'λόγος κτλ.' *NIDNTT*, 3: 1088.

[114] Gramcord.   [115] B. Klappert, 'λόγος κτλ.' *NIDNTT*, 3: 1087.

a series of sounds ('utterance acts') or thoughts ('propositional acts') that came from his mouth, rather it denoted, in some contexts, the efficacious activity of God ('illocutionary acts'). This is well illustrated in Isa. 55:10–11:

> For as the rain and the snow come down from heaven, and do not return there until they have watered the earth, making it bring forth and sprout, giving seed to the sower and bread to the eater, so shall my word [Heb. דְּבָרִי; Gk ῥῆμά] be that goes out from my mouth; it shall not return to me empty, but it shall accomplish that which I purpose, and succeed in the thing for which I sent it.

The author of First Peter reflects this rich background when he indicates that the regeneration of the believer has been brought about by means of (διά) the 'living and enduring word of God' (λόγου ζῶντος θεοῦ καὶ μένοντος, 1:23). Some commentators argue that the two adjectival participles ζῶντος ('living') and μένοντος ('enduring') modify θεοῦ ('God'): 'the word of the living and enduring God'.[116] However, with the majority of commentators it seems best to construe them with λόγος ('word') instead.[117] First, we have already noted parallelism between the two following phrases:

ἐκ   σπορᾶς   φθαρτῆς ἀλλὰ ἀφθάρτου
διὰ   λόγου   ζῶντος θεοῦ καὶ μένοντος

Since ἀφθάρτου ('imperishable') stands at the end of the clause modifying σπορᾶς ('seed'), it is also likely that μένοντος ('enduring'), a parallel idea also standing in the emphatic position in its clause, modifies λόγου ('word', which we have noted is parallel in thought to σπορᾶς). Second, and more importantly, the word 'endure' (μένω) appears again in v. 25 emphasising the enduring quality not of God, but of his word: τὸ ῥῆμα κυρίου **μένει** εἰς τὸν αἰῶνα ('the word of the Lord **abides** for ever'). This word, says Peter in v. 25b, 'is the word [of the gospel] that was proclaimed to you' (τοῦτο δέ ἐστιν τὸ ῥῆμα τὸ εὐαγγελισθὲν εἰς ὑμᾶς).

This 'word' has both propositional content (the dianoetic dimension) and illocutionary force (the dynamic dimension). Its propositional content is indicated by the word εὐαγγελισθέν ('the good news that was proclaimed', v. 25b), the aorist passive participle of εὐαγγελίζω ('announce

---

[116] See Manns, 'La théologie de la nouvelle naissance', 141.
[117] See, e.g., Hamblin, 'Greek Participle', 91; Bénétreau, *Première épître de Pierre*, 112.

good news, proclaim the gospel').[118] The use of the word εὐαγγελισθέν harkens back to the thought of 1:11–12 where the proclamation of the good news (also denoted by the verb εὐαγγελίζω) concerned 'the sufferings [destined] for Christ and the glories after these [sufferings]' (v. 11c). Peter's substitution of the word κυρίου ('Lord') in 1:25a for the LXX's θεοῦ ('God') in his quotation of LXX Isa. 40:8 further strengthens the link between this 'word' and Jesus Christ. The genitive κυρίου is most probably an object genitive ('the word whose object is the Lord [Jesus Christ]') rather than a subject genitive ('the word that was proclaimed by the Lord') since the word was not announced to them by Jesus Christ but by those who proclaimed the sufferings and glorification of Christ (1:11). Thus the 'word' has propositional content: it concerns the suffering, death, resurrection, and glorification of Jesus Christ.

More than that, the 'word' here has illocutionary force (its dynamic dimension). As such it is performative not just informative, effective not just significative, life-giving not just life-revealing. The 'word' here is described as λόγου ζῶντος θεοῦ καὶ μένοντος ('the living and remaining word of God'). It is 'living' (ζῶντος) because it comes from God (λόγου **θεοῦ**), the creator and sustainer of life and, thus, not only speaks about life, but has the power to communicate that life which he has disclosed in a unique way 'through the resurrection of Jesus Christ' (δι' ἀναστάσεως Ἰησοῦ Χριστοῦ, 1:3e) who himself 'has been made alive in the spirit' (ζῳοποιηθεὶς δὲ πνεύματι, 3:18). The 'word' both 'extrinsically reveals the power of the resurrection to those whom God has chosen, and intrinsically gives that power to those who believe'.[119] Thus there is no conflict between 1:3 which says that believers have been 'born anew ... through the resurrection of Jesus Christ from the dead' (ἀναγεννήσας ... δι' ἀναστάσεως Ἰησοῦ Χριστοῦ ἐκ νεκρῶν, v. 3ce) and 1:23 which states that believers have been 'born anew ... through the living and remaining word of God' (ἀναγεγεννημένοι ... διὰ λόγου ζῶντος θεοῦ καὶ μένοντος, v. 23ac). The new life that is communicated to the elect by virtue of Christ's resurrection is the same life that is disclosed in the word of his resurrection. As Boring notes, 'in 1:3 the new birth was by the resurrection of Jesus Christ; here it is through the word that is inseparably bound to this event and mediates it to the believers'.[120] It is this connection that enables Peter to draw an analogy between the 'word' (λόγος) and the life-giving ability of a 'seed' (σπορά). Just as seed sown on a natural level, though perishable, has life-giving power

---

[118] BDAG, 402.   [119] Parsons, 'We Have Been Born Anew', 237.
[120] Boring, *1 Peter*, 88.

within it, so the word of God, which is much superior because it is imperishable, has life-giving power because it communicates that (eternal) life which has been made available to the elect through the resurrection of Jesus from the dead.

Peter then concludes (vv. 24–5) with a quotation from Isa. 40:6–8 in order to validate (διότι, 'for'; cf. 1:16; 2:6) what he has said in v. 23 about the imperishable quality of the word of God: 'For all flesh is as grass and all its glory as the flower of grass; the grass withers and the flower falls, but the word of the Lord remains for ever' (vv. 24–5a). Peter goes on to identify this word as 'the word of the gospel that was proclaimed to you' (v. 25b). Selwyn comments:

> The prophecy which opens II-Isaiah, was addressed to a people exiled and oppressed, and offers them hope and comfort; God promises deliverance to those who are repentant and receptive, and his promise – in contrast to all else in human life – remains sure ... Every leading thought here fits in with what our author has been saying. He too is addressing readers who are exiled ... and oppressed; and he has the same message for them, the contrast between the perishability of all mortal things (cf. φθαρτός in verses 18, 23) and the incorruptibility of the Christian inheritance and hope.[121]

Thus Achtemeier concludes:

> [T]he contrast between what is transitory and what is permanent embodied in the quotation would be highly appropriate for a beleaguered community of Christians facing what gave every appearance of being the permanent, even eternal, power and glory of the Roman Empire. In such a situation, the announcement that the glitter and pomp, and power of the Roman culture was as grass when compared to God's eternal word spoken in Jesus Christ, available through the gospel preached to and accepted by the Christians of Asia Minor, would give them courage to hold fast to the latter while rejecting the former. Even the hostility of that overwhelming power becomes more bearable when its ultimately transitory nature is revealed and accepted.[122]

---

[121] Selwyn, *First Epistle of St. Peter*, 152.
[122] Achtemeier, *1 Peter*, 142.

Summary

The image of 'rebirth', with which the first main division of the letter began, reappears here in v. 23, rather logically, in a context dealing with familial love. The imperative to 'love one another' (ἀλλήλους ἀγαπή-σατε, v. 22b) is only possible because of God's prior saving work in causing believers to be born anew. The means by which this rebirth was brought about is identified by Peter as 'the living and remaining word of God' (λόγου ζῶντος θεοῦ καὶ μένοντος, v. 23c). This 'word' (λόγος), as we have seen, has both propositional content and illocutionary force, dianoetic as well as dynamic dimensions. As propositional it has full Christological content and is thus identified in v. 25 as 'the word of the gospel that was proclaimed to you' (τὸ ῥῆμα τὸ εὐαγγελισθὲν εἰς ὑμᾶς, v. 25b). This gospel proclamation, according to v. 11, has as its content 'the sufferings [destined] for Christ and the glories after these [sufferings]' (τὰ εἰς Χριστὸν παθήματα καὶ τὰς μετὰ ταῦτα δόξα, v. 11c). More than that, this word also has illocutionary force. As the 'living word *of God*' (λόγου ζῶντος *θεοῦ*, v. 23c), it is not only signifi-cative but also effective, not only informative but also performative, not only life-revealing but also life-giving: it has the power to communicate that life which has been disclosed in a unique way 'through the resurrec-tion of Jesus Christ' (δι' ἀναστάσεως Ἰησοῦ Χριστοῦ, 1:3e). As Senior notes: '"The word of God" is a way of speaking of the gospel in its most dynamic and comprehensive sense, ultimately as a metaphor for the sav-ing force of God's own presence in human life, a presence embodied in Jesus and the gospel.'[123]

---

[123] Senior, *1 Peter*, 50.

5

THE EXPECTATION OF SALVATION
Salvation as a future event

1.   Context

1 Peter 1:3–12 forms one unbroken sentence in the Greek and constitutes the first main division of the letter. The main body of the letter opens (1:3–12) on a note of praise and blessing (εὐλογητός; cf. Eph. 1:3; 2 Cor. 1:4). Theologically, this opening blessing continues the theme of the opening salutation (1:1–2) which highlights God's sovereign and saving initiative and grace in the lives of believers. The main theme of the present section (1:3–12) is introduced immediately in v. 3: God is to be praised and thanked for his divine mercy and saving work. The main theme of this passage then is salvation. Significantly, the term σωτηρία ('salvation') itself appears only four times in 1 Peter, and yet three of these occurrences are in this section (1:5, 9, 10; the fourth occurrence is found in 2:2), and in all three cases they are with reference to salvation as a future event. The overall message of 1:3–12 may be summarised as follows: 'Believers have been reborn to an entirely new life that is characterised by hope and joy and that is destined for glory and final salvation.'[1]

Furthermore, it has been clearly demonstrated that this opening section functions as an introduction to the entire letter by anticipating themes in succeeding sections of the letter.[2] 1 Peter 1:3–12 serves as an introduction to 1:13–5:11 in two basic ways. First, the terminology and motifs of 1:3–12 anticipate themes that will be developed in succeeding sections of the letter.[3] Second, in a more general way 1:3–12 serves as a presupposition for 1:13–5:11. That is to say, 1:3–12 serves as the theological 'foundation upon which the author bases his exhortations'.[4] As we have noted above and I will argue below, the main theme

---

[1] Kendall, 'Literary and Theological Function', 115.
[2] See ibid., 103–20; Elliott, *1 Peter*, 330.
[3] See Kendall, 'Literary and Theological Function', 103–20.
[4] Ibid., 114.

of 1:3–12 is salvation. The salvation described (or better, exulted in) here 'requires a distinctive way of life (ἀναστροφή) and the author's concern in 1:13–5:11 is to encourage his readers in this way' (hence the change from the indicative in 1:3–12 to the imperative in vv. 13f., signalled by the consecutive conjunction διό ['therefore'] in v. 13).[5] This being the case, the theme of salvation is not only prominent in the opening section of this letter but in fact pervades the entire letter.

2.   Content

Future salvation as hope and inheritance (1:3–5)

Verses 3–5 comprise the first of the three subunits (3–5, 6–9, 10–12) in this section in which God is 'blessed' (εὐλογητός) for his saving work. In v. 3 the believers' entrance into salvation is spoken of in terms of being 'rebirthed' (ἀναγεννάω). This 'begetting anew' points to the new and unique origin of the believer's salvation (θεός, v. 3). The blessing of this new status is then further defined by two prepositional phrases (each beginning with εἰς) indicating the goal and hence future orientation of this new origin: ἐλπίς (v. 3d) and κληρονομία (v. 4a). Finally, the link with future salvation is made clear with the juxtaposition of the divine (ἐν οὐρανοῖς) preservation (τετηρημένην) of the believers' inheritance (κληρονομίαν) in v. 4 with the divine (ἐν δυνάμει θεοῦ) preservation (φρουρουμένους) of believers (ὑμᾶς) for eschatological salvation (εἰς σωτηρίαν ἑτοίμην ἀποκαλυφθῆναι ἐν καιρῷ ἐσχάτῳ) in v. 5 (suggesting that κληρονομία and σωτηρία are parallel ideas).

ἐλπίς ('hope', v. 3)

Peter begins with the main theme of the passage (vv. 3–12): God is to be 'blessed' (εὐλογητός) for his great mercy (τὸ πολὺ αὐτοῦ ἔλεος) in granting salvation to believers. The reason why he is to be praised is then explained in the next clause: ἀναγεννήσας ἡμᾶς ('he has caused us to be born again'). The first result or benefit of God's begetting is then further defined with the first of two clauses beginning with the preposition εἰς: εἰς ἐλπίδα ('for a living hope'). The word ἐλπίδα is then modified by the adjective ζῶσαν ('living'). This whole prepositional phrase is in turn grounded in another prepositional phrase: δι' ἀναστάσεως Ἰησοῦ Χριστοῦ ἐκ νεκρῶν ('through the resurrection of

---

[5] Ibid., 114.

Jesus Christ from the dead'). Three questions concern us here: (1) What is the nature and content of this hope? (2) What does the author mean when he calls it a *'living* hope' (ἐλπίδα ζῶσαν)? (3) Are the words δι' ἀναστάσεως Ἰησοῦ Χριστοῦ ἐκ νεκρῶν linked to ὁ ἀναγεννήσας ἡμᾶς or ἐλπίδα ζῶσαν?

First, what is the nature and content of this 'hope' (ἐλπίς)? The noun ἐλπίς appears 117 times in the LXX (81× in the OT and 36× in the Apocrypha),[6] commonly rendering, where there is a Hebrew original, תִּקְוָה ('hope'),[7] בָּטַח ('trust'),[8] מִבְטָח ('confidence'),[9] בִּטָחוֹן (see בָּטַח), while the verb ἐλπίζω occurs 117 times (98× in the OT and only 19× in the Apocrypha, normally translating בּוֹטֵחַ [verb בָּטַח] 'trust', [noun בֶּטַח] 'security').[10] In a number of these passages ἐλπίς is used to denote secular objects of hope.[11] Yet as the Old Testament Scriptures repeatedly demonstrate, God's desire is that his people would make him their hope/ the sole object of their hope (e.g. Pss. 14:6 [LXX 13:6]; 40:4 [39:5]; 65:5 [64:6]; 71:5 [70:5]; 73:28 [72:28]; 94:22 [93:22]; 142:5 [141:6]). This comes out most clearly in the Psalms where the noun ἐλπίς and the verb ἐλπίζω represent the attitude of those who look to God alone for salvation (see, e.g., LXX Pss. 61:8 [62:7]; 64:6 [65:5]). Throughout the Psalms God is characteristically ὁ σῴζων τους ἐλπίζοντας ἐπὶ σὲ (lit. 'the Saviour of those who hope in you'; LXX Ps. 16:7 [17:7]). As a divine predicate in the LXX Psalms, ἐλπίς represents the Hebrew מַחְסֶה ('refuge, shelter', 13:6 [14:6]; 60:4 [61:4]; 61:8 [62:8]; 90:9 [91:9]; 141:6 [142:6] translated elsewhere in the LXX by such terms as βοηθός ['helper', 61:9 (62:9)] or καταφυγή ['refuge', 103:18 (104:18)]), מִבְטָח ('confidence', 'trust', 39:5 [40:4]; 64:6 [65:5]; 71:5 [70:5]) and שֵׂבֶר ('hope', 146[145]:5). For the LXX translators, to make God one's 'hope' meant trusting him for saving help or deliverance or protection. Here the difference between hope and trust begins to fade.

While the saving in view here is primarily from troubles and distresses in this life, for some writers the horizon of hope did stretch beyond the present life. It embraced both 'Yahweh's coming in glory, his reign over a new earth, the conversion of Israel and the nations, and the new covenant, based on the forgiveness of sins'.[12] In 2 Maccabees we have both the hope (ἐλπίζομεν [ἐπὶ τῷ θεῷ]) that (ὅτι) God will restore the nation of Israel (ἡμᾶς ἐλεήσει καὶ ἐπισυνάξει ἐκ τῆς ὑπὸ

---

[6] Gramcord.   [7] BDB, 876.   [8] BDB, 105.   [9] BDB, 105.

[10] BDB, 105; R. Bultmann, 'ἐλπίς', *TDNT*, 2: 521.

[11] E.g. a wage (Deut. 24:15), temporal security (Judg. 18:7), other humans (Jer. 17:5), physical health (2 Macc. 9:22).

[12] E. Hoffmann, 'ἐλπίς', *NIDNTT*, 2: 240.

τὸν οὐρανὸν εἰς τὸν ἅγιον τόπον, 2:18) as well as the hope of a glorious resurrection as expressed in 2 Macc. 7:14: καὶ γενόμενος πρὸς τὸ τελευτᾶν οὕτως ἔφη αἱρετὸν μεταλλάσσοντας ὑπ' ἀνθρώπων τὰς ὑπὸ **τοῦ θεοῦ προσδοκᾶν ἐλπίδας πάλιν ἀναστήσεσθαι ὑπ' αὐτοῦ** σοὶ μὲν γὰρ ἀνάστασις εἰς ζωὴν οὐκ ἔσται. The martyr is able to face death with integrity (καθαρός) because he puts his trust entirely in God (παντελῶς ἐπὶ τῷ κυρίῳ πεποιθώς, 2 Macc. 7:40). The mother of the seven brothers martyred in 2 Maccabees, we are told, was able to face this horrific ordeal courageously (εὐψύχως) *διὰ* τὰς ἐπὶ κύριον ἐλπίδας (*'because* of her hope in the Lord', 7:20). What, then, was the content of her hope? She tells us in v. 23: ὁ τοῦ κόσμου κτίστης ... τὸ πνεῦμα καὶ τὴν ζωὴν ὑμῖν πάλιν ἀποδίδωσιν μετ' ἐλέους. By contrast, the ungodly have ἀδήλοις ἐλπίσιν ('uncertain hopes', 2 Macc. 7:34) or κενὴ ἡ ἐλπις ('empty hope', Wis. 3:11) and only the prospect of judgment after death (2 Macc. 7:34–7; Wis. 3:18). The content of ἐλπίς, then, is the twin hope of deliverance at the final judgment and the enjoyment of eternal life.

These two elements reappear in the New Testament. What is distinctive in the New Testament 'is the claim that this hope, founded upon God's promise to Israel, is fulfilled for believers in Christ, whether Jew or Gentile'.[13] In fact, in Acts 26:6 Paul claims to be on trial because of this very hope: ἐπ' ἐλπίδι τῆς εἰς τοὺς πατέρας ἡμῶν ἐπαγγελίας γενομένης ὑπὸ τοῦ θεοῦ (26:6). This hope, he tells us is the ἐλπίδος καὶ ἀναστάσεως νεκρῶν ('hope and resurrection of the dead', 23:6), a resurrection that embraces both the δικαίων τε καὶ ἀδίκων (24:15; implying a coming judgment for the latter, cf. 24:25). This future resurrection can be the content of Christian hope, because, as we shall see, it is grounded in the past resurrection of Jesus Christ from the dead (ἐλπίδα ζῶσαν δι' ἀναστάσεως Ἰησοῦ Χριστοῦ ἐκ νεκρῶν, 1 Pet. 1:3; cf. 1 Pet. 1:21). As Bultmann notes: 'Christian hope rests on the divine act of salvation accomplished in Christ, and, since this is eschatological, hope itself is an eschatological blessing.'[14] While in some passages ἐλπίς retains the more temporal meaning of deliverance in the present life (as we saw in the Psalms), on the whole, the primary benefit denoted by ἐλπίς is the eschatological salvation of believers to eternal life with God. This observation is made by Hoffmann, who notes that '[i]n many passages ἐλπίς denotes not the personal attitude but the objective benefit of salvation towards which hope is directed ... Where v[er]b or noun are

---

[13] Wieland, *Salvation*, 29.   [14] R. Bultmann, 'ἐλπίς', *TDNT*, 2: 532.

used absolutely without further qualification the reference is usually to the eschatological fulfillment.'[15]

The noun ἐλπίς appears three times in 1 Peter (with the verb ἐλπίζω occuring twice, 1:13; 3:5). The close link noted in our Old Testament survey between hoping in God and trusting God also appears in 1:21: ὥστε τὴν πίστιν ὑμῶν καὶ ἐλπίδα εἶναι εἰς θεόν ('so that your faith and hope are in God'). Peter also draws lines of continuity between the Old and New Testaments when he calls upon wives to follow the example of αἱ ἅγιαι γυναῖκες αἱ ἐλπίζουσαι εἰς θεόν ('the holy women who hoped in God', 3:5). Twice this hope is said specifically to be εἰς θεόν ('in God', 1:3; 3:5) and twice it is linked to the resurrection (1:3, 21). In at least three verses it is the subjective side of hope that appears to receive the accent (1:21; 3:5, 15). Elsewhere in the letter, however, there is ample evidence that the author looked towards a future, eternal life which transcended personal feelings of hope in this present life (e.g., 1:4, 5, 7, 9, 10, 13; 2:2, 11–12; 3:9–10, 18–22; 4:6, 13; 5:4, 6, 10). It is therefore reasonable to refer the ἐλπίδα ζῶσαν in 1:3 to the objective, eschatological hope of Christians, that is, their salvation, with the death and resurrection of Christ as the basis and means for attaining it. Three factors point in this direction. First, from the context we noted earlier that εἰς ἐλπίδα (v. 3d) is parallel to εἰς κληρονομία (v. 4a), which is in turn parallel to εἰς σωτηρίαν (v. 5c), suggesting that the 'hope' mentioned here is a reference to final salvation (as in v. 5c). Second, the future, objective sense of ἐλπίς is in keeping with the use of εἰς which can be telic in force. Dupont-Roc rightly notes that '[l]a dynamique de cette naissance oriente alors toute l'existence chrétienne "vers une espérance vivant," espérance qui vise l'avenir (εἰς ἐλπίδα)'.[16] Third, the relationship between the believer's hope and Christ's resurrection from the dead (argued for below) in v. 3 would suggest that the hope being spoken of is the hope of the future resurrection. In sum, the hope mentioned in v. 3 can be described as the goal and result of being rebirthed and has as its content the future salvation of believers.

Second, what does Peter mean when he calls it an ἐλπίδα ζῶσαν ('**living** hope')? While Elliott defines it as a 'lively (*living*) confidence in the power of God',[17] this definition does not square well with our more objective understanding of hope in this passage to denote the believer's future salvation. The immediate context provides the best clue for understanding why this hope is described as 'living' (ζῶσαν): it is living

---

[15] E. Hoffmann, 'ἐλπίς', *NIDNTT*, 2: 241.

[16] Dupont-Roc, 'Le Jeu des prépositions', 205.   [17] Elliott, *1 Peter*, 334.

because it is established and accomplished δι' ἀναστάσεως Ἰησοῦ Χριστοῦ ἐκ νεκρῶν ('through the resurrection of Jesus Christ from the dead', v. 3). While some scholars link the words δι' ἀναστάσεως Ἰησοῦ Χριστοῦ with ἀναγεννήσας (making the resurrection the basis of the new birth),[18] it is probably better to view them as being linked to ἐλπίδα ζῶσαν (though without completely rejecting the former). At least four arguments can be put forward in support of this connection. First, the word order suggests that there is a more direct relationship between the words ἐλπίδα ζῶσαν and δι' ἀναστάσεως Ἰησοῦ Χριστοῦ ἐκ νεκρῶν since the latter immediately follows the former. Second, the addition of the words ἐκ νεκρῶν at the end of the clause (which seem quite redundant if the author was wanting to emphasise rebirth) creates a verbal contrast (ζῶσαν ... ἐκ νεκρῶν) suggesting that such a link was in the mind of the author:

εἰς	ἐλπίδα	ζῶσαν
δι'	ἀναστάσεως Ἰησοῦ Χριστοῦ	ἐκ νεκρῶν

Third, that such a link was in the mind of the author can be suggested by the fact that only eighteen verses later he makes the same connection when he writes, θεὸν τὸν **ἐγείραντα αὐτὸν ἐκ νεκρῶν** καὶ δόξαν αὐτῷ δόντα, **ὥστε** τὴν πίστιν ὑμῶν καὶ **ἐλπίδα** εἶναι **εἰς θεόν** (v. 21). Fourth, the word order of the clause (v. 3, noted above) creates 'an inevitable association in thought between ζῶσαν and ἀναστάσεως: resurrection means life and makes life possible'.[19]

What then is this 'living hope' (ἐλπίδα ζῶσαν)? It can be described in various ways: it is the 'hope of life', the 'hope of eternal life', or the 'hope of resurrection life' (or 'the hope that is resurrection life'). It is the hope and blessing of future resurrection life in the presence of the living God (θεοῦ ζῶντος) grounded in the 'resurrection of Jesus Christ from the dead'. As Kühschelm notes: 'Sie versetzt die Christen in eine "lebendige Hoffnung", weil ihnen dadurch das "durch die Auferstehung Jesu Christi von den Toten" eröffnete, neue, endgültig gesicherte Leben bei Gott zugesprochen ist.'[20] The hope that Peter is talking about, then, is resurrection hope: '[T]he hope we have can be called *living*: it points forward to life eternal by way of our own resurrection'.[21] As Marshall writes: '[T]he hope of future life rests on the fact that God raised Jesus

---

[18] Spicq, *Les Épîtres de Saint Pierre*, 45; Campbell, *Honour, Shame, and the Rhetoric of 1 Peter*, 44.

[19] Michaels, *1 Peter*, 19.   [20] Kühschelm, 'Lebendige Hoffnung', 203.

[21] Scharlemann, 'An Apostolic Descent', 13.

from the dead and on the reasonable inference that, if God raised Jesus, he will also raise those who trust in Jesus'.[22] This hope, then, is the 'hope of life' beyond the grave and therefore it is a '*living* hope'.

κληρονομία ('inheritance', v. 4)

The second result or benefit of the believer's rebirth is a κληρονομία ('inheritance'). The word is a compound of κλῆρος ('land received by lot, allotment', 'lot, portion, share')[23] and νέμω ('to dispense, distribute', 'allot')[24] and refers to the portion that is given,[25] the 'inheritance, possession, property'.[26] The idea of inheritance follows on logically from the metaphor of rebirth: 'Par conséquent ceux que Dieu a engendrés hériteront de plein droit, grâce au Christ.'[27] This relationship between rebirth and inheritance along with the parallelism that we noted between κληρονομία and σωτηρία (and ἐλπίς in v. 3), suggests both its divine origin, eschatological nature, and gracious character.

As most commentators acknowledge, the language of inheritance is drawn principally from the Old Testament.[28] The noun κληρονομία appears 183 times in the Old Testament (and another 41× in the Apocrypha)[29] most of the time (approximately 140×) rendering, where there is a Hebrew original, נַחֲלָה ('possession, property, inheritance'),[30] and in some cases words of the stem יׁרשׁ ('inherit, take possession of'). In the Old Testament the land of Canaan was regarded as the κληρονομία God promised to his people: τὴν γῆν Χανααν αὕτη ἔσται ὑμῖν εἰς **κληρονομίαν** γῆ Χανααν σὺν τοῖς ὁρίοις αὐτῆς (Num. 34:2; cf. Lev. 25:23; Num. 32:19; Deut. 2:12). The promise of the Land of Canaan as an inheritance goes back to God's promise to Abraham in Gen. 12: καὶ ἔλαβεν Αβραμ τὴν Σαραν γυναῖκα αὐτοῦ καὶ τὸν Λωτ υἱὸν τοῦ ἀδελφοῦ ... ἦλθον εἰς γῆν Χανααν ... καὶ ὤφθη κύριος τῷ Αβραμ καὶ εἶπεν αὐτῷ τῷ σπέρματί σου δώσω τὴν γῆν ταύτην (vv. 5–7). The point to be noted right from the outset is that it is God who gives the land to his people (cf. Deut. 3:20; 12:9; 19:14; Josh. 1:15; 17:4; 1 Chron. 16:18; 2 Chron. 20:11). God's right to give the land to his people derives from the fact that, as Schelkle points out, the owner of the land

---

[22] Marshall, *1 Peter*, 37.   [23] BDAG, 548.
[24] E. Hoffmann, 'ἐλπίς', *NIDNTT*, 2: 296.
[25] E. Hoffmann, 'ἐλπίς', *NIDNTT*, 2: 296.
[26] BDAG, 548.   [27] Spicq, *Les Épîtres de Saint Pierre*, 46.
[28] Feldmeier, *Brief des Petrus*, 48; Brox, *Petrusbrief*, 62.
[29] Gramcord.   [30] BDB, 635.

was Yahweh (e.g., Exod. 19:5; Ps. 24:1 [23:1]), and so his giving of the land to them is an act of pure and sovereign grace.[31]

It should also be noted that the giving of land to his people as κληρονομία is much more than just the handing over of a piece of turf. In giving the land as κληρονομία, 'it invests the occupation of the land with greater significance: occupation involves the enjoyment of a filial relationship with God; it is not merely the possession of a piece of real estate'.[32] And so in giving his people *his* land as κληρονομία, 'God reveals that he considers Israel to be his "son"'.[33] For this reason the land is also spoken of as κληρονομίαν κυρίου (2 Sam. 14:16) or τὴν κληρονομίαν μου (Jer. 2:7; cf. Jer. 16:18, τὴν γῆν μου ... τὴν κληρονομίαν μου). Such statements only makes sense 'if the language of inheritance connotes the idea of Israel's "sonship"'.[34] God can give the land to Israel because it belongs to him and not to its current inhabitants. Miller concludes: '[T]he land, then, represents Yahweh's solidarity with the nation to which he has bound himself in covenant'.[35] This intimacy is then mirrored in two related assertions in the Old Testament. First, not only is the land spoken of as Yahweh's inheritance, but also the nation of Israel itself (see, e.g., Deut. 4:20; 32:8–9; 1 Kgs 8:51, 53; 1 Sam. 10:1; 2 Sam. 20:19). Second, not only is Israel referred to as Yahweh's inheritance, and not only is the land spoken of as Israel's inheritance, but Yahweh himself is to be Israel's true inheritance (see, e.g., Num. 18:20; Ps. 16:5 [15:5]; Ezek. 44:28).

In the *koine* period κληρονομία continued to have the idea of inheritance or property (see, e.g., P.Oxy. 14.1638; 19.2231; 27.2474; 63.4390; P.Ryl. 2.108; P.Tebt. 213). In later Judaism the notion of inheritance became a 'Metapher für das *eschatologische Heilsgut* des (ewigen) Lebens'.[36] While it was often still tied to the land, the language of inheritance included such notions as the inheriting of the whole earth (CD I 7; *1 En.* 5:7; *Jub.* 22:14; *4 Ezra* 6:55f.), eternal life (*Pss. Sol.* 14:10; *1 En.* 40:9; *T. Job* 18), the coming aeon (*4 Ezra* 7:96; *2 En.* 50:2; 66:6), and a heavenly inheritance (*4 Ezra* 7:9, 17; *1 En.* 39:8). In the New Testament the noun κληρονομία appears only fourteen times (with the verb κληρονομέω appearing seventeen times). The word occurs outside of 1 Peter (1:4) in Mark (2×) Luke–Acts (4×), the Pauline epistles (5×) and Hebrews (2×). In a number of instances the word κληρονομία is used to speak of the inheritance of property

---

[31] Schelkle, *Petrusbriefe*, 31.   [32] Miller, 'Land', 626.
[33] Ibid., 625.   [34] Ibid., 626.   [35] Ibid.
[36] Feldmeier, *Brief des Petrus*, 48.

or possessions (Mk 12:7 = Mt. 21:38 = Lk. 20:14; Lk. 12:13; Acts 7:5; Gal. 3:18; Heb. 11:8). Once it is used to speak of the saints as God's inheritance (τῆς κληρονομίας αὐτοῦ ἐν τοῖς ἁγίοις, Eph. 1:18). In all of its other occurrences κληρονομία carries soteriological and eschatological connotations (Acts 20:32; Eph. 1:14; 5:5; Col. 3:24; Heb. 9:15; 1 Pet. 1:4).

It is clear that Peter also conceived of the κληρονομία of v. 4 in soteriological and eschatological terms. Five pieces of evidence substantiate this judgment. First, the immediate context, as we noted above (and will argue below), indicates that εἰς κληρονομία is another way of describing the σωτηρίαν ἑτοίμην ἀποκαλυφθῆναι ἐν καιρῷ ἐσχάτῳ (v. 5), which, as the words ἐν καιρῷ ἐσχάτῳ ('in the last time') indicate, is a future event. Second, as Achtemeier rightly points out, 'by definition an inheritance points to the future'.[37] Third, this last point was substantiated by our consideration of inheritance language in the New Testament which, when used to speak of the believers' inheritance, pointed primarily to its eschatological nature. Fourth, the phrase τετηρημένην ἐν οὐρανοῖς εἰς ὑμᾶς suggests an inheritance that is awaiting believers, not one that is here and now in their possession. Fifth, the three adjectives modifying κληρονομία – ἄφθαρτος ('imperishable, incorruptible, immortal'), ἀμίαντος ('undefiled, pure'), and ἀμάραντος ('unfading') – contrast the permanence of this future reward with the transitoriness of the present, once again pointing to its eschatological nature.[38] Perhaps F. W. Beare has best captured the sense of the three alpha privatives when he notes that '[t]he paronomasia of the three verbals is most effective; the inheritance is *un*touched by death, *un*stained by evil, *un*impaired by time'.[39] Each of these words emphasises the fact that the inheritance which Peter is speaking about is an eternal and hence eschatological one. In Israel's history, the 'inheritance' was often lost through foreign invasions and deportations, defiled due to idolatry or immorality, and ravaged by war, pestilence or famine. By contrast, says Peter, this eternal inheritance is imperishable, undefiled and unfading because it is being kept ἐν οὐρανοῖς (lit. 'in heavens'), that is, God's dwelling place.

σωτηρία ('salvation', v. 5)

In discussing the use of the term σωτηρία ('salvation') in an early Christian text, a range of possible backgrounds must be taken into

---

[37] Achtemeier, *1 Peter*, 95. [38] Michaels, *1 Peter*, 20–1.
[39] Beare, *First Epistle of Peter*, 57–8 (emphasis mine).

account. The noun σωτηρία was widely used in the Greco-Roman world to denote deliverance or preservation (Herodotus 5.98; 7.172; Plato, *Leg.* 647b; *Prot.* 321b; 354b; Thucycides 6.83; Euripides, *Orest.* 1178; Aeschines, *Ctes.* 3.134; Aeschylus, *Pers.* 508; Xenophon, *Cyr.* 4.1.2), safety (Thucydides 2.60; Herodotus 4.98; Sophocles, *Aj.* 1080; Aeschylus, *Eum.* 909; Plato, *Resp.* 433c; 425e; *Prot.* 356d; Aristotle, *Pol.* 1321b21), a way or means of safety (Aeschylus, *Sept.* 209; *Pers.* 735; Euripides, *Orest.* 778; Aristophanes, *Eq.* 12), a safe return (Demosthenes, *Poly.* 50:16; 57.20; Aeschylus, *Pers.* 797; *Ag.* 343, 1238), security (Isocrates, *Paneg.* [*Or.*] 4.95; Plato, *Menex.* 240d; *Leg.* 921d), preservation (Aristotle, *Mete.* 355a20; *Metaph.* 396b34; 397a31; 397b6; cf. Plato, *Prot.* 321b), and bodily health or well-being (Hippocrates, *Epid.* 1.12; *Acut.* 11; *Morb.* 2.26; *Fract.* 31; *Prorrh.* 2.14; *Artic.* 65; cf. *BGU*, 2.380, 423, 632). This last sense of the term is well attested in the papyri, appearing mostly in personal letters inquiring after the health of the addressee (P.Oxy. 14.1766; 17.2151; 36.2788; 42.3607; 47.3364; 62.4340; 67.4627), or as a prayer wish (to the gods) for the good health (P.Oxy. 21.2609; 42.3065; 55.3810), safety (P.Oxy. 6.935, 939; 14.1666; cf. 12.1409), or preservation of the addressee (P.Oxy. 1.138; 6.933; 7.1070). Of interest is P.Oxy. 55.3781, a circular letter announcing the σωτηρία of all humankind at the accession of the Roman Emperor Hadrian (25 August AD 117):

> ἐπὶ σωτηρίᾳ τοῦ σύνπαντ[ος] ἀνθρώπων γενους ἴστε
> τὴν ἡγεμονίαν παρὰ τοῦ θεοῦ πατρὸς διαδεδέχθ[ον]
> Αὐτοκράτορα Καίσαρα Τραϊανὸν Ἄριστ[ον] Σεβαστὸν
> Γερμανικὸν Δακικὸν Παρθικόν.

In religious contexts σωτηρία carries all of the same connotations depicted so far, except that in these contexts it is the gods who provide σωτηρία from the various perils of life.[40] For the Gnostics it was the revelation of γνῶσις (the knowledge of god) that brought salvation. Such salvation was understood in terms of the release of the soul from the prison of the body at death.[41] In the mystery religions salvation or deliverance was achieved 'through the initiate's sharing in the experience of the dying and rising god through the actions of the mystery cult'.[42] Initiation into salvation was gained through participation in a sacramental ritual 'by which they [the initiates] were said to die and be born

---

[40] See, e.g., Plato, *Leg.* 903b; Marcus Aurelius, *Med.* 10.1.3.
[41] See R. Bultmann, 'γινώσκω', *TDNT*, 1: 692–6.
[42] J. Schneider, 'σώζω, κτλ.', *NIDNTT*, 3: 205.

again'.[43] The god is the θεὸς σεσῳσμένος as illustrated in the following verse quoted by Julius Firmicus Maternus in his *De errore profanarum religionum* (22.1):

θαρρεῖτε μύσται τοῦ θεοῦ σεσῳσμένου
ἔσται γὰρ ἡμῖν ἐκ πόνων σωτηρία.

According to Green, σωτηρία, for the mysteries, 'meant primarily deliverance from the tyranny of an oppressive and capricious Fate which could quench life at a moment's notice; it meant the promise of a better life beyond the grave'.[44]

In contrast to the broad usage of σωτηρία in the general Greco-Roman milieu, a slightly narrower field of use emerges in the Judaism reflected by the LXX. The noun σωτηρία appears 108 times in the Greek translation of the Hebrew Old Testament (and another 50 times in the Apocrypha),[45] most of the time rendering, where there is a Hebrew original, forms of the stem ישׁע (the basic Hebrew root denoting salvation or deliverance).[46] Chief among these occurrences is the fact that in the vast majority of these 108 verses God is the author of σωτηρία: τοῦ κυρίου ἡ σωτηρία (LXX Ps. 3:9[8]). In a few instances σωτηρία is ascribed to humans (Judg. 15:18; 1 Sam. 14:45; 19:5; 2 Sam. 23:12; 1 Chron. 11:14), but in each case it is made perfectly plain that God is the real Saviour of his people. Although God used human 'saviours', he was not obligated to do so. In order to highlight the fact that God is not dependent on human agents but is altogether sovereign in the work of salvation, he will, at times, dispense altogether with human intermediaries.

The actual content of σωτηρία varies according to context and circumstances; it may denote: deliverance from enemies (e.g., Exod. 14:13; 15:2; Judg. 15:18; 1 Sam. 2:1; 1 Chron. 16:35), victory over enemies (e.g. 1 Sam. 14:45; 2 Sam. 19:2[3]; 2 Kgs 13:17; 1 Chron. 11:14; Ps. 33:17 [32:17]; 1 Macc. 4:25) and vindication (Ps. 71:15 [70:15]; Isa. 45:17, 21), deliverance from death (Isa. 25:8–9; cf. Ps. 6:4–5[5–6]; note also Pss. 18[17], 68[67], 116[114]), deliverance from troubles and calamities (Ps. 69:13[68:14]; Job 30:15; Isa. 33:2; cf. Pss. 18[17]:19; 85[84]:7; 91[90]:16), deliverance from sin (Ps. 51:14[50:15]; cf. Ps. 79[78]:9), escape (2 Sam. 15:14; Job 11:20), help (Ps. 38:22[37:23]; cf. 2 Sam. 10:11; 1 Chron. 19:12), preservation (4 Macc. 15:2), and safety (Ps. 12:5 [11:6]; cf. Tob. 8:4, 5, 17; 2 Macc. 14:3; 4 Macc. 15:8). Furthermore, God's saving action in the past, reproduced repeatedly in the present,

[43] Green, *Meaning of Salvation*, 78.   [44] Ibid.
[45] Gramcord.   [46] See G. Fohrer, 'σῴζω', *TDNT*, 7: 973–8.

will have its climax in the future (cf. Ps. 98:7–9; Isa. 43:1–3; 60:16; 63:9; Jdt. 8:17; Wis. 16:6; 18:7; Sir. 16:1; 1 Macc. 5:62).

The principal example of God's saving intervention, his salvation, was Israel's deliverance at the Red Sea, when 'the Lord saved Israel that day from the Egyptians' (Exod. 14:30). What God's deliverance of his people at the Red Sea also illustrates is the fact that salvation is historical. Unlike the Gnosticism of later centuries, salvation was not based on a secret knowledge of God revealed privately to its initiates. Nor was it based on some mystical union with a god through sacramental ritual as in the mystery religions. Instead salvation was rooted in this historic event of the Exodus where God stepped in to save his people. Green suggests that '[i]t is no exaggeration to say that this rescue from Egypt … determined the whole future understanding of salvation by the people of God'.[47] In fact one of the most distinctive descriptions of God in the Old Testament is: 'I am the Lord your God, who brought you out of the land of Egypt, out of the house of slavery' (Exod. 20:2; Deut. 5:6).

In the New Testament the word σωτηρία appears forty-five times (forty-six if you count the shorter ending of Mark [16:8]). The word occurs outside 1 Peter (1:5, 9, 10; 2:2) in Luke–Acts (10×), the Johannine corpus (1×), the Pauline epistles (18× [Romans 5×, 2 Corinthians 4×, Ephesians 1×, Philippians 3×, 1 Thessalonians 2×, 2 Thessalonians 1×, 2 Timothy 2×]), Hebrews (7×), 2 Peter (1×) Jude (1×), and Revelation (3×).[48] In a number of these citations the more secular-historical sense of deliverance that we saw in the LXX is evident. The initial Old Testament colouring of σωτηρία in the New Testament can be seen in a number of Old Testament quotations and allusions (Lk. 1:69; Acts 7:25; 13:47; 2 Cor. 6:2; Heb. 5:9). Luke 1:69 and 71 refer to σωτηρία in the sense of 'messianic deliverance from the hands of national enemies'.[49] On three occasions it is used in the sense of deliverance from present distress or trouble (2 Cor. 1:6; Phil. 1:19; Heb. 1:7). In Acts 27:34 Paul encourages all those on the ship μεταλαβεῖν τροφῆς· τοῦτο γὰρ πρὸς τῆς ὑμετέρας σωτηρίας ὑπάρχει. 'Otherwise σωτηρία regularly refers to *salvation* in the supernatural-eschatological sense'[50] (see, e.g., Rom. 13:11; 1 Thess. 5:9; 2 Tim. 2:10; Heb. 5:9; 9:28).

In the same way, 1 Peter's use of the word σωτηρία (1 Pet. 1:5, 9, 10; 2:2) is consistently eschatological, and it is clear that Peter conceived of salvation as future here in v. 5. Three pieces of evidence substantiate this judgment. First, Peter describes the believer's salvation (σωτηρία) as

---

[47] Green, *Meaning of Salvation*, 16.   [48] Gramcord.
[49] K. H. Schelkle, 'σωτηρία', *EDNT*, 3: 327.   [50] Ibid.

something that is ἀποκαλυφθῆναι ἐν καιρῷ ἐσχάτῳ ('to be revealed in the last time', 1:5c). Here Peter is not thinking of the 'times' or the 'ages' in a generalised sense (that seems to be more the sense of v. 20 where Peter uses the genitive plural χρόνων, 'times'). Instead, Peter's use of the singular καιρῷ ('time') modified by the adjective ἐσχάτῳ ('last') points to that final point in time when the salvation of believers will take place. This seems to be in keeping with the temporal use of the dative to denote a point in time (with the ἐν being added for clarification).[51] In this case, the adjective ἐσχάτῳ leaves us in no doubt as to what point in time: the 'last' or end point. Moreover, this salvation is described by Peter as now being 'ready' (ἑτοίμην) but still awaiting unveiling (ἀποκαλυφθῆναι) on the last day (ἐν καιρῷ ἐσχάτῳ). The inclusion of the adjective ἑτοίμην ('ready') indicates the writer's sense of imminence with regard to this final unveiling (cf. 4:7, 17). What is decisive here though is that this salvation, while ready, will not be unveiled until the last day (καιρῷ ἐσχάτῳ).

Second, it is clear from the context (see the next point) that the 'salvation' (σωτηρία) mentioned here is another way of describing the 'inheritance' (κληρονομία; see argument [3] below) mentioned in the previous verse (v. 4), which we have already noted is certainly future. Third, salvation is presented here as the divinely apponted goal (telic εἰς) for which believers are presently being protected. Verses 4 and 5 actually form a minor chiasm in which both the verbs of protection and the nouns 'inheritance' and 'salvation' complement each other:

A   εἰς κληρονομίαν
  B   τετηρημένην ... εἰς ὑμᾶς
  B′   τοὺς ... φρουρουμένους
A′   εἰς σωτηρίαν

The divine (θεοῦ) preservation (φρουρουμένους) of Christians (ὑμᾶς ... τούς) described here is parallel to the description of the divine (ἐν οὐρανοῖς) preservation (τετηρημένην) of their inheritance, and adds further certainty to the promise of the new inheritance into which they have been born. As Schelkle points out, '[d]er Gott, der in Himmel das Erbe bewahrt [τετηρημένην], bewahrt [φρουρουμένοῦ] auf Erden die Söhne des Erbes'.[52] Peter wants to assure his readers that they will certainly receive this inheritance, that future salvation will be theirs. But how does God actually protect believers? We know from the broader context that

---

[51] BDF, §200.   [52] Schelkle, *Petrusbriefe*, 32.

he does not keep them from persecution or suffering.[53] Instead we are told that God protects them so that they will receive their inheritance, eschatological salvation.

This raises the question of the relationship of two prepositional phrases ἐν δυνάμει θεοῦ ('by the power of God') and διὰ πίστεως ('through faith'). Both prepositions (ἐν and διά) are dependent on the articular participle τοὺς ... φρουρουμένους, and both depict instrumentality ('by, through, by means of'). However, the word order demonstrates the primacy of the power of God, both by the placement of the words ἐν δυνάμει θεοῦ in the emphatic position at the beginning of the sentence and by their insertion between the article and participle on which they depend (τοὺς **ἐν δυνάμει θεοῦ** φρουρουμένους).[54] The participle φρουρουμένους ('being guarded') is passive indicating that the believer is being guarded by God's power, rather than the believers' use of that power. Robertson suggests that the διά phrase depicts *intermediate* agency ('faith'), while the ἐν phrase portrays *immediate* agency ('the power of God').[55] The prepositional phrase διὰ πίστεως ('through faith') indicates 'the instrument whereby the divine protection becomes a reality'.[56] Christian faith is the visible evidence of the unseen power of God which enables, sustains and preserves that trust. God's power protects believers because his power is the means (ἐν) by which their faith is sustained. While God will not necessarily protect believers from persecution or suffering, he does promise to sustain their faith until they come into their inheritance. In the end it is God's power that enables the believer to remain faithful until the end.

Future salvation and present suffering (vv. 6–9)

These four verses (vv. 6–9) constitute the second of three subunits (vv. 3–5, 6–9, 10–12) in which God is praised for his saving work. The Greek prepositional phrase ἐν ᾧ (lit., 'in this') links this subunit with what has gone before. More than that, it carries the theme of salvation over into the present unit making it the basis for the rejoicing of vv. 6 and 8. So while there appears to be a shift in focus from the future salvation of vv. 3–5 to the problem of present suffering in vv. 6–9, it

---

[53] See the Introduction.

[54] Wendland, '"Stand Fast in the True Grace of God!"', 42–5, refers to this practice of Peter's as 'syntactic' or 'lexical disjunction' (see p. 42 for his definition; he includes 1 Pet. 1:5 among his examples which also include 1:10, 11, 19; 2:12; 3:3, 16; 4:1, 12; 5:1, and I would add 1:13, 14, 15, 18; 2:5, 15, 18; 3:1, 2, 4, 7, 17, 19; 4:2, 8; 5:2).

[55] Robertson, *Word Pictures*, 82.   [56] Achtemeier, *1 Peter*, 97.

is actually the theme of salvation that continues to be the focus. The discussion on suffering, faith and love, while important, is more of a digression.

Structure

The key to the structure of vv. 6–9 is found in the two occurrences of the verb ἀγαλλιᾶσθε (vv. 6, 8), which, in both of its occurrences, is related to the theme of salvation (vv. 3–5, 9). The second ἀγαλλιᾶσθε (v. 8b) is a resumption of the first (v. 6a) with the discussion between them (vv. 6b-8a) being more of a digression (or *concession* ['although...']). The main thought of this passage can be expressed in one sentence: (v. 6a) ἐν ᾧ ἀγαλλιᾶσθε ... (v. 8b) [ἀγαλλιᾶσθε resuming the theme of rejoicing in salvation, v. 6a] χαρᾷ ἀνεκλαλήτῳ καὶ δεδοξασμένῃ [v. 9] κομιζόμενοι τὸ τέλος τῆς πίστεως [ὑμῶν] σωτηρίαν ψυχῶν. The rejoicing of which Peter speaks seems to form something of an *inclusio* (vv. 6a and 8b-9) bracketing his discussion on faith (vv. 6b-7b and vv. 8a-b), which in turn brackets mention of the eschatological reward for faith (v. 7c). The basic structure of vv. 6–9 can be charted like this:

A Rejoicing in salvation (v. 6a)
  B Faith despite trials (vv. 6b-7b)
    C The eschatological reward for faith (v. 7c)
  B′ Faith despite not seeing (v. 8a-b)
A′ Rejoicing in salvation (vv. 8b-9)

Looking at the above structure we note: (1) the theme of eschatological salvation brackets the whole discussion (A, A′) and is found at the heart of it (C), demonstrating the importance of salvation in this passage; (2) B and B′ find their fulfilment in C: the faith that is tried and proved genuine (vv. 6b-7b [B]) will result in (εἰς) eschatological reward (ἔπαινον καὶ δόξαν καὶ τιμήν [C]); the faith that does not see now (v 8a-b [B′]) will one day see because its object (v. 7d, Ἰησοῦ Χριστοῦ) will one day be revealed (v 7d, ἀποκαλύψει [C]); (3) the theme of joy in salvation is the key to the whole discussion. The thought here is: A despite B; A′ despite B′ (joy [A] [v 6a] is possible despite trials [B] [vv. 6b-7b]; joy [A′] [v. 8bc] is possible despite not seeing [B′] [v. 8a-b]). What is the basis for such a joy? The answer is salvation (v. 6a, ἐν ᾧ [= vv. 3–5]; v. 9b, σωτηρίαν ψυχῶν) realised now in Christ (v. 8b, εἰς ὃν) but awaiting consummation at his revelation (v. 7d, ἐν ἀποκαλύψει Ἰησοῦ Χριστοῦ). Elliott writes: 'The exultation or exuberant demonstration of gladness spoken of in verse 6 is the joyous response to the threefold benefactions enumerated in vv. 3–5. In v. 8, the future exaltation (salvation) is the reason for present exultation.'[57]

Digression

The question that concerns us now is this: If the main thought of the passage is salvation, then what is the purpose of the digression on the trying of faith through suffering (especially vv. 6b–7b, but also 8ab)? Perhaps a clue to this answer can be found in 1 Pet. 4:12, which counsels believers to 'not be surprised at the fiery trial coming upon you to test you, as though something strange were happening to you'. Here Peter turns to address the reaction of surprise that believers might be feeling in the face of persistent and intense suffering. Before their conversion, these Gentile believers probably did not experience any form of religious persecution or marginalisation in their tolerant Hellenistic context. But now, having accepted the message of the gospel, they were experiencing social persecution, ostracism, marginalisation, and hostility. They may have regarded these experiences as quite 'strange' (ξένος) or foreign to what they might have expected as the blessing of salvation. They may even have started wondering if something had not gone very wrong indeed. As a result, their experience of suffering may have begun to undermine, to a degree, their experience of salvation. Far from being a sign of God's presence among them, they may have begun to see their suffering as a sign of God's absence. It is possible that such a questioning may lie behind Peter's comments in 1:8: ὃν **οὐκ ἰδόντες** ἀγαπᾶτε, εἰς ὃν ἄρτι **μὴ ὁρῶντες** πιστεύοντες δὲ ἀγαλλιᾶσθε. And so in this present section (1:6–9) Peter explains to his readers that their experience of suffering should not be considered as something 'strange', in fact quite the opposite: it is a badge of their authentic membership in the community of the saved. Peter will explain in this section that suffering is a crucial component in the process of salvation: it authenticates faith (this is the sense of δοκίμιον in v. 7a), which, when proved genuine (v. 7a-b), results in eschatological salvation (vv. 7c and 9).

Content

ἐν ᾧ ἀγαλλιᾶσθε ... ἀγαλλιᾶσθε *(vv. 6–8)*

At the beginning of this new subunit an interest in salvation is signalled by the prepositional phrase ἐν ᾧ, which has its antecedent in the foregoing

---

[57] Elliott, *1 Peter*, 339.

discussion on salvation in vv. 3–5. What, specifically, is the antecedent to which the relative pronoun ᾧ at the beginning of v. 6 refers? Three main interpretations have been put forward: (1) ᾧ is masculine and refers back to either θεός or Ἰησοῦ Χριστοῦ in v. 3; (2) ᾧ is masculine and refers back to καιρῷ [ἐσχάτῳ] in v. 5; (3) ᾧ is neuter and refers back to the entire thought expressed in vv. 3–5. The first view is attractive in that it not only ties vv. 6–9 to the main clause in v. 3, but also finds a parallel in v. 8: εἰς ὃν [Ἰησοῦ Χριστοῦ] … ἀγαλλιᾶσθε ('in whom [= Jesus Christ] … you rejoice'). This view is unlikely, though, because there are too many intervening words between the relative pronoun ᾧ and θεός or Ἰησοῦ Χριστοῦ. This suggests that perhaps view (2) may be better because καιρῷ not only immediately precedes the relative pronoun, but also agrees with it grammatically (in number and possibly gender). The problem is that such an interpretation requires that ἀγαλλιᾶσθε be understood as present in form but future in meaning (i.e., 'at that time [ἐν καιρῷ ἐσχάτῳ] you *will* rejoice'). While that is possible,[58] it is however preferable, with Achtemeier, 'to find a meaning that could allow the present tense its normal function'.[59] The third view, which sees the entire content of vv. 3–5 as the antecedent of the ἐν ᾧ is probably the best. The prepositional phrase ἐν ᾧ is used in four other places in 1 Peter (2:12; 3:16; 3:19; 4:4), and each time it bears an adverbial/conjunctive force 'connect[ing] with the situation described in what precedes'.[60] In 2:12 and 3:16 it is clearly temporal. In 4:4, ἐν ᾧ functions adverbially referring to the circumstances described by the foregoing verses (vv. 2–3), in this case to the fact that Peter's readers are no longer behaving like their Gentile neighbours. Here ἐν ᾧ expresses a causal connection between the believers' new behaviour and the abuse they receive from their unbelieving contemporaries. In a similar way the ἐν ᾧ of 1:6 should also be construed as causal ('for that reason', 'because of that').[61] As such, 'it reaches back to the entire content of vv. 3–5, focusing on the eschatological hope of believers. They rejoice now *because* of the inheritance that most certainly awaits them'.[62]

The verb ἀγαλλιᾶσθε (v. 6a; present middle indicative of ἀγαλλιάω, 'to be exceedingly joyful, exult, be glad, overjoyed'),[63] then, is the 'joyous response to the threefold benefactions enumerated in vv. 3–5'.[64]

---

[58] On the futuristic present see, e.g., BDF, §323; Wallace, *Greek Grammar*, 535–7.
[59] Achtemeier, *1 Peter*, 100.   [60] BDAG, 727.
[61] Brox, *Petrusbrief*, 63; Fink, 'Use and Significance of *en hōi* in 1 Peter', 35.
[62] Schreiner, *1 Peter*, 67 (emphasis mine).   [63] BDAG, 4.
[64] Elliott, *1 Peter*, 339.

The verb ἀγαλλιάω (normally as the middle ἀγαλλιάομαι) and the corresponding noun ἀγαλλίασις ('extreme gladness', 'exultation') occur only in the LXX, New Testament, and those writers dependent on them.[65] These words refer to both the public expression of cultic joy as well as individual rejoicing over God's acts of salvation.[66] While the rejoicing in view here is primarily a rejoicing over God's past acts of salvation, ἀγαλλιάομαι was also used as an eschatological term. In the exilic and post-exilic prophets 'Israel's rejoicing in his God, even in wretched situations, broadened out to include anticipatory gratitude for final salvation and messianic joy'.[67] So, for example, in Isa. 61:10 we read, καὶ εὐφροσύνη εὐφρανθήσονται ἐπὶ κύριον ἀγαλλιάσθω ἡ ψυχή μου ἐπὶ τῷ κυρίῳ ἐνέδυσεν γάρ με ἱμάτιον σωτηρίου καὶ χιτῶνα εὐφροσύνης.

In the New Testament, ἀγαλλιάομαι (11×; 3× in 1 Peter) is used in a similar way to the LXX: it designates the 'joy and exultation over the salvation which God has given and promised through Jesus'.[68] Luke 1:14 speaks of the joy (ἀγαλλίασις) that attended the birth of John the Baptist (cf. 5:35), who himself rejoiced (ἐσκίρτησεν ἐν ἀγαλλιάσει) in his mother's womb when she met the mother of the Messiah (Lk. 1:44), who in turn rejoiced in the work of salvation that had begun in her: Μεγαλύνει ἡ ψυχή μου τὸν κύριον, καὶ **ἠγαλλίασεν** τὸ πνεῦμά μου **ἐπὶ τῷ θεῷ τῷ σωτῆρί μου** (Lk. 1:46–7). In Lk. 10:21 Jesus himself ἠγαλλιάσατο [ἐν] τῷ πνεύματι τῷ ἁγίῳ because of the revelation of God's saving purposes. In Mt. 5:12, rejoicing (χαίρετε καὶ ἀγαλλιᾶσθε) is possible despite persecution because (ὅτι) of the anticipation (by faith) of eschatological reward (ὁ μισθὸς ὑμῶν πολὺς ἐν τοῖς οὐρανοῖς [an idea similar to 1 Pet. 1:6]). In Acts 16:34, it is the present experience of this salvation that is attended with rejoicing: ἠγαλλιάσατο πεπιστευκὼς τῷ θεῷ ('he rejoiced greatly having believed in God'). Other than our present passage (1 Pet. 1:6–9) it is the 'eschatological act of divine salvation which is supremely the theme of rejoicing' (e.g., 1 Pet. 4:13; Jude 24; Rev. 19:7).[69]

The question that now concerns us is: When does the rejoicing of 1 Pet. 1:6 take place? Is it present rejoicing in anticipation of a future salvation, or is it future rejoicing at the consummation of salvation? Some scholars have argued that while ἀγαλλιᾶσθε is present in form, it is future in

---

[65] R. Bultmann, 'ἀγαλλιάομαι, ἀγαλλίασις', *TDNT*, 1: 19.

[66] This is especially prominent in the Psalms, e.g., LXX Pss. 9:15 [9:14]; 12:6 [13:5]; Ps. 20:2 [21:1]; 51:14 [50:14].

[67] E. Beyreuther, 'ἀγαλλιάομαι', *NIDNTT*, 2: 353.

[68] A. Weiser, 'ἀγαλλιάω, ἀγαλλίασις', *EDNT*, 1: 8.

[69] R. Bultmann, 'ἀγαλλιάομαι, ἀγαλλίαισς', *TDNT*, 1: 20.

meaning, and so the rejoicing spoken of occurs in the future.[70] Goppelt is representative of this view: 'It [ἀγαλλιᾶσθε] promises, rather, as a futuristic present tense a coming joy at the consummation.'[71] Yet such an interpretation does not suit the immediate context. Instead, it is more natural to understand ἀγαλλιᾶσθε as being present both in form *and* meaning. Three arguments substantiate this judgment. First, this seems to be the natural way to understand the same verb only two verses later (v. 8). There ἀγαλλιᾶσθε stands in parallel to ἀγαπᾶτε which is clearly a present indicative and not a future (in form or meaning). It would be quite unnatural to translate ἀγαπᾶτε … ἀγαλλιᾶσθε as, '[whom = ὅν] you love … [in whom = εἰς ὅν] you *will* rejoice'. It is better, then, to translate all three indicatives as present: 'you rejoice … you love … you rejoice' (rendering ἀγαλλιᾶσθε … ἀγαπᾶτε … ἀγαλλιᾶσθε [vv. 6a, 8a,b]). Second, this view is also better able to account for the present tense circumstantial participles in v. 8 (i.e., ὁρῶντες and πιστεύοντες). Third, by analogy, the theme of (present) rejoicing in suffering surfaces again in 4:13: ἀλλὰ καθὸ κοινωνεῖτε τοῖς τοῦ Χριστοῦ παθήμασιν **χαίρετε … ἀγαλλιώμενοι** ('but to the degree that you share in the sufferings of Christ, **rejoice with great joy**').

Hence it is not necessary to argue with Martin 'that action of the participle [λυπηθέντες] is [temporally] antecedent to the action of the main verb [ἀγαλλιᾶσθε]'.[72] Instead, the participle and verb should be construed as contemporaneous.[73] The relationship indicated by the use of the aorist participle λυπηθέντες (lit. 'having been afflicted') is that of concession: 'in this you rejoice, ***though*** now for a little while, if necessary, you are afflicted by various trials'.[74] The concessive participle λυπηθέντες implies that the rejoicing is in fact a present reality *in spite of* the suffering. Hence, 'the aorist participle is simultaneous in time with the "rejoicing" earlier in this verse'.[75] Neither should we identify the λυπηθέντες as causal (as Selwyn mistakenly does).[76] This would imply that suffering is intrinsically joyful, not, as λυπηθέντες suggests, rather painful. Instead, as de Villiers points out, 'the main theme in the preceding verses centres round the blessings God has given the Christians and the expectation for the future, which gives them reason for rejoicing despite all their afflictions. It is not the suffering that gives them ground to

---

[70] Michaels, *1 Peter*, 27; Goppelt, *1 Peter*, 88–9; Martin, 'Present Indicative', 310–12.
[71] Goppelt, *1 Peter*, 88–9.   [72] Martin, 'Present Indicative', 309.
[73] Schreiner, *1 Peter*, 66, n. 28.   [74] See Wallace, *Greek Grammar*, 634.
[75] Abernathy, *Exegetical Summary*, 20.
[76] See Selwyn, *First Epistle of St. Peter*, 127.

rejoice.'[77] The basis for rejoicing in suffering, then, is the salvation spoken of in the preceding verses (vv. 3–5): 'Hier in v 6 wird aber noch nicht mehr also ein unvermitteltes "Trotzdem" der Freude formuliert: Trotz der Trauer ist jetzt schon Grund zur Freude (identisch mit dem Grund zum Dank an Gott vv 3–5).'[78] Future salvation (realised now in part), then, is the cause for present rejoicing in spite of present suffering.

That such a contrast is intended by Peter is suggested by the presence of the temporal adverb ἄρτι ('now, at the present time') in combination with the neuter ὀλίγον (used adverbially with the sense of 'for a little while', 'a short while'). The use of ἄρτι suggests that the sufferings denoted by the aorist participle λυπηθέντες are a present reality for Peter's readers and not just a hypothetical possibility.[79] The adverb ὀλίγον refers to the duration of time[80] and not, as Hort suggests, to the 'depreciation of the intrinsic importance of the sufferings endured'.[81] Its combination with ἄρτι suggests, in the context of this letter, a contrast between present suffering and future salvation. The placement of ἄρτι next to ὀλίγον suggests that Peter is making a deliberate contrast between the relative shortness of present suffering in comparison to the σωτηρίαν ἑτοίμην ἀποκαλυφθῆναι ἐν καιρῷ ἐσχάτῳ (v. 5). The note of 'eschatological urgency'[82] is sounded in these two phrases: the idea of a salvation '**ready** to be revealed' (ἑτοίμην ἀποκαλυφθῆναι) is reinforced by the reminder that the sufferings of the present (ἄρτι) are only 'for a little while' (ὀλίγον). The joy that is experienced even now, despite suffering, is an 'anticipatory joy': it rejoices in anticipation of the σωτηρίαν ἑτοίμην ἀποκαλυφθῆναι (v. 5).

The ἵνα plus the subjunctive εὑρεθῇ introduces the divine purpose and final outcome (introduced by εἰς) of the experience of suffering: ἵνα τὸ δοκίμιον ὑμῶν τῆς πίστεως ... εὑρεθῇ εἰς ἔπαινον καὶ δόξαν καὶ τιμὴν ἐν ἀποκαλύψει Ἰησοῦ Χριστοῦ. The purpose (ἵνα) of the various trials (ποικίλοις πειρασμοῖς, v. 6b), then, is 'à tester notre foi, à en vérifier l'authenticité'.[83] The author plays off the words δοκίμιον, denoting the tested genuineness of faith, and δοκιμαζομένου (present passive participle) which refers to the testing of gold διὰ πυρός. The reference to the testing of gold by fire is a stock comparison in Jewish (e.g., Zech. 13:9; Wis. 3:4–6; cf. Sir. 2:1–9) and Greco-Roman literature (e.g., Seneca, *Prov.* 5.10), though it is more likely the former that Peter is drawing on.

[77] De Villiers, 'Joy in Suffering', 72.   [78] Brox, *Petrusbrief*, 63.
[79] As in Hort, *First Epistle of Saint Peter*, 60.   [80] BDAG, 703.
[81] Hort, *First Epistle of Saint Peter*, 41.   [82] Kelly, *The Epistles of Peter*, 54.
[83] Spicq, *Les Épîtres de Saint Pierre*, 49.

The contrast that Peter is making in 1 Pet. 6–7 is between authentic faith and gold. The phrase πολυτιμότερον χρυσίου (v. 7b) stands in apposition to τὸ δοκίμιον ὑμῶν τῆς πίστεως (v. 7a). Faith that is tested 'genuine' (δοκίμιον) is more valuable than gold because the latter is temporary and will one day perish (χρυσίου τοῦ ἀπολλυμένου) while the former has eternal value (as v. 7c indicates). This comparison between gold which is perishable and genuine faith implies an argument from the lesser to the greater: if gold, which is perishable and hence of much less value, is tested, how much more will faith, which is imperishable and of much greater value, be tested. As Achtemeier notes: 'The emphasis here is not on faith itself so much as on the nature of the faith that results from such trials. It is that tested and proved character of faith ... which brings approval from God at the last judgment.'[84] Divine approval at the judgment, then, is the goal toward which genuine faith looks (this is made explicit in v. 9). Present testing by trials, then, points toward (and are preliminary to) eschatological assessment at the judgment (v. 7c).

The verb εὑρεθῇ (aorist passive subjunctive of εὑρίσκω, 'find') along with the prepositional phrase εἰς ἔπαινον καὶ δόξαν καὶ τιμὴν ἐν ἀποκαλύψει Ἰησοῦ Χριστοῦ completes the thought begun in v. 6b. The passive εὑρεθῇ (together with the ἀναγεννήσας ἡμᾶς of v. 3, the three passives [τετηρημένην, φρουρουμένου, ἀποκαλυφθῆναι] in vv. 4–5, and the εἰ δέον of v. 6) along with the result clause (εἰς) of which it is a part points to the sovereign action of God. εὑρεθῇ (like τετηρημένην and φρουρουμένου) is a divine passive indicating God as the subject. Here it is used in the sense of 'to discover through examination' and refers to divine assessment of believers at the final judgment.[85] The basic function of the ἵνα clause (ἵνα ... εὑρεθῇ), then, is 'to extol the value, in God's sight, of this "genuine faith" and to affirm its ultimate (i.e., eschatological) significance'.[86]

That εὑρεθῇ refers, in this context, to eschatological assessment at the final judgment is shown by the two prepositional phrases of which it is a part: εἰς ἔπαινον καὶ δόξαν καὶ τιμήν (lit., 'for praise and glory and honour') and ἐν ἀποκαλύψει Ἰησοῦ Χριστοῦ ('at the revelation of Jesus Christ'). ἔπαινον, δόξαν and τιμὴν, attributes that are normally ascribed to God (4:11; 5:11; cf. 2:12) and Jesus Christ (1:11, 21; 2:4, 6; 5:1) in 1 Peter (and the NT), are bestowed upon believers because of the genuineness of their faith. This eschatological reward is the ultimate confirmation of the genuineness of their faith. The idea of honour receives

---

[84] Achtemeier, *1 Peter*, 102.   [85] BDAG, 412.   [86] Michaels, *1 Peter*, 30.

some illumination from 2:6 where 'honour' (ἔντιμον) is contrasted with 'shame' (καταισχυνθῇ), and the notion of ἔπαινον ('praise') finds its contrast in the ἐκδίκησιν ('punishment') of v. 14. These contrasts support the 'insight that the basic element in all three is vindication "at the time when Jesus Christ is revealed"'.[87] The prepositional phrase ἐν ἀποκαλύψει Ἰησοῦ Χριστοῦ refers to the final revelation of Jesus Christ at the second coming (cf. 1:13; 4:13). This phrase brings us back to a similar prepositional phrase at the end of v. 5 (εἰς σωτηρίαν ἑτοίμην ἀποκαλυφθῆναι ἐν καιρῷ ἐσχάτῳ). As Bigg notes, '[i]n all these passages it denotes the revelation of Christ in his majesty as Judge and Rewarder'.[88] As Judge, he will vindicate true faith, and as Rewarder he will bestow upon it all the blessings (e.g., ἔπαινον καὶ δόξαν καὶ τιμήν) of the σωτηρία he brings. It is this very thought that enables the believer to rejoice despite their trials.

The fact that Jesus Christ will one day be revealed implies that he is now hidden. The relative clause that follows makes this explicit with the ὅν (v. 8a) referring back to Ἰησοῦ Χριστοῦ in the previous verse (v. 7c) and to the words οὐκ ἰδόντες (v. 8a) indicating that Jesus Christ is currently invisible to his people. Here we are confronted with another paradoxical aspect of the Christian life: ὅν οὐκ ἰδόντες ἀγαπᾶτε, εἰς ὅν ἄρτι μὴ ὁρῶντες πιστεύοντες δὲ ἀγαλλιᾶσθε. These two relative clauses are virtually parallel in form:

8a.	ὅν		οὐκ	ἰδόντες		ἀγαπᾶτε
8b. εἰς	ὅν ἄρτι	μὴ		ὁρῶντες	πιστεύοντες δὲ	ἀγαλλιᾶσθε

The ἰδόντες in v. 8a is concessive implying that love (ἀγαπᾶτε) for Christ is a present reality (hence the present active indicative) despite not being able to see him (οὐκ ἰδόντες).[89] Similarly, the adverbial participle ὁρῶντες (v. 8) is also concessive implying that rejoicing (ἀγαλλιᾶσθε) is a present reality (present middle indicative) despite not seeing but believing all the same (μὴ ὁρῶντες πιστεύοντες δέ). As Achtemeier observes, 'that contrast, directly related to a central problem for the readers, namely, the discrepancy between their present experience of suffering and their anticipated future glory, takes the form here of the tension between faith and sight'.[90] The words οὐκ ἰδόντες (v. 8a) indicate, as Goppelt quite rightly points out, 'that the renewal of the individual (2 Cor. 4:18; 5:7) and of creation (Rom. 8:24f.; Heb. 11:3, 27) have not yet taken shape concretely. According to 1 Jn 3:2, one's own salvation

[87] Ibid., 32.   [88] Bigg, *Epistles of St. Peter*, 105.
[89] Wallace, *Greek Grammar*, 634.   [90] Achtemeier, *1 Peter*, 102.

becomes visible together with Christ's becoming visible.'[91] Once again, in the context of this letter, this contrast has an eschatological nuance about it. This is reinforced by the addition of the ἄρτι in the parallel phrase of v 8b:

8a.   ὃν   οὐκ ἰδόντες   ἀγαπᾶτε
8b. εἰς ὃν **ἄρτι** μὴ ὁρῶντες πιστεύοντες δὲ ἀγαλλιᾶσθε

These verses highlight the eschatological tension that exists between the present (ἄρτι) but incomplete experience (characterised by οὐκ ἰδόντες, and μὴ ὁρῶντες) of their salvation (characterised by the words ἀγαπᾶτε, πιστεύοντες and ἀγαλλιᾶσθε) and the future consummation of that salvation (the σωτηρίαν ψυχῶν [v. 9] which will take place at the ἀποκαλύψει Ἰησοῦ Χριστοῦ [v. 7c]). The mention of πιστεύοντες ('believing') here in v. 8b provides a link back to the πίστις of vv. 5 and 7 (where 'faith' is both guarded [v. 5] and tested [v. 7]) as well as a link forward to the mentioned of faith's (πίστις) vindication (σωτηρίαν) in v. 9. In 1 Peter, the verb πιστεύω ('believe', 'trust') and the noun πίστις ('faithfulness, fidelity, commitment'; 'trust, confidence, faith')[92] denote 'fidelity toward and confidence and trust in God (1:5, 7, 21; 5:9) and Jesus Christ (1:8; 2:6, 7)'.[93] It is possible, with Michaels, to construe the preposition εἰς with πιστεύοντες so as to read, 'in [whom] you believe'.[94] The difficulty with this interpretation is that it, (1) leaves no connection between ἀγαλλιᾶσθε and the rest of the clause and (2) it makes the participle πιστεύοντες the main verb in the clause rather than the finite verb ἀγαλλιᾶσθε (as Michaels does).[95] However, ἀγαλλιᾶσθε rather than πιστεύοντες should be seen as the main verb of the clause.[96] While it is true that the words εἰς ὃν are sometimes found (3×) with πιστεύω in the New Testament (e.g., Jn 6:29; Acts 14:23; Rom. 10:14), it is better in this case to construe it with ἀγαλλιᾶσθε. This offers both a better explanation of the relationship between the main verb (ἀγαλλιᾶσθε) and the rest of the clause, and continues the parallel with v. 8b:

7c.   Ἰησοῦ Χριστοῦ
8a.   ὃν   ἀγαπᾶτε
8b.   εἰς ὃν   ἀγαλλιᾶσθε

The parallel intended by the author appears to be between the two finite verbs ἀγαπᾶτε ('[whom] you love') and ἀγαλλιᾶσθε ('[in whom] you

[91] Goppelt, *1 Peter*, 93.   [92] BDAG, 818.   [93] Elliott, *1 Peter*, 343.
[94] Michaels, *1 Peter*, 33.   [95] Ibid.
[96] See Hamblin, 'Greek Participle', 84; Elliott, *1 Peter*, 343.

rejoice'). If this is the case, then, what do we make of the words μὴ ὁρῶντες πιστεύοντες δέ? The adverbial participle πιστεύοντες is most probably causal (rather than adversative), indicating that the believing is the cause of the rejoicing. Hence the δέ should probably be interpreted as contrasting the two participles ([μὴ] ὁρῶντες and πιστεύοντες) rather than linking them (in the sense of 'though you do not see him you believe [in him] *and* you rejoice'). If this is the case, the clause should be translated (lit.): 'in whom, although not seeing but believing, you rejoice'. The joy (χαρᾷ) that characterises their rejoicing is then described as ἀνεκλαλήτῳ καὶ δεδοξασμένῃ ('inexpressible and glorious'). The word δεδοξασμένῃ ('glorious') links back to δόξαν ('glory') in v. 7 hinting at its eschatological dimension. Peter is saying that even now believers experience 'une anticipation de la gloire à venir' and 'goûter par avance le joie du salut'.[97] What Peter is talking about then is a present rejoicing 'lit up by the light of eternity'[98] which 'allows the Christian to be sure of that future salvation with its attendant glory despite present circumstances that militate against such confidence'.[99] For Peter, then, assurance of salvation can be found both in the testing of faith as well as in the rejoicing that accompanies it (both, according to Peter, are marks of a genuine saving faith).

σωτηρίαν ψυχῶν (v. 9)

This rejoicing (ἀγαλλιᾶσθε) in the present experience of salvation in Christ (εἰς ὃν ... πιστεύοντες ... ἀγαλλιᾶσθε) is also prompted by the assurance of salvation in the future (κομιζόμενοι τὸ τέλος τῆς πίστεως [ὑμῶν] σωτηρίαν ψυχῶν, v. 9, which is another way of describing the experience of v. 7c, ἔπαινον καὶ δόξαν καὶ τιμὴν ἐν ἀποκαλύψει Ἰησοῦ Χριστοῦ). Because the 'present participle is normally contemporaneous in time to the action of the main verb',[100] which, in this case, is also present (ἀγαλλιᾶσθε), κομιζόμενοι here is best understood as describing a present activity. The use of the present participle (κομιζόμενοι) should not be taken to mean that the salvation (σωτηρίαν) spoken of here is itself present. The use of the verb κομιζόμενοι (present middle participle of κομίζω, 'receive', 'obtain') in conjunction with its object τέλος ('outcome, end, result') suggests that future salvation is in view. As a middle, κομιζόμενοι means 'to receive as a type of compensation',[101]

---

[97] Bénétreau, *Première épître de Pierre*, 24.
[98] Scharlemann, 'An Apostolic Descent', 14.
[99] Achtemeier, *1 Peter*, 104.   [100] Wallace, *Greek Grammar*, 625.
[101] L&N, 57.126.

'obtain as a reward'.[102] In the New Testament, κομιζόμενοι is almost always used with the sense of 'eschatological recompense'.[103] The verb is used again in 1 Pet. 5:4 with the same eschatological nuance: καὶ φανερωθέντος τοῦ ἀρχιποίμενος **κομιεῖσθε** τὸν ἀμαράντινον τῆς δόξης στέφανον. The use in 1:9 of the present participle κομιζόμενοι ('receiving') in conjunction with τέλος ('end') and σωτηρίαν (denoting eschatological salvation) may suggest 'that we have here the "now" and "not yet" tension so common in the New Testament. The idea here is that Christians *now* obtain *by faith* (τῆς πίστεως [ὑμῶν]) what they will one day fully enter into. Believers *now* enjoy salvation and yet will experience it fully at the revelation of Jesus Christ.'[104]

As with the πιστεύοντες of the previous verse (v. 8b), κομιζόμενοι is causal: the cause of the rejoicing is 'obtaining the goal of your faith, your salvation'. We have already noted that σωτηρία is an eschatological term and hence has a future orientation. The future orientation of this σωτηρία is brought out further by the Greek word τέλος. The word τέλος, functioning as the object of κομιζόμενοι, is used with the sense of 'end', 'goal', or 'outcome'. The noun τέλος appears four times in 1 Peter (with the adverb τελείως ['fully, completely, perfectly'][105] appearing once). In 3:8 τὸ τέλος ('finally') is used adverbially to conclude the final paragraph of the section to which it belongs (2:13–3:12). The rest of its occurrences have an eschatological flavour. In 4:7 (which follows the reference to eschatological judgment in vv. 5–6), its use in conjunction with the verb ἐγγίζω ('draw near, come near, approach')[106] expresses the basic New Testament conviction that the end of the age is viewed as being at hand. The phrase τί τὸ τέλος ('what [will be] the end') in 4:17 denotes the 'end result' or 'outcome' (τέλος) of those who reject the gospel in disobedience (= eschatological punishment). In a similar way, the words τὸ τέλος in 1:9 refer to the eschatological 'outcome', 'intended end' or 'goal' of the believer's faith (τῆς πίστεως [ὑμῶν]).

The intended end or outcome of faith is then identified by the explanatory apposition σωτηρίαν ψυχῶν (lit. 'salvation of souls') making clear the eschatological nature of that goal. What does Peter mean when he speaks of the salvation ψυχῶν ('of souls')? The word ψυχή occurs six times in the comparatively small space of this letter (1:9; 1:22; 2:11, 25; 3:20; 4:19). In each case it refers to the entire person and not a higher or spiritual part of a person in distinction from the body.[107] Best suggests

[102] Elliott, *1 Peter*, 344.   [103] Ibid., 334.   [104] Schreiner, *1 Peter*, 70.
[105] BDAG, 996–7.   [106] BDAG, 270.
[107] Dautzenberg, 'Σωτηρία ψυχῶν', 272–5.

that 'it is almost the equivalent of the personal pronoun (it can be so replaced at 1:9, 22; 2:25; 4:19); it is the man himself ... the whole man, who is saved'.[108] This last thought is clearly illustrated in 3:20 where Peter uses the word ψυχή in conjunction with διασῴζω ('bring safely through', 'save', 'rescue')[109] to denote the 'eight persons' (ὀκτὼ ψυχαί) (in their entirety and not just as disembodied 'souls') who were 'rescued' or 'saved' (διεσώθησαν) from the flood. In classical Greek usage the ψυχή is 'the essential core of man which can be separated from his body and which does not share in the body's dissolution'.[110] By contrast, in Hebrew thought, the soul (most commonly denoted by נֶפֶשׁ) denotes the human being in his or her entirety as a לְנֶפֶשׁ חַיָּה ('living being', Gen. 2:7; [LXX] ψυχὴν ζῶσαν).[111] Peter's usage of ψυχή, then, clearly echoes this typical Hebraic mindset. In light of Peter's adoption of this tradition, the phrase σωτηρίαν ψυχῶν should be understood to denote the salvation of the entire person. For Peter, future salvation implies the hope of personal resurrection (cf. vv. 3, 21) which brings about the transformation of the total person rather than just the release of the 'soul' from the imprisonment of the body (as in much Greek thought). With v. 9 (and the resumptive ἀγαλλιᾶσθε of v. 8d) Peter now concludes the line of thought that he had begun at v. 6 (ἐν ᾧ ἀγαλλιᾶσθε): 'If the present reality is suffering, it will surely result in eschatological redemption. Joy is therefore the appropriate stance however incongruous it may appear in present circumstances.'[112]

Future salvation and past prophecy (vv. 10–12)

Verses 10–12 constitute the last of three subunits (vv. 3–5, 6–9, 10–12) which comprise the opening section of the letter in which God is praised for his work of salvation. The Greek prepositional phrase περὶ ἧς σωτηρίας (lit., 'concerning this salvation', 1:10a) both links (by means of the relative pronoun ἧς ['which, this'] and the link-word σωτηρία ['salvation']) this subunit with what has gone before (σωτηρίαν ψυχῶν, v. 9; cf. v. 5b) and continues the focus (περί) on salvation (ἧς σωτηρίας). While the previous two subunits (vv. 3–5, 6–9) conclude with a reference to salvation (vv. 5b and 9b), the mention of salvation at the beginning

---

[108] Best, *1 Peter*, 80. Dautzenberg, 'Σωτηρία ψυχῶν', 276, offers the following translation of σωτηρία ψυχῶν: 'eure endgültige Rettung' ('your final rescue [or salvation]').

[109] BDAG, 237.

[110] E. Jacob, 'ψυχή κτλ.', *TDNT*, 9: 611.

[111] See Stone, 'The Soul: Possession, Part, or Person?', 47–61.

[112] Achtemeier, *1 Peter*, 104.

of this section (in conjunction with the preposition περί) suggests that the focus here is directly on salvation. As such, it probably represents the climax of the letter opening rather than just an appendix. In this section salvation is presented as the climax of the divine plan foretold by the prophets and now in the process of fulfilment. Michaels suggests a chiastic structure which represents salvation as the object of prophetic and angelic inquiry:

A Inquiries of prophets in the past
(ἐξεζήτησαν καὶ ἐξηραύνησαν … ἐραυνῶντες, vv. 10–11)
    B Divine revelation to prophets in the past
    (οἷς ἀπεκαλύφθη, v. 12a)
    B´ Divine announcement to Christians in the present
    (ἃ νῦν ἀνηγγέλη ὑμῖν, v. 12b)
A´ Inquiries of angels in the present
(ἐπιθυμοῦσιν, v. 12c)[113]

The focus of vv. 10–12 raises the following question: In light of his consistent focus on salvation as a future event, why does Peter now suddenly turn his attention to the prophets of the Old Testament? Michaels suggests that Peter's emphasis on salvation in terms of future vindication and on faith as the appropriate response of those waiting for this salvation 'could give the impression that God's people are no better off now than before Christ had come. Then, as well as now, faith was based on a promise and was pointed toward the future. What difference had the coming of Christ made?'[114] Peter's concern in this passage, then, seems to be to assure his readers (note the εἰς ὑμᾶς of v. 10b and the οὐχ ἑαυτοῖς ὑμῖν δέ of v. 12a) that although the completion of their salvation is something that still lies in the future, even now (note the νῦν of v. 12b) they are living in a time (note the τίνα ἢ ποῖον καιρόν of v. 11b) when the history of salvation is in the process of fulfilment. Achtemeier writes: 'In that way, the readers are comforted by the assurance that their salvation is surely in the hands of God, since it is part of the divine plan that had long ago been set (e.g., 1:20), and that is now at the point of fulfilment.'[115]

Salvation as χάρις

The prepositional phrase περὶ ἧς σωτηρίας (1:10a) at the beginning of this new subunit continues the focus on salvation functioning as a kind

---

[113] Michaels, *1 Peter*, 39.   [114] Ibid., 38–9.   [115] Achtemeier, *1 Peter*, 105.

of heading for vv. 10–12. Standing absolutely at the beginning of the sentence, περί ('concerning') marks a new section of thought around which (the figurative sense of περί) the following discussion will centre. It stresses the idea of salvation mentioned at the end of each of the two previous subunits (vv. 5, 9) but now stands at the head of this new subunit (v. 10). What Peter means by 'salvation' (σωτηρία) here receives further clarification by an almost identical prepositional phrase near the end of v. 10: περὶ τῆς ... χάριτος (v. 10b). We first need to ask what Peter means by the word χάρις in this verse. According to Elliott, *'charis* ("grace") is one of the author's preferred terms for denoting the divine favour and beneficence that believers have experienced as a result of their rebirth into the family of God'.[116] For Hort, 'χάρις here is evidently grace in the simplest and most general sense, the manifestation of what we call graciousness, of favour and acceptance on the part of God, as dependant on his own free good pleasure, not on any covenant obligation'.[117] While these definitions do provide good, general descriptions of 'grace', and while they will shed some light on Peter's choice of the word χάρις here, these more traditional conceptions, however, should 'not obscure the fact that 1 Peter appears to use χάρις in a more specialised sense as a comprehensive term which has the closest connections with σωτηρία'.[118] In its present context, the word χάρις belongs to a prepositional phrase which stands in parallel with another (1:10):

| 1:10a | περὶ | ἧς | σωτηρίας |
| 1:10b | περὶ | τῆς | χάριτος |

The parallelism between the two phrases suggests that the two terms are virtually synonymous in this context. This word χάρις ('favour, grace, gracious care/help', 'gracious deed/gift, benefaction'),[119] then, further expands Peter's list of synonyms used to describe σωτηρία (cf. his use of ἐλπίς in v. 3 and κληρονομία in v. 4). χάρις is more than just God's 'favour and beneficence' (Elliott)[120] or gracious disposition to give (Hort);[121] it is the gift itself. In this context it denotes the gift of eschatological salvation. Arichea and Nida note that '"grace" is used in many ways in the New Testament; in Paul it primarily means "God's love" or "God's favour", but here, it refers primarily to the result of God's love and favour ... and can be taken as synonymous with salvation itself'.[122]

[116] Elliott, *1 Peter*, 345.   [117] Hort, *First Epistle of Saint Peter*, 49.
[118] Kendall, 'Introductory Character', 139.   [119] BDAG, 1079.
[120] Elliott, *1 Peter*, 345.   [121] Hort, *First Epistle of Saint Peter*, 49.
[122] Arichea and Nida, *Handbook*, 29.

Furthermore, the closest parallel to its use here in v. 10 is v. 13, where Peter speaks of τὴν φερομένην ὑμῖν χάριν ἐν ἀποκαλύψει Ἰησοῦ Χριστοῦ ('the grace to be brought you at the revelation of Jesus Christ'). This verse combines the ideas of v. 7 (ἐν ἀποκαλύψει Ἰησοῦ Χριστοῦ) and v. 10 (περὶ τῆς εἰς ὑμᾶς χάριτος), both of which refer to the eschatological gift of salvation. As in 1:7, the words ἐν ἀποκαλύψει Ἰησοῦ Χριστοῦ (1:13) should be understood to refer to the second coming of Christ. In that case, the χάρις of 1:13, like 1:10, denotes the eschatological grace-gift, final salvation.

The word χάρις has a similar nuance in 3:7, where Peter exhorts husbands to show their wives honour since they are συγκληρονόμοις χάριτος ζωῆς ('co-heirs of the grace of life'). That the χάρις spoken of in 3:7 is eschatological in nature is further indicated by the epex-egetical modifier ζωῆς (an object genitive). In this expression (χάριτος ζωῆς), which is unique to the New Testament, the genitive ζωῆς ('of life') should be construed as an epexegetic/appositional/defining geni-tive – 'grace that is life', or 'grace that consists in life'. As Spicq points out, the word 'life' (ζωῆς) here is most probably a shorthand way of referring to 'eternal life': 'Dans cette perspective eschatologique, la "grâce" est le don semblablement accordé par Dieu aux deux époux, et qui consiste dans la vie éternelle (génetif épexégétique; cf. Rm 6,23).'[123] Furthermore, the language of inheriting (συγκληρονόμος ['co-heir']) recalls 1:4, where the eschatological inheritance of believers is men-tioned (the κληρονομίαν … τετηρημένην ἐν οὐρανοῖς) and 3:9 (two verses later), which speaks of inheriting a blessing (εὐλογίαν κληρονομήσητε).

Finally, in 5:5 Peter once again underscores the relationship between χάρις and salvation when he exhorts his readers to clothe themselves with humility 'because [ὅτι] God opposes the proud, but gives grace [χάριν] to the humble'. What does Peter means when he says that God gives grace to the humble? The answer appears to be given in v. 6 (which is closely tied to v. 5 by means of the conjunction οὖν): 'Be humble therefore, under the mighty hand of God, in order that he might exalt you at the appointed time [ἵνα ὑμᾶς ὑψώσῃ ἐν καιρῷ]'. What it means for God to give grace is then made clear by the ἵνα ὑμᾶς ὑψώσῃ ('in order that he will exalt you'). The prepositional phrase ἐν καιρῷ ('at the appointed time') recalls a similar and earlier one, ἐν καιρῷ ἐσχάτῳ ('in the last time', 1:5c), and, in the context of this letter, is clearly a reference

---

[123] Spicq, *Les Épîtres de Saint Pierre*, 124.

to the parousia.[124] 'Grace, therefore, is final vindication and salvation: the exaltation of the surrendered believer at the appropriate time.'[125]

Peter's choice of this word χάρις to denote the eschatological salvation of believers is interesting. Elliott notes that it is one of Peter's 'preferred terms for denoting the divine favor and beneficence that believers have experienced as a result of their rebirth into the family of God (1:2, 10, 13; 3:7; 4:10; 5:5, 10, 12)'.[126] As such it serves to underscore the sovereignty, freedom, and initiative of God in such salvation. It points to the fact that God is the ultimate actor in the drama of salvation and so Peter can describe him near the end of the letter as ὁ θεὸς πάσης χάριτος ('the God of all grace', 5:10). This 'grace' is described as being specifically intended for the readers (εἰς ὑμᾶς, 'meant for you', 1:10). In the present context, this phrase should be given the force of 'the grace *coming to you*' (cf. 1:13)[127] or perhaps better, 'the grace *destined for you*'.[128] This is probably how an identical construction should be understood in v. 11: τὰ εἰς Χριστὸν παθήματα ('the sufferings destined for Christ'):

1:10a	τῆς	εἰς	ὑμᾶς	χάριτος
1:11d	τὰ	εἰς	Χριστὸν	παθήματα

Beare suggests that this 'pregnant use of the preposition [εἰς]' brings out the 'thought of the divine foreordaining'.[129] In the context of the opening portion of this letter with its emphasis on divine election (1:1–2), mercy (v. 3), regeneration (v. 3), and preservation (v. 5), such an understanding best captures the sense of the preposition here. As Achtemeier notes, 'the phrase [τὰ εἰς Χριστὸν παθήματα] points to the continuing dynamic of the divine initiative in such salvation, and illumines both the present and future character of such salvation: its power is already present (in their faith), but not yet fulfilled (e.g., 1:4–5)'.[130]

Salvation as the object of prophetic inquiry

Peter now turns his attention from his present readers (ὑμᾶς), who are the privileged recipients of this 'grace' (τῆς χάριτος), to the prophets of old (προφῆται), who are portrayed as conducting a diligent investigation (ἐξεζήτησαν καὶ ἐξηραύνησαν [v. 10b], ἐραυνῶντες [v. 11a]) into the time and circumstances (εἰς τίνα ἢ ποῖον καιρὸν) in which

---

[124] Achtemeier, *1 Peter*, 339.   [125] Kendall, 'Introductory Character', 140.
[126] Elliott, *1 Peter*, 345.   [127] Achtemeier, *1 Peter*, 108.
[128] Ibid.   [129] Beare, *First Epistle of Peter*, 65, 66.
[130] Achtemeier, *1 Peter*, 108.

this salvation would be fulfilled. The following outline (vv. 10b-11a) shows that the focus in this section is the prophets' diligent inquiry into this grace/salvation. The word 'salvation' functions as a kind of heading for this section (H = heading). The searching and investigating (A, A′) of the prophets ([B] 'prophets'; [B′] 'the ones having prophesied') states the theme of this section functioning as a sort of *inclusio*, with 'grace', the object of this searching, at the very heart (C). The structure looks like this:

H περὶ ἧς σωτηρίας   **(salvation)**
   A ἐξεζήτησαν καὶ ἐξηραύνησαν (searching)
     B προφῆται οἱ   (prophets)
     C περὶ τῆς εἰς ὑμᾶς χάριτος   (grace)
     B′ προφητεύσαντες   (prophets)
   A′ ἐραυνῶντες   (searching)

The two compound verbs ἐξεζήτησαν (ἐκζητέω, 'seek out, search for') and ἐξηραύνησαν (ἐξεραυνάω, 'try to find out') function as a hendiadys emphasising 'the persistence and thoroughness of their search'.[131] This is the only occurrence of ἐξεραυνάω in the New Testament, and its use in combination with ἐκζητέω (and later ἐραυνάω, v. 11a) is another indication of the author's love for alliteration. The same two compound verbs are used in LXX Ps. 118:2 [119:2] with reference to οἱ ἐξερευνῶντες τὰ μαρτύρια αὐτοῦ ἐν ὅλῃ καρδίᾳ ἐκζητήσουσιν αὐτόν. The verb ἐκζητέω is used in combination with ἐρευνάω in 1 Macc. 9:26 with reference to the foreign authorities who ἐξεζήτουν καὶ ἠρεύνων τοὺς φίλους Ιουδου. In all these cases, ἐκζητέω, ἐξεραυνάω, and ἐραυνάω seem to be used interchangeably by the respective authors. In 1:10 Peter has probably used ἐκζητέω in combination with ἐξεραυνάω simply for rhetorical effect. In fact, the single verb ἐραυνάω ('search, examine, investigate') of 1 Pet. 1:11a seems to serve as a recapitulation of the two verbs of v. 10b (ἐκζητέω and ἐξεραυνάω).

Who are these prophets who prophesied about this grace? Selwyn contends 'that it was the Christian prophets who were especially in our author's mind'.[132] Warden concurs, concluding that 'the prophets of 1 Peter 1:10–12 are contemporary prophets among the first readers of the epistle'.[133] As a result both Selwyn and Warden have understood the phrase τὰ εἰς Χριστὸν παθήματα to refer *not* to the sufferings experienced by Christ himself but to the sufferings experienced by Christians

---

[131] Ibid.   [132] Selwyn, *First Epistle of St. Peter*, 134.
[133] Warden, 'The Prophets of 1 Peter', 12.

'for' or 'on behalf of' (εἰς) Christ. By contrast, most commentators agree that Peter is referring to Old Testament rather than New Testament prophets.[134] The following should be noted: First, as I will go on to argue below, the phrase τὰ εἰς Χριστὸν παθήματα more likely refers to the sufferings of Christ (which, according to the following chapter [2:21–5], are also to be experienced by those who follow in Christ's footsteps). Second, the presence of the adverb νῦν ('now') in the phrase ἃ νῦν ἀνηγγέλη ὑμῖν implies a contrast between the message of the prophets in the past (vv. 10–11; note the προμαρτυρόμενον of v. 11c) and the proclamation and reception of the gospel in the present (note the ἀνηγγέλη ὑμῖν and εὐαγγελισαμένων ὑμᾶς of v. 12).[135] This temporal contrast (cf. 2:10, 25; 3:20–1) suggests that Peter is referring to the prophets of ancient Israel and not the New Testament community.[136] And third, the participle προμαρτυρόμενον (present middle participle of προμαρτύρομαι, 'bear witness to beforehand, predict')[137] and its object τὰ εἰς Χριστὸν παθήματα καὶ τὰς μετὰ ταῦτα δόξας (lit. 'the sufferings for Christ and after these things glory') suggests that these prophets preceded Christ and so must be Old Testament.[138] This picture of the Old Testament prophets searching out and investigating the grace/salvation destined for the New Testament community of believers underscores 'la continuité du dessein de Dieu et l'unité de la révélation qui s'y rapporte'.[139] This salvation, presented salvation-historically as the fulfilment of Old Testament prophecy, represents not the 'rêverie de l'Eglise' but the 'volonté éternelle de Dieu',[140] and as such 'underlies the certainty of the announced salvation in Christ in the midst of circumstances that contradict rather than confirm it'.[141]

The adverbial participle ἐραυνῶντες (v. 11), simultaneous with the action of the two main verbs (ἐξεζήτησαν καὶ ἐξηραύνησαν),[142] further defines the activity of the prophets mentioned in the previous verse. The preposition εἰς is linked (as object) with ἐραυνῶντες and not ἐδήλου and 'accents the intensity of the prophets' search in much the same way as the combining of the two verbs prefixed with εκ does in the preceding verse'.[143] The object of the prophets' searching is then specified as τίνα ἢ ποῖον καιρόν (lit. 'which [or whom] or what sort of time'). Peter has previously used the word καιρός ('time, period')[144] in conjunction with ἔσχατος ('last') to denote the time of the final revelation of salvation

---

[134] See Brox, *Petrusbrief*, 69, n. 229; Spicq, *Les Épîtres de Saint Pierre*, 55.
[135] Elliott, *1 Peter*, 349.   [136] Ibid.   [137] BDAG, 872.
[138] See Achtemeier, *1 Peter*, 108.   [139] Margot, *Les Épîtres de Pierre*, 25.
[140] Ibid.   [141] Achtemeier, *1 Peter*, 108–9.
[142] Hamblin, 'Greek Participle', 85.   [143] Michaels, *1 Peter*, 41.
[144] BDAG, 497.

(v. 5). Here again in v. 11 the word καιρός has an eschatological flavour, this time denoting not the consummation of salvation, but its inauguration through τὰ εἰς Χριστὸν παθήματα καὶ τὰς μετὰ ταῦτα δόξας ('the sufferings intended for Christ and the glories to follow'). What are we to make of the phrase τίνα ἢ ποῖον καιρόν? Some commentators have suggested that the τίνα should be translated as a substantive pronoun ('who, whom') rather than as an interrogative adjective coordinate with ποῖον and modifying καιρόν ('what time').[145] If this is correct then the phrase τίνα ἢ ποῖον καιρόν should be rendered something like 'to whom or to what time',[146] or 'to what sort of person or time'.[147] Kilpatrick observes that this construal is supported by the fact that in 1 Peter 'τίς is always a pronoun, 3:13; 4:17; 5:8', a use that 'seems to be in agreement with general New Testament practice'.[148] On the other hand, τίς is often used as an interrogative adjective in the New Testament (e.g. Mt. 5:46; Lk. 14:31; Jn 2:18; Acts 10:21), and this is probably how it should be understood here. ποῖος should probably retain its normal qualitative sense (i.e., 'what sort'; cf. Mk 11:28; Jn 12:33)[149] since its use in conjunction with τίς would suggest that the two words are not completely synonymous in this context.[150] Thus τίνα ἢ ποῖον καιρόν should be translated 'what or what kind of time'[151] (not just 'what or what time').[152] First, as Kendall points out, 'the compound indirect question τίνα ἢ ποῖον should be seen as modifying καιρόν. Thus, the prophets were searching to discover when and under what circumstances the καιρός would come.'[153] Second, the focus of this text is the temporal difference between the ancient prophets of Israel and the New Testament community (suggested by such words as καιρόν [v. 11b] and νῦν [v. 12b]). They prophesied (προφητεύσαντες [v. 10b]; cf. also the προμαρτυρόμενον of v. 11c) about something (i.e., τὰ εἰς Χριστὸν παθήματα καὶ τὰς μετὰ ταῦτα δόξας) that did not find fulfilment in their own day (οὐχ ἑαυτοῖς ὑμῖν δὲ).[154] Third, as Michaels notes, the rendering 'what person or time' is unlikely 'because Peter gives no indication of any mystery or doubt about the "person" in whom the hope of salvation centred. The person was Christ.'[155] It seems that the prophets

---

[145] Kilpatrick, 'TINA 'H ΠΟΙΟΝ KAIΠON', 91–2.
[146] Ibid., 91.   [147] Elliott, *1 Peter*, 345–6.
[148] Kilpatrick, 'TINA 'H ΠΟΙΟΝ KAIΠON', 91.
[149] Wallace, *Greek Grammar*, 346.
[150] See Porter, *Idioms*, 137; Senior, *1 Peter*, 34.
[151] Wallace, *Greek Grammar*, 346; Dupont-Roc, 'Le Jeu de prépositions', 210–11.
[152] As suggested by BDF, §298(2).   [153] Kendall, 'Introductory Character', 142–3.
[154] Schreiner, *1 Peter*, 74.   [155] Michaels, *1 Peter*, 41.

were more concerned about the *when* of fulfilment rather than specifically the *who* (cf. Dan. 12:5–13; Hab. 2:1–4; 4 Ezra 4).[156] Fourth, as Jobes
notes, 'if the two components [τίνα and ποῖον] were different but corresponding, one might expect the conjunction to be καί ... "they looked
into what person *and* what sort of time" – not ἤ (or)'.[157] The words εἰς
τίνα ἤ ποῖον καιρὸν, then, seem to be there for emphasis, once again
highlighting the temporal contrast between the prophets who looked forward to a time when these prophesies would be fulfilled and the New
Testament community which was the privileged recipient of the salvation inaugurated by Christ.

This salvation was inaugurated, as the content of the prophecies indicates, through τὰ εἰς Χριστὸν παθήματα καὶ τὰς μετὰ ταῦτα δόξας
('the sufferings intended for Christ and the glories to follow', v. 11c).
While some commentators argue that the 'sufferings' and 'glories'
referred to here denote the sufferings of Christians for (εἰς) Christ,[158]
it is better here to see a reference to the sufferings destined for Christ
(from the perspective of the prophets) and the glorious events that followed. As Jobes observes, elsewhere in the New Testament 'the prepositional phrase with *eis* adjectivally modifies its head noun by specifying
the recipients of the verbal action implied by the noun'.[159] Moreover, the
syntax of this phrase is paralleled in v. 10 by a similar construction (τῆς
εἰς ὑμᾶς χάριτος) which clearly means 'the grace for you'. Note the
parallels between the two phrases:

| v. 11d | τὰ | εἰς | Χριστὸν | παθήματα |
| v. 10b | τῆς | εἰς | ὑμᾶς | χάριτος |

Beare suggests that 'the weighty εἰς in both cases [vv. 10 and 11] brings
out the thought of foreordering; the sufferings of Christ, like the grace
bestowed upon Christians, came upon him "by the determinate counsel
and foreknowledge of God" (Acts 2:23; cf. Acts 4:28)'.[160] The phrase εἰς
Χριστόν expresses 'the common *Christian* conviction that the OT prophets, and the Sacred Scriptures generally, prophesied beforehand concerning Jesus Christ, his suffering, death, and resurrection ... and in general
the saving events now come to pass'.[161] A related theme appears in 1 Pet.
1:20–1: **προεγνωσμένου** μὲν **πρὸ καταβολῆς κόσμου** φανερωθέντος

---

[156] See Schreiner, *1 Peter*, 74.   [157] Jobes, *1 Peter*, 101.
[158] See Selwyn, *First Epistle of St. Peter*, 263–5; Kilpatrick, 'ΤΙΝΑ 'Η ΠΟΙΟΝ
ΚΑΙΠΟΝ', 2–3, 5–6.
[159] Jobes, *1 Peter*, 100.   [160] Beare, *First Epistle of Peter*, 66.
[161] Elliott, *1 Peter*, 348 (emphasis his).

δὲ ἐπ' ἐσχάτου τῶν χρόνων δι' ὑμᾶς τοὺς δι' αὐτοῦ πιστοὺς εἰς
θεὸν τὸν ἐγείραντα αὐτὸν ἐκ νεκρῶν καὶ δόξαν αὐτῷ δόντα. The
primary point being made here and in v. 10 is that the death and glorification of Christ originated in God's sovereign and eternal plan.

With the word παθήματα we have the first explicit mention of the
sufferings of Christ. The word πάθημα ('suffering, misfortune') occurs
sixteen times in the New Testament, four times in 1 Peter alone. In addition to that, 1 Peter contains 30 per cent (12×) of all occurrences of the
related verb πάσχω ('suffer, endure',[162] appearing 40× in the NT). While
the phrase τὰ εἰς Χριστὸν παθήματα καὶ τὰς μετὰ ταῦτα δόξαςis
unique to 1 Peter, the words τὰ παθήματα are used elsewhere in the
New Testament to denote the sufferings of Christ (2 Cor. 1:5; Phil. 3:10;
Heb. 2:9, 10). Then in conjunction with τὰ παθήματα, Peter makes mention of τὰς μετὰ ταῦτα δόξας ('after these [= sufferings] glories'). The
unusual 'glories' (δόξας) along with the singular 'glory' (δόξης, 4:13;
5:1) denotes, as the larger context of the book indicates, his resurrection
(1:3; 3:18), ascension (3:19, 22), proclamation (3:19), exaltation (3:22;
2:4), and final revelation (4:5, 13; 5:4). The juxtaposition of these two
phrases τὰ παθήματα and τὰς δόξας 'constitutes a Petrine variation on a
common early tradition and conception of Jesus Christ's suffering-death-
resurrection-glorification-life as a single salvatory event'.[163] Elsewhere
in his letter Peter summarises these two chief foci of Christ's life (suffering and death/resurrection and glorification) as θανατωθεὶς μὲν σαρκὶ
ζῳοποιηθεὶς δὲ πνεύματι (3:18) and refers to himself as a μάρτυς τῶν
τοῦ Χριστοῦ παθημάτων, ὁ καὶ τῆς μελλούσης ἀποκαλύπτεσθαι
δόξης κοινωνός (5:1). Then in 4:13 he makes reference to τοῖς τοῦ
Χριστοῦ παθήμασιν and τῇ ἀποκαλύψει τῆς δόξης αὐτοῦ. As Spicq
observes, '[s]ouffrance et gloire résument le mystère pascal, dans lequel
culmine l'économie du salut'.[164] Peter's choice of the word 'sufferings'
to speak of Christ's death enables him, as at 3:18, to link the experience
of Christ in suffering and glory (1:11) with that of believers in order to
encourage them that, like Christ, their present experience of suffering
will one day give way to glory (1:6–7).

The 'gospel' (v. 12)

The εἰς Χριστὸν παθήματα καὶ τὰς μετὰ ταῦτα δόξας, predicted by
the prophets, are now identified by Peter as the gospel that had been

[162] BDAG, 785.   [163] Elliott, *1 Peter*, 348.
[164] Spicq, *Les Épîtres de Saint Pierre*, 56

recently proclaimed to those who are now believers in Asia Minor. The neuter plural relative pronoun ἅ (v. 12b) refers back to the immediately preceding αὐτά (v. 12a), which in turn connects with the words τὰ εἰς Χριστὸν παθήματα καὶ τὰς μετὰ ταῦτα δόξας (v. 11c). The flow of thought looks like this:

τὰ εἰς Χριστὸν <u>παθήματα</u> <u>καὶ</u> <u>τὰς</u> μετὰ ταῦτα <u>δόξας</u>

αὐτα

ἅ νῦν ἀνηγγέλη ὑμῖν

    διὰ τῶν εὐαγγελισαμένων ὑμᾶς

      [ἐν] πνεύματι ἁγίῳ

        ἀποσταλέντι ἀπ’ οὐρανοῦ

εἰς ἃ ἐπιθυμοῦσιν ἄγγελοι παρακύψαι

According to v. 12, the 'things [αὐτά] which have now been announced' (ἃ νῦν ἀνηγγέλη) by the ones 'preaching the gospel' (εὐαγγε-λισαμένων) to them are Christ's 'sufferings and consequent glories' (τὰ παθήματα καὶ τὰς μετὰ ταῦτα δόξας). The adverb νῦν ('now'), marking Peter's transition from past to present, emphasises once again the temporal contrast between 'the previous time of the prophets and the current time of salvation, the anticipation and the final proclamation and reception of the good news'. The verb ἀνηγγέλη (aorist passive of ἀναγγέλλω, 'disclose, announce, proclaim, preach')[165] is a paronym of the verb εὐαγγελισαμένων (aorist middle participle of εὐαγγελίζω, 'bring good news, announce good news', 'proclaim the gospel')[166] and together they denote the proclamation of 'the divine message of salvation'.[167] The verb εὐαγγελίζω (54× in the New Testament) and its noun εὐαγγέλιον ('good news', 76×) are two of the most frequently used terms in the New Testament for denoting the good news 'that God has acted for the salvation of the world in the incarnation, death and resurrection of Jesus'.[168] Peter uses the same verb in two other places in this letter. In 1:25 τὸ ῥῆμα τὸ εὐαγγελισθὲν εἰς ὑμᾶς ('the word which was preached to you') is τὸ ῥῆμα κυρίου ('the word of the Lord'; cf. 4:17, τῷ τοῦ θεοῦ εὐαγγελίῳ) by which believers are

---

[165] BDAG, 59.　[166] BDAG, 402.　[167] BDAG, 402.
[168] U. Becker, 'εὐαγγέλιον, κτλ', *NIDNTT*, 2: 111.

born again (1:23) and nourished unto salvation (2:2). Then in 4:6 we are told that this 'good news' was previously 'proclaimed' (εὐηγγε-λίσθη) to those who are now believers in Asia Minor, including those who have since died (καὶ νεκροῖς), with the purpose that (εἰς τοῦτο γάρ) through their reception of it they might enjoy salvation at the final judgment (ζῶσι κατὰ θεὸν πνεύματι). For this author, then, the proclamation of the gospel (as denoted by εὐαγγελίζω), which has as its essential content the suffering, death, resurrection, and glorification of Jesus Christ, is the key to salvation. This salvation is realised in part now through the proclamation and reception of the gospel by faith but awaits consummation at the revelation of Jesus Christ (cf. 1 Pet. 1:5, 7). Peter's summary of the gospel in terms of Jesus' death and resurrection as the fulfilment of Old Testament prophecy represents the fundamental core of New Testament proclamation (see, e.g., Lk. 24:25–27; 1 Cor. 15:1–5).

The divine origin of the gospel is then once again highlighted by the words [ἐν] πνεύματι ἁγίῳ ἀποσταλέντι ἀπ' οὐρανοῦ ('by the Holy Spirit sent from heaven', v. 12b). It is possible that the passive ἀνηγ-γέλη in conjunction with the words [ἐν] πνεύματι point to God as the originator of the message, while the prepositional phrase introduced by διά designates the messengers as the instruments or agents (διά) through whom the message was delivered (cf. 1:3, 5, 23; 2:14; 3:1; 2 Pet. 1:3, 4).[169] The phrase πνεύματι ἁγίῳ, basically equivalent to the earlier πνεῦμα Χριστοῦ, together with the words ἀποσταλέντι ἀπ' οὐρανοῦ reinforces the divine origin, initiative, and authentication of the gospel proclamation. Peter then concludes with a final qualifying phrase referring back (ἅ) to the αὐτά of v. 12a: εἰς ἃ ἐπιθυμοῦσιν ἄγγελοι παρακύψαι (lit. 'on these [things] angels long to look'). The verb παρ-ακύπτω ('look in/into') is used here with the sense of 'to try to find out someth[ing] intellectually',[170] 'to try to learn, to desire to learn'.[171] Here the angels are portrayed as desiring to comprehend what has now been openly proclaimed in the gospel. The mention here of angelic desire serves to emphasise both the greatness of the gospel proclamation and the exclusive privilege granted to those who have been the recipients of it. Schreiner writes: 'Again, the privilege of enjoying and anticipating salvation comes to the forefront. Old Testament prophets saw it from

---

[169] See Achtemeier, *1 Peter*, 111; Michaels, *1 Peter*, 47.
[170] BDAG, 767.   [171] L&N, 27.39.

afar, and angels also marvel when gazing upon what God has done in Christ, while the Petrine readers actually experience it.'[172]

3.   Summary

In the opening sequence of 1 Peter (vv. 3–5), an interest in salvation was signalled by the description of three saving benefits that believers have received as a result of God's great mercy and regenerating action: a living hope (v. 3), a heavenly inheritance (v. 4), and a salvation ready to be revealed in the last time (v. 5). These three benefits were simply different ways of looking at the same event: the believer's eschatological salvation. The first benefit, hope, was described as 'living' by virtue of God's past action of raising Christ from the dead. This then became the basis and guarantee of the believer's own future resurrection to life (hence a '*living* hope'). The nature of this eschatological hope then received fuller definition in Peter's appropriation of the Old Testament language of 'inheritance' (v. 4). This inheritance, we are told, is being kept in heaven for believers (v. 4b) – who themselves are being 'kept' by God's power (v. 5a) – in anticipation of its final unveiling as a 'salvation ready to be revealed in the last time' (v. 5).

Eschatological salvation was also the underlying theme of vv. 6–9 surfacing at the beginning (v. 6a), middle (v. 7c), and end (v. 9) of the discussion. The digression (vv. 6b-8b), signalled by the concessive λυπηθέντες, also brought the theme of faith to the fore (vv. 7a, 8b, 9; cf. v. 5b). The pairing of the expressions τὸ δοκίμιον ὑμῶν τῆς πίστεως (v. 7a) with εὑρεθῇ εἰς ἔπαινον καὶ δόξαν καὶ τιμὴν ἐν ἀποκαλύψει Ἰησοῦ Χριστοῦ (v. 7c) and τὸ τέλος τῆς πίστεως [ὑμῶν] (v. 9a) with σωτηρίαν ψυχῶν (v. 9b) served to associate the idea of salvation with the concept of faith. The introduction of the theme of faith also gave Peter the opportunity to introduce another important theme for this letter: suffering. In the context of this passage, suffering has the practical effect of authenticating faith, which, if proven authentic (v. 7a), has as its outcome eschatological salvation (vv. 7c, 9b). It is this thought that enables the believer to rejoice even in the midst of suffering (v. 6a; v. 8bc).

Verses 10–12 then brought our passage to a climax with its contrast between the past era of prophetic anticipation and the present age of salvific fulfilment. What the Old Testament prophets looked forward to (vv. 10–11), and angels long to look into (v. 12c), Peter's readers now enjoy (vv. 9–10b). The ancient prophets made careful search and inquiry

---

[172] Schreiner, *1 Peter*, 76.

as to the future time and circumstances of salvation, predicting, under the inspiration of the 'Spirit of Christ', the 'sufferings destined for Christ and the glories to follow'. In doing so, 'it was revealed that they were not ministering to themselves but to you', the future readers of this letter. Peter's main point was that believers are greatly privileged to be living in the time when the prophecies of salvation are being fulfilled. Moreover, in the activity of the prophets the Spirit of Christ bore witness to the fact that saving grace would, as in the experience of Christ, involve a pattern of present suffering followed by future glory. Far from calling into question the reality of their salvation, the believers' present experience of suffering confirms their Christian experience and provides a firm basis for their future hope and glorification (salvation).

6

SALVATION AS FUTURE VICTORY AND VINDICATION

1.   1 Peter 3:18–22: The suffering and vindication of Christ

Without doubt this passage constitutes the greatest challenge to the interpreter of this epistle. Werner Bieder calls it a 'schier unlösbare Rätsel'.[1] Jean Galot refers to it as 'le plus difficile de l'épître ... aussi un des plus obscure de toute la Bible.'[2] Martin Luther's perplexity over this passage is often quoted: 'Das ist ein wunderlicher Text und finsterer Spruch, als freilich einer im Neuen Testament ist, das ich noch nicht gewiss weiss, was St. Peter meint.'[3] This passage raises a number of challenging questions for the exegete concerning its structure, syntax, relationship to the immediate and broader context, conceptual background, coherence, meaning, and relationship to 4:1–6 (especially 4:6). These issues will be explored as we consider this passage's contribution to our understanding of salvation in 1 Peter (3:18 will receive fuller treatment in other parts of this work).

Structure

The ensuing discussion will be based on the following chiastic analysis of 3:18–4:6 (which will be defended in the course of the exegesis):[4]

> **A** **3:18** The suffering and vindication of Christ
> > **B** **3:19** The ascension of Christ and his proclamation of condemnation and victory over the evil spirits
> > > **C** **3:20** The salvation of Noah through water

---

[1] Luther, *WA*, 12: 367 (quoted in Reicke, *Disobedient Spirits*, 1).
[2] Galot, 'La Descente du Christ aux enfers', 473.
[3] Quoted in Scharlemann, 'He Descended into Hell', 90.
[4] For other attempts to discern a chiasmus in 1 Pet. 3:18–4:6, see McCartney, 'The Use of the Old Testament', 149; Johnson, 'The Preaching to the Dead', 50–1; Keener, *Bible Background Commentary*, 717–18.

       C′   **3:21**   The salvation of baptised believers
                            through the resurrection of Jesus Christ
    B′   **3:22**   The ascension of Christ into heaven with
                            cosmic powers subjected to him
A′   **4:1–6**   The suffering and vindication of believers

Context

F. W. Beare argues that this 'passage is in some degree a digression, moving away from the subject immediately in hand, the exposition of the meaning of undeserved suffering. It may at least be said that the thought is not closely sustained and connected.'[5] Yet Selwyn's view that 3:18–22 'fits closely into its context both before and after, and is almost essential to the main argument' receives greater justification from the context.[6] These verses are joined syntactically with the previous section (3:13–17) by means of the causal conjunction ὅτι ('because, for') and the connective καί ('also') as well as the words Χριστός ('Christ', 3:15, 16, 18a), πάσχω ('suffer', 3:14, 17, 18a), and δικαιοσύνη/δίκαιος ('righteousness'/ 'righteous', 3:14/18b). The ὅτι at the beginning of v. 18 provides a Christological basis for the foregoing exposition (3:13–17) for doing what is right despite suffering. In this way 3:18–22 functions in a similar way to 2:21–25 which provides Christological support for 2:18–20. Christ's innocent suffering (3:18b) is presented as both the basis for present salvation (3:18b-c) and the model for innocent suffering (cf. 4:1). Not only that, God's vindication of Christ's suffering (through resurrection, ascension, proclamation, and exaltation at God's right hand [3:18e, 19, 21d, 22]) both indicates Christ's ability to bring believers to God (3:18c) and provides the assurance of their future vindication/salvation (4:6c). Suffering, then, is not a sign of divine displeasure. Instead, as we will see again in this section, it is the pathway to future salvation, vindication and glory.

Content

The suffering of Christ (v. 18a)

The ὅτι at the beginning of v. 18 provides a Christological basis for doing what is right despite suffering (3:13–17). Here Christ's innocent

---

[5] Beare, *First Epistle of Peter*, 144.
[6] Selwyn, *First Epistle of St. Peter*, 195.

suffering (Χριστὸς ... ἔπαθεν, δίκαιος ['Christ ... suffered, a just man'], v. 18ab) is held up as a model for the innocent suffering of believers (3:14, 17; cf. 2:19–20). The verb πάσχω ('suffer, endure') (appearing 12× in this letter – more than other books of the NT) appears three more times in 1 Peter with Christ as the subject (2:21, 23; 4:1). Peter's preference for the word 'suffered' rather than 'died' is explained by his desire to establish a connection between the experience of Christ and the experience of believers in suffering (3:13–17/18–22). In any case, this reference to his suffering also includes reference to his death (cf. 2:21–4), as the next part of the verse indicates (θανατωθεὶς μὲν σαρκί, v. 18d). Even so, Peter's focus is not so much the death of Christ, but God's vindication of his death through resurrection (as the concessive μὲν ... δέ construction will indicate). The implications of all this for believers will be unpacked in 4:1–6: just as Christ's innocent suffering provides a model for the innocent suffering of believers, so also his vindication by God provides suffering believers with the assurance that they too will enjoy future vindication by God.

The vindication of Christ: resurrection (v. 18d-e)

Dalton notes from the outset that 'the right understanding of this phrase is of the greatest importance for the interpretation of the whole passage'.[7] The first part of this phrase (θανατωθεὶς μὲν σαρκί) connects back to the ἔπαθεν of v. 18a reiterating the thought of Christ's suffering/death, while the second part of the phrase (ζῳοποιηθεὶς δὲ πνεύματι) looks forward to vv. 19–22 making explicit Christ's vindication through his resurrection (vv. 18e, 21d), ascension (vv. 19, 22b), proclamation (v. 19; cf. v. 22c), and exaltation to God's right hand (v. 22a). The μὲν ... δέ construction here is most probably concessive and has the effect of 'throw[ing] the emphasis on the second member (indicated by δέ)'.[8] The phrase ζῳοποιηθεὶς δὲ πνεύματι is therefore the climax of the contrast. Thus, in this final part of v. 18 (de) the innocent, suffering Christ gives way to the victorious, vindicated Christ. God's vindication of the innocent, suffering Christ provides suffering believers with the assurance of their own future vindication. For just as his suffering means that they should also be prepared to suffer (4:1), so his being made alive (v. 18e; cf. 1:3; 2:5; 3:7) means that they can be assured of finally being made alive as well (4:6).

---

[7] Dalton, *Christ's Proclamation*, 135 (referring to 3:19–22).
[8] BDF, §447(5).

While the meaning of the two elements of this antithesis are not difficult to understand, complication has arisen due to the attempts of some scholars to associate this verse with the later notion of the descent of Christ, as a disembodied soul, to the world of the dead (according to their interpretation of v. 19). However, as most commentators now rightly recognise, the couplet that comprises v. 18de consists of two parallel phrases asserting the death and resurrection of Christ:

θανατωθεὶς	μὲν	σαρκί
having been put to death		in the flesh
ζῳοποιηθεὶς	δὲ	πνεύματι
having been made alive		in the spirit

This couplet contrasts two aorist passive participles (θανατωθείς and ζῳοποιηθείς) and two dative nouns (σαρκί and πνεύματι). The two (aorist) participial phrases are then followed by a third aorist participle πορευθείς ('having gone', v. 19), creating a logical connection between the death, resurrection, and ascension of Christ:

Χριστός...	('Christ')	
θανατωθείς	('having been put to death')	= crucifixion
ζῳοποιηθείς	('having been made alive')	= resurrection
πορευθείς	('having gone'; cf. v 22b)	= ascension

The 'flesh-spirit' contrast is a familiar one to the New Testament.[9] But what is the contrast that Peter is making here? On the basis of 1:11 (πνεῦμα Χριστοῦ) Schelkle argues that 'spirit' here is a reference to Christ's divine nature: 'In dieser Existenz lebte er von gottlicher Ewigkeit her.'[10] Yet in his discussion on v. 19 he interprets ἐν ᾧ as 'in seinem pneumatischen Personteil, als Geistwesen und ohne Leiblichkeit',[11] indicating that he also wants to see in πνεύματι a reference to Christ's disembodied soul which carried out the activity of 'preaching'. Similarly, Spicq in his commentary on 1 Peter suggests that 'les deux participes aoristes se correspondent rigoureusement (*men ... dé*) et veulent préciser dans quelle condition humaine et divine le Christ a accompli la rédemption des vivants es des morts'.[12] He describes Christ's 'having been made alive in the Spirit', in terms of a 'vitalité nouvelle, c'est-à-dire avec un accroissement de puissance ... libéré de la *sarx* qui est faible', but glorified 'dans

---

[9] See, e.g., Mt. 26:41; Mk 14:38; Lk. 24:39; Jn 3:6; Rom. 1:3–4; 2:28–9; 1 Cor. 5:5; 2 Cor. 7:1; Gal. 3:3; Phil. 3:3.
[10] Schelkle, *Petrusbriefe*, 104.   [11] Ibid.
[12] Spicq, *Les Épîtres de Saint Pierre*, 135.

son âme, avant de la ressusciter, trois jours après, dans son corps'.[13] But to say, as Spicq does, that the work of redemption rests upon the death of Christ and the vivification of his soul while his body lay in the tomb is contrary to the teaching of 1 Peter. According to 1 Peter, the believers' rebirth to a living hope comes δι' ἀναστάσεως Ἰησοῦ Χριστοῦ ἐκ νεκρῶν (1:3e); their being brought to God (προσαγάγη τῷ θεῷ) is a consequence of his ζῳοποιηθεὶς δὲ πνεύματι (3:18e); and their baptism saves (ὑμᾶς νῦν σῴζει βάπτισμα) only δι' ἀναστάσεως Ἰησοῦ Χριστοῦ (3:21d). Wright's comments on this verse are very apt:

> The 'flesh/spirit' antithesis of 3:18 and 4:6 sounds to modern western ears as though it stands for our 'physical/non-physical' distinction; but this would take us down the wrong path. The writer insists that it is the *resurrection* of Jesus that has accomplished salvation. There is no hint in this text that resurrection is being understood any differently to its standard use across both the pagan and Jewish world and in the rest of early Christianity. When, then, the writer says that the Messiah was 'put to death in/by flesh, but made alive in/by spirit', we should not project on to this text the 'physical/non-physical' antithesis that 'flesh/spirit' conjures up for us today.[14]

How then should we understand this σαρκί/πνεύματι contrast in 1 Pet. 3:18? As most commentators now recognise, σαρκί and πνεύματι do not denote the material (body) and immaterial (soul/spirit) parts of Christ's person, but rather his earthly mode of existence and his spiritual mode of existence or resurrected state. Our understanding of this contrast depends largely on how we construe these two datives. One possibility is to construe them as either datives of instrument/means or datives of agency. Construed this way σαρκί would denote human agency while πνεύματι would denote divine agency: '[I]n that case, it means that Christ was put to death by humans but raised by (God's) Spirit'.[15] However, as Jobes rightly points out, the emphasis here is 'not between the agents of the action but between the two states of Christ's existence. Just as Christ emerged from suffering and death into resurrection life, so will Peter's oppressed readers, which is a thought more apt to Peter's purposes.'[16] While it is also possible to read both nouns as datives of sphere (or datives of reference with respect to sphere), it is probably better to construe both σαρκί and πνεύματι as datives of reference with

[13] Ibid., 136.   [14] Wright, *Resurrection*, 469 (emphasis his).
[15] Achtemeier, *1 Peter*, 250.   [16] Jobes, *1 Peter*, 240–1.

respect to two differing modes or states of Christ's existence (viz. in human form before his death and glorified form after his resurrection). Thus σαρκί indicates that it was 'in respect to his physical mortal existence that Christ was put to death (as in 2 Cor. 4:11; Heb. 5:7)'.[17] By contrast, πνεύματι most likely refers to the new spiritual, supernatural mode of Christ's existence, entered through his resurrection. As Hiebert notes, 'perhaps the most probable view is that both terms refer to the whole Christ. Both "flesh" and "spirit", each used without an article, emphasise quality and denote two contrasted modes of the Lord's existence as incarnate, before and after the resurrection.'[18]

It should be noted that in the final analysis the issue is not whether one opts for a dative of reference with respect to sphere or mode of existence, but that one sees in these datives a reference to the death and resurrection of Christ.

The meanings of σαρκί and πνεύματι are further defined by the two aorist participles they modify: θανατωθείς ('having been put to death') and ζωοποιηθείς ('having been made alive'). Once again, the contrast is not between the material and immaterial parts of Christ's person as if to say he was 'put to death' with respect to his body but 'made alive' or 'quickened' with respect to his disembodied 'soul/spirit'.[19] Such an understanding, as Ladd indicates, would be 'contrary to primitive Christian belief, which always thought of the resurrection of the *body*, although of a body transformed by the Holy Spirit'.[20] What Peter is saying, then, is that while Christ was put to death with respect to his mortal physical existence (= crucifixion), he was made alive with respect to his immortal spiritual existence (= resurrection).

The verb θανατόω ('put to death', 'kill, execute') occurs ten times in the New Testament outside of 1 Pet. 3:18.[21] Of those ten occurrences, θανατόω appears six times in the Gospels with reference to the killing of Jesus (Mk 14:55 = Mt. 26:59; 21:1) and the killing of his disciples (Mt. 10:21 = Mk 13:12 = Lk. 21:6).[22] In Mk 14:55 we read that οἱ δὲ ἀρχιερεῖς καὶ ὅλον τὸ συνέδριον ἐζήτουν κατὰ τοῦ Ἰησοῦ μαρτυρίαν εἰς τὸ θανατῶσαι αὐτόν. As Michaels notes, the use of the same verb in 1 Pet. 3:18 'recalls the synoptic accounts of the judicial proceedings

[17] Elliott, *1 Peter*, 645.   [18] Hiebert, 'The Suffering and Triumphant Christ', 150.
[19] Wright, *Resurrection*, 469; Dalton, *Christ's Proclamation*, 136; Achtemeier, *1 Peter*, 249.
[20] Ladd, *Theology of the New Testament*, 647 (emphasis his).
[21] Mt. 10:21; 26:59; 27:1; Mk 13:12; 14:55; Lk. 21:16; Rom. 7:4; 8:13; 8:36; 2 Cor. 6:9.
[22] W. Bieder, 'θανατόω', *EDNT*, 2: 133.

that led to Jesus' death'.[23] That θανατόω in 1 Pet. 3:18 is a reference to Jesus death/crucifixion is clear.

The contrasting phrase that now follows makes Christ's resurrection and vindication explicit: ζῳοποιηθεὶς δὲ πνεύματι ('but made alive with respect to the/his spirit'). The verb ζῳοποιέω ('make alive, give life to') occurs ten times in the New Testament outside of 1 Peter. In seven of those occurrences (70 per cent) it is used with reference to the resurrection (Jn 5:21 [2×]; Rom. 4:17; 8:11; 1 Cor. 15:22, 36, 45). The meaning of ζῳοποιέω is well illustrated in Rom. 8:11 where it is used in parallelism to ἐγείρω ('raise up'): 'If the Spirit of him who raised (ἐγείραντος) Jesus from the dead dwells in you, he who raised (ἐγείρας) Christ from the dead will also give life (ζῳοποιήσει) to your mortal bodies through his Spirit who dwells in you.' The use of ζῳοποιέω in parallelism with ἐγείρω, the verb most frequently used of God raising Jesus from the dead, would suggest that it serves here as a synonym for ἐγείρω. This also appears to be the case in 1 Peter, where an earlier mention of the resurrection employs the verb ἐγείρω: 'God, who raised him [θεὸν τὸν ἐγείραντα αὐτόν = Christ, 1:21] from the dead [ἐκ νεκρῶν] and gave him glory'. It also brings to mind the author's stress on Christ's resurrection at the outset of his letter (ἀναστάσεως Ἰησοῦ Χριστοῦ ἐκ νεκρῶν, 1:3) and prepares us for the same thought in 3:21 (ἀναστάσεως Ἰησοῦ Χριστοῦ) and its elaboration in 3:22. Thus we can be certain that in the expression θανατωθεὶς μὲν σαρκὶ ζῳοποιηθεὶς δὲ πνεύματι, we 'have the common New Testament tradition expressed elsewhere in creedal passages, such as that of Romans 8:34: "Christ Jesus who died, yes, who was raised from the dead, who is at the right hand of God"'.[24]

This couplet (θανατωθεὶς μὲν σαρκὶ ζῳοποιηθεὶς δὲ πνεύματι) prepares us in advance for a similar one in 4:6 (κριθῶσι μὲν κατὰ ἀνθρώπους σαρκὶ ζῶσι δὲ κατὰ θεὸν πνεύματι). As we will see, the experience of Christ in his suffering (v. 18ad) but especially in his vindication (v. 18e), is established as the basis for not only the believers' own suffering (4:1, 6b), but especially their vindication by God (4:6c). Thus, v. 18 comes to a climax with its reference to Christ's resurrection and provides us with 'the determinative event in connection with which vv. 19–21 are to be understood'.[25] Peter's mention of the resurrection at the very end of v. 18 sets the immediate context within which the following verses (esp. v. 19) are to be interpreted.

[23] Michaels, *1 Peter*, 203.   [24] Dalton, *Christ's Proclamation*, 137.
[25] Elliott, *1 Peter*, 647.

The vindication of Christ: proclamation (vv. 19–20b)

ἐν ᾧ καί

The words ἐν ᾧ καί (lit. 'in which also') link vv. 19–20b with 18de. The conjunction καί ('also') connects the aorist participle in this verse (πορευθείς) with the preceding aorist participles in v. 18de (θανατωθείς, ζωοποιηθείς), creating a logical connection between the death, resurrection, and ascension of Christ:

θανατωθείς	('having been put to death')	= crucifixion
ζωοποιηθείς	('having been made alive')	= resurrection
ἐν ᾧ καί	('in which also')	
πορευθείς	('having gone')	= ascension

What exactly is the syntactic function of ἐν ᾧ? It is possible that the antecedent to the dative relative pronoun ᾧ is the preceding πνεύματι. We noted earlier that πνεύματι is most probably a dative of reference and denotes Christ's spiritual mode of existence, that is, his resurrected state (as opposed to Christ as a 'disembodied spirit'). Thus, with πνεύματι as its antecedent, ἐν ᾧ could mean something like 'in which spiritual mode of existence' [of Christ in his resurrected state]. This would immediately rule out any interpretation which understands ἐν ᾧ καί πνεύματι as a reference to either Christ's pre-existent spirit (at the time of Noah)[26] or disembodied spirit (between his death and resurrection).[27] While this interpretation is certainly possible, ἐν ᾧ is probably better construed as having an adverbial/conjunctive force as elsewhere in the letter (cf. 1:6; 2:12; 3:16; 4:4).[28] Contextually, this interpretation makes best sense as it provides the most satisfactory explanation for the relationship between the two aorist participles in 3:18de (θανατωθείς and ζωοποιηθείς) and the one in 3:19 (πορευθείς) and as a result advances the thought in a logical manner (death→ resurrection→ascension). Moreover, as Elliott notes, 'the focus of vv. 19–22 is not on the *mode* of Christ's going ("in his spirit") but on the events involved with the *occasion* of his going, namely his resurrection (vv. 18e, 21d) and ascension in heaven (v. 22)'.[29] The words ἐν ᾧ, then,

---

[26] See Grudem, *First Epistle of Peter*, 158, 159–61; 206–39; 'Christ Preaching through Noah', 3–31; 'He Did not Descend into Hell', 103–13; Feinberg, '1 Peter 3:18–20: Ancient Mythology and the Intermediate State', 303–36.

[27] See Best, *1 Peter*, 42; Schelkle, *Petrusbriefe*, 104

[28] See Wallace, *Greek Grammar*, 343; Robertson, *Grammar*, 587.

[29] Elliott, *1 Peter*, 652 (emphasis his).

provide the link (note the conjunction καί ['also']) between Christ's resurrection in v. 18e (ζῳοποιηθεὶς δὲ πνεύματι) and his ascension (πορευθείς) and proclamation (ἐκήρυξεν) in v. 19.

However we construe the phrase ἐν ᾧ (whether as a causal or temporal conjunction, or as a simple relative referring back to πνεύματι in v. 18e), the important thing is that we see in the words ἐν ᾧ καί a link between Christ's ζῳοποιηθεὶς and πορευθεὶς ἐκήρυξεν 'making Christ's proclamation to the spirits a direct outcome of his resurrection from the dead'.[30] As Michaels notes, '[i]f the emphasis in the preceding verse is indeed on Christ's triumph or vindication, then the proclamation indicated here must have been made in connection with that triumph, not in connection with the suffering and death that preceded it'.[31] Thus the accent rests on the vindication of Christ in his resurrection and ascension into heaven.

πορευθείς

The Greek verb πορευθείς (the aorist passive of πορεύομαι, 'go, proceed, travel') is used here in its simple and primary meaning of 'to go'. This 'going' has traditionally been understood to refer to Christ's descent into the underworld or Hades.[32] While the verb πορεύομαι, in itself, does not reveal the direction of the movement (whether 'ascent' or 'descent', for example), it is significant that it is never used in the New Testament to mean 'go down, descend'. On the other hand, πορεύομαι is used in the book of Acts to refer to Jesus' ascension to heaven (Acts 1:10–11 [2×]) and in John's Gospel to refer to his ascent to God (who is in heaven) (Jn 14:2, 3, 28; 16:28). πορεύομαι should also be understood to refer to Christ's ascension into heaven in 1 Pet. 3:19.[33] Initially, two key arguments substantiate this judgment. First, this interpretation, as we have already noted above, is supported by the logical relation of the aorist participles θανατωθεὶς (3:18d), ζῳοποιηθεὶς (v. 18e), and πορευθεὶς (v. 19): reference to the ascension of Christ logically follows reference to his death and resurrection. A second clue is found in the immediate context. The verb πορευθείς ('having gone') occurs again (also as an aorist passive participle) in v. 22 with a clear reference to Christ's ascension or 'having gone into heaven' (πορευθεὶς εἰς οὐρανόν). Focusing on the **B C C′ B′** part of our chiasm reveals that the double use of πορευθείς forms an *inclusio*

---

[30] Michaels, *1 Peter*, 205–6.   [31] Michaels, *1 Peter*, 205.

[32] Krimmer and Holland, *Petrusbrief*, 120–1; Vogels, *Christi Abstieg in Totenreich*, 116–20, 136.

[33] So, e.g., Dalton, *Christ's Proclamation*, 161–3; Bénétreau, *Première épître de Pierre*, 208.

in which the first use of the word (B) is more easily understood in light of the second (B´) (and indeed is dependent on it for its meaning):

> **B 3:19** **The πορευθείς of Christ** and his proclamation to the spirits in prison
>
> **C 3:20** The salvation of Noah (διεσώθησαν) through (διά) water
>
> **C´ 3:21** The salvation of baptised believers (σώζει) through (διά) the resurrection of Jesus Christ
>
> **B´ 3:22** **The πορευθείς of Christ** into heaven with angels and authorities and powers subjected to him

Recognition of the chiastic structure of this passage (ABCC´B´A´) also removes the difficulty of seeing a reference to the resurrection in this place as disrupting the flow of thought of this passage as whole (vv. 18–22). For some commentators this is exactly what it would do.[34] This is because they are convinced that v. 19 refers to a disembodied journey (descent) by Christ to the underworld (a view rejected in this study). A reference to the ascension, however, best explains Peter's use of the word πορευθείς in this context.[35] The question that now concerns us is this: What is the nature of the proclamation that was made in conjunction with this 'going' (πορευθεὶς ἐκήρυξεν)? In order to answer that question we first need to consider two other questions: (1) who are the recipients of that proclamation? and (2) where did it take place?

τοῖς πνεύμασιν

The recipients of the risen Christ's proclamation are now identified by Peter as πνεύμασιν ('spirits'). Traditionally, the πνεύμασιν here have been identified with the souls of humans who have died.[36] However, a good case can be made for viewing these πνεύμασιν as supernatural beings, understood in early Jewish and Christian tradition as the fallen angels (referred to as 'sons of God' [בְּנֵי הָאֱלֹהִים] in Gen. 6:1–4; often called 'Watchers' [ἐγρήγοροι], 'spirits' [πνεύματα], or 'demons' in Jewish literature [e.g., *1 En.* 10:15; 12:3, 4; *Jub.* 5:1–11; 10:1–14]) who disobeyed God by descending to earth,[37] engaging in illicit intercourse with human women,[38] and together with their offspring (the 'giants' [נְפִלִים] in Gen. 6:4, γίγαντα in *1 En.* 7:2, τιτᾶνας in *1 En.* 9:9]) initiating the evil that led to the Noachic flood.[39] The plural

---

[34] See G. Friedrich, 'κηρύσσω', *TDNT*, 3: 707.
[35] So, e.g., Dalton, *Christ's Proclamation*, 161–3; Elliott, *1 Peter*, 653.
[36] See Krimmer, *Petrusbrief*, 120.   [37] *1 En.* 6:6.
[38] *1 En.* 7:1; 9:7–9.   [39] *1 En.* 10:1–22.

'spirits' (πνεύματα, πνεύμασιν, πνευμάτων) occurs thirty-four times in the New Testament. Yet only once is it used to refer to human beings: πνεύμασι δικαίων τετελειωμένων ('spirits of just [people] made perfect', Heb. 12:23). Here the πνεύμασιν are clearly identified by a qualifying genitive δικαίων τετελειωμένων. On the other hand, the plural 'spirits' frequently denotes supernatural beings in the New Testament, whether malevolent supernatural beings (21×) or benevolent angels (5×). Significantly, not once are humans collectively referred to as 'spirits' in either the Old or the New Testament (even though this is done with ψυχή in 3:20). In light of the biblical tendency either to indicate clearly in the context that the human 'spirits' are being referred to or to supply a qualifying genitive,[40] it is surprising that Peter does not say something like 'the spirits *of those* who once disobeyed' (τοῖς πνεύμασιν ἀπειθη-σάντων), rather than 'spirits who once disobeyed' (τοῖς πνεύμασιν ἀπειθήσασίν), if it is in fact human spirits that he is referring to. It is likely, then, that the plural 'spirits' of 3:19 are not human spirits but malevolent supernatural beings (cf. v. 20). But is this interpretation supported by the immediate context? There are three indicators that make this interpretation most likely: (1) the parallel between the disobedient 'spirits' of v. 19 and the subjugated 'angels' of v. 22, (2) the reference to the 'disobedience' (v. 20a) of the spirits against the backdrop of early Israelite flood traditions, and (3) the reference to their 'imprisonment' as a consequence of this disobedience (v. 19). We will discuss each of these in turn.

πνεύμασιν ... ἀγγέλων (vv. 19, 22c)

Focusing again on the B C C´ B´ part of our chiasm reveals not only a correspondence between the double use of πορευθείς but also a correspondence between the disobedient πνεύμασιν ('spirits') of vv. 19–20a and the subjugated ἀγγέλων καὶ ἐξουσιῶν καὶ δυνάμεων ('angels and authorities and powers') of v. 22:

> **B 3:19** The πορευθείς of Christ and his proclamation to the πνεύμασιν in prison (ἐν φυλακῇ)
>
> **C 3:20** The salvation (διεσώθησαν) of Noah through (διά) water
>
> **C´ 3:21** The salvation of baptised Christians (σῴζει) through (διά) the resurrection of Jesus Christ

---

[40] See, e.g., LXX Dan. 3:86a; Lk. 23:46; Acts 7:59; 1 Cor. 2:11; 1 Cor. 14:32; Heb. 12:23.

B´ 3:22   The πορευθείς of Christ into heaven with ἀγγέλων
καὶ ἐξουσιῶν καὶ δυνάμεων subjected to him
(ὑποταγέντων αὐτῷ)

The presence of ἀγγέλων in the triad ἀγγέλων καὶ ἐξουσιῶν καὶ
δυνάμεων suggests a synonymity between the subjugated angels (ὑποταγέντων αὐτῷ ἀγγέλων) of v. 22 and the disobedient angelic spirits (πνε
ύμασιν ἀπειθήσασίν) of vv. 19–20. The immediate context, then, suggests that the πνεύμασιν of v. 19 denotes malevolent supernatural beings
(subjugated by Christ in v. 22c) and not the spirits of dead humans.

ἀπειθήσασίν (v. 20a)

These πνεύμασιν are then further identified as those who ἀπειθήσασιν
ποτε ('once disobeyed', v. 20a). The dative aorist participle ἀπειθήσασιν ('[the-ones-having-] disobeyed') is best understood as an adjectival
participle (in the predicate position) modifying the dative πνεύμασιν and
therefore should be translated 'the spirits who were disobedient' or perhaps 'the spirits who disobeyed'.[41] Grudem wrongly interprets the participle as temporal ('*when* they disobeyed') arguing that apart from two
narrowly defined exceptions, 'there do not seem to be any clear examples
in the New Testament of anarthrous participles (participles which lack
the definite article in front of them) which have an arthrous antecedent
(i.e. an antecedent with a definite article) and which are adjectival (in
that they modify the noun which is their antecedent)'.[42] While we might
have expected to see an article before ἀπειθήσασιν when it is being used
adjectivally, it is not necessarily required (though admittedly this use of
the participle without the article is rare).[43] Contrary to Grudem, there are a
number of examples of anarthrous adjectival participles modifying articular antecedents in the New Testament (e.g., Mt. 7:14; Lk. 12:28; Acts
7:56; Heb. 4:12; Rom. 12:1;), and this is probably also the case here.

The context within which this disobedience occurred is then indicated
by three qualifying phrases: (1) ὅτε ἀπεξεδέχετο ἡ τοῦ θεοῦ μακρο-
θυμία, (2) ἐν ἡμέραις Νῶε, and (3) κατασκευαζομένης κιβωτοῦ. The
reference to the ἡμέραις Νῶε locates the disobedient spirits in terms
of the historical context within which this disobedience occurred. The
question that now concerns us then is this: Who are these spirits whose
disobedience is somehow related to the 'days of Noah' just preceding the
time of the flood? While Peter says nothing more of these 'spirits' or the

---

[41] See Wallace, *Greek Grammar*, 618–19; Hamblin, 'Greek Participle', 121.
[42] Grudem, *First Epistle of Peter*, 234.
[43] See Wallace, *Greek Grammar*, 618–19; Robertson, *Grammar*, 1108.

nature of their disobedience, there are a number of indications from early Jewish and Christian writings that the disobedience of these angelic spirits included the abandonment of their heavenly dwelling to engage in illicit intercourse with human women.[44] In *1 Enoch* we read:

> And when the sons of men had multiplied, in those days, beautiful and comely daughters were born to them. And the watchers, the sons of heaven, saw them and desired them. And they said to one another, 'Come, let us choose for ourselves wives from the daughters of men, and let us beget for ourselves children.'[45]

From this sexual union between the angels and human women a race of 'giants' (γίγαντας) was born,[46] and together with the Watchers (ἐγρήγοροι) they perpetrated the evil that eventually led to the Flood:

> That in the generation of Jared, my father, they transgressed the word of the Lord/the covenant of heaven, and behold, they went on sinning and transgressing the custom. With women they were mingling, and with them they were sinning. They married some of them, and they went on begetting (children), not like spirits, but fleshly. And there will be great wrath upon the earth and a flood, and there will be great destruction for a year.[47]

Significantly, the book of *1 Enoch* refers to the offspring of the Watchers as 'spirits' and 'evil spirits':

> But now the giants who were begotten by the spirits [ἀπὸ τῶν πνευμάτων] and flesh – they will call them evil spirits [πνεύματα πονηρά] upon the earth, for their dwelling will be upon the earth. The spirits that have gone forth from the body of their flesh are evil spirits [πνεύματα πονηρά], for from humans they came into being, and from the holy watchers was the origin of their creation. Evil spirits they will be on the earth, and evil spirits [πνεύματα πονηρα] they will be called. The spirits of heaven [πνεύματα οὐρανοῦ], in heaven is their dwelling; but the spirits begotten on the earth [τὰ πνεύματα ἐπὶ τῆς γῆς τὰ γεννηθέντα], on earth is their dwelling.[48]

That this is the most probable background to Peter's reference to the πνεύμασιν ἀπειθήσασιν ('spirits who disobeyed') can be seen by the

---

[44] *1 En.* 6:1–8; 9:7–8; 12:4; 15:3; 106:13–14; *Jub.* 7:1; *T. Rub.* 6:6; *T. Naph.* 3:5; Jude 6.
[45] *1 En.* 6:1–2.   [46] *1 En.* 7:1–3.   [47] *1 En.* 106:13–15.   [48] *1 En.* 15:8–10.

nature of their captivity (ἐν φυλακῇ) and the proclamation made to them by the risen Christ (ἐκήρυξεν).

ἐν φυλακῇ (v. 19)

In the New Testament φυλακή (47×) denotes 'the act of guarding' (Lk. 2:8), 'guard' or 'sentinel' (Acts 12:10), 'a watch of the night' (Mt. 14:25; Mk 6:48),[49] a 'haunt', 'lair', or 'dwelling place' (Rev. 18:2),[50] and most commonly 'prison' (36× including Mt. 5:25; 14:3, 10; 25:36, 39, 43–4; Mk 6:27; Lk. 3:20; 21:12; 22:33; Acts 5:19, 22, 25; 8:3; 12:4–5, 6, 10; 2 Cor. 6:5; 11:23; Heb. 11:36; Rev. 2:10; 20:7). Similarly, in the papyri it has the sense of 'care' or 'charge of a thing' (P.Oxy. 1.135; P.Lille. 1.7), 'security' (P.Oxy. 54.3758), 'watch' or 'guard' (P.Tebt. 2.282), 'a guard' (i.e., a person keeping guard, P.Oxy. 16.1853; P.Giss. 1.19), a period of time during which a watch was kept (P.Petr. 2.45), and most commonly 'a prison' (P.Oxy. 2.259; 16.1835, 1919; 19.2238; 27.2478; 56.3870; P.Giss. 1.84). But what does it refer to in 1 Pet. 3:19? If, as some have argued, πνεύμασιν is a reference to the souls of the human dead, then φυλακή here must be a reference to the abode of the dead. According to Krimmer, φυλακή 'ist der Ort, an dem die Toten sind, die auf das Gericht warten'.[51] This place of waiting has been variously interpreted as designating either hell,[52] Hades,[53] or the abode of the dead in general.[54] But as Dalton rightly points out (and as we have just seen in our brief survey of the use of φυλακή in the NT), 'nowhere in biblical literature is the world of the dead, as such, called φυλακή'.[55] To what, then, does φυλακή refer? A clue to this answer may be found in Jude 6 and 2 Pet. 2:4. In 2 Pet. 2:4 we read that 'God did not spare [the] angels [ἀγγέλων] when they sinned, but cast them into hell [ταρταρώσας] and committed them to chains [σειραῖς] of gloomy darkness, to be kept until judgment'. What was the sin committed by these angels? Jude 6–7 gives us an indication:

> And the angels [ἀγγέλους] who did not keep their own position of authority, but abandoned their own dwelling,[56] he has kept[57]

---

[49] BDAG, 1067.   [50] L&N, 85.85.   [51] Krimmer, *Petrusbrief*, 120.

[52] Bigg, *Epistles of St. Peter*, 163; F. Hauck and S. Schulz, 'πορεύομαι', *TDNT*, 6: 577.

[53] Spicq, *Les Épîtres de Saint Pierre*, 137; Boismard, *Quatre hymnes baptismales*, 79.

[54] Galot, 'La Descente du Christ aux enfers', 475, 480; Vogels, *Christi Abstieg in Totenreich*, 43–4

[55] Dalton, *Christ's Proclamation*, 160.

[56] See *1 En.* 6:5.   [57] See *1 En.* 18:4–6; *2 En.* 7:2.

in eternal chains[58] in gloomy darkness[59] until the judgment of the great day,[60] just as Sodom and Gomorrah and the surrounding cities, which, in the manner as they [τὸν ὅμοιον τρόπον τούτοις], indulged in sexual immorality and pursued unnatural desire.[61]

Jude tells us that these angels are the ones who abandoned their (heavenly) dwelling (ἀπολιπόντας τὸ ἴδιον οἰκητήριον) and engaged in sexual immorality (ἐκπορνεύσασαι καὶ ἀπελθοῦσαι) with human women (ὀπίσω σαρκὸς ἑτέρας). Jude's reference here is clearly dependent on *1 Enoch* (cf. his direct quotation of *1 Enoch* in vv. 14–15). 2 Peter's reference is also from the same Enochian material. The reference in 2 Pet. 2:4 to the sin of the angels and their subsequent 'imprisonment' is then followed in v. 5 by a reference to the flood and the salvation of Noah and his seven family members, paralleling exactly the flow of thought in 1 Pet. 3:19–20:

2 Pet. 2:4–5	1 Pet. 3:19–20	*1 Enoch*
v. 4 The casting of angels who sinned (ἀγγέλων ἁμαρτησάντων) during the time of Noah (cf. Jude 6–7) into hell (ταρταρώσας) where they are committed to chains of darkness (σειραῖς ζόφου παρέδωκεν)	**v. 19** The imprisonment of spirits (ἐν φυλακῇ πνεύμασιν) who once disobeyed (ἀπειθήσασίν ποτε) in the days of Noah (ἐν ἡμέραις Νῶε) when the ark was being built (i.e., just preceding the flood).	**10:4–14; 13:2; 14:5; 18:14; 21:6, 10** The casting of angels, whose transgression (οἱ παραβάντες) inaugurated the evil that led to the flood, into darkness (βάλε εἰς τὸ σκότος) where they are bound in the prison house of the angels (ἐδέθησαν … δεσμωτήριον ἀγγέλων)
v. 5 The salvation of Noah and seven others when God brought the flood upon the earth.	**v. 20** The salvation of Noah and seven others through the flood waters.	**67:1–4; 106:15–18** The salvation of Noah and his sons from the water by means of the ark.

---

[58] See *1 En.* 13:1; 14:5; 54:3–4; 56:1–4; 88:1.
[59] See *1 En.* 10:4–6.   [60] See *1 En.* 10:12.
[61] See *1 En.* 2–5; 106:13–15.

The book of *1 Enoch*, then, is the most probable background, not only for 2 Peter and Jude, but also 1 Pet. 3:19–20. Even though *1 Enoch* does not use the word φυλακή, we do have the motif of the angels being 'bound' (δέω), in 'bonds' (δεσμοί), or in 'prison' (δεσμωτήριον). In *1 Enoch* the fallen angels are variously described as being bound 'hand and foot' (δῆσον ... ποσὶν καὶ χερσίν) and 'cast into the darkness' (βάλε εἰς τὸ σκότος),[62] bound (δῆσον) and led away 'to the prison where they will be confined forever' (εἰς τὸ δεσμωτήριον συνκλείσεως αἰῶνος),[63] bound (δῆσαί σε),[64] 'in bonds in the earth' (ἐν τοῖς δεσμοῖς τῆς γῆς) bound (δῆσαι) 'for all the days of eternity' (εἰς πάσας τὰς γενεὰς τοῦ αἰῶνος),[65] in 'a prison for the stars and the hosts of heaven' (δεσμωτήριον τοῦτο ἐγένετο τοῖς ἄστροις καὶ δυνάμεσιν τοῦ οὐρανοῦ),[66] and 'bound' (ἐδέθησαν) in 'a prison for the angels' where 'they will be confined forever' (δεσμωτήριον ἀγγέλων· ὧδε συνσχεθήσονται μέχρι αἰῶνος εἰς τὸν αἰῶνα).[67]

The location of the 'prison' (φυλακή) has been assigned to various locations in Jewish sources: under the earth (*1 En.* 10:4; 14:5; 15:8, 10; 67:7 *Jub.* 5:6), on the earth (*1 En.* 13:9; 15:8), at the end of both heaven and earth (*1 En.* 18:1–16; 21:1–10), and in the heavens (*1 En.* 7:1–3; 18:3; *2 En.* 7:1–3; *T. Levi* 3:1–3). This latter option best fits our passage. First, we have already seen that Christ's 'going' (πορευθείς = ascension) to the 'spirits in prison' (τοῖς ἐν φυλακῇ πνεύμασιν) is an event which is carried out in conjunction with his ascension. Second, the parallels between B and B´ in our chiasm also suggest that Christ's 'having gone to the spirits in prison' is done in conjunction with his 'having gone into heaven' (πορευθεὶς εἰς οὐρανόν). The thematic parallels may be highlighted as follows:

B 3:19 πορευθεὶς ἐν φυλακῇ ἐκήρυξεν πνεύμασιν
B´ 3:22 πορευθεὶς εἰς οὐρανόν ὑποταγέντων αὐτῷ ἀγγέλων

Christ's heavenly ascent to the spirits in prison is paralleled by a similar journey made by Enoch. In *1 En.* 17–18 Enoch tells of how he was taken and led away to a certain place[68] 'beyond the ends of the earth' where 'the heavens come to an end ... and I saw a great chasm'.[69] Beyond that he saw

a place where there was neither firmament of heaven above, nor firmly founded earth beneath it ... 'This place is the end of

[62] *1 En.* 10:4. [63] *1 En.* 10:12–14. [64] *1 En.* 13:2.
[65] *1 En.* 14:5. [66] *1 En.* 18:14. [67] *1 En.* 21:6, 10.
[68] *1 En.* 17:1. [69] *1 En.* 18:10–11.

heaven and earth; this has become a prison for the stars and the hosts of heaven [δεσμωτήριον τοῦτο ἐγένετο τοῖς ἄστροις καὶ ταῖς δυνάμεσιν τοῦ οὐρανοῦ] ... these are they that transgressed the command of the Lord ... And he was angry with them and bound them [καὶ ὀργίσθη αὐτοῖς καὶ ἔδησεν αὐτούς] until the time of the consummation of their sins – ten thousand years'.[70]

According to the book of *2 Enoch*, the disobedient angelic spirits are imprisoned in the second heaven:

> And those men took me up to the second heaven. And they set me down on the second heaven. And they showed me prisoners under guard, in measureless judgment. And there I saw the condemned angels, weeping. And I said to the men who were with me, 'Why are they tormented?' The men answered me, 'They are evil rebels against the Lord, who did not listen to the voice of the Lord, but they consulted their own will'.[71]

That this is the most likely background for our 1 Peter passage can be seen from the final element of this picture: the *proclamation* (ἐκήρυξεν) made by Christ to these imprisoned spirits who once disobeyed God.

ἐκήρυξεν (v. 19)

The aorist active indicative ἐκήρυξεν is the only finite verb in vv. 19–20a and so expresses the main thought of this passage.[72] The sequence of events presented by the preceding participles (θανατωθείς, ζωοποιηθείς, πορευθείς) makes it clear that this proclamation is carried out in conjunction with the ascension of Christ into heaven:[73]

θανατωθείς	('having been put to death')	= crucifixion
ζωοποιηθείς	('having been made alive')	= resurrection
πορευθείς	('having gone' = v. 22)	= ascension
ἐκήρυξεν	**('he proclaimed')**	**= proclamation**

What seems clear from this verse is (1) the proclamation was made by Christ, (2) it was made in conjunction with his resurrection and ascension (and therefore not in conjunction with a descent between his death and resurrection), and (3) the recipients of this proclamation are the spirits who disobeyed in the days preceding the flood (τοῖς ἐν φυλακῇ

---

[70] *1 En.* 18:12–16.   [71] *2 En.* 7:1–3.
[72] Elliott, *1 Peter*, 659.   [73] Ibid.

πνεύμασιν ἀπειθήσασίν). What is not immediately clear is the actual content of that proclamation.

The verb κηρύσσω ('make proclamation as a herald'; related to the nouns κῆρυξ ['herald', 'public messenger, envoy', 'crier'][74] and κήρυγμα ['that which is cried by a herald, proclamation', 'announcement'])[75] was widely used in the Greco-Roman world to denote 'the activity of the herald in the discharge of his office'[76] and carried the basic meaning of 'to proclaim', 'to announce', 'to declare'.[77] κηρύσσω appears thirty-two times in the LXX (with the nouns κῆρυξ ['herald, crier'] and κήρυγμα ['proclamation, message'] appearing four times each) rendering a variety of Hebrew terms (but most frequently קָרָא, 'call, proclaim',[78] 'cry [aloud]'[79]).

The verb κηρύσσω appears sixty-one times (κῆρυξ [3×]; κήρυγμα [9×]) in the New Testament and carries the same basic meaning of 'to make public declarations, proclaim aloud' (1 Pet. 3:19; Mt. 10:27; Lk. 12:3; Rom. 2:21; Rev. 5:2). Other than these few references, κηρύσσω is normally associated in the New Testament with the proclamation of the εὐαγγέλιον ('gospel', or 'the good news of salvation'). Because it is normally associated with the proclamation of the gospel in the New Testament, many commentators assume that this is in fact what Peter is referring to in 3:19. This is strengthened, it is felt, by the fact that εὐαγγελίζω appears in 4:6 (εὐηγγελίσθη), a verse that a number of commentators both associate with and interpret in the light of 3:19.[80] Yet, as we will see below, while there is a correspondence between 3:18 and 4:6, there is no demonstrable correspondence between 3:19 and 4:6. Instead, it is better to allow κηρύσσω here to have its more neutral sense of 'proclaim', 'announce', with no reference to the proclamation of the good news (salvation).

What, then, is the content of this proclamation? There is good reason to believe that Peter is not referring to a proclamation of salvation to these disobedient spirits but to a proclamation of judgment and victory over them. Three arguments can be put forward to defend this interpretation. First, the correspondence between the two occurrences of πορευ-θείς (vv. 19, 22) and the correspondence between the πνεύμασιν of

---

[74] LSJ, 949.   [75] LSJ, 949.

[76] G. Friedrich, 'κηρύσσω', *TDNT*, 3: 697.

[77] Homer, *Il.* 2.438; Aeschylus, *Eum.* 566; Xenophon, *Anab.* 3.4; Plutarch, *Mor.* 2.185a; Sophocles, *El.* 606; Aeschines, *Tim.* 3.246; Euripides, *Hec.* 530; Aristotle, *Ath. pol.* 4.19.

[78] BDB, 894–5.   [79] G. Friedrich, 'κηρύσσω', *TDNT*, 3: 700.

[80] Boismard, *Quatre hymnes baptismales*, 64–5; Krimmer, *Petrusbrief*, 121.

v. 19 and the ἀγγέλων of v. 22 in our chiasm suggest one further parallel between these two verses:

B 3:19 πορευθεὶς ἐν φυλακῇ   **ἐκήρυξεν**   πνεύμασιν
  C 3:20 διεσώθησαν   δι' ὕδατος
  C´ 3:21 σῴζει βάπτισμα   δι' ἀναστάσεως Ἰησοῦ Χριστοῦ
B´ 3:22 πορευθεὶς εἰς οὐρανόν **ὑποταγέντων αὐτῷ** ἀγγέλων

The parallelism between B and B´ would seem to suggest that B should be interpreted in light of B´. That is, Christ's proclamation in v. 19 (B) should be interpreted in light of his subordination of 'angels and authorities and powers' in v. 22 (B´). Since Christ's subordination of the angels, authorities, and powers is the final confirmation of their condemnation, then his proclamation of v. 19 should be seen as having the same content – condemnation of and victory over the evil spirits.

Second, it is interesting to note that when Peter wants to talk about the proclamation of the gospel he uses the word εὐαγγελίζω ('proclaim the divine message of salvation', 'proclaim the gospel'; generally, 'bring good news', 'announce good news').[81] Peter uses this verb in 1:12, 25, and 4:6 (two references before and one reference after our text, 3:19):

  1:12 ἃ νῦν ἀνηγγέλη ὑμῖν διὰ τῶν **εὐαγγελισαμένων**
  1:25 τοῦτο δέ ἐστιν τὸ ῥῆμα τὸ **εὐαγγελισθὲν**
  3:19 [τοῖς ἐν φυλακῇ πνεύμασιν] [**ἐκήρυξεν**]
  4:6 νεκροῖς   **εὐηγγελίσθη**

This naturally raises the following question: Why has Peter used εὐαγγελίζω three times (1:12, 25; 4:6) to denote the preaching of the gospel, but then suddenly changed to κηρύσσω (which has a broader semantic range) in 3:19 if in fact he wanted to say that this was also another instance of the preaching of the gospel? If Peter had wanted to unambiguously communicate that this was another instance of the preaching of the gospel, then surely he would have employed his favoured term εὐαγγελίζω a fourth time instead of changing to κηρύσσω only here (or at least he would have qualified κηρύσσω). By changing from εὐαγγελίζω to κηρύσσω in this verse Peter seems to be indicating that this is a different type of proclamation (here a proclamation of judgment and victory).

Third, this interpretation of κηρύσσω is supported in the LXX and *1 Enoch* (which we have now established as the most important

[81] BDAG, 402.

conceptual background for 1 Pet. 3:19–20). Like 1 Pet. 3:19, the book of Jonah uses both πορεύομαι ('to go' [3×]) along with κηρύσσω ('to proclaim' [3×]) to refer to God's commissioning of Jonah to go to Nineveh and to proclaim to them a message (κήρυγμα, Jon. 3:2) of judgment and doom because of their 'wickedness' (τῆς κακίας, Jon. 1:2 = ἀπειθήσασιν, 1 Pet. 3:20).

Once again, however, the most important conceptual background for Christ's proclamation to the disobedient spirits is *1 Enoch*. Even though *1 Enoch* does not use the word κηρύσσω (it generally uses πορεύομαι with εἶπον, e.g., 12:4 [πορεύου καὶ εἶπε]; 13:1 [εἶπεν πορεύου]; 13:3 [πορευθεὶς εἴρηκα]; 15:2 [πορεύθητι καὶ εἶπε]), we do have the motif of Enoch undertaking a journey to heaven,[82] during the course of which he went (was sent by God)[83] to the evil angel spirits or 'Watchers' (in the second heaven in *2 Enoch* 7) and announced to them their condemnation and doom (*1 Enoch* 12:4–6; 13:1–10; 14:1–7; 15:1–16). God's words to Enoch are:

> Enoch, righteous scribe, go and say [πορεύου καὶ εἶπε] to the watchers of heaven [τοῖς ἐγρηγόροις τοῦ οὐράνου] – who forsook the highest heaven, the sanctuary of the(ir) eternal station, and defiled themselves with women. As the sons of earth do, so they did and took wives for themselves. And they wrought great desolation on the earth – 'You will have no peace or forgiveness'.[84]

In obedience to God's command Enoch first went to Asael, the leader of the fallen angels, and announced God's judgment to him: 'And, Enoch, go and say [εἶπεν πορεύου] to Asael, "You will have no peace. A great sentence [κρίμα μέγα] has gone forth against you, to bind you [δῆσαί σε]".'[85] Then he proceeded to address all of the fallen angels: 'Then I went and spoke [πορευθεὶς εἴρηκα] to all of them together. And they were all afraid, and trembling and fear seized them.'[86] Once again the message was a message of judgment: '[F]rom now on you will not ascend into heaven for all the ages; and it has been decreed to bind you in bonds in the earth for all the days of eternity [ἐν τοῖς δεσμοῖς τῆς γῆς ἐρρέθη δῆσαι ὑμᾶς εἰς πάσας τὰς γενεὰς τοῦ αἰῶνος].'[87] Just as Enoch was sent by God to announce to the evil angelic spirits or 'Watchers' their condemnation and doom, so Peter presents Christ as the new Enoch (or

---

[82] *1 En.* 14–15; *2 En.* 7.   [83] *1 En.* 15:2.   [84] *1 En.* 12:4–5.
[85] *1 En.* 13:1–2.   [86] *1 En.* 13:3.   [87] *1 En.* 14:5; see also *Jub.* 5.

the antitype of which Enoch is the type), as going and proclaiming to the evil spirits his victory and their condemnation.

The vindication of Christ: exaltation (v. 22)

1 Peter 3:18–22 reaches a climax in v. 22 with its mention of Christ's ascension into heaven (v. 22b), exaltation to the right hand of God (v. 22a), and superiority over the cosmic powers (v. 22c). Mention of Christ's ascent into heaven (πορευθεὶς εἰς οὐρανόν) recalls v. 19 where the same verb (πορεύομαι) was used to refer to Christ's heavenly journey and proclamation to the imprisoned spirits (τοῖς ἐν φυλακῇ πνεύμασιν πορευθεὶς ἐκήρυξεν). Peter again picks up this word πορευθείς ('having gone') in order to spell out further implications of Christ's resurrection. The immediate implications of Christ's resurrection (v. 21d) and ascension (v. 22b) are expressed in the two clauses that frame the participial expression πορευθεὶς εἰς οὐρανόν (v. 22b):

> A. ὅς ἐστιν ἐν δεξιᾷ [τοῦ] θεοῦ (v. 22a)
> **B. πορευθεὶς εἰς οὐρανόν** (v. 22b)
> C. ὑποταγέντων αὐτῷ ἀγγέλων καὶ ἐξουσιῶν καὶ δυνάμεων (v. 22c)

Framing the reference to Christ's 'ascension into heaven' (B) is mention of his exaltation (A) and his subjugation of the cosmic powers (C):

> A. Exaltation
> **B. Ascension**
> C. Subjugation

This dislocation of the normal order (viz. ascension→exaltation) is possibly due to the author's desire to express the following two implications of Christ's resurrection–ascension: (1) his divine vindication and exaltation at the right hand of God (A) and (2) the subjugation of cosmic powers to the resurrected and exalted Christ (C). This concluding stress on Christ's resurrection (v. 21d), ascension (v. 22b), exaltation (v. 22a), and subjugation of cosmic powers (v. 22c), together with the earlier mention of his resurrection (v. 18e), ascension (v. 19), and victorious proclamation over the disobedient angelic spirits (v. 19) sets this entire passage (vv. 18–22) within the context of these glorious events. This suggests that the function of vv. 18–22 is to explain the implications of these events for both the evil spirits (subjugation and condemnation) and suffering believers (victory and vindication), but with the emphasis on the latter (as we will now see in 4:1–6).

2. 1 Peter 4:1–6: the suffering and vindication of believers

Context

Having established the divine vindication of Christ through innocent suffering (3:18–22), Peter returns once more to the fact of Christ's suffering (v. 18a) and death (v. 18d) as a model (4:1ab, 6b) for innocent suffering 'in the flesh' (v. 1c), and his vindication by God (3:18e, 19, 21d, 22) as the assurance that those who suffer innocently as Christians will enjoy future vindication (salvation) by God (v. 6c). As we will see, the language of vv. 1 and 6 in this passage recalls that of 3:18, indicating a relationship not only with that verse but the entire discussion growing out of it. At the same time, 4:1–6 is distinguished from 3:18–22 by its hortatory style as Peter seeks to develop the moral and soteriological implications of the latter for his readers.

Content

The innocent suffering of believers (4:1–4)

The idea of the believer's identification with Christ in suffering (cf. also 2:18–20, 21–5) now receives explicit emphasis in the opening words of this passage: Χριστοῦ οὖν παθόντος σαρκὶ καὶ ὑμεῖς τὴν αὐτὴν ἔννοιαν ὁπλίσασθε ('therefore, since Christ suffered in the flesh, you also [must] arm yourselves with the same way of thinking', 4:1ab). Having ended the previous section (3:18–22) with the glorious outcome of Christ's suffering (v. 22), Peter now brings his readers back to the theme of v. 18 in order to highlight the point he now wants to apply to their lives: 'Christ suffered in the flesh' (Χριστοῦ οὖν παθόντος). The inferential conjunction οὖν ('therefore') at the beginning of v. 1 resumes the thought of v. 18 regarding Christ's innocent suffering (as the genitive absolute construction indicates) and seeks to draw a conclusion from it. 1 Peter 3:18 and 4:1 appear to form an *inclusio*, suggesting the possibility that Peter wants to draw a conclusion from the entire previous section (3:18–22). If that is the case, the description of Christ's innocent suffering followed by divine vindication in 3:18–22 is meant to strengthen the resolve of his readers, who should also prepare themselves for suffering (4:1–4, 6b) knowing that suffering is the pathway to eschatological reward (4:6c). While it is true that Peter will develop the implications of both Christ's suffering *and* vindication for believers (4:6bc), the focus in v. 1 is more directly related to the connection between the innocent suffering of Christ (3:18) and the innocent suffering of believers (4:1). This is indicated by the repeated use of πάσχω and σάρξ in 3:18ad and 4:1a and c:

3:18ad	Χριστὸς...	ἔπαθεν... θανατωθεὶς	σαρκί
4:1a	Χριστοῦ οὖν	παθόντος	σαρκί
4:1c	ὅτι ὁ	παθὼν	σαρκί

In each case, σάρξ is a dative of respect (lit., 'with respect to the flesh') modifying the foregoing participle and denoting the human mode of existence in which Christ, and consequently his followers, suffer. As Achtemeier notes, 'the qualifying σαρκί points to Christ's human suffering, and reminds the readers that Christ shares a fate exemplary for, and, because it was human suffering, comparable to the kind of suffering they undergo at the hands of their hostile contemporaries'.[88]

The emphatic καί ὑμεῖς ('you also') that now follows begins Peter's exhortation to his readers in which he encourages them to follow the example of Christ: **καὶ ὑμεῖς** τὴν αὐτὴν ἔννοιαν ὁπλίσασθε ('**you also** [must] arm yourselves with the same way of thinking'). Once again the experience of Christ serves as a paradigm for believers. This correspondence between the experience of Christ and the experience of believers receives emphasis from the words καί ὑμεῖς ('you also') and αὐτήν ('same'). The verb ὁπλίσασθε ('arm yourselves with'), found only here in the New Testament, is the verbal counterpart of ὁπλίτης ('heavy armed soldier, warrior', Num. 32:21)[89] and ὅπλον ('weapon', Jn 18:3; cf. its metaphorical use in Rom. 13:12; 2 Cor. 6:7; 10:4).[90] The figure of arming oneself employs a military metaphor to describe the struggle of the Christian life (the use of military metaphors is quite common to the NT[91] and Greco-Roman philosophy[92]). As the remainder of the passage will reveal, 'the martial language indicates that discipline and grit are needed to live the Christian life, particularly in view of the suffering believers encounter'.[93]

Peter then indicates what it is that believers should arm themselves with: τὴν αὐτὴν ἔννοιαν ('the same mind'). The noun ἔννοια ('thought, knowledge, insight'),[94] an accusative of thing (content), is found in the New Testament only here and in Heb. 4:12 (plural). In the LXX, ἔννοια occurs fourteen times and is a favourite word in Proverbs (12×) where it

---

[88] Achtemeier, *1 Peter*, 277.   [89] LEH, 441; LSJ, 1239.
[90] See BDAG, 716; Robertson, *Word Pictures*, 121.
[91] See, e.g., 1 Pet. 2:11; Lk. 11:22; Rom. 6:13; 2 Cor. 6:7; Eph. 6:11–17; 1 Thess. 5:8.
[92] See, e.g., Plato, *Apol.* 28d.5–29a.1; Seneca, *Ep.* 59.7–8.
[93] Schreiner, *1 Peter*, 199.   [94] BDAG, 337.

occurs with the sense of 'consideration', 'insight', 'perception', 'under-standing', or 'thinking'. It is used to render a number of Hebrew words: מְזִמָּה ('purpose, discretion, device', Prov. 1:4; 3:22), בִּינָה ('understand-ing', 4:1; 23:4), תְּבוּנָה ('understanding', 2:11), שֵׂכֶל ('prudence, insight', 16:22), and דַּעַת ('knowledge', 18:15). In addition, it is coupled with such terms as βουλή ('counsel, advice, plan, decision', 2:11; 3:21; 8:12), παιδεία ('teaching, instruction', 4:1; 16:22), σοφία ('wisdom', 24:7), σοφός ('clever, prudent, wise', 23:19), φρόνιμος ('understand-ing, prudent, wise', 18:15), and αἴσθησις ('perception, knowledge', 5:2; 18:15). Both the noun (ἔννοια) and the verb ἐννοέω ('have in mind, consider') are related to νοῦς ('mind, intelligence, attitude, understand-ing') and, along with other such terms in 1 Peter as διάνοια ('mind', 1:13) and ἄγνοια ('ignorance', 1:14), express 'the cognitive dimension of behaviour'.[95] As its use in Proverbs indicates, the cognitive activity indicated by ἔννοια has less to do with concepts and ideas (as in the philosophical use of ἔννοια) and more to do with 'intention or dispos-ition in the sphere of moral actions'.[96]

The identifying adjective αὐτήν ('same'), in conjunction with the emphatic καὶ ὑμεῖς ('you also'), indicates that the 'understanding', 'insight', or, perhaps even better, 'intention' that believers are to arm themselves with should correspond to that of Christ. The premise for this exhortation can be found in the previous statement (v. 1a), where the word παθόντος ('suffered') gives us a clue as to what this 'understanding' or 'intention' should consist in. The aorist participle παθόντος is causal and so indicates the *reason* or *ground* for the action of the imperative ὁπλίσασθε ('arm yourselves with').[97] Hence v. 1ab should be translated 'since [or perhaps better, "because"][98] Christ suffered, you also must arm yourselves with the same intention'. Basically what Peter is saying is this: *because Christ* suffered, *you also* should be mentally prepared to suffer. 'Once again an inseparable connection is affirmed between the suffering of Christ and the suffering of his followers.'[99] The main point of this verse, then, is that those who want to follow Christ must arm themselves with the intention to suffer, the implication being that just as Christ suffered in obedience to the will of God, so also will Christians.

[95] Elliott, *1 Peter*, 713.   [96] Achtemeier, *1 Peter*, 277.
[97] See Robertson, *Grammar*, 1128; Wallace, *Greek Grammar*, 631–2.
[98] See Wallace, *Greek Grammar*, 631.
[99] Elliott, *1 Peter*, 712 (see 2:18–20/21–25; 3:13–17/18–22).

The final clause of v. 1 (v. 1c), along with vv. 2–3, indicates that it is obedience to God's will (v. 2b) that leads to suffering (vv. 1c, 4, 6b). The ὅτι at the beginning of v. 1c is most probably causal ('because') giving the reason for what precedes: ὅτι ὁ παθὼν σαρκὶ πέπαυται ἁμαρτίας ('*because* the one having suffered with respect to the flesh has ceased from sin'). That is, believers are to arm themselves with the intention to suffer *because* the one having suffered with respect to the flesh has ceased from sin. But what exactly does Peter mean by this phrase? A number of interpretations have been offered. First, a number of commentators have suggested that 'the one having suffered' is Christ himself.[100] Michaels interprets the phrase πέπαυται ἁμαρτίας as ' "is through with sin" in the sense that he [Christ] has finished dealing with it, once and for all; he has put it behind him, says Peter, and so should we'.[101] However, (1) it is syntactically more likely that believers, and not Christ, are the subject of the participle, and (2) 4:1–6, as we noted above, is to be distinguished from 3:18–22 by its hortatory style as Peter seeks to develop the moral and soteriological implications of the latter for his readers (thus the focus is believers and not Christ).[102]

Second, the one 'having suffered' is a reference to the believers' metaphorical 'death' in baptism.[103] Feldmeier suggests '[d]ie für den 1Petr ungewöhnliche Rede von der Sünde im Singular macht es wahrscheinlich, dass es sich hier um die Reformulierung paulinischer Gedanken handelt, wie sie der Apostel etwa in Röm 6,1–11 entfaltet: Durch die Taufe partizipieren die Glaubenden am Tod Jesu und werden so als Gestorbene von der Sünde frei.'[104] This interpretation, however, should be rejected on three grounds: (1) Peter is speaking of actual physical suffering and not metaphorical death in baptism;[105] (2) Peter consistently uses the word ἁμαρτία to denote concrete acts of sin (cf. 2:22, 24; 3:18; 4:8) and not, as in Paul, a power that controls humans;[106] and (3) as the context indicates (4:2–4), Peter is talking about ceasing (πέπαυται) from concrete sinful behaviour, and not liberation from the power of sin.[107]

---

[100] See Strobel, 'Macht Leiden von Sünden frei?', 419; Thurén, *Argument and Theology*, 166.
[101] Michaels, *1 Peter*, 228.
[102] See Elliott, *1 Peter*, 711; Jobes, *1 Peter*, 263–4; Michaels, *1 Peter*, 225.
[103] See Spicq, *Les Épîtres de Saint Pierre*, 144; Feldmeier, *Brief des Petrus*, 141.
[104] Feldmeier, *Brief des Petrus*, 141.
[105] Elliott, *1 Peter*, 716; Achtemeier, *1 Peter*, 279.
[106] See the discussion in Chapter 3.
[107] Elliott, *1 Peter*, 716; Wallace, *Greek Grammar*, 109.

Third, some scholars see here a reference to 'the purifying effect on the spirit of bodily suffering'.[108] As a proverb, the clause would carry the idea that innocent suffering purifies the sufferer from sin. While this explanation is attractive, it does however raise some doubts: (1) It is difficult to see how this interpretation fits the immediate context. The aim of this passage (3:18–4:6) is not to offer teaching on the purifying value of suffering (which would be to insert an entirely new and unrelated thought into this passage), but to remind believers that their suffering is an indication of their solidarity with Christ who also suffered innocently (and therefore to give certain evidence of their break with a life of sin). (2) The notion that suffering is a necessarily purifying experience has rightly been called into question by some commentators.[109] (3) The consistent message of 1 Peter is that the suffering and death of Christ deals with the problem of sin, not human suffering.[110] Hence, it is unlikely that this phrase bears that meaning here.

What, then, does Peter mean by the phrase ὁ παθὼν σαρκὶ πέπαυται ἁμαρτία? The immediate context provides the best clue. The inseparable connection between the suffering of Christ and the suffering of believers indicated in this verse (and elsewhere in 1 Peter)[111] suggests that those who, like Christ, are committed to following God's will (θελήματι θεοῦ, v. 2b) and not human desires (ἀνθρώπων ἐπιθυμίαις, v. 2a) will suffer. Therefore, says Peter, 'the one having suffered … has ceased from sin'. That is to say, suffering, in this context, is an indication (or evidence) that a person has broken with sin (πέπαυται ἁμαρτίας); that is, their behaviour is no longer ruled by sinful human desires (ἀνθρώπων ἐπιθυμίαις) but by the will of God (θελήματι θεοῦ).[112] In this verse, then, Peter is calling upon believers to arm themselves with a mental readiness to suffer, because if, like Christ, they are committed to following God's will, then, like Christ, they too will suffer. Suffering, then, is a sign of their solidarity with Christ, and for that reason they must be prepared to suffer.

The believers' purpose (εἰς τὸ … βιῶσαι) in arming themselves with such an understanding (v. 1c) is then stated in v. 2: εἰς τὸ μηκέτι ἀνθρώπων ἐπιθυμίαις ἀλλὰ θελήματι θεοῦ τὸν ἐπίλοιπον ἐν σαρκὶ βιῶσαι χρόνον ('so as to live out the remaining time in the flesh no

---

[108] Selwyn, *First Epistle of St. Peter*, 209.
[109] See Jobes, *1 Peter*, 264; Selwyn, *First Epistle of St. Peter*, 209.
[110] See 1:3–4, 18–20; 2:24; 3:18.
[111] See 1 Pet. 2:18–20/21–25; 3:13–17/18–22; 3:18/4:1, 6.
[112] See Jobes, *1 Peter*, 265.

longer according to human desires but according to the will of God'). Christians are to arm themselves with an intention to suffer for the purpose of being able to live out (βιῶσαι) the remainder of their time (τὸν ἐπίλοιπον ... χρόνον) governed no longer by human desires (μηκέτι ἀνθρώπων ἐπιθυμίαις) but by the will of God (ἀλλὰ θελήματι θεοῦ). Conversely, those who do not arm themselves with an intention to suffer will probably not be prepared to live out their lives for the will of God because, as v. 4 indicates, such a commitment will probably entail suffering.

The contrasting datives [ἀνθρώπων] ἐπιθυμίαις ('human desires') and θελήματι [θεοῦ] ('will of God') are most probably datives of rule (in conformity with)[113] denoting two 'opposing standards that govern the believers' lives before and after conversion'.[114] The phrase μηκέτι ἀνθρώπων ἐπιθυμίαις ('no longer according to human desires', 4:2) recalls an earlier use of ἐπιθυμία ('desire, longing, craving, lust' [in the negative sense])[115] where it once again denotes those desires that characterised the Petrine readers before their conversion: ταῖς πρότερον ἐν τῇ ἀγνοίᾳ ὑμῶν ἐπιθυμίαις ('the desires of your former ignorance', 1:14). In the following verse (v. 3) Peter will give a representative list of sins typical of a life lived in accord with 'human desires' (ἀνθρώπων ἐπιθυμίαις). The phrase ἀλλὰ θελήματι θεοῦ ('but according to the will of God'), recalling the earlier expression ἀλλὰ κατὰ τὸν καλέσαντα ὑμᾶς ἅγιον ('but in conformity with the Holy One who called you', 1:15), indicates the standard that they are to live in conformity with. The point is, Christians are to live out their lives in conformity with God's will despite the suffering that may result from such a commitment.

The γάρ ('for') at the beginning of v. 3 then explains why believers should live out their remaining time in the flesh for the will of God (τὸ ... θελήματι θεοῦ τὸν ἐπίλοιπον ἐν σαρκὶ βιῶσαι χρόνον). The reason is because they have already spent 'more than enough' (ἀρκετὸς ... χρόνος) time in the past 'carrying out the will of the Gentiles' (τὸ βούλημα τῶν ἐθνῶν κατειργάσθαι). Goppelt aptly notes that the phrase ' "the will of the Gentiles" (τὸ βούλημα τῶν ἐθνῶν) manifests itself especially in those forms of social and religious custom that become requirements through the power of habit and the pressure for conformity'.[116] The list of vices that follows enumerates the types of conduct characteristic of a lifestyle opposed to the will of God: πεπορευμένους ἐν ἀσελγείαις

---

[113] Selwyn, *First Epistle of St. Peter*, 210.   [114] Elliott, *1 Peter*, 719.
[115] BDAG, 372.   [116] Goppelt, *1 Peter*, 284.

('live licentiously'),[117] ἐπιθυμίαις ('cravings, lusts'),[118] οἰνοφλυγίαις ('drunkenness'),[119] κώμοις ('excessive feasting, revelry'),[120] πότοις ('drinking parties, carousing'),[121] καὶ ἀθεμίτοις εἰδωλολατρίαις ('and unlawful idolatries').[122] Goppelt notes that 'the whole catalogue [of v. 3b] is not one of "vices" on the edge of society, but of the social and religious lifestyle of society as a whole. By renouncing this way of life, Christians remove themselves from the life in society that they have shared before.'[123]

The consequence of this cultural non-participation by Christians is now stated in v. 4. The relative construction ἐν ᾧ (lit., 'in which') which begins v. 4 is probably causal and refers back to the situation described in the previous verses (vv. 2–3) explaining why the Christians' pagan contemporaries are 'surprised'. As such, ἐν ᾧ, in this context, can be rendered 'therefore', 'because of this', or 'for which reason'. As Achtemeier observes, the ἐν ᾧ is also anticipatory of the genitive absolute phrase μὴ συντρεχόντων ὑμῶν κτλ. ('you do not join with etc.').[124] The verb συντρέχω ('run together, go with'), used figuratively here, indicates the cause of the surprise: μὴ συντρεχόντων ὑμῶν εἰς τὴν αὐτὴν τῆς ἀσωτίας ἀνάχυσιν ('you do not join with them in the same flood of dissipation'). The words τὴν αὐτὴν τῆς ἀσωτίας ἀνάχυσιν provide an apt summary of the vices listed in the previous verse. The noun ἀνάχυσις (found only here in the NT) literally means 'pouring out' (cf. ἀναχέω, 'pour out') and is used here as a 'figurative description of immoral behaviour' with the more active sense of 'flood' or 'wild outpouring (of dissipation)'.[125] The noun ἀσωτία ('debauchery, dissipation, prolificacy'; cf. also Eph. 5:18; Tit. 1:6)[126] is summarised by Foerster as 'wild and disorderly living'.[127] Together, these terms describe the unrestrained excesses involved in the vices enumerated in v. 3.

The believers' disassociation from these former practices provokes a twofold reaction from their unbelieving contemporaries. First, they are described as being 'surprised' (ξενίζονται). This surprise is not mere 'amazement', but astonishment with the overtone of resentment and hostility. That this is so can be seen by the second reaction (which is related to the first): 'they malign [you]' (βλασφημοῦντες). When used in relation to humans βλασφημέω can mean 'slander, revile, defame', or

---

[117] BDAG, 141.　[118] BDAG, 372.　[119] BDAG, 701.
[120] BDAG, 580.　[121] BDAG, 857.　[122] BDAG, 280.
[123] Goppelt, *1 Peter*, 285.　[124] Achtemeier, *1 Peter*, 283.
[125] Elliott, *1 Peter*, 726.　[126] BDAG, 148.
[127] W. Foerster, 'ἄσωτος, ἀσωτία', *TDNT*, 1: 507.

'malign'.[128] When God is the object of this verb it is generally rendered 'blaspheme' (i.e., 'speak irreverently/impiously/disrespectfully of or about').[129] While a number of commentators understand βλασφημοῦντες as a reference to blaspheming God,[130] the immediate and broader context[131] of 1 Peter suggests that Peter is speaking of the verbal abuse that is directed against Christians for their cultural nonparticipation. βλασφημοῦντες, then, is an adverbial (or circumstantial) participle and is to be translated as a main verb: 'they are astonished and they malign you'. This verse provides us with an important key for understanding the nature of the persecution alluded to in 1 Peter. The difficulties being experienced by many of the Petrine readers resulted not from an official policy of state-organised persecution, but instead involved various forms of social persecution beginning with astonishment and suspicion and leading to resentment, ostracism, verbal abuse, and perhaps in isolated cases more serious forms of persecution.

The vindication of suffering believers (4:5–6)

The parenetic material contained in vv. 1–4 exhorted believers to arm themselves with the intention to suffer just as Christ suffered (4:1), because the decision to suffer shows that they are prepared to live in conformity with the will of God (v. 2) rather than the expectations of contemporary culture (vv. 2–3). This decision to break with their pagan past astonished their nonbelieving contemporaries, whose astonishment quickly turned to slander (βλασφημοῦντες, v. 4), criticism, and condemnation (κριθῶσι, v. 6b). However, at the final judgment there will be a great reversal. Even though the believer may have been the object of an unfavourable and unjust judgment against them by unbelievers (κριθῶσι κατὰ ἀνθρώπους, v. 6b), God will have the final say at the eschatological judgment when he passes an unfavourable but just judgment on the oppressor (οἳ ἀποδώσουσιν λόγον τῷ ἑτοίμως ἔχοντι κρῖναι, v. 5) but honours and vindicates the believer (ζῶσι δὲ κατὰ θεὸν πνεύματι, v. 6c).

Condemnation for the oppressor (v. 5)

Those who malign believers will be judged on the last day. The formulation ἀποδώσουσιν λόγον ('give an account')[132] has eschatological overtones and recalls similar expressions in the New Testament (Mt.

---

[128] BDAG, 178.   [129] BDAG, 178.   [130] BDAG, 178.
[131] See 2:12; 3:9, 14, 16; 4:14, 16.   [132] BDAG, 110.

12:36; Rom. 14:12). The statement in v. 5 forms a foil to v. 6b where the word κρίνω appears again but this time with reference to the negative assessment of believers by nonbelievers. The flow of thought proceeds as follows:

> Divine judgment on unbelievers (4:5)
> Judgment of believers by unbelievers (4:6b; cf. v. 4)
> Divine vindication of believers (4:6c)

The unfavourable and unjust judgment of believers by unbelievers is sandwiched between two statements pointing to the ultimate and definitive judgment of God. At the final judgment there will an 'eschatological turning of the tables':[133] those who sought to pass a negative judgment on believers in this life (4:6b) will soon be the recipients of a negative judgment themselves (v. 5). On the other hand, those believers who have been maligned and judged by humans in this life (v. 6b; cf. v. 4) will enjoy divine vindication at the day of judgment (v. 6c). The one to whom account is to be rendered is described as τῷ ἑτοίμως ἔχοντι κρῖναι ζῶντας καὶ νεκρούς ('the one ready to judge the living and the dead'). The stereotypical expression ζῶντας καὶ νεκρούς, a reference to the final judgment, underscores the universality of this judgment from which none – whether the physically alive or the physically dead – will be exempt. In the context of this passage (4:1–6), Peter's statement provides his readers with the assurance that their persecutors (cf. vv. 3–4) will not escape God's just judgment.

Vindication for the believer (v. 6)

This verse (v. 6) is linked to the previous (v. 5) by the inferential conjunction γάρ ('for, therefore'), and also by the words καί ('also'), κρίνω ('judge', vv. 5, 6b) and νεκρός ('dead', vv. 5, 6a). The words εἰς τοῦτο, on the other hand, point forward to the ἵνα ('so that') clause and indicate the purpose ('for this reason', 'to this end') for which 'the gospel was proclaimed to the dead' (νεκροῖς εὐηγγελίσθη). The ultimate purpose for which the gospel was proclaimed to them was so that (ἵνα + subjunctive ζῶσι) its recipients might enjoy resurrection life (ζῶσι δὲ κατὰ θεὸν πνεύματι). The inference (denoted by the inferential γάρ) to be drawn from v. 5, then, is this:

premise: (v. 5)   God is the judge of the living and the
                        dead

---

[133] A phrase borrowed from Elliott, *1 Peter*, 729.

> **conclusion:** (v. 6)   therefore (γάρ) the 'believing dead' (i.e.
> those who responded positively to the
> gospel during their lifetime but have
> since died) can be assured that they will
> receive a favourable verdict (i.e., be
> vindicated by God) at the judgment.

Two initial conclusions about the 'dead' can be drawn from the immediate context: (1) The use of the word νεκροί in both vv. 5 and 6 suggests that the 'dead' of v. 6 are in some way related to the 'dead' of v. 5. Since νεκροί refers to the physically dead in v. 5, it should probably be understood to carry the same meaning here in v. 6. (2) While νεκροί in v. 5 is a reference to the dead in general, the νεκροί of v. 6 should be understood as a subset of this group. There νεκροῖς is the object of the aorist passive εὐηγγελίσθη and the implied subject of ζῶσι ('they might live') in the purpose/result clause indicating that the 'dead' must be limited to those who are the recipients of the gospel and the life it confers. The question is, when did they hear and respond to the gospel? While a number of commentators see here a reference to the preaching of the gospel to the dead *while in a state of death* (i.e., as disembodied souls in Hades),[134] it is more likely, for contextual reasons (see below), that Peter is referring to a group from among the letter's addressees who heard and responded to the gospel during their lifetime but had since died (again see below).

There are, nevertheless, a considerable number of commentators who insist on seeing a correspondence between the proclamation of the gospel to the dead (νεκροῖς εὐηγγελίσθη) in 4:6 and Christ's proclamation to the imprisoned spirits (τοῖς ἐν φυλακῇ πνεύμασιν ἐκήρυξεν) in 3:19.[135] Cranfield remarks, 'by far the most likely explanation is that there is a reference back to 3:19, and the νεκροί of 4:6 are to be identified with the πνεύματα of 3:19 … and that εὐηγγελίσθη refers to the preaching [ἐκήρυξεν] by Christ which is spoken of in 3:19'.[136]

The differences between 3:19 and 4:6, however, are quite substantial, making such an identification very unlikely. (1) I have argued that the proclamation (denoted by ἐκήρυξεν) made in 3:19 is one of condemnation, while in 4:6 it is clearly the 'good news' (εὐηγγελίσθη) leading to resurrection life (ἵνα … ζῶσι δὲ κατὰ θεὸν πνεύματι). (2) The

---

[134] See Horrell, 'Interpretation of 1 Pet. 4.6', 70–89.

[135] Klumbies, 'Die Verkündigung unter Geistern und Toten', 223; Feldmeier, *Brief des Petrus*, 144; Vogels, *Christi Abstieg in Totenreich*, 81, 142–59; Windisch, *Die katholischen Briefe*, 75.

[136] Cranfield, 'The Interpretation of 1 Peter 3:19 and 4:6', 371.

πνεύμασιν of 3:19, I have argued, are not the souls of deceased humans, but malevolent supernatural beings whose disobedience, according to early Jewish tradition, led to the Noachic flood. There is thus no correspondence between the πνεύμασιν of 3:19 and the νεκροί of 4:6. (3) The context demands that we see the preaching and reception of the gospel as preceding the judging by humans (4:6b) since the latter actually presupposes the former: Christians are being maligned and judged precisely because of their adherence to the gospel. Their reception of the gospel has meant that they no longer live as they once did and as a result they are maligned and judged by their unbelieving contemporaries (vv. 4, 6b). The preaching of the gospel is thus an event that occurred during their lifetime.

Why then does Peter use the word 'dead' (νεκροῖς)? To begin with, the use of the word 'dead' (νεκροῖς) in v. 6, parallels Peter's use of the same word in v. 5 (νεκρούς), where the focus is also on those who have since died. The reason for this focus on those who have since died stems from the fact that Peter is considering these two groups from the perspective of the final judgment. As Bénétreau notes,

> l'Evangile a été annoncé à des hommes et des femmes, mort depuis. C'est précisément le fait qu'ils sont morts depuis cette évangélisation qui rend ce groupe digne de considération dans la perspective de la sanction. Le v 5 s'intéressait au sort des calomniateurs et des blasphémateurs, actuellement vivants, mais peut-être morts au jour de jugement.[137]

As Bénétreau observes, the reference to the 'dead' (νεκρούς) in v. 5 includes those who malign Christians in this life but who, by the day of judgment, will have since died. At the final judgment God will judge those who have died (the 'dead') because of their mistreatment of Christians while they were still alive. Then picking up on the word 'dead' at the end of v. 5 Peter turns his focus to the believing 'dead'. Peter's use of the word 'dead' in both cases serves to draw a contrast between the fate of these two different groups: those who wrongfully judged believers in their lifetime (as indicated by the words βλασφημοῦντες in v. 4 and κριθῶσι κατὰ ἀνθρώπους in v. 6b) will one day be judged themselves (κρῖναι); those believers who were maligned and judged during their lifetime will be vindicated by God at the final judgment. According to the immediate context, that future vindication is tied directly to their

---

[137] Bénétreau, *Première épître de Pierre*, 222–3.

reception of this gospel in this life (just as the future judgment of non-believers is tied directly to their persecution of believers in this life).

(4) As our chiasm indicates (A and A´), 4:6 does not parallel 3:19 but 3:18. There exists a clear parallelism between the two couplets of balanced antithetical statements in 3:18 and 4:6:

A 3:18	θανατωθεὶς	μὲν			σαρκί
	ζῳοποιηθεὶς	δὲ			πνεύματι
A´ 4:6	κριθῶσι	μὲν	κατὰ	ἀνθρώπους	σαρκί
	ζῶσι	δὲ	κατὰ	θεὸν	πνεύματι

Any interpretation of 4:6, then, needs to take into account the parallel formulation of 3:18 (and not 3:19). Before considering the relationship between 3:18 and 4:6, we need to examine the two parallel statements of 4:6bc in their own right. Having done that, we will seek further illumination from their relationship to the parallel statements in 3:18de.

The final part of v. 6 (bc) is linked to what goes before by the conjunction ἵνα, which, along with the subjunctive ζῶσι, denotes the purpose and, by implication, the intended result ('so that') of the proclamation of the gospel. The ἵνα clause is then made up of two contrasting but parallel clauses set in opposition to one another by a μέν … δέ construction (cf. 1:20; 2:4; 3:18). As most commentators recognise, the μέν clause is concessive ('though') and, like 3:18, has the effect of subordinating the first member (κριθῶσι κατὰ ἀνθρώπους σαρκί) and accentuating the second (ζῶσι κατὰ θεὸν πνεύματι). As Spicq remarks, the first member of the couplet, '"ayant été jugés … dans la chair" … ce n'est qu'une parenthèse'.[138] The δέ clause, on the other hand, indicates the purpose or intended result towards which the εἰς τοῦτο at the beginning of the verse points (= resurrection life). Regarding the μέν clause as parenthetical avoids 'the strange notion that the gospel was proclaimed to the dead "in order that they might be judged"'.[139] Instead, the gospel was preached so that they might live in the spirit (thus the ἵνα with the subjunctive ζῶσι), *even though* they were judged in the flesh.[140] As Spicq again observes, 'le but de l'intervention suprême du Christ n'est pas de juger et de condamner, mais de donner la vie éternelle, c'est-à-dire "selon Dieu"'.[141] We begin with the parenthetical part of the couplet.

[138] Spicq, *Les Épîtres de Saint Pierre*, 147.
[139] Horrell, 'Interpretation of 1 Pet. 4.6', 82.
[140] Abernathy, *Exegetical Summary*, 156.
[141] Spicq, *Les Épîtres de Saint Pierre*, 147.

κριθῶσι κατὰ ἀνθρώπους σαρκί

The first question that concerns us here is the meaning of κρίνω in the present context. Peter's use of the same verb in v. 5 to speak of the eschatological judgment of God has led some commentators to contend that Peter is making a similar reference here in v. 6.[142] However, the accompanying prepositional phrase κατὰ ἀνθρώπους (lit. 'according to human standards') indicates that it is human judging and not divine judging that is in view here (see below). Other commentators see in κριθῶσι a reference to death itself as the judgment spoken of here, whether in terms of martyrdom (as the outcome of formal legal proceedings)[143] or death as a judgment on sin in general.[144] However, since death as a judgment on sin represents a divine judgment this view is unlikely for the same reason as the previous one. The former view (martyrdom) is also unlikely since there is nothing in 1 Peter to suggest that, at this time, there existed an official policy of state-organised persecution resulting in martyrdom.

What then does Peter intend for us to understand by his use of the word κρίνω? To begin with, Peter's use of the word κρίνω in v. 6 does suggest that he wants to relate what he is saying to what he has already said in v. 5 with respect to the theme of judgment (where the verb κρίνω also appears). In v. 5 we saw that the focus of the judgment was primarily on those who malign believers (βλασφημοῦντες... οἳ ἀποδώσουσιν λόγον τῷ ἑτοίμως ἔχοντι κρῖναι). With the present phrase, κριθῶσι κατὰ ἀνθρώπους σαρκί, Peter retains his focus on the maligning of believers by nonbelievers, but here he uses the word κρίνω instead of βλασφημέω (which he used in v. 4). His choice of this word enables him to draw a sharp contrast between the fate of the Gentile persecutors and those whom they persecute: those who judged (κριθῶσι [v. 6]) believers in their lifetime will one day themselves be judged (κρῖναι [v. 5]) by God; those who were wrongfully judged during their lifetime will be vindicated at the final judgment (as the δέ clause indicates). In light of the immediate context with its focus on the maligning of believers by non-believers, the verb κρίνω most likely carries the sense of to 'pass an unfavourable judgment upon, criticize, find fault with, condemn',[145] and so continues the focus (from vv. 1–4) on the suffering of believers at the hands of their maligning nonbelieving contemporaries.

---

[142] Reicke, *Disobedient Spirits*, 206–8; Frings, '1 Petr 3,19 und 4,6', 85.
[143] See Spicq, *Les Épîtres de Saint Pierre*, 147.
[144] See Dalton, *Christ's Proclamation*, 238; Goppelt, *1 Peter*, 291.
[145] BDAG, 567 (s.v. 2.b).

This interpretation is made all the more certain by the prepositional phrase κατὰ ἀνθρώπους (lit. 'according to human standards') that follows it. The preposition κατά here (with the accusative) is a 'marker of norm of similarity or homogeneity'[146] and 'expresses conformity to some standard, model, rule, or will'.[147] The norm or standard by which this judgment is made is expressed by the noun that follows it: viz., ἀνθρώπους ('humans'). Hence the best translation for the phrase κατὰ ἀνθρώπους is 'according to human standards'. This construal makes best sense in the immediate context where the Gentiles are described as maligning Christians because they 'do not join with them [μὴ συντρεχόντων] in the same [τὴν αὐτὴν] flood of dissipation' (v. 4). The verb συντρέχω ('run together, go with') along with the identifying adjective αὐτήν ('same') here expresses the idea of conformity. Because believers no longer conform to the norms or standards of Gentile society around them the result is that they are maligned (βλασφημοῦντες, v. 4). The reason why believers no longer conform to the norms of society is because their lives are now regulated by a different norm (v. 2): 'so as to live the remaining time in the flesh no longer *according to* **human desires** [ἀνθρώπων ἐπιθυμίαις] *but* **for the will of God**' (v. 2). The idea expressed in v. 6, then, is that believers are being judged, criticised, and faulted (κριθῶσι) according to (κατά) the norms of society (ἀνθρώπους, 'human standards'), norms that they no longer live in accordance with. Once again σαρκί is a dative of respect (lit., 'with respect to the flesh') and denotes one's physical mortal existence. This is another indication that the judging that is taking place here relates to the maligning of believers during their lifetime. The phrase κριθῶσι μὲν κατὰ ἀνθρώπους σαρκί, then, indicates the type of suffering that was being experienced by the believers in Asia Minor: they were being maligned (βλασφημοῦντες) and judged (κριθῶσι) because of their cultural nonconformity and non-participation.

ζῶσι δὲ κατὰ θεὸν πνεύματι

The phrase ζῶσι δὲ κατὰ θεὸν πνεύματι supplies the content of τοῦτο and indicates the purpose or intended result (ἵνα, 'so that') for which the gospel was proclaimed: eschatological salvation. With this final contrasting (δέ) phrase the focus now shifts from suffering (v. 1), being maligned (v. 2), and being judged (v. 6b) to the prospect of final salvation, life in

---

[146] BDAG, 512 (s.v. 5).   [147] Selwyn, *First Epistle of St. Peter*, 215.

the spirit according to God's standard. The verb ζάω ('live') appears in six other places in 1 Peter (1:3, 23; 2:4, 5, 24; 4:5) and 'denotes the life of resurrection conferred by God'.[148] In 3:18 we are told that Christ was 'made alive [ζωοποιέω] with respect to the spirit [πνεύματι]' and became, according to 2:4, a 'living stone [λίθον ζῶντα] chosen and honoured [ἐκλεκτὸν ἔντιμον] in God's sight [παρὰ θεῷ]'. In the very next verse, Peter then draws a comparison between Christ as the 'living stone' (λίθον ζῶντα, 2:4) and believers as 'living stones' (λίθοι ζῶντες, 2:5). By being in relationship with the living stone, believers themselves also (καὶ αὐτοί) share in his identity (λίθοι) and life (ζῶντες). Moreover, because believers share in his identity and life, they will also one day share in his destiny: resurrection life (2:6; 4:6c). In the present passage, this is borne out by the correspondence between ζωοποιηθεὶς δὲ πνεύματι in 3:18e (A2 in the chiasm) and ζῶσι δὲ πνεύματι in 4:6c (A2′):

3:18e	ζωοποιηθεὶς	δὲ		πνεύματι
	made alive			with respect to the spirit
4:6c	ζῶσι	δὲ	(κατὰ θεὸν)	πνεύματι
	might live		(according to God)	with respect to the spirit

The experience of Christ in his resurrection and vindication (3:18e) is established as the basis for the believer's own resurrection and vindication by God (4:6c). Like 3:18e, πνεύματι here is a dative of respect and denotes the new spiritual, supernatural mode of the believer's existence, entered through resurrection. Elliott writes: '[H]ere, as in 3:7, the final realisation of resurrection life is in view. Within the overall context of 1 Peter, this life is synonymous with the final salvation (1:5, 9, 10; 2:2; 4:18), exaltation (5:6b), and glorification (1:7c; cf. 5:10) in store for all believers, the deceased as well as those presently living.'[149]

The phrase κατὰ θεόν stands in direct parallel to κατὰ ἀνθρώπους and therefore should probably be translated 'according to God's standard'. Similar expressions appear in two other places in 1 Peter. Earlier we were told that it was 'according to his great mercy [ὁ κατὰ τὸ πολὺ αὐτοῦ ἔλεος]' that God 'has given us a new birth into a living hope through the resurrection of Jesus Christ from the dead' (1:3). Then in 5:2 Peter exhorts elder-shepherds to exercise their oversight 'in accordance with the will of God [κατὰ θεόν]'. In 2:4 we have the expression παρὰ θεῷ ('before God, in God's sight') and once again (cf. 3:18) there is a contrast (μέν … δέ) between the world's estimation and treatment of

---

[148] Elliott, *1 Peter*, 738. [149] Ibid.

Christ in terms of rejection (ὑπὸ ἀνθρώπων μὲν ἀποδεδοκιμασμένον) and God's estimation and treatment of Christ in terms of election and honour (παρὰ δὲ θεῷ ἐκλεκτὸν ἔντιμον). These conflicting judgments about Christ (e.g., 3:18; 2:4) also find a correspondence in the conflicting judgments about those who identify with Christ (4:6). It is likely, then, that the phrase κατὰ θεόν (v. 6c) refers to God's favourable judgment (in terms of vindication) of those who have chosen to identify with Christ in contrast to the world's unfavourable judgment against them (v. 6b; just as v. 5 refers to his unfavourable judgment against those who malign believers). 'In any case the point is that God's impartial judgment (1:17; 4:17), will (2:15; 3:17; 4:2, 19), intention (1:2b), and disposition of mercy (1:3; 2:10) supersede and reverse all erroneous and malicious human criticism.'[150]

The structure and content of 4:6 echoes that of 3:18 with the result that the experience of Christ in terms of suffering and vindication is reproduced in the lives of believers. In fact the entire chiasm (from 3:18–4:6) is held together by the experience of Christ in terms of suffering and vindication at one end (3:18) and the experience of the believers in terms of suffering and vindication at the other (4:6), with the experience of baptism in the middle uniting the two (3:21):

A   Christ

A1 θανατωθεὶς μὲν   σαρκί
       put to death   with respect to the flesh

A2 ζωοποιηθεὶς δὲ   πνεύματι
       made alive   with respect to the spirit

   [C-]C′ Baptism
       σώζει βάπτισμα ... δι' ἀναστάσεως 'Ιησοῦ Χριστοῦ
       baptism saves you ... through the resurrection of Jesus
       Christ

A′ Believers

A1′ κριθῶσι   μὲν κατὰ ἀνθρώπους σαρκί
        judged   according to humans with respect to the flesh

A2′ ζῶσι   δὲ   κατὰ θεὸν   πνεύματι
        might live according to God   with respect to the spirit

Peter draws a direct correspondence between the experience of believers and the experience of Christ in order to provide believers with the assurance that just as God raised and vindicated (3:18e, 19, 21d) the 'living stone rejected by humans' (2:4), so God will raise and vindicate those

---

[150] Ibid., 739.

believers (4:6c) who have suffered (4:1), been maligned (4:4), and been judged by humans (4:6b). Our passage comes to something of a climax, then, with this depiction of the believer's final salvation in terms of vindication through resurrection to eternal life.

3.   Summary of 3:18–4:6

In this passage (3:18–4:6) Peter has presented Christ's innocent suffering (3:18ad) as both the basis for present salvation (3:18bc) and as a model for believers who suffer unjustly (3:18ad/4:6b; 4:1ab). Not only that, God's vindication of Christ's innocent suffering through his resurrection (3:18e, 21d), ascension (vv. 19, 22b), victorious proclamation (v. 19), and exaltation to God's right hand (v. 22), provides suffering believers with the assurance that God will one day vindicate them also by raising them from the dead (3:18e/4:6c) and bestowing upon them praise, glory, and honour (see 1:7). The believer's solidarity with Christ means that they can anticipate the same glorious future as their suffering but vindicated Lord. Thus Peter's unique presentation of the believers' final salvation in terms of future vindication and victory through suffering is designed to engender hope amongst a small minority group of believers facing the reaction of a hostile world against their faith.

PART III

Intercatholic conversation

7

DIVINE ELECTION

1.   Introduction

It is appropriate that we begin our theological discussions with the doctrine of election, since it is chronologically the beginning of God's personal dealing with believers in grace. Therefore it is rightly considered the first step in God's sovereign and gracious plan in bringing salvation to believers individually. As such the doctrine of election calls attention to the gracious initiative of God in the plan of salvation. We experience salvation, insists Grenz, 'because the triune God, who is relational in his own nature, *chooses* to enter into relationship with us his creatures. He calls sinful humans to share in the divine fellowship (2 Pet. 1:4). This central dimension of God's *eternal intention* leads us to the concept of election.'[1] It is thus no wonder that Peter begins his letter – a letter which is rich in salvation language – with a bold declaration of the believers' eternal election (1:1–2) cast in a Trinitarian framework that presupposes the electing initiative of God the Father (1:2a), the consecrating action of God the Spirit (1:2b), and the atoning work of God the Son (1:2c).

But what does election signify? As we seek to bring 1 Peter into conversation with the concerns of systematic theology, the following important issues relating to the doctrine of election surface for examination. These issues include: What is the relationship between the doctrine of the Trinity and the doctrine of election? What is the relationship between election and ethics? Is election *conditional* (i.e., based on God's foresight of human faith) or *unconditional* (based entirely on God's sovereign will and good pleasure)? What is the role of Jesus Christ in the divine programme of election? (or What does it mean to say that election took place 'in Christ'?) Is election to salvation *individual*, *corporate*, or both? Is election *single* (unto salvation), *double* (unto salvation *and* damnation), or something else? If it is double, does God stand behind

---

[1] Grenz, *Theology for the Community of God*, 584 (emphasis mine).

the decree of election to salvation in the same way he stands behind the decree of election to damnation (i.e., are the two decrees symmetrical)? With these questions in mind we begin with the role of the Trinity in election.

2.   Election: a Trinitarian basis

When we are talking about *divine* election (as the title of this chapter indicates) we are indicating that the subject of election is *God*. To talk about God in Christian theology is to talk about the one God who *is* Father, Son, and Spirit. That this triune God is the subject (and object?) of election suggests that just as there is both a unity and a diversity in God, so we should also expect to see a unity and diversity in election. What then is the role of the Father, Son, and Spirit in the divine elective programme? The one theologian that perhaps stands above all in his attempt to relate the doctrine of election to the doctrine of the Trinity is Karl Barth. One of the more interesting features of Barth's theology in general, and of his doctrine of election in particular, is the manner in which he interacts with the theology of Reformed orthodoxy. The seriousness with which Barth engaged the writings of this period has given rise to the term 'neo-orthodoxy'. Barth's treatment of the Reformed doctrine of predestination is especially interesting, observes McGrath, 'in that it demonstrates the manner in which he can take traditional terms, and give them a radical new meaning within the context of his theology'.[2] In terms of the doctrine of election, Barth reacted against Reformed orthodoxy, insisting that 'the static, abstract decree of Augustine and Calvin must be replaced by a dynamic, concrete decree that has its reality in Jesus Christ'.[3]

Bruce McCormack suggests that for Barth the primary question is: 'Who is the God who elects and what does a knowledge of this God tell us about the nature of election?'[4] The starting point is God's self-revelation in Jesus Christ. According to Barth, '[t]he doctrine of the Trinity states that our God, namely, He who makes Himself ours in His revelation, is really God'.[5] In making himself known to us in revelation, both the identity of the God who elects and the content of that election have been made known to us: Jesus Christ: 'Not an abstract providence or all-powerful Will, Barth argued, but the *triune* God is the God who elects. The doctrine of election must be materially determined by ...

[2] McGrath, *Christian Theology*, 470.
[3] Lewis and Demarest, *Integrative Theology*, 1: 297.
[4] McCormack, 'Grace and Being', 93.   [5] Barth, *CD*, I/1: 401.

God's self-revelation in Jesus Christ.'[6] Barth writes: 'The doctrine of election is the sum of the Gospel because of all words that can be said or heard it is the best: that God elects man; that God is for man to the One who loves in freedom. It is grounded in the knowledge of Jesus Christ because he is both the electing God and elected man in One.'[7] In *freedom* God makes a self-determination for *love*. It consists both of the fact that 'God has elected fellowship with man for Himself' and that 'God has elected fellowship with Himself for man'.[8] For Barth, then, predestination concerns the primal act of freedom or self-determination 'by means of which God determines to be God, from everlasting to everlasting, in covenantal relationship with human beings and to be God in no other way'.[9] Put simply, it is 'the freedom to be for us in Jesus Christ'.[10]

The crucial phrase in the quotation from Barth above is that Christ is both 'the electing God and elected man in One'. He is both 'the agent of election (in his identity as God) and ... the concrete object of election (in his identity as God's human covenant partner)'.[11] What is important to note here is that the subject-cum-object of divine election is 'neither God the Father in the abstract, nor even the Son considered apart from the incarnation, but *Jesus Christ*, the historical person crucified outside the walls of Jerusalem'.[12] In other words, for Barth there can be no thought of an election which has its locus in a *deus absconditus* or hidden God who subsequently becomes incarnate in the person of Jesus of Nazareth. Rather, the subject of both election and the incarnation is the Son as he is identified by reference to his historical, saving work on the cross. For this reason, writes Barth, 'He is the Lamb slain, and the Lamb slain from the foundation of the world. For this reason, the *crucified* Jesus is the "image of the invisible God".'[13] In this way the doctrine of election serves to answer the question: 'Who is the God who elects?'[14] 'The one true God is the One who has freely bound himself in a covenant with human beings, and will never take back that choice. The covenant of grace enters into God's "self-definition".'[15] For this reason, notes Barth, '[the doctrine of election] is part of the doctrine of God because originally God's election of man is a predestination not merely of man but of himself. Its function is to bear testimony to eternal, free, and unchanging grace as the beginning of all the ways and works of God.'[16]

[6] Mangina, *Karl Barth*, 69.   [7] Barth, *CD*, II/2: 3.
[8] Barth, *CD*, II/2: 162.   [9] McCormack, 'Grace and Being', 98.
[10] Mangina, *Karl Barth*, 70.   [11] Ibid., 69.   [12] Ibid., 70 (emphasis his).
[13] Barth, *CD*, II/2: 123.   [14] McCormack, 'Grace and Being', 93.
[15] Mangina, *Karl Barth*, 70–1.   [16] Barth, *CD*, II/2: 3.

In what sense can it be said to be a predestination of himself? According to Barth, God is both subject and object of a double predestination (*praedestinatio gemina*) in that both the decision of election and reprobation proceed from him and fall upon him (rather than upon two separate groups of people as in Calvin [see the discussion below]):

> If the teachers of predestination were right when they spoke always of a duality, of election and reprobation, of predestination to salvation or perdition, to life or death, then we may say already that in the election of Jesus Christ which is the eternal will of God, God has ascribed to man the former, election, salvation, and life; and to Himself he has ascribed the latter, reprobation, perdition, and death.[17]

Thus for Barth, election and atonement are intimately related (in that the latter represents God as the eternally rejected one in the place of sinners). For while he can speak of God's 'eternal election', he cannot do so in abstraction apart from its realisation in Jesus Christ. And while '[e]lection is indeed before all things … it is also with all things; it is God's sovereign will actualising itself in our midst. And the content of that activity is simply Jesus Christ, the electing God and the electing human being in one.'[18] In the end, what unites election and redemption is the fact that the same subject stands at the centre of both: 'Jesus Christ, the same Jesus Christ who was "crucified under Pontius Pilate"'.[19]

Barth also went on to affirm the subjective dimension of election as 'both a work of the Spirit within us and a work of the human subject who is acted upon by grace'.[20] However, the intimate link that we saw between election and redemption in Christ is not so evident between election and calling (or vocation) by the Spirit (and hence between election and conversion). This is shown in the fact that '[n]ot every one who is elected lives as an elect man'.[21] The difference between those who live as the elect and those who do not resides in 'their calling … [t]here are, in fact, two classes of men the called and the uncalled, the believing and the godless, and therefore the elect and the *apparently* rejected, the community of God and the world'.[22] Thus, while all are objectively elect in Christ, not all are subjectively called by the Spirit. Or to put it another way, all are elected to be 'in Christ' *de jure* but not all are 'in Christ' *de facto*. Barth writes:

---

[17] Barth, *CD*, II/2: 163.   [18] Mangina, *Karl Barth*, 72.   [19] Ibid.
[20] Bloesch, *Jesus is Victor*, 35.   [21] Barth, *CD*, II/2: 321.
[22] Barth, *CD*, II/2: 345, 351 (emphasis mine).

> The sanctification of man, his conversion to God, is, like his justification, a transformation, a new determination, which has taken place *de jure* for all the world and therefore for all men. *De facto*, however, it is not known by all men, just as justification has not *de facto* been grasped and acknowledged and known and confessed by all men, only by those who are awakened to faith.[23]

What contribution does Peter offer to the discussion and in what way might our understanding of 1 Peter's doctrine of election be sharpened as we engage in dialogue with Barth? The following points can be made: (1) Peter would also affirm that the starting point for an adequate doctrine of election is the doctrine of the triune God (see 1:1–2; 2:4–10). Thus he begins his letter with the words (1:1–2): 'To the elect ... [elect] according to the foreknowledge of *God the Father*, by [means of] the consecration of the *Spirit*, for [the purpose of] obedience and sprinkling of the blood of *Jesus Christ*'. The word 'elect' (ἐκλεκτός) here is qualified by three prepositional phrases, each of which presuppose the activity of the triune God: the electing initiative of the Father (1:2a), the consecrating action of the Spirit (1:2b), and the atoning work of the Son (1:2c). Thus in a very qualified sense it may be possible with Barth to refer to Christ as 'the electing God'. However, as 1 Pet. 1:1–2 indicates, the Son's role in election relates to his atoning work (1:2c) and not his choosing initiative which alone is ascribed to God the Father (1:2a). As Bruce McCormack correctly points out, '[t]hat Jesus Christ, the God-human in His divine-human unity, should be conceived of as the subject of election, is a claim that finds no *direct* confirmation in the New Testament'.[24]

(2) By making the triune God and not humans the central focus of his doctrine of election, Barth is able to effectively affirm the sovereignty and freedom of God in election. As we have seen, for Barth, election is the primal act of divine freedom or self-determination: 'Primarily God elected or predestined Himself'.[25] For this reason, he insists, it is an 'election of grace'.[26] Barth explains:

> In the beginning, before time and space as we know them, before there was any reality distinct from God which could be the object of the love of God or the setting for his acts of freedom, God anticipated and determined within Himself (in the power of His love and freedom, of His knowing and willing) that the

[23] Barth, *CD*, IV/2: 511. [24] McCormack, 'Grace and Being', 94 (emphasis his). [25] Barth, *CD*, II/2: 162. [26] Barth, *CD*, II/2: 101.

goal and meaning of all his dealings with the as yet non-existent universe should be the fact that in his Son he would be gracious towards man, uniting Himself with him. *In the beginning it was the choice of the Father* Himself to establish this covenant with man by giving up his Son for him … *In the beginning it was the choice of the Son* to be obedient to grace, and therefore to offer up himself and to become man in order that this covenant might be made a reality. *In the beginning it was the resolve of the Holy Spirit* that the unity of God, of Father and Son should not be disturbed or rent by this covenant with man, but that it should be made the more glorious, the deity of God, the divinity of His love and freedom, being confirmed and demonstrated by this offering of the Father and this self-offering of the Son. This choice was in the beginning.[27]

As the one who accomplishes and fulfils the divine covenant through his self-offering, Jesus Christ is the agent of reconciliation. More than that, for Barth, reconciliation is to be equated with the concrete person of Jesus Christ: 'Jesus Christ is the reconciliation' (*Jesus Christus die Vorsöhnung*).[28] In saying that, Barth is seeking 'to subvert the assumption that Christ's work sets up a possibility which humans must now actualise in faith – the basic error he saw at work in Bultmann's theology'.[29] Instead, at the cross nothing short of the end of human history took place: 'Human history was actually terminated at this point'.[30] As Mangina notes, 'Barth's account of the world ending at the cross depends on an inclusive Christology, in which the Son of God assumes flesh in the widest possible sense: the life-story of every person, indeed the sweep of human history'.[31] Thus, as Gunton points out, there is an 'almost platonic realism' to his conception of Jesus' death and its effect on all humans.[32] Barth writes:

> We died: the totality of all sinful men, those living, those long dead, and those still to be born, Christians who necessarily know and proclaim it, but also Jews and heathen, whether they hear and receive the news, or whether they tried and still try to escape it. His death was the death of all, quite independently of their attitude or response to this event.[33]

---

[27] Barth, *CD*, II/2: 101–2.   [28] Barth, *CD*, IV/1: 34.
[29] Mangina, *Karl Barth*, 119.   [30] Barth, *CD*, IV/1: 734.
[31] Mangina, *Karl Barth*, 127.   [32] Gunton, 'Salvation', 147.
[33] Barth, *CD*, IV/1: 295.

It is at this point, however, that we part company with Barth. On the one hand, like Barth, Peter's casting of the doctrine of election in Trinitarian terms enables him to underscore the sovereignty and freedom of God in election. Election for Peter, to use Barthian language, is also an instance of divine freedom or self-determination, wholly undetermined from without himself, in which he chooses, in Christ (on election 'in Christ' see below), and on the basis of his eternal foreknowledge (1:2a) and mercy (2:10; cf. 1:3) alone, to be gracious to some (and in this sense it is unconditional – see below). On the other hand, unlike Barth, Peter also leaves room for the divine rejection of others (2:8; see below). For Barth, God's freedom to reject some is compromised by his insistence that because Christ is *the* elect and rejected one, no one can finally be rejected. For Peter, however, God's freedom actually consists in his sovereign freedom to save some (1:1–2) and to reject others (2:8). For the moment we can say, to rephrase 1 Pet. 1:1–2 in Barthian language, that:

> In the beginning it was the choice of the Father (1:2a) to establish a (new) covenant with his chosen ones by giving up his Son for them (v. 2c). In the beginning it was the choice of the Son, in obedience to the Father, to become man and to offer himself up as an atoning and substitutionary sacrifice (see 3:18; cf. 2:24) in order that this new covenant might be made a reality (1:2d). In the beginning it was the resolve of the Spirit that the unity of the Father's electing will (1:2a) and the Son's atoning work (1:2c) should not be rent asunder by effectively applying the benefits of Christ's atoning work to the Father's elect alone (1:2b).

(3) Barth correctly specifies Christ as the true object of election (see 1:20; 2:4d, 6b) in whom all others are elect (1:2c; 2:5a, 9a). Moreover, Christ is, in a very qualified and Barthian sense, the object of a double predestination (on which see below). For Barth, the terms 'elect' and 'rejected' refer not to two separate groups of people, but primarily to one person: Jesus Christ. 'As the elect, he is precisely the rejected one – the "Lamb of God, who takes away the sins of the world".'[34] This much Peter would affirm (1:2d, 20; 2:4cd, 6b/7c): 'Coming to him, a living stone, *rejected by humans but elect*, honoured, in the sight *of God*' (2:4); 'You were ransomed … with the precious blood of Christ, the one having been chosen before the foundation of the world' (1:18–20). The difference between Peter and Barth, however, is the scope of election and, as a

---

[34] Mangina, *Karl Barth*, 71.

result, the objects of election and rejection (for if election is limited to a certain group then rejection of the rest necessarily follows).

For Peter, election is clearly limited to those (the ἐκλεκτοῖς, 1:1) whom the Father has foreknown (1:2a) and whom the Spirit has set apart (v. 2c) for the purpose of covenant relationship – by faith – on the basis of the Son's atoning work (v. 2d). Saving faith (represented by the word ὑπακοήν here) is thus the divine goal/result (the εἰς here in v. 2d denotes both) of election. The opposite truth is that those who do not finally come to faith (i.e., before they die) are not elect. That all do not come to faith in God (something that both Peter and Barth admit) is a fact that Peter ascribes to election (something Barth cannot admit), positively in 1:1–2 and negatively in 2:8. Unlike Barth, Peter not only limits the elect to those come to saving faith in Christ (1:2d; 2:4; cf. 1:5, 7, 9, 21; 5:9), but he also allows for the eternal rejection of those who reject this relationship in unbelief (2:8). To put it another way, those who do not act as the elect are *in reality* (not just *apparently* as in Barth) rejected by God (2:8). Peter would therefore limit those who are 'in Christ' to those who have 'come to him [in faith]' (2:4; cf. 1:2d) on the basis of election (1:2; 2:4–5, 9).

(4) Thus, for Peter, there exists an inseparable link between the Father's electing initiative (1:2a) and the Spirit's consecrating action (1:2b). This point is worth underlining, for as we have just seen in Barth, while all are objectively elect in Christ, not all are subjectively called by the Spirit. Such an approach lends credence to the Arminian accusation that the doctrine of unconditional election (which I will argue below is in agreement with 1 Peter) undermines any motivation to holiness. John Wesley argued that '[predestination] directly tends to destroy that holiness which is the end of all the ordinances of God ... that doctrine itself – that every man is either elected or not elected from eternity, and that one must inevitably be saved, and the other inevitably damned – has a manifest tendency to destroy holiness in general'.[35] For the author of 1 Peter, however, there is an inseparable link between election and ethics: believers have been chosen on the basis of (κατά) God's eternal, pre-determining love (1:1b, 2a), by means of (ἐν) the Spirit's consecrating action (v. 2b) *for the purpose of obedience* (εἰς ὑπακοήν; v. 2c). It is on this basis (διό, 'therefore', v. 13) that Peter can issue the injunction (and note the connection between calling and holiness), 'but as he who *called* you is holy, you also *be holy* in all your conduct' (v. 15). Election and holiness reappear again side by side in the very next chapter: 'But you

---

[35] Wesley, 'Free Grace', *Works*, 7: 376.

are an elect race ... a holy nation' (2:9). Thus, writes Calvin (following his citation of 1 Pet. 1:2):

> If election has as its goal holiness of life, it ought rather to arouse and goad us eagerly to set our mind upon it than to serve as a pretext for doing nothing. What a great difference there is between these two things: to cease well-doing because election is sufficient for salvation, and to devote ourselves to the pursuit of good as the appointed goal of election![36]

3.   Election: conditional or unconditional?

Throughout the history of the church Christian thinkers have viewed salvation synergistically in which the human will freely cooperated with God. In order to maintain this synergism and at the same time accommodate the biblical doctrine of election, they have made God's foreknowledge (viewed as prescience) of free human actions the basis of God's predestination. Thus Origen (c.185–c.254) writes:

> Foreknowledge precedes foreordination ... God observed beforehand the sequence of future events, and noticed the inclination of certain men towards piety which followed on this inclination; and he foreknew them, knowing the present and foreknowing the future ... if anyone in reply asks whether it is possible for the events which God foreknew not to happen, we shall answer, Yes, and there is no necessity determining this happening or not happening.[37]

For Origen, God's foreknowledge is not the cause of future events but vice versa:

> Celsus imagines that an event, predicted through foreknowledge, comes to pass because it was predicted; but we do not grant this, maintaining that he who foretold it was not the cause of its happening, because he foretold it would happen; but the future event itself, which would have taken place though not predicted, afforded the occasion to him, who was endowed with foreknowledge, of foretelling its occurrence.[38]

[36] Calvin, *Institutes*, 3.23.12.
[37] Origen, *Commentary on the Epistle to the Romans*, 1.
[38] Origen, *Against Celsus* 2.20 (*ANF*, 4: 440).

In the sixteenth to seventeenth centuries James Arminius (1560–1609) also made God's foreknowledge the basis of his decision to save some and damn others:

> To these succeeds the fourth decree by which God decreed to save and damn certain particular persons. This decree has its foundation in the foreknowledge of God, by which he foreknew from all eternity those individuals who *would*, through his preventing grace, *believe*, and, through his subsequent grace *would* persevere.[39]

Similarly, in the eighteenth century, John Wesley (1703–91) based election on God's omniscient foreknowledge of who would believe, and, thus, who would become elect. This is illustrated with reference to his mother's analogy of the sun:

> But observe … Just as I … now know the sun shines: Yet the sun does not shine because I know it, but I know it because it shines. My knowledge supposes the sun to shine; but does not in anyway cause it … In a word, God looking on all ages, from creation to the consummation, as a moment, and seeing at once whatever is in the hearts of all the children of men, knows everyone that does or does not believe, in every age or nation. Yet what he knows, whether faith or unbelief, is in nowise caused by his knowledge. Men are as free in believing or not believing as if he did not know it at all.[40]

Cottrell, a modern Arminian theologian, sees this as the very heart of the issue:

> How is it possible that God could determine even before the creation which individuals will be saved, and could even write their names in the book of life? The answer is found in the fact and nature of God's foreknowledge. The Bible explicitly relates predestination to God's foreknowledge, and a correct understanding of this relationship is the key to the whole question of election to salvation.[41]

Election is thus conditional in that it is contingent upon persons meeting the conditions for being in Christ: faith in Christ and union with him

---

[39] Arminius, *Works* 1:589 (emphasis his).
[40] Wesley, 'On Predestination', *Works*, 6: 227.
[41] Cottrell, 'Conditional Election', 58.

in baptism. God then 'elects' those whom he foresees will meet these conditions. Thus, for Arminians such as Thomas Oden, election does not denote God's eternal and unconditional choosing of believers for salvation, but rather denotes the weaker sense of God *naming* or *designating* those who, as a result of the right use of their free-will, have chosen to believe. The doctrine of election thus denotes the act of God whereby he *names* or *labels* those who have freely chosen to believe as 'the elect': 'Those who not only hear the invitation, but respond to it in repentance, faith, and obedience, are characteristically denoted in Scripture as "the chosen (*eklektos* ...)".'[42]

Reformed theology, on the other hand, has always taught that election is unconditional:

> God, before the foundation of the world was laid, according to his eternal and immutable purpose, and the secret counsel and good pleasure of his will, hath chosen, in Christ, unto everlasting glory, out of his mere free grace and love, without any foresight of faith, or good works, or perseverance in either of them, or any other thing in the creature, as conditions, or causes moving him thereunto; and all to the praise of his glorious grace.[43]

John Calvin (1509–64) discussed predestination in both his *Institutes* (3.21–4) and his *A Treatise on the Eternal Predestination of God*. Calvin noted the following characteristics of election: (1) '[T]hat God by his eternal goodwill (for which there was no other cause than his own purpose), appointed those whom he pleased unto salvation, rejecting all the rest'.[44] (2) That election is founded upon God's 'free mercy'[45] and 'mere generosity'.[46] As such, God is under no obligation to save anyone: 'We shall never be clearly persuaded, as we ought to be, that our salvation flows from the wellspring of God's free mercy until we come to know his eternal election, which illumines God's grace by this contrast: that he does not indiscriminately adopt all into the hope of salvation but gives to some what he denies to others.'[47] (3) That election is not based on foreseen faith but vice versa. Calvin rejects the view of those who 'say that when Paul [in Rom. 8:29] affirms that those were predestinated whom God foreknew, he means that each one was chosen in respect of his future faith when he should believe'.[48] Instead, he rightly affirms 'that

---

[42] Oden, *Transforming Power of Grace*, 129.
[43] *Westminster Confession of Faith*, 3.5.
[44] Calvin, 'A Treatise on the Eternal Predestination of God', 31.
[45] Calvin, *Institutes*, 3.21.1.   [46] Ibid., 3.21.1, 6.   [47] Ibid., 3.21.1.
[48] Calvin, 'A Treatise on the Eternal Predestination of God', 48.

by the term foreknowledge we are to understand the counsel of God by which he predestinates *his* own to salvation'.[49] Thus, concludes Calvin, '[God] was so far from being moved by any faith in them to come thus to adopt them, that this his election is the cause and beginning of all faith in them; and that, therefore, election is, in order, before faith'.[50] (4) That election is absolutely certain as to its outcome: 'God's unchangeable plan, by which he predestined for himself those whom he willed, was in fact intrinsically effectual unto salvation for these spiritual offspring alone'.[51]

In the following century, Francis Turretin (1623–87) in his *Institutes of Elenctic Theology* (1679–85) affirmed the same characteristics of election through a series of affirmations and denials: (1) 'Are there conditional decrees? We deny ... every decree of God is eternal; therefore it cannot depend upon a condition which takes place only in time', but rather 'God's decrees depend on his good pleasure ... Therefore they are not suspended upon any condition outside of God'.[52] (2) 'Is election from the foresight of faith, or works; or from the grace of God alone? The former we deny; the latter we affirm.'[53] It is '[b]y the unanimous consent of the church', notes Turretin, that 'the Reformed maintain election to be purely gratuitous and that no foresight can be granted of faith or of works or of merit', rather, '[f]aith and obedience are the fruit and effect of election'.[54] (3) 'Is the election of certain men to salvation constant and immutable? We affirm.'[55] Or to put the question differently: 'Is the decree of election so sure and immutable that the elect must necessarily and infallibly be brought to salvation at last? ... we affirm.'[56]

What contribution can our exegesis of 1 Peter make to this discussion? The following points suggest that, for Peter, election represents God's *unconditional* choice of certain persons for salvation: (1) In 1:1–2 Peter notes that God's election of certain individuals (on the issue of whether election is individual or corporate see below) was carried out on the basis of or in accordance with (κατά) 'the foreknowledge of God the Father' (1:2a). While it is true in principle that, as Boettner notes, 'foreknowledge presupposes foreordination',[57] I noted in my exegesis of this verse that when 1 Peter (and the NT in general) speaks of divine 'foreknowledge' it is actually referring to (God's loving) 'foreordination'. Thus when Peter speaks of election 'according to the foreknowledge of God the Father', he is saying that nothing outside of God was the cause of his choice of

---

[49] Ibid. (emphasis his).   [50] Ibid., 46.   [51] Calvin, *Institutes*, 3.21.7.
[52] Turretin, *Institutes*, 4.3.3.   [53] Ibid., 4.11.   [54] Ibid., 4.11.8, 10.
[55] Ibid., 4.12.   [56] Ibid., 4.12.5.
[57] Boettner, *Reformed Doctrine of Predestination*, 46.

certain persons for salvation (i.e., it is unconditional). Rather, God the Father has elected for salvation those upon whom he has eternally (as the πρό- in πρόγνωσις suggests) and thus freely chosen in himself to set his covenantal affection.

(2) This finds support in Peter's insistence that obedience is the result or effect of God's foreknowledge or foreordination, and not its cause. While the human response is plainly presupposed in 1:2d (εἰς ὑπακοήν ['for *obedience*', i.e., conversion]), the preposition εἰς with ὑπακοήν denotes goal/purpose indicating that it is the outcome and not the cause of God's electing initiative. If the latter were the case we would, at the very least, expect a preposition denoting cause rather than purpose (i.e., 'elect ... according to the foreknowledge of God the Father ... *because of* obedience [διὰ ὑπακοήν]'). Commenting on this verse, Calvin notes that 'when Peter calls them elect *according to the foreknowledge of God*, he is showing that the cause of it depends on God alone, because he of his own free will has chosen us. Thus the foreknowledge of God excludes every worthiness on the part of man.'[58]

(3) God's election of believers on the basis of/in conformity with (κατά) his foreknowledge in v. 2, is paralleled in v. 3 by his regenerating of believers on the basis of/in conformity with (κατά) his 'great mercy' (ὁ τὸ πολὺ αὐτοῦ ἔλεος) and not the believer's obedient response in faith (this is in agreement with v. 2c which indicates that it is the Spirit's consecrating and regenerating action that results in [εἰς] conversion, and not vice versa). In my exegesis of this verse I noted that the addition of the adjective πολύ ('great') in the formulation κατὰ τὸ πολὺ αὐτοῦ ἔλεος ('according to his great mercy') highlights the magnitude of this divine generosity and grace which has resulted in the believers' new birth (1:3; cf. 1:23). This stress on divine mercy appears again in our other election passage (2:4–10), where the elect (ὑμεῖς γένος ἐκλεκτόν, 'you are an elect race', 2:9a) are described as those who 'once were not shown mercy, but now have been shown mercy'. In sum, Peter would want to affirm that God's election of believers is founded upon God's freely given mercy without any regard to (foreseen) human worth, merit, or faith, and in this sense it is unconditional.

4.   Election: in Christ

Of central importance to Barth's doctrine of election is the notion that we are elect *in Christ*. For Barth, unlike Calvin, predestination does not refer

---

[58] Calvin, *Epistles of St. Peter*, 230.

to 'a decision of God in which the human race is divided into elect and reprobate, but to God's self-election and God's election of humanity, both actual *in Jesus Christ*'.[59] As we have already seen, this means first of all that 'in Jesus Christ we are to discern election as the divine self-election', in which God freely chooses to be for us *in Jesus Christ*.[60] Election is thus the 'primal decision'[61] or eternal 'Self-determination by means of which God chooses *in Jesus Christ* love and mercy for the human race and judgment (reprobation) for himself'[62] (in this sense predestination is double for Barth – see below). Then secondly, 'in Jesus Christ we are to discern election as the election of humanity'.[63] A person's election consists in the fact that 'he belongs eternally to Jesus Christ and therefore is not rejected, but elected by God *in Jesus Christ*; that the rejection which he deserves on account of his perverse choice is born and cancelled by Jesus Christ; and that he is appointed to eternal life with God on the basis of the righteous, divine decision'.[64] Since this election takes place 'in Christ' it cannot be rejected or annulled by human choice:

> [I]ndividuals recognise the election of Jesus Christ as their own election … he may indeed behave and conduct himself … as the man who is rejected by God … But he cannot reverse or change the eternal decision of God … he for his part may deny and annul everything else by his own choice, but cannot possibly deny or annul the gracious choice of God.[65]

Thus while explicitly rejecting the doctrine of universal salvation, Barth's thought logically leads there. Furthermore, Barth wrongly leaves no room for the rejection of some individuals by God (thus undermining God's freedom in election).

While Barth's doctrine of election tended to emphasise the divine choice to the exclusion of the human choice, Arminian-Wesleyan theology has tended to move in the opposite direction. Like Barth, Cottrell affirms that 'the election of Jesus is the central and primary act of election. All other aspects of election are subordinate to it. It is the very heart of the redemptive plan.'[66] However, unlike Barth, the election of individuals in Christ takes place according to God's foreknowledge of who will meet the conditions of *being in Christ* (by an act of free will). Cottrell explains: '[God] foreknows whether an individual will meet the

---

[59] Webster, *Barth*, 91 (emphasis added).   [60] Ibid.
[61] McCormack, 'Barth, Karl', 66.
[62] McCormack, 'Grace and Being', 98 (emphasis mine).
[63] Webster, *Barth*, 91.   [64] Barth, *CD*, II/2: 306 (emphasis added).
[65] Barth, *CD*, II/2: 314, 316–17.   [66] Cottrell, 'Conditional Election', 52.

conditions for salvation … What are these conditions? The basic and all-encompassing condition is whether a person is *in Christ*, namely, whether one has entered into a saving union with Christ …'[67] In order to be *in Christ* other conditions must also be met: 'Of course, there are other conditions which one must meet in order to *be* in Christ … The basic condition, of course, is faith.'[68] He concludes: 'Thus having set forth these conditions for being in Christ, God foreknows from the beginning who will and who will not meet them. Those whom he foresees as meeting them are predestined to salvation.'[69]

While I have rejected a number of conclusions that both Barth and Cottrell came to on the matter of election, they are right to see the election of Jesus Christ as a crucial aspect of the doctrine of election in general. In 1 Peter Jesus is expressly referred to as elect on at least three occasions. In 1:20 we are told that '[Christ] was destined [προεγνωσμένου] before the foundation of the world [μὲν πρὸ καταβολῆς]'. Then in ch. 2 Christ is referred to as 'a living stone, rejected by humans but elect, honoured, in the sight of God' (v. 4bcd) and 'a cornerstone elect, honoured' (v. 6b). Furthermore, the election of believers is linked with the election of Christ. Peter's description of Jesus as an 'elect stone' (λίθον … ἐκλεκτόν) in v. 4d and an 'elect cornerstone' (λίθον ἀκρογωνιαῖον ἐκλεκτὸν) in v. 6d is paralleled by his description of believers as an 'elect race' (γένος ἐκλεκτόν) in v. 9a. Moreover, as I noted in my exegesis of this passage, this parallelism coincides with another in vv. 4–5 in which the divine election of Christ as λίθον ζῶντα ('a living stone', v. 4) is linked (καὶ αὐτοί ['yourselves also'], v. 5a) with that of believers who are 'also' (καί) described ὡς λίθοι ζῶντες ('as living stones', v. 5a). The parallelism, however, is not symmetrical, as Jewett notes: 'Yet there is obviously a difference between the Head and the members of the body in this respect as in all others. We are elect as living stones, but Christ is elect and precious as the chief cornerstone (1 Pet. 2:4ff.). In other words, we are chosen in him, not he in us.'[70] So what exactly does it mean to say that we are elect in Christ? What is the relationship between Christ's election and ours?

To say that we are elect in Christ means at least two things for Peter: (1) It means that God determined that believers would experience salvation through Jesus Christ and his atoning work. Jesus is God's elect or chosen (cf. 1 Pet. 1:20; 2:4, 6) 'agent and person through whom the electing work of God would come to fruition. When God planned to

---

[67] Ibid., 61 (emphasis his).   [68] Ibid. (emphasis his).   [69] Ibid.
[70] Jewett, *Election and Predestination*, 55.

save some, he intended from the beginning that their salvation would be effected through the work of Christ.'[71] Thus in 1 Pet. 1:20 we are told that '[Christ] was destined [lit. 'foreknown', προεγνωσμένου] before the foundation of the world [πρὸ καταβολῆς κόσμου] but was made manifest in the last of times for your sake [δι' ὑμᾶς]'. The emphatic position of the δι' ὑμᾶς ('for your sake') at the end of the verse stresses that both the foreordaining of Christ from before history and his eschatological appearing at the climax of salvation history occurred for the sake of believers (δι' ὑμᾶς). Moreover, as Michaels points out, 'what is decided from all eternity is not simply that Jesus Christ should come into the world, but that he should fulfil a certain role, the role intimated already in v. 19'.[72] There we read that 'you were ransomed (v. 18) ... with the precious blood of Christ as a lamb flawless and faultless' (v. 19). The point of the text, then, was that Christ was chosen from eternity to die as a ransom (a substitutionary sacrifice) for all God's elect (ἐκλεκτοῖς ['elect', 1:1] = ὑμᾶς ['you', v. 20]). In other words, when God eternally elected a people for himself, his intention was that they should experience salvation only through what Christ would accomplish on the cross for them ('for your sake', 1:20). Thus the election of Christ was functional; he was chosen for a specific task, and that task was, through his death and resurrection, to provide salvation for all God's elect. Storms concludes: 'Therefore, we are chosen "in Christ" in the sense that this Son to whom the Father has given us is he through whom this election life is made ours in experience. His sinless life, atoning death, and glorious resurrection were the means through which God's electing purpose was put into effect.'[73]

(2) It means that God elected believers to be 'in Christ', that is, for incorporation into Christ or union with Christ. In our second election passage (2:4–10) believers are portrayed as 'coming [προσερχόμε-νοι] to [πρός] him [= Christ, 2:3]', an expression which most probably denotes a coming to him in faith (i.e., drawing near to him in salvation) and hence an entering into union and solidarity with Christ (as the next part of the verse indicates – see above). This coming to Christ in faith, we noted earlier, is a result (εἰς) of the believers' election by God (1:2). It is not without significance that 1 Peter is the only letter outside of the Pauline corpus to use the expression 'in Christ' (ἐν Χριστῷ, 3×; 3:16; 5:10, 14). In 3:16 Peter speaks of the believers' good conduct 'in Christ' (ἐν Χριστῷ). Then in 5:10 he refers to believers as those who have been

---

[71] Schreiner, 'Individual Election unto Salvation', 103.
[72] Michaels, *1 Peter*, 66–7.   [73] Storms, *Chosen for Life*, 96.

'called [καλέσας] to his eternal glory in Christ [ἐν Χριστῷ]'. Finally in 5:14 Peter wishes peace 'to all of you who are in Christ [ἐν Χριστῷ]'. Best suggests that the phrase 'in Christ' is used by Peter 'to denote the action of God in redeeming men through Christ and to denote Christians as joined together in fellowship with Christ; ... the Christian is united to Christ in fellowship on the basis of what God has done for him in the death and resurrection of Christ'.[74] Thus the second sense in which the believers' election can be said to be 'in Christ' is that they have been elected for fellowship with Christ.

Seen in this light, the doctrine of election is pastorally significant. I note briefly two points: (1) In addressing a church in which suffering was not just a real threat but the experience of many, it is a great comfort to know that salvation does not depend on our initiative or choice but on God's eternal, irrevocable election in Christ. (2) Because we are chosen in Christ, the certainty of our election derives not from trying to penetrate the mystery hidden in God's eternal decree and secret counsel, but by looking to Christ (in faith) in whom we have been chosen (or as Calvin put it, 'the mirror [i.e., Christ] wherein we must ... contemplate our own election').[75] As Jewett notes, 'when we receive Christ, our faith brings the assurance that we are elect. Knowing that Christ has been chosen as our Prophet, Priest, and King, we know that we have been chosen as the beneficiaries of his saving work'.[76]

5. Election: individual or communal?

Having surveyed the relevant New Testament data, William Klein in his *The New Chosen People: A Corporate View of Election* concludes that the writers of these documents 'present election from two basic perspectives – corporate and individual'.[77] Individual election, he argues, relates to 'God's appointment of individuals to perform tasks, functions, or ministries in his service'.[78] It is not, however, an election to salvation. Instead, concludes Klein, 'the New Testament writers address salvific election in primarily, if not exclusively, corporate terms'.[79] Again he writes: 'Our study of the New Testament documents demands that we view election to salvation corporately ... God has chosen the church as a body rather than specific individuals who populate that body.'[80] Klein, however, is

---

[74] Best, *1 Peter*, 134.   [75] See Calvin, *Institutes*, 2.24.5.
[76] Jewett, *Election and Predestination*, 56.
[77] Klein, *New Chosen People*, 257.
[78] Ibid., 268.   [79] Ibid., 257.   [80] Ibid., 258, 259.

still content to speak of *individuals* who make up that elect body (e.g.): 'All believers find their identity as *one of* God's chosen ones through participation and incorporation in the body of Christ. *An individual* finds "chosenness" "in Christ".'[81] But how does an individual find *chosenness* 'in Christ'? 'The body is chosen; one enters that body through faith in Christ.'[82] Faith in Christ, in turn, is a matter of free choice: 'God has chosen a people in Christ, but individuals must decide whether or not to accept God's salvation and so enter that body'.[83] Thus for Klein, the 'church' appears to be nothing more than 'an abstract entity or a concept that God chose. Those who become part of that entity are those who exercise faith. God simply chose that there be a "thing" called the church, and then he decided that all who would put their faith in Christ would become part of the church.'[84]

Klein is right to stress the corporate nature of election. This seems quite clear from 1 Pet. 2:9–10, which, as Klein notes, 'applies a series of corporate terms' to the new elect people of God:[85] 'But you are an elect race, a royal priesthood, a holy nation, a people for God's special possession … You who once were no people, but now you are the people of God; once you were not shown mercy, but now have been shown mercy.' However, 1 Peter does not portray the church as an empty class, an abstract entity or an intangible concept, for in the preceding verses the church, as an elect (cf. v. 9) corporate entity (referred to as a 'spiritual house', v. 5c) is made up of elect (v. 5, 9) individuals (referred to as 'living stones' [v. 5a], believers [v. 7a], those who come to Christ [2:4a], are built up [v. 5b], and offer spiritual sacrifices [v. 5e]). Furthermore, as my exegesis of 1:1–2 (along with my theological reflection on these verses above) has indicated, election clearly involves the choosing of people not of an abstract concept. There we saw that the elect are those who (1) have been chosen on the basis of God's loving predetermination (1:2a), (2) by means of the Spirit's action of setting them apart (v. 2b), and (3) for the purpose of conversion and covenant relationship with God (v. 2c). This can hardly be said of an abstract entity or empty class. The point of all this is to say that, for 1 Peter (and the NT in general), a corporate election presupposes an individual election and vice versa (in this case, the election of a 'spiritual house' [2:5c] presupposes the election of both the 'cornerstone' [v. 6b] and the individual 'living stones' [v. 5a] that make it up). In the end it is unnecessary to choose between the two. Since the

---

[81] Ibid., 265 (emphasis mine).   [82] Ibid., 266–7 (emphasis mine).
[83] Ibid., 267.   [84] Schreiner, 'Individual Election unto Salvation', 102.
[85] Klein, *New Chosen People*, 243.

divine decrees are eternal, it is not possible to speak of one being before the other in terms of order. In the end it is probably best to say that in choosing a group (the church) God also chooses the individuals that make up that group.

6.   Election: is predestination double?

A number of theologians have concluded (correctly, I believe) from the doctrine of unconditional election that its logical correlate must be the decree of reprobation. The historical origins of this view can be traced back to the ninth-century writings of Godescalc of Orbais (also known as Gottschalk [*c.* 805–69]), who maintained that '[t]here is a twofold predestination, of the elect to blessedness, and of the reprobate to death'.[86] This view gained a number of significant supporters during the Reformation. The Swiss reformer Ulrich Zwingli (1484–1531) wrote: 'The bliss of everlasting life and the pain of everlasting death are altogether matters of free election or rejection by the divine will.'[87] The German reformer Martin Luther (1483–46) taught that 'God rejected a number of men and elected and predestined others to everlasting life, such is the truth'.[88] John Calvin (1509–64) accepted the logic of double predestination when he wrote: 'Indeed many, as if they wished to avert a reproach from God, accept election in such terms as to deny that anyone is condemned. But they do this very ignorantly and childishly, since election itself could not stand except as set over against reprobation.'[89] He thus defined predestination as 'God's eternal decree, by which he compacted with himself what he willed to become of each man. For all are not created in equal condition; rather, eternal life is foreordained for some, eternal damnation for others. Therefore, as any man has been created to one or the other of these ends, we speak of him as predestined to life or to death.'[90] Theodore Beza (1519–1605), Calvin's successor in Geneva, taught predestination as 'God's eternal and unchangeable ordinance, which came before all of the causes of salvation and damnation, and by which God has determined to glorify himself – in some men by saving them through his simple grace in Christ and in other men by damning them through his rightful justice in Adam and in themselves'.[91] The particular view of predestination held by these theologians has been

[86] Cited in Custance, *The Sovereignty of Grace*, 37.
[87] Cited in Stephens, *Theology of Huldreich Zwingli*, 99.
[88] Cited in Buis, *Historic Protestantism and Predestination*, 47.
[89] Calvin, *Institutes*, 3.23.1.   [90] Ibid., 3.21.5 (cf. 3.23.7).
[91] Beza, *Quaestiones*, 116 (cited in Bray, *Beza's Doctrine of Predestination*, 88).

labelled *supralapsarianism*, which, as the name suggests, represents the decree to save some and damn others as *preceding* the decree to permit the fall ('*supra lapsum*: above or prior to the fall').[92]

Karl Barth, who also held to a form of supralapsarianism, reacted against the Reformed doctrine of double predestination (*praedestinatio gemina*), arguing that the double decree of election and reprobation had as its object not humans viewed as two separate groups – the elect and reprobate – but one person: Jesus Christ. As *the* elect one, Christ elects himself alone for rejection with the result that '[r]ejection cannot again become the portion or affair of man … There is no condemnation – literally none – for those that are in Christ Jesus.'[93] Since the decree of reprobation fell upon Christ and not humans, Barth cannot speak of anyone as rejected, but only as 'apparently rejected'[94] or 'liv[ing] as one rejected in spite of his election'.[95] As Jewett points out, at this point Barth's doctrine of election takes 'more than a furtive glance in the direction of universalism'.[96] While explicitly rejecting the doctrine of universal salvation (*apokatastasis*) himself, Barth's thought logically leads there.[97]

However, despite the celebrated names associated with the supralapsarianism view of predestination, *infralapsarianism*, which represents the decree to save some and damn others as *following* the decree to permit the fall (*infra lapsum*: below or subsequent to the fall), became the dominant view of the Reformed church. This view found an able expositor in Francis Turretin (1623–87), who held the chair of theology (earlier held by Calvin and Beza) at the Geneva Academy from 1653 until his death in 1687. For Turretin, the question of 'the object of predestination' is 'not simply "what" the object of predestination was … for it is evident that here we speak of the human race … Rather the question is "of what kind" it was … with regard to quality, i.e., how man was considered in the mind of God predestining and with what qualities he was clothed; whether those before the creation and fall or after.'[98] In Turretin's scheme the latter represents the biblical view: 'The Scripture certainly leads us to this. It says that we are chosen out of the world; therefore not as creatable or capable of failing, but as fallen and in the corrupt mass.'[99] However, like the supralapsarians, Turretin also taught that predestination was double: '[N]ot only does election necessarily prove reprobation (because the

[92] Muller, *Dictionary of Latin and Greek Theological Terms*, 292.
[93] Barth, *CD*, IV/1: 747.   [94] Barth, *CD*, II/2: 351.
[95] Barth, *CD*, II/2: 321.   [96] Jewett, *Election and Predestination*, 51.
[97] See Bloesch, *Jesus is Victor*, 63.
[98] Turretin, *Institutes*, 4.9.1.   [99] Ibid., 4.9.15.

election of some cannot be said without the preterition of others) and the damnation of the wicked…but the Scripture so clearly establishes it'.[100]

Recently, in his *The Cross and Salvation* (1997), Bruce Demarest has argued against the double predestinarianism of what he labels as 'Hyper-Calvinism' and 'Barthianism' insisting that 'the biblical evidence leads us to posit an *asymmetrical* view of soteriological purpose – namely, unconditional election to life and conditional election to damnation. When we speak about damnation, we mean that God predestines persons not to sin and disobedience but to *condemnation* that issues from sin.'[101] Thus Demarest opts for what he labels *unconditional single election*:

> The weight of biblical and historical evidence rests in favor of a single unconditional election to life. This position holds that out of the mass of fallen and responsible humanity – for reasons known to himself – God in his grace chose some to be saved and to permit others to persist in their sin.[102]

However, Demarest has clearly misunderstood the supralapsarian view (and wrongly labels what should probably be termed 'High-Calvinism' as 'Hyper-Calvinism'). Supralapsarians like Theodore Beza, for example, also held to an 'asymmetrical' view of election and reprobation. According to Beza, the reprobate are not simply condemned to damnation but to *just* damnation. So while no one is damned except those whom God has ordained to damnation, Beza could also say that 'no one is damned except those who "are found to have in themselves just causes of damnation"'.[103] 'The reprobate are condemned because of their corruption, unbelief, and sin.'[104] It seems that Beza could hold these two ideas together (damnation as ordained by God but also the fault of the reprobate) by distinguishing between the decree of reprobation (which is the first cause of reprobation) and its execution (which takes into account secondary causes, i.e., sin and unbelief). Beza writes:

> Likewise, the mention made of the damnation of the reprobate, it is usually stressed that the fault of the reprobate is to be found in themselves. In spite of this, sometimes it is necessary for Scripture to declare the great power of God, his patience, and the riches of his glory towards the vessels of mercy by leading

[100] Ibid., 4.14.2.   [101] Demarest, *Cross and Salvation*, 138.

[102] Ibid., 137–8.

[103] Beza, *Quaestiones*, 127 (cited in Bray, *Theodore Beza's Doctrine of Predestination*, 89).

[104] Bray, *Theodore Beza's Doctrine of Predestination*, 89.

us to the high secret: the secret decree of God which is the first cause of the damnation of the reprobate. The only cause of this decree known to man is the just will of God. We must all obey his will reverently as it comes from him who is just and incomprehensible. It is necessary that we note a difference between the decree of reprobation and reprobation itself. It is the will of God that the secret of his decree should be kept hidden from us. At the same time, God's word expresses very clearly the causes of reprobation and damnation: corruption, lack of faith, and iniquity. These causes are both necessary and voluntary in the vessels made to dishonour.[105]

How is our exegesis of the election passages in 1 Peter pertinent to this discussion? (1) Since, as we have seen, election for Peter is eternal (1:2, 20), it is therefore not possible to speak of 'an order of decrees'. However, if pushed to choose between the two options, we would have to say that supralapsarianism is the more biblical and logical of the two. For as even Turretin himself (an ardent defender of infralapsarian) rather inconsistently admits, 'Although predestination did not precede the decree to create man and permit his fall, *it does not follow that God made man with an uncertain end.* For if God did not have the manifestation of mercy and justice in salvation and damnation as an end, it must not straightway be said that he had not end at all.'[106] To say, as Turretin does, that God did not make humans 'with an uncertain end' is to say, positively, that he *did* make them with a certain end and this is supralapsarianism. In the end it hardly matters whether we say that God's election takes into account humans as uncreated, created, or fallen, because since his election is eternal these latter categories have no bearing on God's decision – considered uncreated, created or fallen, the elect remain the same. Thus priority must be given to God's eternal election of some for salvation and rejection of others for damnation over these other categories.

(2) Election for Peter is clearly double. To argue that election is merely single (as Demarest does) on the basis that reprobation occurs merely by (passive) divine permission is, as Luther points out, merely 'double talk'.[107] We have seen in my exegesis of 1 Pet. 2:8 that Peter holds two ideas in tension: divine predestination and human responsibility in reprobation. In 1 Pet. 2:8–9 we read: 'They stumble because they are disobeying the

---

[105] Beza, *Tractationes*, I:176–7 (cited in Bray, *Beza's Doctrine of Predestination*, 91–2).

[106] Turretin, *Institutes*, 4.9.21 (emphasis mine).

[107] Luther, 'Romans', *LW*, 25:83, n. 18.

word, to which also they were appointed [ὃ καὶ ἐτέθησαν]' (2:8c, 9a). I noted in my exegesis of these verses that the verb τίθημι ('decree, ordain, appoint') denotes divine appointment, while the prepositional phrase εἰς ὅ ('to which') refers back to the entire preceding thought, namely, believers stumble over the stone because of their disobedience. The force of this text, then, is that those who stumble over Christ the stone because of their disobedience to the word, were indeed divinely appointed to such. Two things thus seem clear from this: (1) that God is in sovereign control of all things, including both the disobedience and ultimate fate of unbelievers (and not just the latter), and (2) that while all of this is clearly in accord with God's sovereign and eternal will, it does not exclude the responsibility of those who stumble over Christ. Since that stumbling is rooted in human disobedience (note the causal participle ἀπειθοῦντες), the implication is clear: those who reject Christ in disobedience to the word (τῷ λόγῳ) will have to take responsibility for it at the final judgment (4:17). Neither truth should be emphasised at the expense of the other. If we emphasise the first, we both make God the author of human disobedience (and hence sin) and we remove responsibility from humans for their disobedience (an important biblical truth). However, if, on the other hand, we emphasise only the second truth (as Arminians and some Calvinists tend to do), we do violence to the biblical teaching (represented here) that God is in sovereign control of all things, the evil as well as the good, the disobedience as well as the obedience, from the decisions made by kings (Prov. 21:1) to the throw of the dice (Prov. 16:33). These two ideas (divine determination and human responsibility) are well illustrated in Lk. 22:22, Acts 2:23, and in the prayer of Acts 4:27–8 (respectively), again with reference to human rejection of Christ:

> For the Son of Man is going as it has been determined, but woe to that one by whom he is betrayed!

> This man [= Jesus of Nazareth], handed over to you according to the definite plan and foreknowledge of God, you crucified and killed by the hands of those outside the law.

> For in this city, in fact, both Herod and Pontius Pilate, with the Gentiles and the peoples of Israel, gathered together against your holy servant Jesus, whom you anointed, to do whatever your hand and your plan had predestined to take place.

We can see here that even though the writer believes that God ordained the killing of Christ, he nevertheless does not exempt those who killed him from responsibility. As Schreiner observes,

Peter indicted those who crucified Christ, even though the execution was predestined by God himself (Acts 2:23). It seems fair to conclude that Peter indicted them because in killing Christ they carried out their own desires. They were not coerced into crucifying Jesus against their wills. No, in putting him to death they did just what they wanted to do. Similarly, Peter criticized those who stumble over Christ the cornerstone for their unbelief and disobedience. He did not argue that their unbelief is free from any guilt because it was predestined. He had already emphasised that they chose not to obey him and that they refused to believe in him. Peter articulated a common theme in the Scriptures that human beings are responsible for their sin and sin willingly, and yet God controls all events in history.[108]

7.   Conclusion

Our dialogue with systematic theology has enabled us to sharpen our understanding of 1 Peter's doctrine of divine election. The theological significance of the doctrine for 1 Peter is signalled by both its strategic placement at the beginning (1:1–2), middle (2:4–10), and end of the letter (5:13) and the Trinitarian framework within which he sets it right at the outset of the letter (1:2). Each of the three Trinitarian members fulfils a specific role in the one divine programme of election: the Father elects, the Spirit sets the elect apart for obedience, and the Son provides atonement for God's elect and set apart people. It is in this sense that we can say that election is unconditional: it finds its origin in the eternal will of the Triune God and not the finite will of humans. It is unconditional because it has no cause outside of God; it is rooted in his sovereign will and good pleasure. Thus the human turning to God in conversion is the effect and not the cause of election. Because humans are the objects of the triune God's electing activity, it has both an individual and corporate dimension; God chooses individuals for community (he does not merely choose an abstract concept called 'the church' and then leave it up to individual persons to populate it). The consequence, however, of selecting certain individuals (whether as individuals or a group) for salvation is that certain others are passed by (are left to stumble in their own disobedience, 1 Pet. 2:8). For reasons known only to God himself, God

---

[108] Schreiner, *1 Peter*, 113.

has, in his mercy (2:10), chosen some to be his special possession (2:9) while leaving the rest to persist in their disobedience and reap its divinely ordained eternal consequences (2:8). The former should be a cause for great rejoicing and praise to God (1 Pet. 1:1–3; cf. Eph. 1:3–6), while the latter brings great sorrow to God (cf. Ezek. 33:11; also Rom. 9:1–2). In the end, election is important to Peter for the following reasons: (1) It underscores the sovereign freedom and grace of God in the salvation of his people. (2) It underscores the continuity between ancient Israel and the New Testament church as the elect people of God and in doing so emphasises the continuity of God's purpose in history, which in its turn underlines the certainty of the believers' salvation since it is part of the divine plan that had been set in eternity but has now found fulfilment in Jesus Christ and the church. (3) Finally, it thus underscores one of Peter's main purposes for writing this letter: '[T]he readers live in a time firmly under God's control when history is about to reach its climax. They therefore have reason rather to rejoice than to despair.'[109]

---

[109] Achtemeier, *1 Peter*, 112.

8

THE ATONEMENT

1.   Introduction

Early Christian tradition affirms that Jesus' death was 'for us'. That is to say, the earliest followers of Jesus were never content with the bare fact that Jesus died but were always concerned with the *meaning* and *significance* of that fact. Thomas Oden writes: 'Christianity proclaims not merely that Christ died, but that his death had significance for the otherwise apparently absurd course of human history.'[1] As Paul Fiddes asks: 'We are really asking the question we have often posed before: how does the particular death of Christ so long ago have a crucial effect on our life before God?'[2] The meaning and significance of the death of Jesus is the subject of the topic of 'the atonement'. As both 1 Peter and the history of interpretation demonstrate, the meaning and impact of the atonement is a rich and complex subject that cannot be grasped by any one theory, nor fully by any combination of them. By allowing 1 Peter to sit down at the conference table and dialogue with some of the theologies and theologians of the atonement it is hoped that a greater appreciation for the complexity, richness, meaning, and significance of the atonement in general, and in 1 Peter in particular, will emerge.

2.   Jesus' death as victory

Many early church fathers and a few contemporary theologians interpret the atonement in terms of Christ's victory over sin, death, and the devil. In fact Gustaf Aulén (1879–1977), the Lutheran theologian from Lund, claimed in his book *Christus Victor* that it was the 'classic' view of the atonement (he also referred to it as the 'dramatic' view).[3] The theory itself actually assumes at least two basic forms: (1) some interpreters

---

[1] Oden, *Systematic Theology*, 2: 345.
[2] Fiddes, *Past Event and Present Salvation*, 95.
[3] See Aulén, *Christus Victor*, 20–3.

(generally patristic writers) interpreted Christ's death as a ransom paid to the devil (see [§3] below), (2) while others, guided by such texts as Col. 2:15, 1 Cor. 15:24–28, 1 Jn 3:8, and Heb. 2:14–15, emphasise Christ's victory over sin, death, and the devil through the cross and resurrection with no recourse to the notion of a ransom paid to the devil.[4] Aulén explains the central theme of this idea of the atonement 'as a divine conflict and victory; Christ – Christus Victor – fights against and triumphs over the evil powers of the world, the tyrants under which mankind is in bondage and suffering, and in him God reconciles the world to himself'.[5] Reconciliation is achieved, he suggests, because in his victory over the powers of evil Christ has both taken away their power to harm believers and keep them in bondage (salvation and deliverance) and, as a result, has removed God's judgment (made atonement).[6]

Aulén's book highlights a number of elements in the *Christus victor* theme which find support in 1 Peter: (1) its *relative* dualism between Christ and powers of evil,[7] (2) its understanding of the evil powers as 'quasi-spiritual beings endowed with distinctive existence',[8] and (3) its understanding of 'the cross as constitutive of divine victory'.[9] Indeed Peter tells us that it was by virtue of his death and resurrection that the risen Christ went and proclaimed his victory over the once disobedient but now subjugated angelic spirits of the flood: 'Having been put to death in the flesh, but having been made alive in the spirit, having gone, he made proclamation [of his victory] to the spirits in prison, who once disobeyed … having gone into heaven, with angels and authorities and powers subjected to him' (3:19–20a, 22).

However, as I bring my exegesis of the relevant passages in 1 Peter to bear on the *Christus victor* model, a number of inadequacies very quickly appear. (1) As we shall see below, 1 Peter provides us with an important reminder that the *Christus victor* model does not exhaust a truly biblical understanding of the redemptive significance of Christ's atoning work (*pace* Aulén, Boyd [?]). (2) Proponents of this model (like Aulén) fail to provide a rational and biblical explanation for the necessity of the cross of Christ in the defeat of the powers of evil: 'Why the cross? Why not some other manner?'[10] (3) If the powers of evil have been defeated then

---

[4] See, e.g., Aulén, *Christus Victor*; Boyd, *God at War* (esp. 238–68).

[5] Aulén, *Christus Victor*, 20.

[6] See ibid., 87.

[7] I use the word 'relative' because there is no *real* dualism between Satan, as a created being, and God, the omnipotent Creator.

[8] Blocher, 'Agnus Victor', 71–2.

[9] Boersma, *Violence, Hospitality, and the Cross*, 187.

[10] McGrath, *Christian Theology*, 418.

how can Peter still write: 'Your adversary the devil prowls about as a roaring lion seeking someone to devour' (1 Pet. 5:8)? (4) Related to this is the problem that the *Christus victor* model often tends to focus primarily on the cosmic nature of the conflict and victory in isolation from the ongoing earthly one. 1 Peter, however, reminds us that both stories are intertwined: the suffering and victory of Christ becomes the basis of the believers' own suffering and victory. The believer's solidarity with Christ means that, like Christ, even though they suffer now they can anticipate the same glorious and victorious future as their resurrected Lord. Thus there is a now-and-not-yet dimension to this victory: the past victory of Christ is the guarantee of the believer's future victory 'at the revelation of Jesus Christ' (1 Pet. 1:7). (5) Aulén's book, as interpreters have noted, strikes too triumphalist a note in its depiction of the atonement, failing to 'emphasise enough the human and even tragic elements of the story'.[11] A theme more central to 1 Peter is that of the suffering of Christ (along with the overall thematic emphasis on suffering that pervades the letter) which is, in fact, constitutive of this victory. In the end we are brought back to point (2) above: Why the cross? The main problem is that the *Christus victor* metaphor rightly describes the outcome of Christ's death and resurrection as a victory gained over the forces of evil; however, what it does not tell us is how the battle was fought, in what way was the victory gained, and why was the cross necessary? Peter's first letter provides us with at least three hints to answer this, two relating to his death as atoning and one relating to his resurrection (without which his death would not be atoning).

(1) As we will see below (§5), central to 1 Peter's doctrine of the atonement is his presentation of Jesus' death as penal substitution. The doctrine of penal substitution provides an important key to understanding in what sense Jesus' death constitutes a victory over sin and Satan. In order to see the connection between these two ideas we will need to spread our net a little wider than 1 Peter. In Rev. 12 Satan is referred to as 'the accuser of our brothers [and sisters] … who accuses them day and night before our God' (v. 10). As a result of the redemptive-historical victory of Christ in his life and death (vv. 5, 10–11), we are told that 'the accuser … has been thrown down' (v. 10). Through his death on the cross Christ frees sinners from the just penalty of the law (see [§5] below) thus rendering Satan's accusations against believers groundless and baseless. This idea seems most explicit in Col. 2:14–15 (an important text for Aulén), where we are told that when Jesus was crucified

---

[11] Gunton, *Actuality of the Atonement*, 58.

'he cancelled out the bond that stood against us with its decrees which was opposed to us and has set it aside by nailing it to the cross. He disarmed the rulers and authorities exposing them to public disgrace, leading them in triumph in him.'[12] Bruce comments: 'Not only has he blotted out the record of their indebtedness but he has subjugated those powers whose possession of that damning indictment was a means of controlling them [believers].'[13] Accordingly, the crucifixion can be seen as a victory over Satan because in his substitutionary penal suffering (cf. 1 Pet. 2:24; 3:18) Christ bore the consequences of the believers' sin (cf. 1 Pet. 2:24), thus cancelling their debt and rendering as empty and baseless Satan's accusations against them. Only in this way can believers expect to share in Christ's victory and vindication (3:18e/4:6c). For as Jeffery, Ovey, and Sach observe, 'it makes sense that Jesus should be vindicated: he led a perfect human life. What is less clear is how believers, who will share in his resurrection, come to be vindicated' (especially since they do not deserve to be).[14] The basis for the believers' confidence that God will one day vindicate them is the fact that Christ bore in their place the penal consequences of their sin (1 Pet. 2:24). *In this way God both maintains the standards of his perfect justice and vindicates sinful humans.*

(2) Jesus' death as a covenant sacrifice (1 Pet. 1:2c; cf. 3:18a-c) represents the second way in which the atonement constitutes a victory over sin and Satan. I noted in my exegesis of the expression αἵματος 'Ἰησοῦ Χριστοῦ ('blood of Jesus Christ') in 1 Pet. 1:2c, that Exod. 24:3–8 formed the most probable background pointing to Jesus' death as a covenant sacrifice. This, I also noted, was associated with the Spirit's work in bringing people into covenant relationship with God (established on the basis of Jesus' death), along with its renewing, cleansing, empowering, and life-changing implications (1 Pet. 1:2b; cf. 1:3, 23). The death of Christ, then, may be considered a victory because it makes possible God's new covenant gift of the Holy Spirit, with its promise of a new heart and a new empowerment to walk in holiness, thus providing liberation from the tyranny of sin and Satan.

(3) Jesus' resurrection from the dead (1 Pet. 1:3, 11; 2:4; 3:18, 21) and exaltation to God's right hand (1 Pet. 3:22) represents a third and important way in which the atonement constitutes a victory. It is interesting to note that in Zech. 3:1 the 'right hand of God' is the very place from which Satan used to accuse God's people: 'Then he showed me the high

---

[12] Blocher, 'Agnus Victor', 86.   [13] Bruce, *Colossians*, 110.
[14] Jeffery, Ovey, and Sach, *Pierced for our Transgressions*, 135.

priest Joshua standing before the angel of the Lord, and Satan standing at his right hand to accuse him.' As a direct result of his death on the cross and resurrection (3:18de, 21d), Peter tells us that Jesus is now 'at the right hand of God, having gone into heaven, with angels and authorities and powers subjected to him' (3:22). The elevation and enthronement of Jesus to a position of privilege at God's right hand also entails the subjugation of those forces that oppose and accuse God's people, who, as a result of Christ's death and resurrection, have received forgiveness of sins (cf. 1 Pet. 2:24d; Acts 5:31). Moreover, God's vindication of Christ's innocent suffering through resurrection (3:18e, 21d), ascension (vv. 19, 22b), victorious proclamation (v. 19), and exaltation to God's right hand (v. 22), provides suffering believers with the assurance that he will one day vindicate them by raising them from the dead (3:18e; 4:6c) and bestowing upon them praise, glory and honour (1:7). Peter's presentation of the believer's salvation in terms of future victory and vindication is designed to engender hope amongst a small group of suffering believers. Their solidarity with Christ assures them that his victory will one day be theirs also. Thus the appropriate attitude in the present is hope (an important word associated with Christ's victorious resurrection in 1 Peter, 1:3, 21; cf. 1:13; 3:15).

3.   Jesus' death as ransom

Often associated with the theme of victory is the notion of ransom. The concept of ransom became a metaphor of central importance in patristic interpretations of Christ's death. The notion of 'ransom' implies three related ideas:

1.   *Liberation*: A ransom is something which achieves freedom for a person who is held in captivity.
2.   *Payment*: A ransom is a sum of money which is paid in order to achieve an individual's liberation.
3.   *Someone to whom the ransom is paid*: A ransom is usually paid to an individual's captor, or his agent.[15]

Most patristic writers followed Origen in interpreting Christ's death as the liberation of humans from bondage (to Satan) by the payment of a ransom price (the blood of Jesus) to Satan. Origen (*c.* 185–253) comments on Eph. 1:7:

---

[15] McGrath, *Christian Theology*, 415.

> *Apolutrōsis* or *lutrōsis* concerns captives and those who have
> been brought under the power of their enemies; but we have
> been brought under the power of enemies, namely, of the prince
> of this world and of the powers subject to him, and we need
> redemption, therefore, and someone who will redeem us by
> giving as a price (*lutron*) his own blood; we have redemption,
> therefore, through his blood and remission of our sins.[16]

This price, explains Origen commenting on Mt. 20:28, is to be paid to
the prince of this world, Satan: 'But to whom did he give his life as the
price of redemption for many? Not to God; maybe to the evil spirit? For
he was holding us under his power, until Jesus would give his life on
our behalf.'[17] Commenting on 1 Pet. 1:18 Ambrose writes: '[The devil]
without doubt demanded the price, so that he might set free those he was
holding bound, but the price of our liberation was the blood of our Lord
Jesus, which necessarily had to be paid to him to whom we had been sold
because of our sins.'[18] Satan, however, was deceived. Attracted by what
he perceived to be a more valuable prize, Satan, according to Gregory of
Nyssa (330–*c*.395), 'chose [Christ] as a ransom for those who were shut
up in the prison of death'.[19] He did not realise, however, that the deity of
Christ was concealed in his humanity: 'The Deity was hidden under the
veil of our nature, so that, as with ravenous fish, the hook of the deity
might be gulped down with the bait of fish.'[20] For Gregory the atonement thus represents 'a manifestation both of God's justice and of his
wisdom'.[21] The justice of God is manifested in the offering of a ransom
(a 'fair exchange')[22] while the wisdom (= 'cunning') of God is displayed
in the concealing of Christ's divinity in the flesh of his humanity.[23]

In their exposition of the ransom theme the patristic writers highlight
a number of important elements which both find support in and sharpen
our understanding of 1 Peter: (1) As my exegesis of 1 Pet. 1:18–19 has
indicated, the patristic writers correctly highlight the importance of the
price (the blood of Christ) that was paid for the believers' redemption
(from their bondage to a sinful [= 'futile', v. 18] past). By contrast, a
number of modern interpreters have sought to divest the metaphor of
just about all of its metaphorical elements and as a result see it simply

---

[16] Origen, *Catenae in Eph.*   [17] *PG*, 13.1397.   [18] *PL*, 16.1299.
[19] Gregory of Nyssa, *The Great Catechism* 23.
[20] Gregory of Nyssa, *The Great Catechism* 24.
[21] Boersma, *Violence, Hospitality, and the Cross*, 190.
[22] Gregory of Nyssa, *The Great Catechism* 22.
[23] Gregory of Nyssa, *The Great Catechism* 23.

as a metaphor for deliverance or setting free and no more. Lyonnet and Sabourin, for example, write:

> For when the hagiographers designated the saving work of Christ by the terms *lutrousthai, apolutrōsis*, and so forth, they wanted to evoke, by the force of the very terms, the source itself out of which proceeded the whole economy of redemption, namely, God himself, the Father, not, however, as that merchant who does not grant freedom unless he has first been paid the corresponding price, but as he who quite gratuitously frees us from every slavery, so that we become 'his own': in other words, not as one who does not set free unless he does not lose anything, but as he who grants freedom for no other reason than because he loves, who does not wish anything else than to communicate his own life to all and to make us participate in his own beatitude provided that we wish to accept that gift by a free act, by an act of faith in the Pauline and Johannine sense.[24]

However, if God can grant freedom without the payment of a price but rather simply as the one 'who quite gratuitously frees us from every slavery ... for no other reason than because he loves',[25] then why the cross?[26] Why not in some other (less costly) manner? If liberation can be granted without the payment of a price, then the cross is hardly necessary. 1 Peter 1:18–19, however, is emphatic that a very high price has been paid for the believers' redemption ('the precious blood of Christ'), with the implication being that had not the ransom price been paid, redemption would not have been effected. This leads on to the next point.

(2) The patristic writers correctly point out that in the work of redemption God does not act in an arbitrary fashion, but in a way that is consistent with his just and holy character. Lyonnet and Sabourin are correct to point out that God 'quite gratuitously frees us from every slavery', but wrongly go on to suggest that he 'grants freedom for no other reason than because he loves'.[27] For, as Carson rightly points out, 'the theme of the love of God, as precious as it is, is not all that the Bible says about God ... It is irresponsible to talk about the love of God without considering the holiness ... and even the wrath of God as it would be ... to focus on his wrath without listening attentively to what the Bible says about

---

[24] Lyonnet and Sabourin, *Sin, Redemption, and Sacrifice*, 103.   [25] Ibid.
[26] Balthasar, *Theo-drama*, 4: 312: 'Why the Cross, if God Forgives in any Case?'
[27] Lyonnet and Sabourin, *Sin, Redemption, and Sacrifice*, 103.

his love'.[28] 1 Peter has much to say about the holiness and justice of God (1:14–16, 17; 2:23; 3:12; 4:5, 17). As Grenz observes: 'God is holy, in that he is just and totally righteous in all he does [cf. 1 Pet. 1:14–16]. God is always fair with all creatures [cf. 1:17]. Consequently, God seeks justice. And one day he will judge each human being according to his righteous standard [cf. 4:5; 2:23]'.[29] In fact the two ideas are closely related in the ransom text of 1 Peter and its immediate context:

> [B]e holy in all your conduct, for it is written [that], 'You shall be holy, because *I am holy*'. And if you call upon a father *who judges impartially* according to the work of each person, conduct yourselves *with fear* … knowing that *you were ransomed* from the futile way of life … with the precious blood of Christ, as a lamb flawless and faultless (1:16–19).

The just judgment of God (1:17; 4:5; cf. 2:7) against a life lived in sin (1 Pet. 1:18; cf. 1:14; 4:2–3) is demanded by his holiness (cf. 1:15–16). Yet liberating sinners from sin (its consequences but also its power) would mean not punishing them. Yet how can he do this without compromising his holiness and justice when they are in fact guilty and deserving of judgment? He did this by providing Christ as the ransom payment who paid the price (i.e., death = 'blood', v. 19) owed by guilty sinners. Sin is thus punished and guilty sinners are liberated. The patristic writers correctly highlighted the element of exchange or substitution here.[30] As I noted in my exegesis of 1 Pet. 1:18–19, the idea communicated here by the language of ransom is that of equivalence or substitution. Christ's death redeems because he takes the believers' place as the ransom price, that is, he dies the death that they should have died (see further the discussion in §5 below).

(3) The patristic writers were thus right to ask the question: Who demanded the payment of a price? Many wrongly insisted it was the devil. Instead, as I have argued, it was God who demanded that a ransom be paid for the liberation of sinner. This fact receives further support from 1 Pet. 1:20 (the verse immediately following our ransom passage, vv. 18–19), which indicates that God's decision to provide Christ as the ransom payment (a decision arising from his holy and just demand that sin be paid for) stems from his sovereign and eternal purpose. 1 Peter 1:18–19 is joined to v. 20 by the adjectival participle προεγνωσμένου

---

[28] Carson, *Gagging of God*, 241.

[29] Grenz, *Theology for the Community of God*, 122.

[30] See esp., e.g., Gregory of Nyssa, *The Great Catechism* 23.

(from προγινώσκω, 'choose beforehand'): προεγνωσμένου μὲν πρὸ καταβολῆς κόσμου ('who [= Χριστοῦ, v. 19] was foreknown/chosen before the foundation of the world', v. 20a). As Beare notes, '[t]he fore-knowledge of God conveys the thought of will and purpose; that Christ is "foreknown" means that his work in the world was ordained by God, that the fulfilment of God's purpose for the world was destined to be accomplished through him, through his sacrifice of himself'.[31] The passive voice of the participle indicates that 'all of this was God's doing … the redemption brought about by the death of Jesus … was due to the divine initiative'.[32] We saw the development of a similar theme in 1:10–12 which spoke of the 'spirit of Christ' predicting (προμαρτυρόμενον) through the prophets 'the sufferings destined for Christ [τὰ εἰς Χριστὸν παθήματα] and the glories after these sufferings'. As Achtemeier again notes, 'the phrase [τὰ εἰς Χριστὸν παθήματα] points to the continuing dynamic of the divine initiative in such salvation'.[33] The demand that sin be paid for was thus an eternal demand.

4.   Jesus' death as sacrifice

Drawing on Old Testament imagery and expectation, the New Testament interprets the death of Jesus on the cross as a sacrifice. Unlike the Old Testament sacrifices, Christ's sacrificial offering 'was the final sacrifice, dealing with all the sins of the world … it was an act of God from beyond [humans], achieving what they could not do, and it was also a "once-for-all" event in the past'.[34] In 1 Pet. 3:18 we are told that 'Christ also suffered [as a sacrifice] for sins [περὶ ἁμαρτιῶν] once for all [ἅπαξ]'. Then earlier in 1:18–19 Christ's death is compared to the sacrificing of the Passover lamb on the eve of Israel's redemption: 'you were ransomed … with the precious blood of Christ, as a lamb flawless and fault-less'. Finally, in 1:2, Christ's death is likened to a covenant sacrifice: 'to the elect … according to the foreknowledge of God the Father, by means of the consecration of the Spirit, for the purpose of obedience and sprink-ling of the blood of Jesus Christ'. As we seek to unpack the significance of Jesus' death as a sacrifice we are confronted with the following two questions: (1) How does the idea of Jesus' death on the cross as a sacrifice throw light on the manner in which God deals with the problem of human sin? (2) Can it explain how the problem of human sin was so decisively dealt with by this one past event?

---

[31] Beare, *First Epistle of Peter*, 80.   [32] Achtemeier, *1 Peter*, 131.
[33] Ibid., 108.   [34] Fiddes, *Past Event and Present Salvation*, 67.

As we saw in my exegesis of 1:19, a number of scholars contend that the phrase 'the blood of Christ' (see 1:2c, 19) stands not for his death but for his *life* released through death (with the accent on life). Paul Fiddes suggests that 'the ritual act [of sacrifice] gave the assurance that God would surely accomplish what the sacrifice portrayed; it was *he* who broke the link between sin and its otherwise inevitable consequence of calamity ... through the sacrificial death God was believed to "cleanse away" or "cover over" the uncleanness of the sin that lay upon the lives of his people'.[35] How does the blood of sacrifice actually achieve this? 'A hint is given here when blood is described as containing life. The idea seems to be that the tainted and unclean life of the offending community is renewed by the pouring out of fresh life present in the blood of the animal.'[36] This interpretation is based on Lev. 17:11–14: 'For the life [Heb. נֶפֶשׁ; Gk ψυχή] of the flesh is in the blood; and I have given it to you for making atonement [Heb. כַּפֵּר; Gk ἐξιλάσκεσθαι] for your lives on the altar; for, as life, it is the blood that makes atonement ... For the life of every creature – its blood is its life' (cf. Gen. 9:4; Deut. 12:23).

In response it should be noted that Lev. 17:11 does not simply say that 'life is in the blood' but that the 'life **of the flesh** [הַבָּשָׂר]] is in the blood' suggesting that if the blood is spilled then life 'in the flesh' will cease. Stibbs remarks:

> A careful examination of the contexts reveals that in each of the three cases [Gen. 9:4; Lev. 17:11; Deut. 12:23] these statements say not that 'blood' is 'life' in isolation, but that blood is the life of the flesh. This means that if the blood is separated from the flesh, whether in man or beast, the present physical life in the flesh will come to an end. Blood shed stands, therefore, not for the release of life from the burden of the flesh, but for the bringing to end of life in the flesh. It is a witness to physical death, not an evidence of spiritual revival.[37]

This is in keeping with the predominant use of the term αἷμα in Scripture to denote death (generally by violence). As Schweizer notes, '[d]abei ist im Neuen Testament aber nicht das Blut als "Stoff" wichtig, sondern als Zeichen für die Tat das freiwillig in den Tod gehenden Herrn'.[38] When speaking of 'the blood of Christ', the New Testament writers were not interested in the material substance as if it could communicate anything

---

[35] Ibid., 69 (emphasis his).   [36] Ibid.
[37] Stibbs, *The Meaning of the Word 'Blood' in Scripture*, 12.
[38] Schweizer, *Petrusbrief*, 33.

in and of itself (such a view reflects more the blood mysticism of the mystery religions than it does biblical theology), but instead in the shed blood of Jesus as a reference to his violent, sacrificial death. In the New Testament generally the salvation accomplished by the blood of Jesus is equally said to be accomplished by the death of Jesus (see Rom. 3:21–6; 5:6–9; Eph. 1:7; Heb. 2:14; Rev. 5:9; cf. Acts 22:20). Thus when Peter tells his readers in 1:18–19 that they have been ransomed 'with the precious blood of Christ' (τιμίῳ αἵματι Χριστοῦ), he means that the price paid, the blood of Christ, was his violent sacrificial death on the cross. Moreover, the idea communicated here by the language of sacrifice is that of substitution. A little later in the same letter we read that 'Christ also suffered [as a sacrifice] [περὶ ἁμαρτιῶν] for sins ... a righteous one in the place of [ὑπέρ] unrighteous ones' (3:18). The death of Christ is substitutionary because, as the sacrifice, he dies the death that believers should have died on account of their sin (on the implications of this see §5 below).

5.   Jesus' death as penal substitution

In previous sections we noted that Christ's death redeems because in his death he takes the believers' place as both the ransom price (§3 above) and atoning sacrifice (§4 above); in dying he suffers the punishment (divine judgment) against sin that sinners themselves should have undergone. This naturally brings us to Peter's description of Jesus' death as a penal substitution. Gunton explains: 'It is here that legal imagery has a part to play in the theology of both sin and salvation. Sin is often conceived as transgression of the law of God, and, correlatively, salvation is understood as freedom from the consequences or penalties of that transgression.'[39] However, it is on this very point that the penal substitution view has been most heavily criticised by some authors. Morna Hooker labels it a 'crude interpretation[s] of the atonement'.[40] Green and Baker call it 'unbiblical',[41] contending that it is unable to communicate much more than the fact that 'God the Father was willing to kill his Son to save others'.[42] Some feminist theologians have gone so far as to label it a case of 'divine child abuse'.[43] For Fiddes, the notion of 'changing

[39] Gunton, *Actuality of the Atonement*, 84.
[40] Hooker, *From Adam to Christ*, 26.
[41] Green and Baker, *Recovering the Scandal*, 148.   [42] Ibid., 141.
[43] See, e.g., Brown and Parker, 'For God So Loved the World?', 2; Brock, 'And a Little Child Will Lead Us: Christology and Child Abuse', 42–61.

places' in the penal view wrongly reduces the doctrine of the atonement to 'a mere formula'.[44] He explains:

> Theories of legal satisfaction set a law above the character of God. The theory runs that God cannot forgive us until the punishment demanded by justice is exacted. This conceives justice as law with ultimate authority; even when the law is said to be God's own law, the theory still requires God to act in a way which is confined by legal restraints. Law has ceased to be a useful guideline to the purpose of God for his creatures, and has become a supreme principle.[45]

Proponents of this view, complains Fiddes, turn God into a cosmic accountant who must balance the books: 'Some preaching thus reduces the event of the cross to a factor in an equation, formulated by a divine mathematician; a death is needed to balance the cosmic sum, and a death is provided.'[46] In response to Fiddes (and Green and Baker, Hooker, and others) the following should be noted from 1 Peter:

(1) My exegesis of 1 Pet. 2:23–4 clearly demonstrates that Christ endured the penal consequences of human sin. In v. 23 Peter testifies that God is 'the one who judges justly', and then in the very next verse (v. 24) he affirms that 'he [Christ] himself bore our sins in his body on the cross'. The expression 'to bear sin', I noted in my exegesis of this verse, signifies 'to bear the consequences of sin' or 'to bear the penalty of sin'. This – the text itself – provides the starting point for any discussion on the nature of the atonement, regardless of what difficulties we may have with the notion of penal substitution.

(2) Fiddes' criticism of the penal theory as being 'too "objective"', at the expense of the "subjective" dimension of the atonement',[47] only holds true if we reduce the meaning of the atonement to the penal view alone. However, as we have already seen, the atonement also has a very clear subjective aspect to it (which itself is inseparably related to its more objective aspect) because it makes possible God's new covenant gift of the Holy Spirit with its promise of a new heart and a new empowerment to walk in holiness (1:2), thus providing liberation from the tyranny of sin (1:18–19; 2:24), reconciliation and relationship with God (3:18; 2:25), and an example to be followed (2:21).

(3) Fiddes is right to be concerned about any theory of 'legal satisfaction [that] set[s] a law above the character of God'.[48] He is wrong,

---

[44] Fiddes, *Past Event and Present Salvation*, 84.   [45] Ibid., 101.
[46] Ibid., 83.   [47] Ibid., 99.   [48] Ibid., 101.

however, to presume that the penal substitution view actually does this. On the contrary, 'the consistent biblical understanding of the law' is that it is not something that is above or outside of God but that it is something that 'mirrors the very being of God, and is therefore inextricably related to his character'.[49] The 'Father who judges impartially' (1 Pet. 1:17; cf. 2:23; 4:5), writes Peter, is also '*the Holy One* who called you' (1:15). Therefore, says Peter quoting Lev. 19:2, 'You shall be holy, because I am holy' (1:16). Consequently, the judgment of God against sin is demanded by his holiness, and the justice of his judgment is ensured because it is exercised in conformity with the perfection of his holiness and not some alien law.

(4) Fiddes, on the other hand, espouses a very impersonal and mechanistic view of divine punishment when he consistently speaks of it as 'the natural consequences of their own sin',[50] 'the tragedy of people's self-inflicted wounds',[51] and 'the bitter harvest they were inevitably sowing for themselves'.[52] Behind this lies his rejection of retributive punishment 'as penalty inflicted from the outside' (i.e., 'that God directly *inflicts* some kind of penalty').[53] Instead he prefers to speak of judgment as 'not a penalty imposed from outside human life, but a natural consequence flowing from the sin itself'.[54] Thus, writes Fiddes, '[w]hen the judgment of God is understood as his personal consent to the natural outworking of people's estrangement from God and each other, then we can think of Christ as participating in our experience of being "accursed" without any suggestion that the Father is punishing the Son on our behalf'.[55]

This view (sometimes referred to as the 'immanentist' view) shows more the influence of Deism and an Enlightenment worldview rather than a biblical (and hence Peter's) worldview and results in an impersonal doctrine of the atonement. 1 Peter, however, suggests that God acts at a level beyond that of merely natural consequence, but in his holiness (cf. 1:15–16) he personally acts to pursue, confront, and punish sinners (4:5, 17; cf. 1:17; 2:23; cf. 2:13–14). This is further suggested by 1 Peter's use of Isa. 53, which indicates that the consequences inflicted upon the Servant (Jesus Christ) because of the sin of others were the result of God's direct involvement: 'Yet it was *the will of the Lord* [וַיהוָה חָפֵץ, lit., 'Yahweh was pleased'] to crush him with pain' (Isa. 53:10). This statement cannot be separated from the following two expressions found in vv. 11 and 12: וַעֲוֹנֹתָם הוּא יִסְבֹּל ('and their guilt he will bear',

---

[49] Williams, 'The Cross and Punishment of Sin', 85.
[50] Fiddes, *Past Event and Present Salvation*, 92.
[51] Ibid.   [52] Ibid., 95.   [53] Ibid. (emphasis his).   [54] Ibid., 93.
[55] Ibid., 104.

v. 11d) and וְהוּא חֵטְא־רַבִּים נָשָׂא ('and he the sin of many bore', v. 12d). '[T]he close identification of God with the law and with the act of punishment made in Scripture shows that he is thoroughly involved in both, and thus proves that penal substitution, being formed by such categories, is not as a consequence impersonal or mechanistic.'[56] The result is a much more personal (and biblical) doctrine of the atonement (after all, says Peter, he is 'a *Father* who judges impartially', 1:17).

The following quotation from John Owen's *The Death of Death in the Death of Christ* provides an apt summary of the Petrine understanding of Jesus' death as a penal substitution. He writes: 'Christ so took and bare our sins, and had them laid upon him, so that he underwent the punishment due unto them, and that in our stead: therefore, he made satisfaction to the justice of God for them'.[57] As Owen goes on to point out, there are three basic parts to this doctrine, each of which have been confirmed by my exegesis of 1 Peter: 'First, that Christ took and bare our sins, God laying them on him. Secondly, that he so took them as to undergo the punishment due unto them. Thirdly, that he did this in our stead.'[58]

6. Jesus' death as reconciliation

Stanley Grenz suggests that the 'focus on reconciliation between sinful humans and the righteous God must always remain central in our theological reflections'.[59] In fact for Hendrikus Berkhof, the terms 'representation' and 'reconciliation' best describe the atonement: 'Guilt is a relational concept. Our debt (guilt) before God is enormous, and representation signifies that in him [Christ] the relationship is restored, that is, that which from our side obstructed the relationship simply does not count anymore in the light of his perfect love and obedience.'[60] How exactly is this reconciliation effected? Berkhof is not sure: 'Why is representation possible? And why does this require the total sacrifice of a life? And how is this sacrifice related to the assumption of the guilt? The NT asserts the "that", but has no answer to the "why" and the "how". That is God's secret.'[61] What he is certain of, however, is that it does not come through the transfer of the consequences of the believer's sin to Christ. 'Did Jesus bear the punishment for our sins?' he asks. 'In Isa. 53:5 this word is used incidentally. The NT does not make use of it ...

---

[56] Williams, 'The Cross and Punishment of Sin', 94.
[57] Owen, *Works*, 10: 280. [58] Ibid.
[59] Grenz, *Theology for the Community of God*, 453.
[60] Berkhof, *Christian Faith*, 305. [61] Ibid.

For Jesus identifies himself with the estrangement from God and all its consequences. But the juridical interpretation and extrapolation of the concept of punishment … is foreign to the NT.'[62]

Berkhof, however, is wrong to assert that the New Testament makes no use of the concept of Christ bearing the punishment for our sins (and as it is found in Isa. 53). We have already established that Isa. 53 is the most likely source of Peter's conviction that Christ 'bore [the consequences of] our sins in his body on the tree [cross]' (1 Pet. 2:24). We noted that this idea is also communicated in 1 Peter by the language of sacrifice. According to 1 Pet. 3:18, it is Christ's sacrificial, substitutionary, and therefore sin-bearing death (see above) which is the very means by which reconciliation between God and humans is effected: 'For Christ also suffered [as a sacrifice] for sins once for all, the righteous in the place of [ὑπέρ] the unrighteous, *in order to bring you to God*'. The expression 'in order to bring you to God' (ἵνα ὑμᾶς προσαγάγῃ τῷ θεῷ) expresses the intended result (ἵνα) of Christ's substitutionary, sin-bearing death in terms of 'access to' and 'reconciliation with' God (cf. 2 Cor. 5:19–21). Thus the work of reconciliation is primarily a divine act in which believers are received into God's favour. Berkhof, however, suggests that 'representation signifies that in him the relationship is restored, that is, that which *from our side* obstructed the relationship simply does not count anymore in light of his perfect love and obedience (2 Cor. 5:19)'.[63] However, as Erickson rightly notes, 'as important as it is for humans to turn to God, the process of reconciliation primarily involves God's turning in favour toward them'.[64] It is not only human unwillingness and sin which obstructs relationship with God but also God's righteous wrath against that sin (and sinner). Because sin is an affront to a holy God it must be expiated, and God must be propitiated before there can be reconciliation. Jesus' sacrificial death achieves both: 'By offering himself as a sacrifice, by substituting himself for us, actually bearing the punishment that should have been ours, Jesus appeased the Father and effected reconciliation between God and humanity.'[65]

7.   Jesus' death as example

Faustus Socinus (1539–1604) in his *De Jesu Christo Servatore* (1578) reacted against the doctrine of Christ's satisfaction, arguing that God, as absolute *dominus*, is above compulsion and therefore not constrained

---

[62] Ibid.   [63] Ibid.   [64] Erickson, *Christian Theology*, 832–3.
[65] Ibid., 833.

by nature to punish sin. Punitive justice, he argued, is not an attribute of God but an effect of his will. Therefore it is 'simply God's decision to punish sin'. In the same way God can simply choose to forgive sinners who repent and turn from their sin:

> Quòd si Deus propter delinquentis non veram poenitentiam, sed poenae formidinem, & coram ipsius maiestate externam demissionem, sententiam iam adversus illum latam revocare solet, quid eum facere consueuisse dicendum est, cum is, qui deliquit, ex animo delictorum poenitentiam agit, adeò ut resipiscat, & in posterum purè & innocenter vivat?[66]

Thus, as Erickson points out, for Socinus, the 'new covenant of which Jesus spoke involves an absolute forgiveness rather than some sort of substitutionary sacrifice'.[67] Even though God's forgiveness is absolutely free, 'being righteous in God's sight involves a real change in our conduct'.[68] The real value of Jesus' death lies in that he provides us with a perfect example of the type of righteous conduct we are to practice. Thus salvation is obtained by following (or imitating) Christ's example: 'Demonstratur … nos Christum imitari posse, hancque esse aeternae salutis viam: ob idque Christum iurè Servatorem nostrum appellari.'[69] Socinus correctly pointed to 1 Pet. 2:21 for proof of the meaning of Christ's death as an example: 'Christ also suffered for you, leaving you an example, so that you should follow in his steps'.

The exemplarist approach gained great popularity in rationalist circles throughout nineteenth-century Europe. This was due largely to a form of Christology which, because of its denial of the two natures of Christ, tended to view Jesus as a normal human being who nevertheless 'embod[ied] certain qualities which are present, actually or potentially, in all other human beings, the difference lying in the superior extent to which he embodied them'.[70] Thus, as McGrath notes, '[t]he person who died on the cross was a human being, and the impact of that death is upon human beings. The impact takes the form of inspiration and encouragement to model ourselves upon the moral example set us in Jesus himself.'[71] The most significant exponent of the exemplarist approach in the following century was Hastings Rashdall who, in his *Idea of Atonement*

---

[66] Socinus, *De Jesu Christo Servatore* 3.2.
[67] Erickson, *Christian Theology*, 801.
[68] Gomes, 'De Jesu Christo Servatore', 223.
[69] Socinus, *De Jesu Christo Servatore* 1.3 2.
[70] McGrath, *Christian Theology*, 426.   [71] Ibid., 427.

in Christian Theology (1919), argued that 'the theory of the atonement associated with the medieval writer Peter Abelard was more acceptable to modern thought forms than traditional theories which made appeal to the notion of substitutionary sacrifice'.[72] Rashdall writes:

> The eternal meaning of the Christian doctrine of salvation through Christ alone is that in the acceptance of this supreme revelation lies the way of being saved and attaining the full-est deliverance from sin, and the highest perfection, of which human nature is capable. Translated into still more modern lan-guage the meaning of the church's early creed, 'There is no other name given among men by which we may be saved', will be something of this kind: 'There is no other ideal given among men by which we may be saved except the moral ideal which Christ taught by his words, and illustrated by his life and death of love'.[73]

The important truth being affirmed here is that 'Christ also suffered for you leaving you an example in order that you might follow in his footsteps' (1 Pet. 2:21). However, as Martin Kähler in his *Doctrine of Reconciliation* (1898) asks: 'Did Christ just make known some insights concerning an unchangeable situation – or did he establish a new situation?'[74] Or as McGrath reframes it: 'Does the cross of Christ illus-trate the saving will of God? Or does it make such a salvation possible in the first place? Is it constitutive or illustrative?'[75] As 1 Pet. 2:21–5 illustrates, the answer is that it is both, for as Peter goes on to write: 'He himself bore our sins in his body upon the tree so that [ἵνα] we, having abandoned wrongdoing, might live for doing what is right; by whose wounds you have been healed' (2:24; cf. 3:18). As this text indicates, the atonement is illustrative because it is constitutive (that is to say, it can only be considered illustrative once it has been considered constitutive); believers are able to 'live for doing what is right' (which is exemplified by Christ in 2:21–3) because Christ bore the believers' sins in his body on the cross (the ἵνα with the subjunctive ζήσωμεν indicates purpose/ result, v. 24b) resulting in their spiritual healing (v. 24d). The crucial weakness with subjective theories of the atonement, is (1) that they tend to trivialise sin and evil, and (2) they can tend, as a result, to degenerate into moralism (or as Luther put it, it 'make[s] Christ into a Moses'). Sin and evil, as we have seen, as objective realities are implied in all of the

---

[72] Ibid., 105.   [73] Rashdall, *The Idea of Atonement*, 463.
[74] Cited in McGrath, *Historical Theology*, 293.   [75] Ibid.

Petrine metaphors for the atonement. They represent a bondage from which believers have been ransomed (1:18–19), an offence from which they have been acquitted (2:25), a power from which they have been freed (2:24) and over which Christ has achieved victory (3:18–22), and a source of alienation from God which has been set right (2:25; 3:18). As Gunton notes,

> [These metaphors] reveal that the problem which the atonement engages is primarily *theological*. It does not consist primarily in morally wrong acts whose effect is on human life alone and which therefore can be rectified by merely human remedial action, but in a disrupted relationship with the creator. As a result of the disruption there is an *objective* bondage, pollution and disorder in personal and social life, encompassing all dimensions of human existence and its context. By virtue of both truths, that the problem is one we cannot solve and that our being clean and free and upright is the gift of the creator, there needs to be a recreative, redemptive, divine initiative in which the root of the problem, the disrupted personal relationship, is set to rights.[76]

In the end, neither truth must be lost. In establishing a case for an objective, past atonement, it cannot be at the cost of denying its subjective and exemplary implications, and vice versa, 'because Christ also suffered for you leaving you an example in order that you might follow in the footsteps of him … who himself bore our sins in his body upon the tree so that we, having abandoned wrongdoing, might live for doing what is right; by whose wounds you have been healed' (1 Pet. 2.21, 24). In light of Christ's exemplary and sacrificial offering of himself, notes Jüngel,

> [t]he whole life of the Christian can be metaphorically characterized as a sacrifice … The writer of 1 Peter exhorts Christians themselves to be built into a 'holy priesthood, to offer spiritual sacrifices acceptable to God through Jesus Christ' (1 Pet. 2.5f.). The addition of the word 'spiritual' makes the metaphorical use of the language altogether clear. It is not specific 'sacrifices' which are meant, but rather the offering to God of the whole life that has been sanctified by God (1 Pet. 1.15).[77]

---

[76] Gunton, *Actuality of the Atonement*, 159 (emphasis his).
[77] Jüngel, 'The Sacrifice of Jesus', 182.

This offering up of one's life, he correctly notes, is not *primarily* about performance but praise, not occupation but celebration, not action but adoration, not works but worship.

8.   Conclusion

This brief dialogue between 1 Peter and some of the major theologies and theologians of the atonement has highlighted three key issues: (1) That one single metaphor by itself is insufficient to capture the richness and truth of all that Christ accomplished on the cross. To limit the atonement simply to the notion of victory, or example, or forgiveness, or even penal substitution, would result in both a distortion of the biblical teaching and an impoverished view of the atonement. (2) The different metaphors (victory, ransom, sacrifice, penal substitution, reconciliation, example, etc.) actually complement rather than compete against each other. 1 Peter exposes the degree to which they are mutually complementary and corroborative. We saw that Christ's victory over sin and Satan was achieved primarily through his death on the cross which 1 Peter (and the NT generally) portrays as both a covenant sacrifice (with its associated gift of the cleansing, transforming and empowering Spirit) and a penal substitution (by which Satan's accusations against believers is rendered groundless). Other metaphors drawn from the slave market or the buying back of prisoners of war and the Old Testament sacrificial system (also substitutionary in character) further fill out the picture providing us with a richer and more rounded understanding of the atonement. The result is an understanding of Christ's atoning death in terms of liberation from the tyranny of sin and Satan, redemption from enslavement to the past, freedom from the law's penalty, entrance into a new covenant with its associated gift of the Spirit, reconciliation with God, and an example of perfect dedication to God's will and its associated call to imitation. (3) While the different models complement each other, the penal substitution model must be seen as central, for, as we have seen, without it the other metaphors (such as victory, ransom, sacrifice, reconciliation, and example) make little sense. As Jeffery, Ovey, and Sach observe: 'Far from being viable *alternatives* to penal substitution, they [the other metaphors] are outworkings of it. As the hub from which all of these other doctrines fan out, penal substitution is surely central.'[78]

---

[78] Jeffery, Ovey, and Sach, *Pierced for our Transgressions*, 211.

CONCLUSION

1.   Review

The object of this study has been to investigate the understanding of salvation in the first letter of Peter. This study has confirmed the importance and richness of this theme, which plays a vital role in relation to the letter's purpose. 1 Peter's soteriological outlook exhibits a salvation-historical framework, in which salvation is rooted in the eternal, sovereign, and gracious electing purpose of God (1:1–2; 2:4–19), revealed in the historical Christ event (1:10–12, 18–21; 2:21–5; 3:18), realised existentially through the proclamation of the message of salvation (1:12, 23), the experience of the new birth (1:3, 23) and baptism (3:20–1), and which will reach its consummation at the return of Christ when suffering and death will give way to life and vindication (1:3–12; 3:18–4:6). While this salvation is offered to all through the proclamation of the gospel (cf. 1:12), it is appropriated (by faith; cf. 1:7, 9, 21) only by those who have been chosen (1:1–2; cf. 2:4–10) and rebirthed (1:3; cf. v. 23) by God, and who, as a result of their election and rebirth, have reoriented their lives to its eschatological promise and present ethical demands through baptism (3:20d–1).

This study has been carried out on two levels: first, by examining the content of the concept of salvation expressed in 1 Peter (chapters 2–6), and then second, given that content, by considering 1 Peter's contribution to the broader theological conversation (at the level of systematic theology) and by allowing that conversation to shape and sharpen our own understanding of 1 Peter's soteriology (chapters 7–8). Underlying this conversation was the desire to explore a means by which a more fruitful dialogue between New Testament studies and systematic theology might be pursued. In doing so I have sought to call into question the notion that biblical theology is necessarily more biblical than systematic theology (contra Gabler, Wrede). Instead I have endeavoured to demonstrate that the two are mutually enriching and correcting (to the extent that both seek to be truly biblical).

The methodological distinctiveness of this study has been the use of what Vanhoozer has termed 'theological criticism'[1] and what I have called 'theological-critical exegesis' (and others have similarly referred to as 'theological interpretation' or 'theological exegesis'). Theological-critical exegesis, as we have already noted, does not dispense with existing methodologies (such as the historical-critical or historical-grammatical method) but provides a sharper criterion for their application. In chapter 1 the presuppositions, methodology, and aims of theological-critical exegesis were explained, its implications for biblical interpretation were explored, and its particular contribution to an understanding of the concept of salvation in 1 Peter was examined. In the end, theological criticism, with its governing interest in God and a desire to do justice to the priority of God, is ideally suited to the study of salvation which itself is rooted in the person, purpose, plan, power, and promise of God.

2.   Theological criticism as a tool for understanding the biblical text

The theological-critical approach to exegesis has proved to be a useful tool at every stage of this investigation. The strongest claim to be made for it in this study is that it is only such an approach that ultimately does justice to the subject matter of the text itself. Because 1 Peter is ultimately concerned about the reality of God (the word θεός itself appears thirty-nine times in 1 Peter with the word πατήρ occurring three times), its readers, therefore, must have a similar interest. Peter's model readers, as Green points out, are those who hear their names in the letter opening: 'to the elect [of God], strangers of the Diaspora' (1:1b).[2] As Green goes on to note, '[f]irst Peter is addressed to just such people and is read best by those who share its theological assumptions and those who hear its opening as an invitation to embody its world'.[3] 1 Peter thus calls for a style of reading that proceeds from faith and seeks theological understanding. 'To read the biblical texts theologically is to read the texts as they wish to be read, and as they should be read in order to do them justice.'[4] This means that to read the text theologically is to read it as its divine and human authors intended it to be read. The assumption, then, of this study, has been that it is the authors (divine and human) whose actions determine the meaning of a text. That is to say, the meaning of

---

[1] See Vanhoozer, 'Introduction', 22.
[2] See Green, 'Theological Interpretation', 328.
[3] Ibid.   [4] Vanhoozer, 'Introduction', 22.

the text is the authorially intended meaning (i.e., the meaning that has been placed in the text by the authors). Treating the text as a divine–human communicative action has provided for us an entry point into the hermeneutical spiral.

My approach to theological-critical exegesis has helped to avoid the extremes of, on the one hand, absolute disinterestedness (objective knowledge) claimed by many historical critics (e.g., Gabler, Wrede, Funk, and Hoover), and, on the other hand, the absolute interestedness (subjective preference) of many so-called postmoderns (e.g., Fish, Derrida, Holland). Instead I opted for a mediating position that recognised the knowability of the text (a reality principle), but also took account of the partiality of the reader (a bias principle). This was achieved by approaching the text at various levels (literal, canonical, catholic), all of which had as their goal the elucidation of the meaning placed in the text by the divine and human authors. The first level at which I approached the text was that of 'literal sense exegesis'. The literal sense, I noted, is the authorially intended sense. Scripture, I said, represents a divine–human communicative action embodied in written discourse. The theological exegete, I argued, must therefore be oriented toward the subject matter of Scripture and committed to determining the meaning placed there (i.e., in the text) by its divine and human authors. The second level at which I approached the text was at a canonical level (my first conference table) and it involved, in a more limited way, bringing Peter into dialogue with other biblical authors. This conversation sought, on the one hand, to provide a thicker description of the text (such as using Isa. 53, words studies, etc., for example), and, on the other hand, to highlight 1 Peter's own distinctive contribution to the conversation (this was done throughout chapters 2–7). The third level (my second conference table), and most distinctively for this study, involved bringing the results of my exegetical study into dialogue with the writings of systematic theologians from various theological traditions (chapters 7–8). While the use of theological criticism has not eliminated all subjectivity from the process of exegesis, it has, I believe, provided us with an adequate understanding of 1 Peter's soteriology. I now turn to summarise briefly the results of this theological-critical study of salvation in the first letter of Peter.

Election

The thematic and theological significance attached to the concept of election by Peter is signalled both by the strategic position it occupies at the beginning (1:1–2), middle (2:4–10) and end of the letter

(5:13), and by the Trinitarian framework within which it is cast right at the outset of the letter (1:2). Each of the three members of the Trinity fulfils a specific role in the one divine programme of election: The Father elects, the Spirit sets the elect apart for obedience, and the Son provides atonement for God's elect and set-apart people. The Trinitarian character of the believers' election then carried over into 2:4–10 where the divine election and honouring of Christ is presented as the basis of the believers' own election and honour. Believers, I said, are elect both *through* Christ (i.e., God determined that believers would experience salvation through the atoning work of Christ) and *in* Christ (i.e., God chose believers for fellowship with Christ/incorporation into Christ). The believers' election in Christ was then contrasted with the divine rejection and shaming of unbelievers. It is at this point that Peter's doctrine of election exhibits a 'compatibilistic' outlook, which affirms, on the one hand, the absolute sovereignty of God in the election of some (believers) and the rejection of others (unbelievers), and, on the other hand, the moral responsibility of humans who will be held accountable for their belief or unbelief (see 2:8). Interaction with theologians from both 'Calvinistic' and 'Arminian' perspectives has encouraged me to hold both truths in tension. In the end, I noted that Peter intends the doctrine of election as a comfort for all believers facing rejection by a hostile and unbelieving world. For despite the precariousness of their situation in society (a fact resulting from their election; see 1:1–2), the believer's election could not be more sure, based as it is on the immutable and eternal purpose of the triune God. The significance of their election as God's elect people is underscored by a number of appellations that were used previously to describe ancient Israel as the elect people of God (2:9–10) thus underscoring the continuity between ancient Israel and the New Testament church as the elect people of God and in doing so emphasising the continuity of God's sovereign purpose in history. But as important as that identification with ancient Israel is, it is even more important that believers grasp that 'the narrative of Israel is itself determined by the story of Jesus and by the soteriological journey and eschatological hope it engenders. The Israel into whose history Peter writes his audience is *Israel as interpreted* by the suffering, death, resurrection, ascension, and pending revelation of Jesus Christ.'[5] I thus turned next to the doctrine of the atonement.

---

[5] Green, 'Faithful Witness in the Diaspora', 288 (emphasis his).

Atonement

My study of the atonement in 1 Peter further confirmed the importance and richness of its soteriological language. Morris asserts that '[f]or a short writing, 1 Peter has an astonishing amount to say about the atonement. Most of the epistle bears on the problem in one way or another, for Peter is concerned throughout with the salvation that God has wrought in Christ.'[6] Peter presents us with almost a mini 'systematic theology' of the atonement by employing no less than six different metaphors in his depiction of the saving significance of the death of Christ: (1) Jesus' death as victory over sin, death, and the forces of evil; (2) Jesus' death as a ransom payment liberating believers from the bondage of a futile, empty, and aimless past; (3) Jesus' death as a covenant sacrifice which is offered up in the place of guilty sinners; (4) Jesus' death as a penal substitution which bears the consequences or penalty (judgment) which our sins merited; (5) Jesus' death as a sacrifice effecting reconciliation between God and sinners; (6) Jesus' death as an example or model of doing what is right despite suffering. In sum, the saving significance of Jesus' death may be summed up as a sin-bearing, substitutionary sacrifice which bore the divine consequences of the believers' sin so that they might enjoy reconciliation with God now (3:18) and eschatological salvation (as opposed to judgment; cf. 4:5) 'at the revelation of Jesus Christ' (1:7). Furthermore, Jesus' death was the means of (in many cases pervaded by an 'already ... not yet' tension) securing victory over sin and Satan, purchasing liberation from bondage to a futile and foolish past, securing entrance into the new covenant with its associated gift of the Spirit, and providing believers, empowered by the Spirit, with an example of perfect dedication to the will of God.

Eschatological salvation

According to 1 Peter, the believers' salvation rests on two related aspects of Christ's activity: (1) his atoning death (1:18–21; 2:21b, 24; 3:18ab) and (2) his subsequent resurrection, exaltation, and vindication by God (1:3, 11, 21; 2:4d, 7d; 3:18e, 19, 21d–22; 4:13; 5:1, 4, 10). His suffering and death, we noted, was victorious, redemptive, sacrificial, substitutionary, reconciliatory, and exemplary. His resurrection, ascension, proclamation, vindication, and exaltation to God's right hand witness to the efficacy of God's saving power and provide believers with the

---

[6] Morris, *The Cross in the New Testament*, 316.

assurance that, like Christ, God will one day vindicate them also by raising them from the dead (3:18e/4:6c) and bestowing upon them praise
and glory and honour (1:7). The believer's solidarity with Christ means
that they too can anticipate the same glorious future as their suffering but
resurrected, vindicated and glorified Lord. Peter's unique presentation
of the believers' eschatological salvation in terms of future resurrection,
vindication, and the bestowal of honour and glory is designed to engender hope amongst a small minority of believers facing the onslaught of a
hostile world against their faith.

3.   Suggestions for further study

Given the constraints of time, space, and focus imposed by the nature of
this study, there is an inevitable variation in the depth to which the tools
of theological-critical exegesis (and, to an even lesser degree, canon
criticism and speech act theory) have been used on Peter's first letter,
and this provides the fuel for further research. The findings of this study
suggest that it might prove fruitful to apply the same methodology to
other aspects of the theology and concerns of this letter. Moreover, the
usefulness of theological-critical exegesis in studying 1 Peter raises the
question of whether this is due to the particular nature of the book itself.
Theologically, 1 Peter is a particularly rich letter, and traditionally theologians have tended to derive their theology almost exclusively from the
New Testament letters. The most closely related contexts elsewhere in
the New Testament would be the Pauline letters, which could similarly
be subject to comparable treatment using the tools of theological-critical
exegesis. But it would also be of interest to attempt to apply the methodology of theological-critical exegesis to the exegesis of the other biblical genres (both OT and NT) such as narrative, prose, poetry, prophecy,
wisdom, gospel, parable, and apocalyptic.

In the nineteenth century Charles Hodge sought to compare the Bible
to a 'store-house of facts', and the method for gathering those facts to the
scientific induction of the natural philosopher.[7] The problem with such a
method, however, is that the theologian can tend to either make almost
exclusive use of those genres that are more conducive to theological formulation (i.e., NT letters) or to treat the different portions of Scripture as
if they were all cut from the same literary cloth. The result is that either
some literary genres are focused on at the exclusion of others or that the
distinctiveness of the different literary genres becomes blurred and the

---

[7] See Hodge, *Systematic Theology*, 1: 10.

biblical witness becomes flattened. Theological-critical exegesis, however, seeks, on the one hand, to interpret the different books of the Bible on their own generic (i.e., pertaining to genre) terms and, on the other hand, to preserve the meaning of the various canonical discourses in a conceptual framework that will enable the theologian to articulate the Christian vision or worldview (as presented through the diverse literary forms) to people today. Vanhoozer suggests that this is done 'by initiating a dialogue between the various canonical forms [conference table 1] and between canonical forms and contemporary forms of thought [conference table 2]'.[8] This can only be achieved through the realisation that the so-called 'iron curtain separat[ing] Bible from theology'[9] is not only illusory, but is undesired, and that a more conscious and serious effort at a methodological level is needed to bridge the present divide between the two disciplines.

But perhaps the greatest challenge posed by this study, and one that is not solved simply by bringing biblical studies and systematic theology together, is how we can communicate Peter's message relevantly, read it meaningfully, and embody it practically in the context of our own believing communities. Fowl rightly contends that 'for Christians, scriptural interpretation should shape and be shaped by the convictions, practices, and concerns of Christian communities as part of their ongoing struggle to live and worship faithfully before God'.[10] While this study represents more (though I hope not solely) an attempt at discerning what salvation *meant* for the author of 1 Peter, it takes the Christian community to truly display 'what it *means*'.[11] Theological criticism is thus both a science (knowledge) and a practice (wisdom): it is both *scientia* and *sapientia*.[12] Or as Peter put it at the end of his letter: 'This is the true grace of God [*scientia*]. Stand fast in it! [*sapientia*]' (5:12).

---

[8] Vanhoozer, 'From Canon to Concept', 122.
[9] Childs, *Biblical Theology*, xvi.　[10] Fowl, *Engaging Scripture*, 62.
[11] Vanhoozer, *Meaning*, 430.　[12] Vanhoozer, 'From Canon to Concept', 123.

BIBLIOGRAPHY

PRIMARY SOURCES

The Apostolic Fathers. LCL. 2 vols. Edited and translated by B. D. Ehrman. Cambridge, Mass.: Harvard University Press, 2003.

Apuleius. *Metamorphoses*. 2 vols. Edited and translated by J. A. Hanson. LCL. Cambridge, Mass.: Harvard University Press, 1989.

2 Baruch. Translated by A. F. Klijn. *OTP* 1: 615–2.

Black, M. (ed.) *Apocalypsis Henochi Graece*. Vol. 3 of *Pseudepigrapha Veteris Testamenti Graece*. Edited by A. M. Denis and M. De Jonge. Leiden: Brill, 1970.

Burnett, R. E. 'Historical Criticism', *DTIB*, 290–3.

Charles, R. H. *The Book of Enoch*. London: SPCK, 1917.

Chilton, B. D. *The Isaiah Targum: Introduction, Translation, Apparatus and Notes*. Edinburgh: T&T Clark, 1987.

Copenhaver, B. P. *Hermetica: The Greek Corpus Hermeticum and the Latin Asclepius in a New English Translation with Notes and Introduction*. Cambridge: Cambridge University Press, 1992.

Diodorus of Sicily. *Diodorus of Sicily*. 12 vols. Translated by C. H. Oldfather. LCL. Cambridge, Mass.: Harvard University Press, 1953.

Dittenberger, W. *Orientis graeci inscriptiones selectae*. 2 vols. Leipzig, 1903–5.

Epictetus. *The Discourses as Reported by Arian, the Manual, and Fragments*. 2 vols. Translated by W. A. Oldfather. LCL. Cambridge, Mass.: Harvard University Press, 1926–8.

Epstein, I. (ed.) *The Babylonian Talmud vols. 1–18*. 18 vols. London: Soncino Press, 1948–52.

Eusebius. *The Ecclesiastical History*. 2 vols. Translated by K. Lake (vol. 1) and J. E. L. Oulton (vol. 2). LCL. Cambridge, Mass.: Harvard University Press, 1949, 1953.

The Fathers According to Rabbi Nathan. Translated by J. Goldin. YJS 10. New Haven: Yale University Press, 1955.

The Fathers According to Rabbi Nathan (Abot de Rabbi Nathan) Version B. Translation and commentary by A. J. Saldarini. SJLA 11. Leiden: Brill, 1975.

Freedman, H., and M. Simon. *Midrash Rabbah*. 10 vols. London: Soncino Press, 1939.

García Martínez, F. *The Dead Sea Scrolls Translated: The Qumran Texts in English*. 2nd rev. edn. Leiden: Brill; Grand Rapids: Eerdmans, 1996.

280

García Martínez, F., and E. J. C. Tigchelaar. *The Dead Sea Scrolls: Study Edition.* 2 vols. Leiden: Brill; Grand Rapids: Eerdmans, 1997, 1998.

Hennecke, E., and W. Schneemelcher (eds.) *New Testament Apocrypha.* 2 vols. Translated and edited by R. McL. Wilson. London: Lutterworth Press, 1965.

Hesychius. *Hesychii Alexandrini Lexicon.* 4 vols. Edited by M. Schmidt. Amsterdam: Adolf M. Hakkert, 1965.

Joseph and Asenath. Translated by C. Burchard. *OTP* 2: 177–247.

Joseph et Aséneth: Introduction, texte critique, traduction, et notes. Edited by Marc Philonenko. StPB 13. Leiden: Brill, 1968.

Josephus. 9 vols. Translated by H. St. J. Thackeray, R. Marcus, A. Wikgren, and H. Feldman. LCL. Cambridge, Mass.: Harvard University Press, 1926.

Marcus Aurelius. *The Comings with Himself of Marcus Aurelius Antonius, Emperor of Rome: Together with his Speeches and Sayings.* Edited and Translated by C. R. Haines. LCL. Cambridge, Mass.: Harvard University Press, 1916.

Melito of Sardis. *On Pascha and Fragments.* Texts and translations edited by S. G. Hall. Oxford: Oxford University Press, 1979.

Nauck, A. *Aristophanis Byzantii Grammatici Alexandrini Fragmenta.* Hildesheim: Georg Olms Verlagsbuchhandlung, 1963 (original edn 1848).

Neusner, J. *The Mishnah: A New Translation.* New Haven, London: Yale University Press, 1988.

Nickelsburg, G. W. E., and J. VanderKam. *1 Enoch: A New Translation: Based on the Hermeneia Commentary.* Minneapolis: Fortress Press, 2004.

Nock, A. D., and A.-J. Festugière. *Corpus Hermeticum.* 4 vols. Collection des Universités de France. Published under the patronage of l'Association Guillaume Budé. Paris: Les Belles Lettres, 1954–60.

Paton, W. R., and E. L. Hicks. *The Inscriptions of Cos.* Oxford: Clarendon, 1891.

Philo. 10 vols. Translated by F. H. Colson, G. H. Whittaker, J. W. Earp, and R. Marcus. 2 supp. vols. by R. Marcus. LCL. Cambridge, Mass.: Harvard University Press, 1929–53.

Philodemus. *De ira liber.* Edited by C. Wilke. Lipsiae: In aedibus B. G. Teubneri, 1914.

Plato. *Plato in Twelve Volumes.* Translated by H. N. Fowler, W. R. M. Lamb, and R. G. Bury. LCL. London: William Heinemann, 1914.

Plutarch. *Moralia.* 15 vols. Translated by F. C. Babbitt, *et. al.* LCL. Cambridge, Mass.: Harvard University Press, 1927–69.

Polybius. *The Histories.* 6 vols. Translated by W. R. Paton. LCL. London: William Heinemann; New York: G. P. Putnam's Sons, 1927.

Pritchard, J. B. (ed.) *Ancient Near Eastern Texts Relating to the Old Testament.* 2nd edn. Princeton, N.J.: Princeton University Press, 1955.

Sallustius. *Concerning the Gods and the Universe.* Edited with Prolegomena and Translation by A. D. Nock. Cambridge: Cambridge University Press, 1926.

Schaff, P. (ed.) *A Select Library of Nicene and Post-Nicene Fathers of the Christian Church.* 1st series. 14 vols. Edinburgh: T&T Clark; Grand Rapids: Eerdmans, 1983–98.

Sibylline Oracles. Translated by J. J. Collins. *OTP* 1: 317–472.

Sifre to Deuteronomy: An Analytical Translation. Translated by Jacob Neusner. 2 vols. BJS 98, 101. Atlanta: Scholars Press, 1987.

Welles, C. B. *Royal Correspondence in the Hellenistic Period: A Study in Greek Epigraphy*. Chicago: Ares Publishers, 1974.

Whitaker, E. C. *Documents of the Baptismal Liturgy*. 2nd edn. London: SPCK, 1970.

Ziegler, J. *Septuaginta*, vol. 14, *Isaias*. 3rd edn. Göttingen: Vandenhoeck & Ruprecht, 1983.

SECONDARY SOURCES

Abernathy, D. *An Exegetical Summary of 1 Peter*. Dallas: Summer Institute of Linguistics, 1998.

'Exegetical Considerations in 1 Peter 2:7–9'. *Notes* 15 (2001): 24–39.

'Translating 1 Peter 3:18–22'. *Notes* 15 (2001): 28–46.

Abraham, W. *Divine Revelation and the Limits of Historical Criticism*. Oxford: Oxford University Press, 1981.

Achtemeier, P. J. 'Newborn Babes and Living Stones: Literal and Figurative in 1 Peter'. Pages 207–36 in *To Touch the Text: Biblical and Related Studies*. J. A. Fitzmyer Festschrift. Edited by M. P. Horgan and P. J. Kobelski. New York: Crossroad, 1988.

'Suffering Servant and Suffering Christ in 1 Peter'. Pages 176–88 in *The Future of Christology. L. E. Keck Festschrift*. Edited by A. J. Malherbe and W. A. Meeks. Minneapolis: Fortress Press, 1993.

1 Peter. Hermeneia. Minneapolis: Fortress Press, 1996.

Agnew, F. H. '1 Peter 1:2: An Alternative Translation'. *CBQ* 45 (1983): 68–73.

Alexander, T. D., and B. S. Rosner (eds.) *New Dictionary of Biblical Theology*. Downers Grove: IVP, 2000.

Arichea, D. C. Jr, and E. A. Nida. *A Translator's Handbook on the First Letter From Peter*. Helps for Translators. New York: United Bible Societies, 1980.

Arminius, J. *The Works of James Arminius*. 3 vols. Translated by J. Nichols. London: Longman, Hurst, Rees, Orme, Brown, and Green, 1825.

Ashcraft, M. 'Theological Themes in 1 Peter'. *TE* 13 (1982): 55–62.

Aulén, G. *Christus Victor: An Historical Study of the Three Main Types of the Idea of the Atonement*. Translated by A. G. Hebert. London: SPCK, 1931.

Austin, J. L. *How to Do Things with Words*. Oxford: Clarendon Press, 1962.

Balthasar, Hans Urs von. *Theo-drama: Theological Dramatic Theory*, vol. 4, *The Action*. San Francisco: Ignatius Press, 1994.

Balz, H., and G. Schneider (eds.) *Exegetical Dictionary of the New Testament*. 3 vols. Grand Rapids: Eerdmans, 1990–3.

Barr, J. *The Semantics of Biblical Language*. Oxford: Oxford University Press, 1961.

Barrett, C. K. *A Critical and Exegetical Commentary on the Acts of the Apostles*. ICC. 2 vols. Edinburgh: T&T Clark, 1994.

Bartchy, S. S. *Mallon Chrēsai: First-Century Slavery and the Interpretation of 1 Corinthians 7:21*. Missoula: Society of Biblical Literature, 1973.

Barth, K. *The Epistle to the Romans*. Translated from the 6th edn by E. C. Hoskyns. London: Oxford University Press, 1933.

Church Dogmatics. 13 vols. Edinburgh: T&T Clark, 1956–75.

Bartholomew, C. G. 'Uncharted Waters: Philosophy, Theology, and the Crisis in Biblical Interpretation'. Pages 1–39 in *Renewing Biblical Interpretation*. Edited by C. Bartholomew, C. Greene, and K. Möller. Carlisle: Paternoster Press; Grand Rapids: Zondervan, 2000.

Barton, J. M. T. 'What Are we to Understand by the "Spirits that were in Prison" Referred to in 1 Peter 3:19?'. *Scripture* 4 (1950): 181–2.

Bauckham, R. J. *Jude, 2 Peter*. WBC. Waco, Tex.: Word, 1983.

'James, 1 and 2 Peter, Jude'. Pages 303–17 in *It is Written: Scripture Citing Scripture*. Edited by D. A. Carson and H. G. M. Williamson. Cambridge: Cambridge University Press, 1988.

Beare, F. W. *The First Epistle of Peter: The Greek Text with Introduction and Notes*. 3rd edn. Oxford: Blackwell, 1970.

Bénétreau, S. *La Première épître de Pierre: Commentaires évangéliques de la Bible*. Vaux-sur-Seine: EDIFAC, 1984.

Bengel, J. A. *Gnomon of the New Testament*. 7th edn. 5 vols. Edinburgh: T&T Clark, 1877.

Berkhof, H. *Christian Faith: An Introduction to the Study of the Faith*. Revised edn. Grand Rapids: Eerdmans, 1986.

Best, E. '1 Peter 2:4–10: A Reconsideration'. *NovT* 11 (1969): 270–93.

1 Peter. NCB. London: Oliphants; Grand Rapids: Eerdmans, 1971.

Bible and Culture Collective. *The Postmodern Bible*. New Haven, Conn.: Yale University Press, 1995.

Bigg, C. A. *A Critical and Exegetical Commentary on the Epistles of St. Peter and St. Jude*. ICC. 2nd edn. Edinburgh: T&T Clark, 1902.

Bishop, E. F. F. 'The Word of a Living and Unchanging God: 1 Peter 1,23'. *The Muslim World* 43 (1953): 15–17.

Blazen, I. T. 'Suffering and Cessation from Sin according to 1 Peter 4:1'. *AUSS* 21 (1983): 27–50.

Blocher, H. 'Agnus Victor: The Atonement as Victory and Vicarious Punishment'. Pages 67–91 in *What Does it Mean to be Saved? Broadening Evangelical Horizons of Salvation*. Edited by J. G. Stackhouse. Grand Rapids: Baker, 2002.

Bloesch, D. *Jesus is Victor! Karl Barth's Doctrine of Salvation*. Nashville: Abingdon Press, 1976.

Boersma, H. *Violence, Hospitality, and the Cross: Reappropriating the Atonement Tradition*. Grand Rapids: Baker, 2004.

Boettner, L. *The Reformed Doctrine of Predestination*. Grand Rapids: Eerdmans, 1936.

Boismard, M.-E. *Quatre hymnes baptismales dans la première épître de Pierre*. LD 30. Paris: Cerf, 1961.

Bömer, F. *Untersuchungen über die Religion der Sklaven in Griechenland und Rom*. 4 vols. Wiesbaden: Steiner, 1957–63.

Boring, M. E. *1 Peter*. ANTC. Nashville: Abingdon Press, 1999.

Boyd, G. A. *God at War: The Bible and Spiritual Conflict*. Downers Grove: IVP, 1997.

Boyer, J. L. 'Relative Clauses in the Greek New Testament: A Statistical Study'. *GTJ* 9 (1988): 233–56.

Bray, G. *Biblical Interpretation: Past and Present*. Downers Grove: IVP, 1996.

Bray, J. S. *Theodore Beza's Doctrine of Predestination*. BHR 12. Nieuwkoop: B. De Graaf, 1975.

Brock, R. N. 'And a Little Child Will Lead Us: Christology and Child Abuse'. Pages 42–61 in *Christianity, Patriarchy, and Abuse: A Feminist Critique*. Edited by Joanne Carlson Brown and Carole R. Bohn. New York: Pilgrim Press, 1989.

Brown, J. C., and R. Parker. 'For God So Loved the World?'. Pages 1–30 in *Christianity, Patriarchy, and Abuse: A Feminist Critique*. Edited by Joanne Carlson Brown and Carole R. Bohn. New York: Pilgrim Press, 1989.

Brox, N. *Der erste Petrusbrief*. EKKNT 21. 2nd edn. Zurich: Benzinger; Neukirchen-Vluyn: Neukirchner Verlag, 1986.

Bruce, F. F. *The Epistles to the Colossians, to Philemon, and to the Ephesians*. NICNT. Grand Rapids: Eerdmans, 1984.

Buis, H. *Historic Protestantism and Predestination*. Philadelphia: Presbyterian and Reformed, 1958.

Bultmann, R. 'Is Exegesis without Presuppositions Possible?'. Pages 289–96 in *Existence and Faith: Shorter Writings of Rudolf Bultmann*. Selected, translated, and introduced by S. M. Ogden. London: Hodder & Stoughton, 1961.

Busch, E. *The Great Passion: An Introduction to Karl Barth's Theology*. Translated by G. W. Bromiley. Edited and annotated by D. L. Guder and J. J. Guder. Grand Rapids: Eerdmans, 2004.

Byron, J. *Slavery Metaphors in Early Judaism and Pauline Christianity: A Traditio-Historical and Exegetical Examination*. WUNT 2/162. Tubingen: Mohr Siebeck, 2003.

Caird, G. B. *New Testament Theology*. Completed and edited by L. D. Hurst. Oxford: Clarendon Press, 1995.

Calloud, J., and F. Genuyt, *La Première épître de Pierre: Analyse sémiotique*. LD 109. Paris: Cerf, 1982.

Calvin, J. 'A Treatise on the Eternal Predestination of God'. Pages 25–206 in *Calvin's Calvinism*. Translated by H. Cole. London: Sovereign Grace Union, 1927.

    The Institutes of Christian Religion. 2 vols. Translated by F. L. Battles. Philadelphia: The Westminster Press, 1960.

    The Epistle of Paul to the Hebrews and the First and Second Epistles of St. Peter. Translated by W. B. Johnston. Grand Rapids: Eerdmans, 1963.

Campbell, B. L. *Honour, Shame, and the Rhetoric of 1 Peter*. SBL Dissertation Series 160. Georgia: Scholars Press, 1998.

Carson, D. A. *Divine Sovereignty and Human Responsibility: Biblical Perspectives in Tension*. Grand Rapids: Baker, 1981.

    'Unity and Diversity in the New Testament: The Possibility of Systematic Theology'. Pages 65–95 in *Scripture and Truth*. Edited by D. A. Carson and J. D. Woodbridge. Leicester: IVP, 1983.

    How Long, O Lord? Reflections on Suffering and Evil. Grand Rapids: Baker, 1990.

    'The Role of Exegesis in Systematic Theology'. Pages 39–76 in *Doing Theology in Today's World: Essays in Honour of Kenneth S. Kantzer*. Edited by J. D. Woodbridge and T. E. McComiskey. Grand Rapids: Zondervan, 1991.

The Gospel According to John. Leicester: IVP; Grand Rapids: Eerdmans, 1991.

Exegetical Fallacies. 2nd edn. Grand Rapids: Baker, 1996.

'New Testament Theology'. Pages 796–814 in *DLNT*.

The Gagging of God: Christianity Confronts Pluralism. Leicester: Apollos, 1996.

Childs, B. S. *Biblical Theology of the Old and New Testaments: Theological Reflection on the Christian Bible.* Minneapolis: Fortress Press, 1993.

Chilton, B. D. *The Isaiah Targum: Introduction, Translation, Apparatus and Notes.* Edinburgh: T&T Clark, 1987.

'Toward Recovering Theological Exegesis'. *ProEccl* 6 (1997): 16–26.

Chin, M. 'A Heavenly Home for the Homeless: Aliens and Strangers in 1 Peter'. *TynBul* 42 (1991): 96–112.

Cottrell, J. W. 'Conditional Election'. Pages 51–73 in *Grace Unlimited.* Edited by C. H. Pinnock. Minneapolis: Bethany Fellowship: 1975.

Cranfield, C. E. B. *The First Epistle of Peter.* London: SCM Press, 1950.

'The Interpretation of 1 Peter 3:19 and 4:6'. *ExpTim* 62 (1958): 269–72.

Custance, A. C. *The Sovereignty of Grace.* Phillipsburg, N.J.: Presbyterian and Reformed Publishing, 1979.

Dalton, W. J. *Christ's Proclamation to the Spirits: A Study of 1 Peter 3:18–4:6.* AnBib 23. 2nd rev. edn. Rome: Pontifical Biblical Institute, 1989.

Dana, H. E., and J. R. Mantey. *A Manual Grammar of the Greek New Testament.* Toronto: Macmillan, 1927.

Dautzenberg, G. 'Σωτηρία ψυχῶν (1 Petr 1, 9)'. *BZ* n.s. 8 (1964): 262–76.

Davids, P. H. *1 Peter.* NICNT. Grand Rapids: Eerdmans, 1990.

Davis, E. F., and R. B. Hays (eds.) *The Art of Reading Scripture.* Grand Rapids: Eerdmans, 2003.

'Nine Theses on the Interpretation of Scripture'. Pages 1–5 in *The Art of Reading Scripture.* Edited by E. F. Davis and R. B. Hays. Grand Rapids: Eerdmans, 2003.

Deissmann, G. A. *Bible Studies: Contributions Chiefly from Papyri and Inscriptions to the History of the Language, the Literature, and the Religion of Hellenistic Judaism and Primitive Christianity.* Translated by A. Grieve. Peabody: Hendrickson, 1988.

Light From the Ancient East: The New Testament Illustrated by Recently Discovered Texts of the Graeco-Roman World. Translated by L. R. M. Strachan. London: Hodder and Stoughton, 1910.

Demarest, B. *The Cross and Salvation: The Doctrine of Salvation.* Wheaton: Crossway, 1997.

Denny, J. *The Death of Christ.* London: Tyndale Press, 1951.

de Villiers, J. L. 'Joy and Suffering in 1 Peter'. *Neot* 9 (1975): 64–86.

Dubis, M. 'Research on 1 Peter: A Survey of Scholarly Literature Since 1985'. *CBR* 4 (2006): 199–239.

Dunn, J. D. G. *Romans 1–8, Romans 9–16.* WBC. Waco, Tex.: Word Books, 1988.

The Christ and the Spirit, vol. 1, *Christology.* Grand Rapids: Eerdmans, 1998.

Dupont-Roc, R. 'Le Jeu des prépositions en 1 Pierre 1,1–12: De l'espérance finale à la joie dans les épreuves présentes'. *EstBib* 53 (1995): 201–12.

Dürr, L. *Die Wertung des göttlichen Wortes im Alten Testament und im Antiken Orient.* MVAG 42.1. Leipzig: Hinrichs, 1938.

Eichrodt, W. *Theology of the Old Testament.* 2 vols. Translated by J. A. Baker. London: SCM Press, 1961–7.

Elliott, J. H. *The Elect and the Holy: An Exegetical Examination of 1 Peter 2:4–10 and the Phrase basileion hierateuma.* NovTSup 12. Leiden: Brill, 1966.

   A Home for the Homeless: A Social-Scientific Criticism of 1 Peter, its Situation and Strategy, with a New Introduction. Minneapolis: Fortress Press, 1990.

   1 Peter. AB. New York: Doubleday, 2000.

Erickson, M. J. *Christian Theology.* 2nd edn. Grand Rapids: Baker Books, 1998.

Ernesti, J. A. *Elements of Biblical Criticism and Interpretation.* Translated by M. Stuart. 3rd edn. Andover: Mark Newman, 1827.

Evans, C. A. *Mark 8:27–16:20.* WBC. Nashville: Thomas Nelson, 2001.

Fagbemi, S. A. A. *Who are the Elect in 1 Peter? A Study in Biblical Exegesis and its Application to the Anglican Church of Nigeria.* Studies in Biblical Literature 104. New York: Peter Lang, 2007.

Feinberg, J. S. '1 Peter 3:18–20: Ancient Mythology and the Intermediate State'. *WTJ* 48 (1986): 303–36.

Feldmeier, R. *Der erste Brief des Petrus.* THKNT 15/1. Leipzig: Evangelische Verlagsanstalt, 2005.

Fiddes, P. S. *Past Event and Present Salvation: The Christian Idea of Atonement.* Louisville, Ky.: Westminster/John Knox, 1989.

Fink, P. R. 'The Use and Significance of *en hōi* in 1 Peter'. *Grace Journal* 8 (1967): 33–39.

Ford, D. *Theology: A Very Short Introduction.* Oxford: Oxford University Press, 1999.

Fowl, S. E. *Engaging Scripture: A Model for Theological Interpretation.* Oxford: Blackwell, 1998.

   'The Role of Authorial Intention in the Theological Interpretation of Scripture'. Pages 71–87 in *Between Two Horizons: Spanning New Testament Studies and Systematic Theology.* Edited by J. B. Green and M. Turner. Grand Rapids: Eerdmans, 2000.

Fowl, S. E., and L. G. Jones, *Reading in Communion: Scripture and Ethics in Christian Life.* Grand Rapids: Eerdmans, 1991.

Frings, J. 'Zu 1 Petr 3,19 und 4,6'. *BZ* 17 (1925): 75–88.

Funk, R. W., and R. W. Hoover (eds.) *The Five Gospels: The Search for the Authentic Words of Jesus.* Sonoma, Calif.: Polebridge; New York: Macmillan, 1993.

Gabler, J. P. 'Oratio de iusto discrimine theologiae biblicae et dogmaticae regundisque recte utriusque finibus'. 2: 179–98 in *Kleinere theologische Schriften.* Edited by T. A. Gabler and J. G. Gabler. 2 vols. Ulm: Verlag des Stettinischen Buchhandlung, 1831.

Gadamer, H.-G. *Truth and Method.* 2nd rev. edn. Translation revised by J. Weinsheimer and D. G. Marshall. London/New York: Continuum, 2004.

Galot, J. 'La Descente du Christ aux enfers (1 P 3:18–20)'. *NRTh* 83 (1961): 471–91.

Gelb, I. J., *et. al.* (editorial board), *The Assyrian Dictionary of the Oriental Institute of the University of Chicago.* Chicago: The Oriental Institute, 1956–.

Glare, P. G. W. (ed.) *Oxford Latin Dictionary*. Oxford: Clarendon Press, 1982.

Goldstein, H. 'Die Kirche als Schar derer, die ihrem leidenden Herrn mit dem Ziel der Gottesgemeinschaft nachfolgen: Zum Gemeinverständnis von 1 Petr 2,21–25 und 3,19–22'. *BibLeb* 15 (1974): 38–54.

Gomes, A. W. 'De Jesu Christo Servatore: Faustus Socinus on the Satisfaction of Christ'. *WTJ* (1993): 209–31.

Goppelt, L. *A Commentary on 1 Peter*. Edited by F. Hahn. Translated and augmented by J. E. Alsup. Grand Rapids: Eerdmans, 1993.

Green, E. M. B. *The Meaning of Salvation*. London: Hodder & Stoughton: 1965.

Green, J. B. 'Scripture and Theology: Uniting the Two So Long Divided'. Pages 23–43 in *Between Two Horizons: Spanning New Testament Studies and Systematic Theology*. Edited by J. B. Green and M. Turner. Grand Rapids: Eerdmans, 2000.

'Modernity, History and the Theological Interpretation of the Bible'. *SJT* 54 (2001): 208–329.

Salvation. UBT. St. Louis: Chalice, 2003.

'Faithful Witness in the Diaspora: The Holy Spirit and the Exiled People of God according to 1 Peter'. Pages 282–95 in *The Holy Spirit and Christian Origins: Essays in Honour of James Dunn*. Edited by G. N. Stanton, B. W. Longenecker, and S. C. Barton. Grand Rapids: Eerdmans, 2004.

Green, J. B., S. McKnight, and I. H. Marshall (eds.) *Dictionary of Jesus and the Gospels*. Downers Grove: IVP, 1992.

Green, J. B., and M. D. Baker. *Recovering the Scandal of the Cross: Atonement in New Testament and Contemporary Contexts*. Downers Grove: IVP, 2000.

Green, J. B., and M. Turner (eds.) *Between Two Horizons: Spanning New Testament Studies and Systematic Theology*. Grand Rapids: Eerdmans, 2000.

Grenz, S. *Theology for the Community of God*. Nashville: Broadman & Holman Publishers, 1994.

Groves, J. A. 'Atonement in Isaiah 53: "For He Bore the Sins of Many"'. Pages 61–89 in *The Glory of the Atonement: Biblical, Historical and Practical Perspectives. Roger Nicole Festschrift*. Edited by C. E. Hill and F. A. James III. Downers Grove: IVP, 2004.

Grudem, W. A. 'Christ Preaching through Noah: 1 Peter 3:19–20 in the Light of Dominant Themes in Jewish Literature'. *TrinJ* (1986): 3–31.

The First Epistle of Peter. TNTC. Grand Rapids: Eerdmans, 1988.

'He Did not Descend into Hell: A Plea for Following Scripture instead of the Apostles' Creed'. *JETS* 34 (1991): 103–13.

Systematic Theology: An Introduction to Biblical Doctrine. Leicester: IVP, 1994.

Gunton, C. E. *The Actuality of the Atonement: A Study of Metaphor, Rationality, and the Christian Tradition*. Edinburgh: T&T Clark, 1988.

'Salvation'. Pages 143–58 in *The Cambridge Companion to Karl Barth*. Edited by John Webster. Cambridge: Cambridge University Press, 2000.

Hamblin, R. L. 'An Analysis of First Peter with Special Reference to the Greek Participle'. ThD dissertation, Southwestern Baptist Theological Seminary, 1959.

Harris, J. R. *Testimonies*. 2 vols. Cambridge: Cambridge University Press, 1916–20.

Harris, M. J. 'Prepositions and Theology in the Greek New Testament'. Pages 1171–215 in vol. 3 of *The New International Dictionary of New Testament Theology*. Edited by Colin Brown. 4 vols. Exeter: Paternoster Press, 1980.

　Slave of Christ: A New Testament Metaphor for Total Devotion to Christ. NSBT 8. Nottingham: Apollos, 1999.

　'Salvation'. Pages 762–7 in *New Dictionary of Biblical Theology*. Edited by T. D. Alexander and B. S. Rosner. Downers Grove: IVP, 2000.

Hart, J. H. A. 'The First General Epistle of Peter'. Pages 3–80 in vol. 5 of *The Expositors Greek Testament*. Edited by W. R. Nicoll. Grand Rapids: Eerdmans, 1974.

Hatch, E., and H. A. Redpath. *A Concordance to the Septuagint*. Oxford: Clarendon Press, 1897.

Hawthorne, G. F., R. P. Martin, and D. G. Reid (eds.) *Dictionary of Paul and his Letters*. Downers Grove: IVP, 1993.

Hays, R. B. 'The Corrected Jesus'. *First Things* 64 (1996): 44–6.

Hiebert, D. E. 'Selected Studies from 1 Peter. Part 2: The Suffering and Triumphant Christ: An Exposition of 1 Peter 3:18–22'. *BSac* 139 (1982): 146–58.

Hill, C. E., and F. A. James III (eds.) *The Glory of the Atonement: Biblical, Historical and Practical Perspectives. Roger Nicole Festschrift*. Downers Grove: IVP, 2004.

Hill, D. *Greek Words with Hebrew Meanings: Studies in the Semantics of Soteriological Terms*. Cambridge: Cambridge University Press, 1967.

Hillyer, N. ' "Rock-Stone" Imagery in 1 Peter'. *TynBul* 22 (1971): 58–81.

Hirsch, E. D. *Validity in Interpretation*. New Haven: Yale University Press, 1967.

　The Aims of Interpretation. Chicago: University of Chicago Press, 1976.

　'Meaning and Significance Reinterpreted'. *Critical Inquiry* 11 (1984): 202–24.

　'Transhistorical Intentions and the Persistence of Allegory'. *NLH* 25 (1994): 549–67.

Hodge, C. *Systematic Theology*. 3 vols. London: Thomas Nelson and Sons, 1883.

Hoehner, H. W. *Ephesians: An Exegetical Commentary*. Grand Rapids: Baker, 2002.

Holland, N. N. 'Unity Identity Text Self'. *PMLA* 90.5 (1975): 813–22.

Hooker, Morna, D. 'Interchange in Christ'. *JTS* 22 (1971): 349–61.

　'Interchange and Atonement'. *BJRL* 60 (1977–8): 462–80.

　From Adam to Christ: Essays on Paul. Cambridge: Cambridge University Press, 1990.

　Not Ashamed of the Gospel: New Testament Interpretations of the Death of Christ. Didsbury Lectures. Carlisle: Paternoster Press, 1994.

Horrell, D. 'Who are ' "The Dead" and When was the Gospel Preached to Them? The Interpretation of 1 Pet. 4.6'. *NTS* 49 (2003): 70–89.

Hort, F. J. A. *The First Epistle of Saint Peter: I:1-II:17*. New York: Macmillan, 1898.

Jeffery, S., M. Ovey, and A. Sach, *Pierced for our Transgressions: Rediscovering the Glory of Penal Substitution*. Leicester: IVP, 2007.

Jewett, P. K. *Election and Predestination*. Grand Rapids: Eerdmans, 1985.

Jobes, K. H. *1 Peter*. BECNT. Grand Rapids: Baker Academic, 2005.

Jobes K. H., and M. Silva. *Invitation to the Septuagint*. Grand Rapids: Baker, 2000.

Johnson, S. E. 'The Preaching to the Dead'. *JBL* 79 (1960): 48–51.

Jüngel, E. 'The Sacrifice of Jesus as Sacrament and Example'. Pages 163–90 in *Theological Essays II*. Edited by J. B. Webster. Translated by A. Neufeldt-Fast and J. B. Webster. Edinburgh: T&T Clark, 1995.

Keener, C. S. *The IVP Bible Background Commentary: New Testament*. Downers Grove: IVP, 1993.

The Gospel of John: A Commentary. 2 vols. Peabody: Hendrickson, 2003.

Kelly, J. N. D. *The Epistles of Peter and of Jude*. London: A. & C. Black, 1969.

Kendall, D. W. 'The Introductory Character of 1 Peter 1:3–12'. ThD dissertation, Union Theological Seminary, 1984.

'The Literary and Theological Function of 1 Peter 1:3–12'. Pages 103–20 in *Perspectives on First Peter*. Edited by C. H. Talbert. Macon, Ga.: Mercer University Press, 1986.

Kennard, D. W. 'Petrine Redemption: Its Meaning and Extent'. *JETS* 30 (1987): 399–405.

Kilpatrick, G. D. '1 Peter 1:11 TINA 'H ΠOION KAIΠON'. *NovT* 28.1 (1986): 91–2.

Kirkpatrick, W. D. 'The Theology of First Peter'. *SwJT* 25 (1982): 58–81.

Kittel, G., and G. Friedrich (eds.) *Theological Dictionary of the New Testament*. Translated by G. W. Bromiley. 10 vols. Grand Rapids: Eerdmans, 1964–76.

Klein, W. W. *The New Chosen People: A Corporate View of Election*. Grand Rapids: Zondervan/Academia Books, 1990.

Klein, W. W., C. L. Blomberg, and R. L. Hubbard. *Introduction to Biblical Interpretation*. Revised and expanded edn. Nashville: Thomas Nelson, 1993.

Klumbies, P.-G. 'Die Verkündigung unter Geistern und Toten nach 1 Petr 3,19f und 4,6'. *ZNW* 92 (2001): 207–28.

Köstenberger, A. J. *John*. BECNT. Grand Rapids: Baker Academic, 2004.

Krimmer, H., and M. Holland. *Erster unde zweiter Petrusbrief*. BibelKommentar 20. Neuhausen-Stuttgart: Hänssler, 1992.

Kühschelm, R. ' "Lebendige Hoffnung" (1 Petr 1,3–12)'. *BL* 56 (1983): 202–6.

Kümmel, W. G. *The Theology of the New Testament According to its Major Witnesses: Jesus–Paul–John*. Translated by J. E. Steely. Nashville: Abingdon Press, 1973.

Ladd, G. E. *A Theology of the New Testament*. Revised by D. A. Hagner. Grand Rapids: Eerdmans, 1993.

Lampe, G. W. H. (ed.) *A Patristic Greek Lexicon*. Oxford: Clarendon Press, 1961–8.

Lane, W. L. *Hebrews 1–8*. Dallas: Word, 1991.

Hebrews 9–13. Dallas: Word, 1991.

LaSor, W. S. *The Dead Sea Scrolls and the Christian Faith*. Chicago: Moody Press, 1962.

LaVerdiere, E. A. 'A Grammatical Ambiguity in 1 Pet. 1:23'. *CBQ* 36 (1974): 89–94.

Lewis, G. R. 'Response to Presuppositions of Non-Evangelical Hermeneutics'. Pages 613–26 in *Hermeneutics, Inerrancy and the Bible*. Edited by E. D. Radmacher and R. D. Preus. Grand Rapids: Zondervan, 1984.

Lewis, G. R., and B. A. Demarest. *Integrative Theology*. 3 vols. Grand Rapids: Baker, 1996.

Liddell, H. G., and R. Scott. *A Greek–English Lexicon*. 9th edn with supplement. Revised by H. S. Jones. Oxford: Oxford University Press, 1968.

Lindbeck, G. *The Nature of Doctrine: Religion and Theology in a Postliberal Age*. Philadelphia: Westminster Press, 1984.

Lonergan, B. J. F. *Method in Theology*. London: Darton, Longman & Todd, 1972.

Longenecker, R. N. *The Christology of Early Jewish Christianity*. Grand Rapids: Baker, 1970.

Louw, J. P., and E. A. Nida. *A Greek–English Lexicon of the New Testament Based on Semantic Domains*. 2 vols. New York: United Bible Societies, 1988.

Lust, J., E. Eynikel, and K. Hauspie (eds.) *Greek English Lexicon of the Septuagint*. Rev. edn. Stuttgart: Deutsche Bibelgesellschaft, 2003.

Luther, M. *Works*. 55 vols. Edited by J. Pelikan. St. Louis: Concordia: 1955–86.

   Commentary on Peter and Jude. Grand Rapids: Kregel, 1990.

Lyonnet, S., and L. Sabourin. *Sin, Redemption, and Sacrifice: A Biblical and Patristic Study*. AnBib 48. Rome: Biblical Institute Press, 1970.

Mangina, J. L. *Karl Barth: Theologian of Christian Witness*. Aldershot: Ashgate, 2004.

Manns, F. 'La Maison où réside l'Esprit, 1 P 2,5 et son arrière-plan juif'. *SBFLA* 34 (1984): 207–24.

   'La théologie de la nouvelle naissance dans la première lettre de Pierre'. *SBFLA* 45 (1995): 107–41.

Mantey, J. R. 'Unusual Meanings for Prepositions in the Greek New Testament'. *Exp* 25 (1923): 453–60.

   'The Causal Use of Eis in the New Testament'. *JBL* 70 (1951): 45–8.

   'On Causal Eis Again'. *JBL* 70 (1951): 309–11.

Marcus, R. 'The Elusive Causal Eis'. *JBL* 71 (1952): 43–4.

Margot, J. C. *Les Épîtres de Pierre: Commentaire*. Geneva: Labor et Fides, 1960.

Marshall, I. H. 'The Development of the Concept of Redemption in the New Testament'. Pages 153–69 in *Reconciliation and Hope. Leon Morris Festschrift*. Edited by R. Banks. Grand Rapids: Eerdmans, 1974.

   1 Peter. IVP New Testament Commentary. Downers Grove: IVP, 1991.

   'The Nature of Christian Salvation'. *EuroJT* 4 (1995): 29–43.

Martin, D. B. *Slavery as Salvation: The Metaphor of Slavery in Pauline Christianity*. New Haven: Yale University Press, 1990.

Martin, R. P., and P. H. Davids (eds.) *Dictionary of the Later New Testament and its Developments*. Downers Grove: IVP, 1997.

Martin, Troy W. 'The Present Indicative in Eschatological Statements of 1 Peter 1:6, 8'. *JBL* 111 (1992): 307–12.

McCartney, D. G. 'The Use of the Old Testament in the First Epistle of Peter'. PhD dissertation, Westminster Theological Seminary, 1989.

McCormack, B. 'Grace and Being: The Role of God's Gracious Election in Karl Barth's Theological Ontology'. Pages 92–110 in *The Cambridge Companion to Karl Barth*. Edited by John Webster. Cambridge: Cambridge University Press, 2000.

    'Barth, Karl'. Pages 64–7 in *The Oxford Companion to Christian Thought*. Edited by A. Hastings, A. Mason, and H. Pyper. Oxford: Oxford University Press, 2000.

McGrath, A. E. *The Genesis of Doctrine: A Study in the Foundation of Doctrinal Criticism*. Grand Rapids: Eerdmans; Vancouver: Regent College Publishing, 1990.

    Historical Theology: An Introduction to the History of Christian Thought. Oxford: Blackwell, 1998.

    Christian Theology: An Introduction. 3rd edn. Oxford: Blackwell, 2001.

McKnight, S. *1 Peter*. NIV Application Commentary. Grand Rapids: Zondervan, 1996.

Metzger, B. M. *A Textual Commentary on the Greek New Testament*. 2nd edn. Stuttgart: Deutsche Bibelgesellschaft, 1995.

Michaels, J. R. *1 Peter*. WBC. Waco, Tex.: Word Books, 1988.

Miguéns, M. 'La "passion" du Christ total (1 P 2,20b-25)'. *AsSeign* 25 (1969): 26–31.

Miller, D. G. 'Land'. Pages 623–7 in *NDBT*.

Moffatt, J. *The Moffatt Translation of the Bible*. 2nd edn. London: Hodder, 1935.

Moo, D. J. 'The Problem of *Sensus Plenior*'. Pages 179–211 in *Hermeneutics, Authority and Canon*. Edited by D. A. Carson and J. D. Woodbridge. Leicester: IVP, 1986.

    The Epistle to the Romans. NICNT. Grand Rapids: Eerdmans, 1996.

Morgan, R. *The Nature of New Testament Theology*. SBT 2nd series 25. London: SCM Press, 1973.

Moriarty, F. L. 'Word as Power in the Ancient Near East'. Pages 345–62 in *A Light Unto My Path: Old Testament Studies in Honour of Jacob M. Myers*. Edited by H. N. Bream, R. D. Heim, and C. A. Moore. Gettysburg Theological Studies 4. Philadelphia: Temple University Press, 1974.

Morris, L. L. *The Apostolic Preaching of the Cross*. 3rd edn. London: Tyndale, 1960.

    The Cross in the New Testament. Grand Rapids: Eerdmans, 1965.

    The Atonement: Its Meaning and Significance. Downers Grove: IVP, 1983.

    The Gospel According to John. Rev. edn. Grand Rapids: Eerdmans, 1995.

Motyer, J. A. *The Prophecy of Isaiah: An Introduction and Commentary*. Downers Grove: IVP, 1993.

Moule C. F. D. *An Idiom Book of New Testament Greek*. 2nd edn. Cambridge: Cambridge University Press, 1959.

Moulton, J. H. [W. F. Howard and N. Turner]. *A Grammar of New Testament Greek*. 4 vols. Edinburgh: T&T Clark, 1908–76. Vol. 1 (3rd edn, 1908): *Prolegomena*, by J. H. Moulton. Vol. 2 (1929): *Accidence and Word*

Formation, by W. F. Howard. Vol. 3 (1963): *Syntax*, by N. Turner. Vol. 4 (1976): *Style*, by N. Turner.

Moulton, J. H., and G. Milligan. *Vocabulary of the Greek Testament*. London: Hodder & Stoughton, 1930.

Mounce, W, D. *Pastoral Epistles*. WBC. Nashville: Thomas Nelson, 2000.

Muller, R. A. *Dictionary of Latin and Greek Theological Terms: Drawn Principally from Protestant Scholasticism*. Grand Rapids: Baker, 1985.

Murray, J. *Redemption: Accomplished and Applied*. Grand Rapids: Eerdmans, 1955.

Nauck, W. 'Freude im Leiden: Zum Problem einer urchristlichen Verfolgungstradition'. *ZNW* 46 (1955): 68–80.

Nickelsburg, G. W. E. *1 Enoch 1: A Commentary on the Book of Enoch Chapters 1–36; 81–108*. Hermeneia. Minneapolis: Fortress Press, 2001.

O'Brien, P. T. *Introductory Thanksgivings in the Letters of Paul*. NovTSup 49. Leiden: E. J. Brill, 1977.

Oden, Thomas C. *Systematic Theology*, vol. 2, *The Word of Life*. San Francisco: Harper & Row, 1989.

The Transforming Power of Grace. Nashville: Abingdon Press, 1993.

Olson, V. S. 'The Atonement in 1 Peter'. ThD dissertation, Union Theological Seminary, Richmond, Virginia, 1979.

Omanson, R. 'Suffering for Righteousness' Sake (1 Pet. 3:13–4:11)'. *RevExp* 79 (1982): 439–50.

Osborne, G. R. *The Hermeneutical Spiral: A Comprehensive Introduction to Biblical Interpretation*. Downers Grove: IVP, 1991.

Oswalt, J. *Isaiah*. NIV Application Commentary. Grand Rapids: Zondervan, 2003.

Owen, J. *The Works of John Owen*. 16 vols. London: Banner of Truth, 1961. First published by Johnstone & Hunter, 1850–3.

Packer, J. I. 'What Did the Cross Achieve? The Logic of Penal Substitution'. *TynBul* 25 (1974): 3–45.

'Preaching as Biblical Interpretation'. Pages 187–203 in *Errancy and Common Sense*. Edited by J. R. Michaels and R. Nicole. Grand Rapids: Baker, 1980.

Pannenberg, W. *Systematic Theology*. 3 vols. Grand Rapids: Eerdmans, 1991.

Panning, A. J. 'Exegetical Brief: What Has Been Determined (ἐτέθησαν) in 1 Peter 2:8?' *Wisconsin Lutheran Quarterly* 98 (2002): 48–52.

Parsons, S. P. 'We Have Been Born Anew: The New Birth of the Christian in the First Epistle of St. Peter (1 Petr. 1:3, 23)'. Doctoral dissertation, Pontificia Studiorum Universita a S. Thomas Aquino in Urbe. Rome, 1978.

Perdelwitz, R. *Die Mysterienreligion und das Problem des I. Petrusbriefes: Ein literarischer und religionsgeschichtlicher Versuch*. Religionsgeschichtliche Versuche und Vorarbeiten Giessen 9.3. Giessen: Töpelmann, 1911.

Perrot, C. 'La descente aux enfers et la prédication aux morts'. Pages 231–46 in *Études sur la première lettre de Pierre*. Edited by C. Perrot. LD 102. Paris: Cerf, 1980.

Peterson, D. (ed.) *Where Wrath and Mercy Meet: Proclaiming the Atonement Today*. Carlisle: Paternoster Press, 2001.

Philipps, K. *Kirche in der Gesellschaft nach dem 1. Petrusbrief*. Gütersloh: Gütersloher Verlagshaus–Gerd Mohn, 1971.

Pietersma, A., and B. G. Wright (ed.) *New English Translation of the Septuagint* (NETS). Oxford: Oxford University Press, 2007.

Pilch, J. J. ' "Visiting Strangers" and "Resident Aliens" '. *TBT* 29 (1991): 357–61.

Piper, J. 'Hope as the Motivation of Love: 1 Peter 3:9–12'. *NTS* 26 (1980): 212–31.

Plumpe, J. C. 'Vivum saxum, vivi lapides: The Concept of "Living Stone" in Classical and Christian Antiquity'. *Traditio* 1 (1943): 1–14.

Porter, S. E. *Idioms of the Greek New Testament*. 2nd. edn. Sheffield: Sheffield Academic Press, 1994.

Puig Tarrech, A. 'Le milieu de la première épître de Pierre'. *RCT* 5 (1980): 95–129, 331–402.

Rakestraw, R. V. 'John Wesley as a Theologian of Grace'. *JETS* 27 (1984): 193–203.

Ramsay, W. M. *The Church in the Roman Empire before A.D. 170*. 5th edn. London: Hodder and Stoughton, 1897.

Rashdall, H. *The Idea of Atonement in Christian Theology*. London: Macmillan, 1920.

Rees, T. *The Racovian Catechism*. London: Longman, Hurst, Rees, Orme, and Brown, 1818.

Reicke, Bo. *The Disobedient Spirits and Christian Baptism: A Study of 1 Peter 3:19 and its Context*. Copenhagen: Munksgaard, 1946.

The Epistles of James, Peter, and Jude. AB. Garden City, N.Y.: Doubleday, 1964.

Rengstorf, K. H. (ed.) *A Complete Concordance to Flavius Josephus*. 4 vols. Leiden: Brill, 1983.

Reventlow, H. G. *Problems of Old Testament Theology in the Twentieth Century*. Translated by J. Bowden. London: SCM Press, 1985.

Reymond, R. L. *A New Systematic Theology of the Christian Faith*. Nashville: Thomas Nelson, 1998.

Rice, J. R. *Our God-Breathed Book: The Bible*. Murfreesboro, Tenn.: Sword of the Lord, 2000.

Richard, E. J. *Reading 1 Peter, Jude, and 2 Peter: A Literary and Theological Commentary*. Reading the New Testament. Macon, Ga.: Smith & Helwys, 2000.

Robertson, A. T. *A Grammar of the Greek New Testament in the Light of Historical Research*. 4th edn. New York: Hodder and Stoughton, 1923.

Word Pictures in the New Testament, vol. 4, *The General Epistles and the Revelation of John*. Nashville: Broadman, 1933.

The Minister and His Greek New Testament. Nashville: Broadman, 1977.

Rogers, C. L., Jr., and C. L. Rogers III. *The New Linguistic and Exegetical Key to the Greek New Testament*. Grand Rapids: Zondervan, 1998.

Rogers, E. F. 'How the Virtues of an Interpreter Presuppose and Perfect Hermeneutics: The Case of Thomas Aquinas'. *JR* 76 (1996): 64–81.

Ryle, G. *Collected Papers*, vol. 2, *Collected Essays 1929–1968*. London: Hutchinson, 1971.

Sandys-Wunsch, J., and L. Eldredge. 'J. P. Gabler and the Distinction between Biblical and Dogmatic Theology: Translation, Commentary and Discussion of his Originality'. *SJT* 33 (1980): 133–58.

Sawyer, J. F. A. 'Theological Dictionary of the New Testament, v 5'. *SJT* 23 (1970): 240–2.

Scalise, C. J. *From Scripture to Theology: A Canonical Journey into Hermeneutics.* Downers Grove: IVP, 1996.

Schaff, P. *The Creeds of Christendom.* 3 vols. 6th rev. edn. Grand Rapids: Baker, 1977.

Scharlemann, M. H. 'He Descended into Hell: An Interpretation of 1 Peter 3: 18–20'. *CTM* 27 (1956): 81–94.

——— 'An Apostolic Descent: An Exegetical Study of 1 Peter 1:3–12'. *ConJ* 2 (1976): 9–17.

Schelkle, K. H. *Der Petrusbriefe—Das Judasbrief.* HTKNT. Freiburg: Herder, 1980.

Schlatter, A. *Petrus und Paulus nach dem I. Petrusbrief.* Stuttgart: Calwer, 1937.

Schlosser, J. 'Ancien Testament et christologie dans la prima Petri'. Pages 65–96 in *Études sur la première lettre de Pierre.* Edited by C. Perrot. LD 102. Paris: Cerf, 1980.

Schlosser, J. (ed.) *The Catholic Epistles and the Tradition.* BETL 176. Leuven: Leuven University Press, 2004.

Schneider, J., and C. Brown. 'σῴζω, κτλ.' Pages 205–21 in vol. 3 of *NIDNTT.*

Schrage, W., and H. Balz. 'Der erste Petrusbrief'. Pages 59–117 in *Die 'katholischen' Briefe: Die Briefe des Jakobus, Petrus, Judas and Johannes.* 11th edn. NTD 10. Göttingen: Vandenhoeck & Ruprecht, 1973.

Schreiner, T. R. *Romans.* BECNT. Grand Rapids: Baker, 1998.

——— 'Does Romans 9 Teach Individual Election unto Salvation?'. Pages 89–106 in *Still Sovereign: Contemporary Perspectives on Election, Foreknowledge, and Grace.* Grand Rapids: Baker, 2000.

——— 'Does Scripture Teach Prevenient Grace in the Wesleyan Sense?' Pages 229–46 in *Still Sovereign: Contemporary Perspectives on Election, Foreknowledge, and Grace.* Grand Rapids: Baker, 2000.

——— *1, 2 Peter, Jude.* NAC. Nashville: Broadman and Holman: 2003.

——— 'Penal Substitution View'. Pages 67–98 in *The Nature of the Atonement.* Edited by J. Beilby and P. R. Eddy. Downers Grove: IVP, 2006.

Schreiner, T. R., and A. B. Caneday, *The Race Set Before us: A Biblical Theology of Perseverance and Assurance.* Downers Grove: IVP, 2001.

Schreiner, T. R., and B. A. Ware (eds.) *Still Sovereign: Contemporary Perspectives on Election, Foreknowledge, and Grace.* Grand Rapids: Baker, 2000.

Schutter, W. L. *Hermeneutic and Composition in 1 Peter.* WUNT 2/30. Tübingen: Mohr (Seibeck), 1989.

Schwank, B., A. Stöger, and W. Thüsing. *The Epistles of St. Peter, St. John and St. Jude.* NTSR 11. London: Sheed and Ward, 1969.

Schwank, P. B. 'Diabolus tamquam leo rugiens'. *Erbe und Auftrag* 38 (1962): 15–20.

Schweizer, E. '1 Petrus 4:6'. *TZ* 8 (1952): 152–4.

——— *Lordship and Discipleship.* SBT 28. London: SCM Press, 1960.

——— *Der erste Petrusbrief.* 3rd edn. ZBK. Zurich: Theologischer Verlag, 1972.

Searle, J. R. 'Austin on Locutionary and Illocutionary Acts'. *The Philosophical Review* 77 (1968): 405–24.

Speech Acts: An Essay in the Philosophy of Language. Cambridge: Cambridge University Press, 1969.

Seland, T. "πάροικος καὶ παρεπίδημο": Proselyte Characterisations in 1 Peter?' *BBR* 11 (2001): 239–68.

Strangers in the Light: Philonic Perspectives on Christian Identity in 1 Peter. Leiden: Brill, 2005.

Selwyn, E. G. *The First Epistle of St. Peter: The Greek Text with Introduction, Notes, and Essays.* 2nd edn. London: Macmillan; New York: St. Martins, 1947.

'The Persecutions in 1 Peter'. *BSNTS* 1 (1950): 39–50.

Senior, D. P., and D. J. Harrington. *1 Peter, Jude and 2 Peter.* SP. Collegeville, Minn.: The Liturgical Press, 2003.

Sharpe, S. *Egyptian Inscriptions from the British Museum and other Sources.* London, 1837.

Shimada, K. 'The Formulary Material in First Peter: A Study According to the Method of Traditionsgeschichte'. ThD dissertation, Union Theological Seminary, New York, 1966.

'A Critical Note on 1 Peter 1,12'. *AJBI* 7 (1981): 146–50.

Sieffert, E. A. 'Die Heilsbedeutung des Leidens und Sterbens Christi nach dem ersten Briefe des Petrus'. *Jahrbücher für deutsche Theologie* 20 (1875): 371–440.

Silva, M. *Biblical Words and their Meaning: An Introduction to Lexical Semantics.* Rev. edn. Grand Rapids: Zondervan, 1994.

'The Case for Calvinistic Hermeneutics'. Pages 251–69 in *An Introduction to Biblical Hermeneutics: The Search for Meaning.* W. C. Kaiser and M. Silva. Grand Rapids: Zondervan, 1994.

Sjöberg, E. 'Wiedergeburt und Neuschöpfung in palästinischen Judentum'. *ST* 43 (1951): 44–85.

Skinner, Q. 'Motives, Intentions and the Interpretations of Texts'. *NLH* 3 (1972): 393–408.

Sleeper, C. F. 'Political Responsibility According to 1 Peter'. *NovT* 10 (1968): 270–86.

Smart, J. D. *The Strange Silence of the Bible in the Church: A Study in Hermeneutics.* Philadelphia: Westminster Press, 1970.

Smith, J. W. 'Some Notes on Wesley's Doctrine of Prevenient Grace'. *Religion in Life* 34 (1964–5): 68–80.

Smyth, H. W. *Greek Grammar.* Rev. by G. M. Messing. Cambridge, Mass.: Harvard University Press, 1956.

Snodgrass, K. R. '1 Peter II.1–10: Its Formulation and Literary Affinities'. *NTS* 24 (1977): 97–106.

The Parable of the Wicked Tenants. WUNT 27. Tübingen: Mohr Siebeck, 1983.

Spicq, C. *Les Épîtres de Saint Pierre.* SB 4. Paris: Gabalda, 1966.

Theological Lexicon of the New Testament. 3 vols. Peabody, Mass.: Hendrickson, 1994.

Spinoza, B. de., *The Chief Works of Benedict de Spinoza.* Translated with an introduction by R. H. M. Elwes. 2 vols. London: Bell, 1889–91.

Spörri, T. *Der Gemeindegedanke im ersten Petrusbrief: Ein Beitrag zur Struktur der urchristlischen Kirchenbegriffs*. NTF 2/2. Gütersloh: Bertelsmann, 1925.

Stanton, G. N. 'Presuppositions in New Testament Criticism'. Pages 60–71 in *New Testament Interpretation: Essays on Principles and Methods*. Edited by I. H. Marshall. Grand Rapids: Eerdmans, 1977.

Stephens, W. P. *The Theology of Huldreich Zwingli*. Oxford: Clarendon Press, 1986.

Stibbs, A. M. *The Meaning of the Word 'Blood' in Scripture*. London: Tyndale Press: 1947.

Stone, L. G. 'The Soul: Possession, Part, or Person? The Genesis of Human Nature in Genesis 2:7'. Pages 47–61 in *What About the Soul? Neuroscience and Christian Anthropology*. Edited by J. B. Green. Nashville: Abingdon Press, 2004.

Storms, C. S. *Chosen for Life: An Introductory Guide to the Doctrine of Divine Election*. Grand Rapids: Baker, 1987.

Stott, J. R. W. *The Cross of Christ*. Leicester: IVP, 1986.

Stout, J. 'What is the Meaning of a Text?' *NLH* 14 (1982): 1–12.

Strack, H. L., and P. Billerbeck. *Kommentar zum Neuen Testament aus Talmud und Midrasch*. 4 vols. Munich: Beck, 1922–8.

Strobel, A. 'Macht Leiden von Sünden frei?: Zur Problematik von 1 Petr 4,1f.' *TZ* 19 (1963): 412–25.

Tanner, K. *Theories of Culture: A New Agenda for Theology*. Minneapolis: Fortress Press, 1997.

Thielman, F. *Theology of the New Testament: A Canonical and Synthetic Approach*. Grand Rapids: Zondervan, 2005.

Thiselton, A. C. *The Two Horizons: New Testament Hermeneutics and Philosophical Description*. Grand Rapids: Eerdmans, 1980.
　New Horizons in Hermeneutics. Grand Rapids: Zondervan 1992.
　The First Epistle to the Corinthians. NIGTC. Grand Rapids: Eerdmans, 2000.

Thurén, L. *Argument and Theology in 1 Peter: The Origins of Christian Paraenesis*. JSNTSup 114. Sheffield: Sheffield Academic Press, 1995.

Thurston, R. W. 'Interpreting First Peter'. *JETS* 17 (1974): 171–82.

Tillich, P. *Systematic Theology*. 3 vols. Chicago: University of Chicago Press, 1951–63.

Torrance, J. B. 'Authority, Scripture and Tradition'. *EvQ* 87 (1987): 245–51.

Towner, P. H. *1–2 Timothy and Titus*. Downers Grove: IVP, 1994.

Trebilco, P. R. 'When Did the Early 'Christians' First Call Themselves 'the Believers'? Unpublished paper, in the author's possession, 1–33.

Turner, N. *Syntax*. Vol. 3 of J. H. Moulton, *A Grammar of New Testament Greek*. 4 volumes. Edinburgh: T&T Clark, 1963.

Turretin, F. *Institutes of Elenctic Theology*. 3 vols. Translated by G. M. Giger. Edited by J. T. Dennison. Phillisburg, N. J.: Presbyterian and Reformed Publishing. 1992–7.

Van der Watt, J. G. (ed.) *Salvation in the New Testament: Perspectives on Soteriology*. NovTSup 121. Leiden: Brill, 2005.
　'Soteriology of the New Testament: Some Tentative Remarks'. Pages 505–22 in *Salvation in the New Testament: Perspectives on*

Soteriology. Edited by J. G. Van der Watt. NovTSup 121. Leiden: Brill, 2005.

Van Dyk, L. 'Do Theories of the Atonement Foster Abuse?' *Dialog* 35 (1996): 21–5.

Vanhoozer, K. J. 'From Canon to Concept: "Same" and "Other" in the Relation between Biblical and Systematic Theology'. *SBET* 12 (1994): 96–124.

Is there a Meaning in this Text? the Bible, the Reader, and the Morality of Literary Knowledge. Grand Rapids: Zondervan, 1998.

First Theology: God, Scripture and Hermeneutics. Downers Grove: IVP, 2002.

'Scripture and Tradition'. Pages 149–69 in *The Cambridge Companion to Postmodern Theology*. Cambridge: Cambridge University Press, 2003.

'Introduction: What is Theological Interpretation of the Bible?' Pages 19–25 in *DTIB*.

The Drama of Doctrine: A Canonical-Linguistic Approach to Christian Theology. Louisville: Westminster John Knox, 2005.

Vanhoozer, K. J., C. G. Bartholomew, D. J. Treier, and N. T. Wright (eds.) *Dictionary for Theological Interpretation of the Bible*. Grand Rapids: Baker, 2005.

Vanhoye, A. 'La Maison spirituelle (1 Pt 2:1–10)'. *AsSeign* 43 (1964): 16–29.

van Itterzon, G. P. *Franciscus Gomarus*. The Hague: M. Nijhoff, 1930.

van Rensburg, F. J. J. 'Metaphors in the Soteriology in 1 Peter: Identifying and Interpreting the Salvific Imageries'. Pages 409–35 in *Salvation in the New Testament: Perspectives on Soteriology*. Edited by J. G. Van der Watt. NovTSup 121. Leiden: Brill, 2005.

van Unnik, W. C. 'The Critique of Paganism in 1 Peter 1:18'. Pages 129–42 in *Neotestamentica et Semitica*. M. Black Festschrift. Edited by E. E. Ellis and M. Wilcox. Edinburgh: T&T Clark, 1969.

Vogels, H.-J. *Christi Abstieg in Totenreich und das Läuterung an den Toten*. Freiburger Theologische Studien 101. Freiburg: Herder, 1976.

Volf, M. 'Soft Difference: Theological Reflections on the Relation between Church and Culture in 1 Peter'. *ExAud* 10 (1994): 15–30.

Wall, R. W. 'Reading the Bible from within our Traditions: The "Rule of Faith" in Theological Hermeneutics'. Pages 88–107 in *Between Two Horizons: Spanning New Testament Studies and Systematic Theology*. Edited by J. B. Green and M. Turner. Grand Rapids: Eerdmans, 2000.

'Canonical Context and Canonical Conversations'. Pages 165–82 in *Between Two Horizons: Spanning New Testament Studies and Systematic Theology*. Edited by J. B. Green and M. Turner. Grand Rapids: Eerdmans, 2000.

Wallace, D. B. *Greek Grammar beyond the Basics: An Exegetical Syntax of the New Testament*. Grand Rapids: Zondervan, 1996.

Wand, J. W. C. *The General Epistles of St. Peter and St. Jude*. London: Methuen, 1934.

Warden, D. 'The Prophets of 1 Peter 1:10–12'. *ResQ* 31 (1989): 1–12.

Ware, B. A. 'Effectual Calling and Grace'. Pages 203–27 in *Still Sovereign: Contemporary Perspectives on Election, Foreknowledge, and Grace*. Edited by T. R. Schreiner and B. A. Ware. Grand Rapids: Baker, 2000.

Webster, J. *Barth*. London: Continuum: 2000.

Word and Church: Essays in Christian Dogmatics. Edinburgh: T&T Clark, 2001.

'Confession and Confessions'. Pages 119–31 in *Nicene Christianity: The Future for a New Ecumenism.* Edited by C. R. Seitz. Grand Rapids: Brazos Press, 2001.

Holy Scripture: A Dogmatic Sketch. Cambridge: Cambridge University Press, 2003.

Barth's Earlier Theology: Four Studies. London/New York: T&T Clark International, 2005.

Wendland, E. R. '"Stand Fast in the True Grace of God!" A Study of 1 Peter'. *JOTT* 13 (2000): 25–102.

Wenham, G. J. *The Book of Leviticus.* NICOT. Grand Rapids: Eerdmans, 1979.

Wesley, J. *Predestination Calmly Considered.* London: Printed at the Conference Office, 1818.

The Works of the Rev. John Wesley. 15 vols. London: Wesleyan Conference Office, 1872.

White, R. E. O. *The Biblical Doctrine of Initiation.* London: Hodder & Stoughton, 1960.

Wieland, G. M. *The Significance of Salvation: A Study of Salvation Language in the Pastoral Epistles.* Carlisle: Paternoster Press, 2006.

Williams, D. S. *Sisters in the Wilderness: The Challenge of Womanist God-Talk.* Maryknoll, N.Y.: Orbis Books, 1993.

Williams G. J. 'The Cross and the Punishment of Sin'. Pages 68–99 in *Where Wrath and Mercy Meet: Proclaiming the Atonement Today.* Edited by D. Peterson. Carlisle: Paternoster Press, 2001.

Williams, M. 'The Five Points of Arminianism'. *Presbyterion* 30 (2004): 11–36.

Willoughby, H. R. *Pagan Regeneration: A Study of Mystery Initiations in the Graeco-Roman World.* Chicago: University of Chicago Press, 1929.

Windisch, H. *Die katholischen Briefe.* HNT 4/2. 3rd edn. Revised and Edited by H. Preisker. Tübingen: Mohr (Siebeck), 1951.

Wohlenberg, G. *Der erste und zweite Petrusbriefe und der Judasbrief.* Leipzig: Deichert, 1923.

Wolterstorff, N. *Divine Discourse: Philosophical Reflections on the Claim that God Speaks.* Cambridge: Cambridge University Press, 1995.

Wrede, W. 'The Task and Methods of "New Testament Theology"'. Pages 68–116 in R. Morgan, *The Nature of New Testament Theology.* SBT 2nd series 25. London: SCM Press, 1973.

Wright, D. 'The Atonement in Reformation Theology'. *EuroJT* 8 (1999): 37–48.

Wright, N. T. 'The Meaning of περὶ ἁμαρτίας in Romans 8.3'. Pages 453–9 in *Studia Biblica 1978: Sixth International Congress on Biblical Studies, Oxford, 3–7 April.* vol. 3, *Papers on Paul and other New Testament Authors.* Edited by E. A. Livingstone. JSNT Sup 3. Sheffield: JSOT Press, 1980.

Jesus and the Victory of God. London: SPCK, 1996.

'Five Gospels but No Gospel: Jesus and the Seminar'. Pages 83–120 in *Authenticating the Activities of Jesus.* Edited by B. Chilton and C. A. Evans. Leiden: Brill, 1999.

The Resurrection of the Son of God. London: SPCK, 2003.

Wright, R. K. M. *No Place for Sovereignty: What's Wrong with Freewill Theism.* Downers Grove: IVP. 1996.

Zerwick, M. *Biblical Greek Illustrated by Examples.* Rome: Pontificii Instituti Biblici, 1963.

Zerwick, M., and M. Grosvenor. *A Grammatical Analysis of the Greek New Testament.* 5th rev. edn. Rome: Editrice Pontificio Istituto Biblica, 1996.

Ziegler, J. *Untersuchungen zur Septuaginta des Buches Isaias.* Münster: Verlag der Aschendorffschen Verlagsbuchhandlung, 1934.

Zorrell, F. *Lexicon graecum novi testamenti.* Rome: Pontifical Biblical Institute, 1963.

INDEX OF NAMES

Abelard, Peter 270
Abernathy, D. 70, 71
Abraham, W. 17
Achtemeier, P. J. 57, 74, 91, 139, 147, 157, 165, 169, 170, 175, 178, 210, 215, 262
Agnew, F. H. 57
Alexander the Great 95
Ambrose 259
Arichea, D. C., Jnr. 176
Aristophanes of Byzantium 48
Arminius, James 238
Asael 207
Attalus III 95
Augustine 230
Aulén, Gustaf 254, 255, 256
Austin, J. L. 19

Baker, M. D. 264, 265
Barrett, C. K. 53
Barth, Karl 17, 230, 231, 232, 233, 234, 235, 236, 241, 242, 243, 248
Bauckham, R. J. 67
Bauernfeind, O. 96
Beare, F. W. 67, 88, 90, 104, 157, 178, 182, 189, 262
Bénétreau, S. 55, 63, 88, 219
Berekiah, Rabbi 131
Berkhof, Hendrikus 267, 268
Best, E. 71, 74, 173, 245
Beza, Theodore 247, 248, 249
Bieder, Werner 188
Bigg, C. A. 90, 102, 103, 170
Boettner, L. 240
Boring, M. E. 135, 137, 146
Boyd, G. A. 255
Bruce, F. F. 257
Büchsel, H. M. F. 134, 135
Bultmann, R. 152, 234
Bunyan, John xii

Caird, G. B. 34
Calvin, John 17, 51, 230, 232, 237, 239, 240, 241, 245, 247, 248
Carson, D. A. 14, 33, 36, 133, 260
Celsus 237
Cha, Youn Soon xii
Childs, Brevard 12, 14
Claudius 50
Clement of Alexandria 100
Clement of Rome 100
Cottrell, J. W. 238, 242, 243
Cranfield, C. E. B. 105, 218

Dalton, W. J. 122, 125, 190, 201
Davidson, Ivor xi, 6
de Villiers, J. L. 167
Deissmann, G. A. 85, 104
Demarest, Bruce 249, 250
Demosthenes 84
Denny, J. 103
Derrida, Jacques 21, 26, 275
Diodorus of Sicily 95, 96
Dionysus 129
Domitian 5
Dubis, M. 2
Dunn, J. D. G. 54, 110, 112
Dupont-Roc, R. 153

Ellil 144
Elliott, J. H. 5, 6, 7, 47, 49, 50, 51, 57, 73, 76, 77, 78, 80, 96, 109, 116, 119, 125, 131, 132, 153, 163, 176, 178, 195, 223
Erickson, M. J. 268, 269
Ernesti, J. A. 13
Evans, C. A. 64

Fagbemi, Stephen 2
Feldmeier, R. 212
Fiddes, Paul 254, 263, 264, 265, 266
Fish, Stanley 21, 26, 275

Foerster, W. 215
Ford, David 1
Fowl, Stephen 24, 25, 26, 31, 279
Funk, R. W. 275

Gabler, J. P. 13, 14, 36, 273, 275
Gadamer, Hans-Georg 22, 23
Galot, Jean 188
Godescalc of Orbais (Gottschalk) 247
Goppelt, L. 51, 95, 130, 167, 170, 214, 215
Green, Joel 1, 159, 160, 264, 265, 274
Gregory of Nyssa 259
Grenz, Stanley 229, 261, 267
Grudem, Wayne A. 49, 55, 58, 199
Gunton, C. E. 234, 264, 271

Hadrian 158
Harris, M. J. 57, 104
Harris, Rendel 70
Heidegger, Martin 22
Heracles 95, 96
Hesychius 128
Hiebert, D. E. 125, 193
Hill, D. 83
Hillyer, N. 70
Hirsh, E. D. 33
Hodge, Charles 278
Hoffmann, E. 152
Holland, Norman 20, 275
Hooker, Morna D. 110, 112, 264, 265
Hoover, R. W. 275
Hort, F. J. A. 82, 168, 176

Ignatius 101, 118
Irenaeus 110

Jeffery, S. M. 257, 272
Jeremias, Joachim 93
Jesus Seminar, The 20, 21
Jewett, P. K. 243, 245, 248
Jobes, K. H. 47, 49, 50, 51, 56, 60, 65, 66, 100, 102, 182, 192
Jones, L. G. 24, 26
Jose, Rabbi 131
Josephus 84, 128, 141
Jüngel, E. 271

Kähler, Martin 270
Kelly, J. N. D. 82, 91, 102
Kendall, D. W. 181
Kilpatrick, G. D. 181
Kittel, G. 143
Klein, William 245, 246

Krimmer, H. 201
Kühschelm, R. 154

Ladd, G. E. 193
Laubach, F. 116
LaVerdiere, E. A. 140
Lee, Chun Bae xii
Lewis, G. R. 23
Lindbeck, G. 26
Lonergan, Bernard 21
Longenecker, R. N. 122
Luther, Martin 188, 247, 250, 270
Lyonnet, S. 260

Mangina, J. L. 234
Marduk 144
Margot, J. C. 90
Marshall, I. H. 1, 87, 154
Martin, Troy W. 167
Maternus, Julius Firmicius 159
Maurer, C. 68
McCormack, Bruce 230, 233
McGrath, Alister E. 19, 81, 230, 269, 270
Meier, Beat xii
Meier, Susanne xii
Michaels, J. R. 56, 58, 59, 76, 104, 111, 115, 126, 140, 171, 175, 181, 193, 196, 212, 244
Miguéns, M. 110
Miller, D. G. 156
Morris, L. L. 86, 87, 92, 93, 98, 102, 123, 277
Moule, C. F. D. 88

Nero 5, 6
Nida, E. A. 176

Oden, Thomas 239, 254
Olson, V. S. 105
Origen 100, 237, 258, 259
Osborne, G. R. 35
Osiris 129
Ovey, M. 257, 272
Owen, John 267

Packer, J. I. 36
Panning, A. J. 70
Parsons, S. P. 129, 131, 142
Philip 84
Philo 74, 84, 128, 130, 141
Plato 45, 100, 129
Pliny 6
Plutarch 83, 129

Polycarp 100, 101
Porphyry 96
Priestley, Joseph 33
Ptah 143

Rashdall, Hastings 269, 270
Rice, John 17
Robertson, A. T. 124, 162
Ryle, Gilbert 29

Sabourin, L. 260
Sach, A. 257, 272
Sallustius 128, 129
Schelkle, K. H. 104, 142, 155, 161, 191
Schmidt, K. L. 125
Schneider, J. 107
Schreiner, T. R. 54, 91, 185, 251
Schrenk, G. 43, 111, 121
Schweizer, E. 263
Searle, John 19, 30, 31
Selwyn, E. G. 5, 54, 55, 109, 125, 147,
     167, 179, 189
Semler, J. S. 13
Senior, D. P. 148
Siede, B. 108
Silva, Moisés 3, 22
Snodgrass, K. R. 66
Socinus, Faustus 268, 269
Spener, J. P. 12
Spicq, C. 60, 69, 91, 118, 177, 183, 191,
     192, 220
Spinoza, B. de 13, 36

Stibbs, A. M. 263
Storms, C. S. 244
Stratonice 95

Tanner, K. 26
Thucydides 45
Thurston, R. W. 6
Tiedtke, E. 94
Trajan 5, 6
Trebilco, Paul xi
Turner, N. 123
Turretin, Francis 240, 248, 250

van Rensburg, F. J. J. 2
van Unnik, W. C. 96
Vanhoozer, K. J. 15, 21, 27, 28, 29, 31, 33,
     34, 35, 274, 279
Vanhoye, A. 63
Vespasian 5
Volf, Miroslav 50

Wall, Robert 25, 27
Warden, D. 179
Webster, John 15, 16, 18, 19, 28
Weiss, K. 103
Wesley, John 236, 238
Wrede, William 14, 19, 21, 36, 273, 275
Wright, N. T. 20, 120, 192

Zachariä, G. T. 13
Ziegler, Joseph 66
Zwingli, Ulrich 247

INDEX OF REFERENCES

Old Testament

Genesis

1   144
1:1–2:4   144
1:1–3   144
1:11   108
1:17   68
2:7   174
2:9   108
3:23   113
4:23   113
6:1–4   197
6:4   197
6:5   133
6:14   108
8:21   133
9:4   89, 90, 263
9:6   89
12:5–7   155
17:5–6   69
17:5   69
18:19   54
19:19   136
20:17   113
22:3   108
23:4   48
23:6   45
28:11   62
29:2   62
29:8   62
31:46   62
32:13   69
40:19   108
49:11   89

Exodus

6:6   86, 92
7–12   92
7:17   89

7:19   89
7:20   89
7:21   89
10:22   78
12:5   91
12:7   89
12:13   89
12:22   89
12:23   89
12:27   92
12:31–3   92
13:11–13   84
13:13   86
13:15   86
14:7   45
14:13   159
14:30   160
15:2   159
15:27   113
19:3–6   125
19:4   125
19:5–6   75
19:5   75–6, 156
19:6   73–4
19:10   138
20:2   160
20:5–6   136
20:6   136
20:12   125
21:6   124
21:25   113
21:29   85
21:30   85
23:18   89
24:3–8   59–60, 257
24:3   59
24:5   59
24:6   59
24:7   59
24:8   59
24:25   92

25:10   108
28:38   105
28:43   105
29:4   125
29:8   125
29:10   124
30:10   89
32   136
33:17   54
34:6   136
34:20   86
34:25   89
40:2   67
40:3   67
40:4   67
40:5   67
40:6   67
40:12   125
40:17   67
40:18   67
40:20   67
40:21   67
40:22   67
40:24   67
40:26   67
40:29   67
40:33   67

Leviticus

1:2   124
3:17   89
5:1   105
5:17   105
6:23   120
7:18   105
8:24   125
14:3   113
14:19   120
14:48   113
16:1   125
16:20–2   104
17:5   76
17:7   94
17:11–14   90, 263
17:11   89, 90, 263
17:14   89
19:2   266
19:4   101
19:31   101
20:6   101
20:19   105
20:20   105
22:9   105

24:15   105
25:8–34   85
25:13–34   84
25:23   155
25:35–55   85
27:9–13   85
27:14–15   85
27:16–25   85
27:16–21   84
27:26–7   86
27:30–1   85

Numbers

3:46–51   86
3:46   86
3:48   86
3:49   86
3:51   86
5:31   105
6:3   138
8:9–10   125
8:9   125
8:21   138
9:7   91
9:13   91, 105
11:12   133
11:15   136
14:19   136
14:24   101
14:33–5   105–6
18:1   105
18:15   86, 89
18:20   156
18:22   105
19:12   138
25:67   124
27:5   124
31:23   138
32:19   155
32:21   210
34:2   155

Deuteronomy

2:12   155
3:20   155
4:20   156
4:28   62
4:30   115
5:6   160
5:9–10   136
5:10   136
7:6   46, 86

7:7   46
7:8   86
9:26   86
11:24   101
12:9   155
12:23   89, 90, 263
12:30   101
13:6   86
15:15   86
16:1–8   92
19:14   155
21:22–3   108
21:23   108, 109
24:15   151
24:16   123
24:18   86
28:25   51
28:27   113
28:35   101
28:40   136
30:2   115
30:3   113
30:4   51
32:6   133
32:8–9   156
32:14   89
32:18   133
32:42   89

Joshua

1:15   155
10:26   108
14:9   101
14:14   101
17:4   155

Judges

15:18   159
18:7   151
20:15   45

Ruth

2:20   85
3:12–13   85
4:1–9   85

1 Samuel

1:29   86
2:1   159
2:12   54

10:1   156
14:32   89
14:45   159
17:40   62
19:5   159
24:3[24:2]   45

2 Samuel

1:10   74
7:14   133
10:11   159
14:16   156
15:14   159
19:2[19:3]   159
20:5   113
20:19   156
23:12   159
23:17   89

1 Kings

6:7   62
6:15   108
8:51   156
8:53   156
9:3   69
10:2   62
18:28   89
22:35   89

2 Kings

3:19   45
3:22   89
5:7   113
7:23   86
8:12   45
9:35   101
13:17   159
16:15   89
19:23   45
19:29   141

1 Chronicles

7:40   45
11:14   159
11:19   89
16:18   155
17:9   69
17:13–14   133
19:12   159
22:8   89

22:10   133
28:4   74
28:6   133

2 Chronicles

2:14   113
11:15   94
14:13   75
20:11   155
23:11   74
31:18   138

Esther

2:23   108
5:14   108

Job

10:12   69
11:20   159
19:21   136
30:15   159
33:11   108
38:10   68

Psalms

1:3   108
2:6   65
2:7   133
3:9[3:8]   159
6:3[6:2]   113
6:4–5[6:5–6]   159
9:13   89
9:15[9:16]   77, 166
11:6   69
12:5[11:6]   159
13:5[12:6]   166
14:6[13:6]   151
16:5[15:5]   156
17:7[16:7]   151
18[17]   159
18:19[17:20]   159
18:37[17:38]   101
18:43   54
20:10   69
21:1[20:2]   166
24:1[23:1]   156
24:22   86
26:6   136
26:11   86
29   144

30:2[29:3]   113
32:7   68
33   144
33:6   61
33:9   61
33:13–17   61
33:17[32:17]   159
33:23   86
34:6[33:6]   144
34:9[33:9]   144
37:6   113
37:23[36:23]   159
39:13[38:14]   48
40:4[39:5]   151
40:7[39:8]   120
41:4[40:5]   113
41:10   133
43:27   86
48:16   86
50:3[49:3]   136
50:14[49:14]   159
50:15[49:15]   115
51:10   108
51:14[50:16]   159
61:4[60:5]   151
62:7[61:10]   151
62:8[61:11]   151
62:9[61:9]   151
62:10[61:9]   94
65:5[64:6]   151
68[67]   159
68:6   133
68:19   86
69:13[68:14]   159
71:5[70:5]   151
71:15[70:15]   159
73:2   86
73:28[72:28]   151
78:31[77:31]   45
78:42[77:42]   86
79:9[78:9]   159
85:7[84:8]   159
88:1–2   136
88:28   69
88:30   69
89:8   69
89:26–7   133
91:5–6   78
91:9[90:9]   151
91:16[90:16]   159
94:11[93:11]   94
94:22[93:22]   151
98:7–9   160
102:4   86

103:3[102:3] 113
103:9 68
104:18[103:18] 151
104:22–3 78
105:10 86
105:23[104:23] 45
106:2 86
106:33 68
106:35 69
107:20 144
109:1 69
110:2 65
110:3 133
116[114–15] 159
118[117] 64
118:22–3[117:22–3] 64
118:22[117:22] 62, 64, 67
119:2[118:2] 179
119:49 144
119:74 144
119:81 144
119:114 144
119:134[118:134] 86
119:147 144
129:7–8 86
130:5 144
136:24[135:24] 86
141:4[140:4] 45
142:5[141:6] 151
142:6[141:7] 151
146:5[145:5] 151

Proverbs

1:4 211
2:11 211
2:12 78
3:21 211
3:22 211
4:1 211
5:2 211
5:5 101
8:12 211
8:25 133
9:10 54
16:22 211
16:33 251
18:15 211
18:19 74
21:1 251
23:4 211
23:19 211
24:7 211
30:19 101

Song of Solomon

5:15 45
8:2 131

Isaiah

1:6 113
2:20 94
6:10 113–14
7:14 66
8:14 62, 63, 65, 66, 67
9:2 78
13:18 136
14:8 108
19:22 115
25:8–9 159
26:1 69
26:16 65
28 64
28:3 65
28:14–22 65
28:16–19 65
28:16 61, 62, 63, 65, 66–7, 69
31:6–7 115
31:6 115
33:2 159
40:6–8 142, 147
40:8 146
40:30 45
42:6 78
42:12 77
42:16 78
43:1–3 160
43:1 78
43:3–4 123
43:20 45, 73, 74, 77
43:21 75–6, 77
43:22 78
44:3 133
44:22 86
45:4 45
45:10 133
45:17 159
45:21 159
45:22 115
48:12 78
48:15 78
49:1 78
49:4 94
49:6 69, 78
49:21 133
51:2 78
52:2 87

52:3   86, 87
53   27, 31–3, 100, 105, 106–7, 120,
     122, 266, 268, 275
53:4–5   106–7
53:4   103, 106
53:5   106, 112–14, 122, 267
53:6   115, 122
53:9–11   120
53:9–10   121
53:9   107, 111
53:10   107, 120, 266
53:11   103, 106, 107, 122
53:12   103, 106, 122, 266
53:16   106
54:6   78
54:8   136
54:12   45
55:7   115
55:10–11   145
57:6   76
58:10   78
59:21   133
60:16   160
61:10   166
63:7   136
63:9   86, 160
65:12   78
65:15   46
66:4   78

Jeremiah

1:5   53, 54, 69
2:5   94
2:7   156
2:27   133
3:4   133
3:12   136
3:19   45, 133
3:22   115
8:19   94
10:15   94
13:23   133
15:7   51
15:21   86
16:18   156
17:5   151
18:3   62
18:8   115
23:5   121
23:6   121
24:7   116
31:9   133

31:15   45
31:18   116
31:29–34   133
32:6–15   85
33:5   121
38:11   86
41:17   51
50:42   136

Lamentations

1:15   45
2:24   94
3:22   136
3:32   136
4:16   136
5:21   116

Ezekiel

5:5   69
11:19–20   133
13:6–19   94
18:20   105, 106
20:32   62
23:4   133
27:24   45
32:17   101
33:11   253
34:5–6   115
34:16   116
36:25–7   133
37:14   69
43:7   101
44:28   156

Daniel

2:23–4   62
2:34   63
3:42   136
3:86   198
4:34   74
12:5–13   182

Hosea

1:6   79
1:8   79
1:9   79
2:1[1:10]   79
2:3[2:1]   79
2:23   79

2:25   79
3:5   115
5:3   53
6:1   115
6:6   136
13:5   54
13:14   86
14:2[14:1]   115

Joel

2:12   115

Amos

3:2   54
3:3   53

Jonah

1:2   207
2:9   94
3:2   207
3:20   207

Micah

1:7   69
4:10   86
6:4   86
6:8   136

Habakkuk

2:1–4   182

Haggai

2:7   45
2:9   75

Zechariah

3:1   257
3:9   65
9:9   121
10:2   94
13:9   168

Malachi

3:17   75, 76

Apocrypha

1 Esdras

5:49   76

2 Esdras

11:10   86
15:18   45

Tobit

8:4   159
8:5   159
8:15   46
8:17   159
13:4   133

Judith

2:15   45
6:4   101
8:12   123
8:17   160
9:6   52–3
9:13   113
11:16   52–3
14:4   101

Wisdom of Solomon

2:13   133
2:16   133
2:18   122, 133
3:4–6   168
3:9   46
3:11   152
3:18   152
4:15   46
5:5   133
5:10   101
7:2   89
9:16–18   133
12:5   89
16:6   160
18:7   160

Sirach

2:1–9   168
4:10   133
16:1   160
17:25   115
21:6   101

23:1 133
23:4 133
23:10 113
28:17 113
46:1 46
47:22 46
50:24 86
51:10 133

1 Maccabees

4:1 45
4:11 86
4:25 159
5:62 160
9:26 179
16:3 123

2 Maccabees

1:18 76
2:18 152
2:28 100
7:14 152
7:20 152
7:23 152
7:34–7 152
7:34 152
7:40 152
9:22 151
12:16 89
14:3 159
14:45 89

New Testament

Matthew

3:9 62, 63
4:3 62
5:12 166
5:25 201
5:46 181
7:14 199
9:36 115
10:6 115
10:13 116
10:21 193
10:27 205
10:38 101
12:36 216
12:44 69, 116
13:3–9 142
13:15 114
13:18–23 142
14:3 201

14:10 201
14:25 201
15:24 115
16:17 89
16:24 101
17:12 118
19:28 129, 133
20:16 78
20:19 113
20:28 259
21:1 193
21:24 64
21:33–46 64
21:38 157
21:42 62, 64, 65
21:44 62
21:45 64
22:14 46
23:20 89
23:35 89
24:2 62
24:22 46
24:24 46
25:36 201
25:39 201
25:43–4 201
26:17–18 92
26:28 89
26:41 191
26:47 108
26:55 108
26:59 193
27:1 193
27:19 122
27:24 89
27:25 89
27:26 113
27:60 62

Mark

4:3–9 142
4:12 114
4:14–20 142
5:5 62
6:27 201
6:48 201
8:31 53
8:34 101
10:12 65
11:28 181
12:1–12 64
12:6 64
12:7 157
12:10 62, 64

12:36 69
13:1 62
13:6 116
13:12 193
13:20 46
13:22 46
13:27 46
14:14–16 92
14:38 191
14:43 108
14:48 108
14:55 193
15:15 113
15:46 62
16:8 160
16:20 101

Luke

1:14 166
1:16 116
1:17 116
1:44 166
1:46–7 166
1:69 160
1:71 160
2:8 201
2:20 116
3:8 62, 63
3:20 201
4:3 62
4:11 62
4:27 101
5:35 166
8:5–8 142
8:11–15 142
9:23 101
9:35 46
9:41 124
10:6 115
11:22 210
11:50 89
11:51 89
12:3 205
12:13 157
12:28 199
13:1 89
14:31 181
17:2 62
18.7 46
19:40 63
19:44 62
20:9–18 64
20:14 157
20:17 62, 64, 65

20:18 63
20:43 69
21:6 62, 193
21:12 201
21:16 193
22:11–15 92
22:15 118
22:22 53, 251
22:33 201
22:51 108
22:52 108
23:35 46
23:46 198
24:2 62
24:21 87
24:25–7 185
24:39 191
24:46 118

John

1:12–13 142
1:13 133
1:29 93
1:34 46
2:18 181
3:3–5 132–3
3:3 133
3:6 191
3:9–10 132–3
3:36 68
5:21 194
5:39 27
6:29 171
7:38–9 133
11:38 62
11:50 123
11:55 138
12:33 181
12:40 114
13:36 101
14:2 196
14:3 196
14:26 16
14:28 196
16:28 196
18:3 210
19:1 113
19:14–42 93
21:19 101

Acts

1:3 118
1:7 69

1:10–11   196
2:19   89
2:20   89
2:23   53, 182, 251, 252
2:25   69
3:14   122
3:18   118
3:19   116
4:8–12   64
4:11   62, 64, 65
4:22   251
4:27–8   251
4:28   182
5:19   201
5:22   201
5:25   201
5:30   108
5:31   258
7:5   157
7:25   160
7:52   122
7:56   199
7:59   198
8:3   201
9:35   116
10:21   181
10:39   108
11:21   116
11:30   71
12:4–5   201
12:6   201
12:10   201
13:29   108
13:32–3   53
13:33   133
13:46   69
13:47   69, 160
14:2   68
14:11–14   94
14:15   94, 115, 116
14:23   171
15:3   116
15:16   115
15:19   116
15:20   89
16:20   124
16:24   108
16:34   166
17:29   62, 63
19:9   68
20:28   69, 89
20:32   157
21:24   138
21:25   89
21:26   138

22:14   122
22:20   89, 264
23:6   152
24:15   152
24:18   138
24:25   152
26:5   53
26:6   152
26:10   71
26:18–20   116
26:18   78, 116
26:20   116
26:23   118
27:3   118
27:27   124
27:34   160
28:27   114

Romans

1:1–4   53
1:3–4   191
1:5   58
1:21   78
2:21   205
2:28–9   191
3:15   89
3:21–6   264
3:25   89
4:12   101
4:17   69, 194
5:2   125
5:6–9   264
5:6   123
5:7   123
5:8   123
5:9   89
5:12–21   110
6   112
6:1–11   110
6:1   110
6:2   110, 111
6:7   110, 111
6:8   110
6:9   110
6:10   110, 111, 119
6:13   210
6:23   177
7:4   193
8:3   120
8:11   194
8:13   193
8:24–5   170
8:29–30   53
8:29   53, 239

8:30 78
8:33 46
8:34 194
8:36 193
9:1–2 253
9:32–3 63
9:33 67, 69
10:14 171
10:16 58, 59
11:2 53
12:1 77, 199
13:11 160
13:12 210
14:12 216
14:15 123
15:18 58
15:31 68
16:13 46

1 Corinthians

1:1 78
1:9 78
2:11 198
3:12 108
3:19 94
3:20 94
5:5 191
5:7 93
6:11 56
11:23 71
12:18 69
12:28 69
14:32 198
15:1 71
15:1–5 185
15:17 94, 95
15:20–8 110
15:22 110, 194
15:23 71
15:24–8 255
15:25 69
15:31 110
15:34 53
15:36 194
15:45 194
15:50 89
15:58 82

2 Corinthians

1:4 149
1:5 183
1:6 160
3:16 116

4:4 78
4:6 78
4:11 193
4:18 170
5:7 170
5:14 110, 123
5:19–21 268
5:19 69, 268
6:2 160
6:5 201
6:7 210
6:9 193
7:1 191
10:4 210
11:23 201
11:25 119
12:18 101

Galatians

1:15 78
1:16 89
2:10 71
3:3 191
3:13 108, 109, 123
3:18 157

Ephesians

1:3–6 253
1:3 149
1:7 258, 264
1:14 75, 157
1:18 157
2:18 125
2:20 62
3:12 125
4:1 78
4:4 78
5:5 157
5:8 78
5:18 215
6:8–9 82
6:11–17 210
6:12 89

Philippians

1:19 160
2:17 77
3:3 191
3:10 183
3:20 51
4:8 77

Colossians

1:13   78
1:29   71
2:14–15   256
2:15   255
3:12   46
3:15   78
3:24   82, 157
4:1   82
4:3   71

1 Thessalonians

1:9   115, 116
2:12   78
2:18   119
4:3   56
4:4   56
4:7   78
5:8   210
5:9   69, 75, 160
5:10   123

2 Thessalonians

1:8   59
1:11   71
2:13   56
2:14   71, 75

1 Timothy

1:12   69
2:6   123
2:7   69, 71
2:15   56
5:10   101
5:21   46
5:24   101

2 Timothy

1:9–10   53
1:11   69, 71
2:10   46, 160
2:23   82
3:14   82

Titus

1:2   46
1:6   215
2:14   87

3:5   129, 134
3:9   94, 95
3:11   82

Hebrews

1:2   69
1:5   133
1:13   69
2:9   183
2:10   183
2:14–15   255
2:14   89, 264
4:12   199, 210
5:1   120
5:3   120
5:5   133
5:7   193
5:9   160
6:5   134
7:27   76, 103, 119,
     120
9:7   89
9:12   89, 119
9:13   89
9:15   157
9:18   89
9:19   89
9:20   89
9:22   89
9:25   89, 119
9:26   118, 119
9:27–8   119
9:28   103, 160
10:4   89
10:6   120
10:8   120
10:13   69
10:18   120
10:26   120
10:39   75
11:3   170
11:8   157
11:13   48
11:27   170
11:28   89
11:36   201
12:14   56
12:23   198
13:11   89, 120
13:12   118
13:15   77, 103
13:16   77

James

1:26 94, 95
2:21 103
3:1 82
5:6 122

1 Peter

1:1–3 73, 253
1:1–2 43, 61, 65, 73, 74, 127, 135,
  139, 149, 178, 229, 233, 235, 236,
  240, 246, 252, 273, 275, 276
1:1 xii, 7, 45–52, 56, 60, 73, 236,
  244, 274
1:2 7, 47–8, 50, 52–60, 61, 109, 128,
  135, 139, 178, 224, 229, 233, 235,
  236, 237, 240, 241, 244, 246, 250,
  252, 257, 262, 263, 265, 276
1:3–12 4, 127, 137, 149–50, 273
1:3–5 57, 127, 150–62, 163, 164, 165,
  168, 174, 186
1:3–4 213
1:3–2:10 136, 137
1:3 4, 48, 57, 63, 73, 127–37, 139,
  140, 142, 146, 148, 149, 150–5,
  169, 174, 176, 178, 183, 185, 186,
  190, 192, 194, 223, 224, 235, 241,
  257, 258, 273, 277
1:4–5 169, 178, 243
1:4 128, 130, 137, 150, 153, 155–7,
  161, 165, 176, 177, 186, 243
1:5 4, 57, 73, 134, 137, 149, 150,
  153, 157–62, 165, 168, 170, 171,
  174, 176, 177, 178, 185, 186, 223,
  236, 243
1:6–9 150, 162–74, 186
1:6–8 163, 164–72, 186
1:6–7 5, 163, 164, 169–70, 183
1:6 162, 163, 165, 166–8, 169, 174,
  186, 195, 243
1:7 4, 57, 73, 109, 134, 135, 153, 163,
  164, 169, 170, 171, 172, 177, 185,
  186, 223, 225, 236, 256, 258, 273,
  277, 278
1:8–9 163
1:8 52, 162, 163, 164, 165, 167,
  170–2, 173, 186
1:9–10 187
1:9 149, 153, 160, 163, 164, 169,
  171, 172–4, 176, 186, 223, 236,
  243, 273
1:10–12 32–3, 150, 162, 174–87,
  262, 273

1:10–11 175, 179, 180, 186
1:10 149, 153, 160, 162, 174, 175,
  176–7, 178, 179, 181, 182, 223
1:11–12 146
1:11 146, 148, 162, 169, 175, 178–9,
  180–3, 184, 191, 257, 277
1:12 56, 78, 82, 99, 137, 175, 180,
  181, 183–6, 206, 273
1:13–25 138
1:13–21 81–2
1:13–17 82
1:13–14 150
1:13 81, 82, 138, 150, 153, 162, 170,
  177, 178, 236, 258
1:14–16 74, 81, 138, 261
1:14 58, 94, 128, 140, 162, 214, 261
1:15–16 261, 266
1:15 55, 74, 78, 94, 99, 162, 214, 236,
  266, 271
1:16–19 261
1:16 138, 147, 266
1:17–21 82, 138
1:17–19 81
1:17–18 51
1:17 60, 81–2, 97, 128, 140, 224, 261,
  266, 267
1:18–21 82, 273, 277
1:18–20 213, 235
1:18–19 4, 27, 81–97, 259–60, 261,
  262, 264, 265, 271
1:18 8, 81, 82, 88, 91, 93–7, 147, 162,
  244, 259, 261
1:19 34, 53, 104, 109, 162, 244, 261,
  263
1:20–1 182
1:20 53, 61, 65, 73, 96, 134, 161, 175,
  220, 235, 243–4, 250, 261,
  262
1:21 16, 73, 82, 152, 153, 154, 169,
  171, 174, 236, 258, 273, 277
1:22–5, 11.1
1:22–3 82, 138
1:22 57, 58, 138–40, 148, 173
1:23–5 138–48
1:23 4, 68, 73, 127, 128, 136, 138,
  139, 142, 145, 146, 147, 148, 185,
  223, 241, 257, 273
1:24–5 138, 142, 147
1:25 17, 54, 58, 68, 78, 99, 137, 138,
  141, 142, 145, 146, 147, 148,
  185, 206
2:1–10 79–80
2:1 236
2:2–4 236

2:2 128, 131, 137, 149, 153, 160, 185, 223
2:3 61, 138, 244
2:4–19 273
2:4–10 34, 43, 61–80, 134, 138, 233, 241, 244, 252, 273, 275
2:4–8 243
2:4–5 72, 77
2:4 46, 61, 63, 64, 65, 72, 79, 137, 169, 183, 220, 223, 224, 235, 236, 243–4, 246, 257, 277
2:5–10 72
2:5–6 271
2:5 57, 61, 62, 63, 65, 72–9, 103, 125, 162, 190, 223, 235, 246
2:6–10 77
2:6–8 67
2:6–7 64
2:6 46, 61, 62, 63, 65, 67, 68, 69, 72, 73, 147, 169, 171, 223, 235, 243–4, 246
2:7–8 73
2:7 57, 62, 64, 67, 68, 72, 73, 79, 171, 235, 246, 261
2:8 2, 27, 43, 57, 62, 63, 67–72, 235, 236, 250, 251, 252, 253, 276
2:9–10 61, 72–9, 139, 246, 276
2:9 46, 54, 57, 61, 62, 65, 72–8, 80, 99, 235, 236, 237, 241, 246, 253
2:10 64, 72, 76, 79, 136, 180, 224, 235, 253
2:11–3:12 98
2:11–12 7, 60, 98, 153
2:11 xii, 48, 60, 64, 173, 210
2:12 7, 8, 94, 98, 162, 165, 169, 195, 216
2:13–5:11 149
2:13–3:12 173
2:13–22 72
2:13–17 98
2:13–14 266
2:14–16 8
2:14 57, 170, 185
2:15 7, 8, 111, 162, 224
2:16 100
2:17 138, 139
2:18–25 72, 113
2:18–20 5, 82, 85, 98, 99, 189, 209, 213
2:18 59, 113, 162
2:19–20 98, 99, 190
2:19 99
2:20 99, 111, 113, 117
2:21–5 4, 27, 81, 82, 97–117, 120, 122, 180, 189, 209, 213, 270, 273

2:21–4 100, 190
2:21–3 98–102, 270
2:21 54, 57, 98–100, 101, 102, 103, 109, 111, 113, 115, 116, 117, 118, 119, 190, 265, 269, 270, 271, 277
2:22–5 31–3
2:22–4 122
2:22 102, 107, 111, 116, 212
2:23–5 270
2:23–4 265
2:23 7, 102, 111, 190, 261, 265, 266
2:24–5 98, 102–16
2:24 63, 98, 99, 102–14, 115, 117, 122, 134, 212, 213, 223, 235, 257, 258, 265, 268, 270, 271, 277
2:25 98, 114–16, 117, 173, 180, 265, 271
3:1–6 98
3:1 5, 59, 94, 162, 185
3:2 94, 162
3:3 162
3:4 162
3:5 153
3:6 111
3:7 57, 98, 135, 162, 177, 178, 190
3:8–12 98
3:8 173
3:9–10 153
3:9 7, 54, 57, 78, 99, 177, 216
3:10–12 61, 138
3:11–12 111
3:11 111
3:12 111, 261
3:13–17 5, 82, 99, 117, 189, 190, 213
3:13–14 8
3:13 181
3:14 111, 112, 117, 118, 119, 189, 190, 216
3:15 6, 8, 117, 153, 189, 258
3:16 7, 8, 94, 117, 162, 165, 189, 195, 216, 244
3:17 111, 117, 118, 119, 162, 189, 190, 224
3:18–4:6 xi, 4, 188–9, 213, 224, 225, 273
3:18–22 82, 99, 117–18, 153, 188–208, 209, 212, 213, 271
3:18 4, 27, 63, 81, 99, 109, 110, 111, 113, 117–26, 135, 146, 183, 188, 189–94, 195, 196, 205, 208, 209, 210, 212, 213, 220, 223–5, 235, 257, 258, 262, 264, 265, 268, 270, 271, 273, 277, 278
3:19–22 34, 190, 195
3:19–21 194

3:19–20   195–208, 255
3:19   xi, 4, 26, 117, 162, 165, 183,
   189, 190, 191, 195, 196, 197,
   198–9, 201–8, 209, 218–19, 224,
   258, 277
3:20–1   4, 180, 273
3:20   173, 189, 197, 198, 199–201,
   206
3:21–2   277
3:21   4, 117, 134, 189, 190, 192, 194,
   195, 197, 198, 206, 208, 209, 224,
   257, 258
3:22   4, 117, 183, 189, 190, 191, 194,
   195, 196, 197, 198–9, 203, 205,
   206, 208, 209, 225, 255, 257, 258
4:1–6   5, 72, 117, 188, 189, 190, 217
4:1–4   117, 209–16, 221
4:1   111, 117, 118, 119, 162, 189, 190,
   194, 209, 210, 211, 212, 213, 216,
   222, 225
4:2–4   50–1, 212
4:2–3   50, 60, 165, 212, 215, 216,
   261
4:2   57, 162, 212, 213, 216, 222,
   224
4:3–4   8, 51, 217
4:3   214, 215
4:4   7, 8, 165, 195, 212, 214, 215, 216,
   217, 219, 221, 222, 225
4:5–6   173, 216–25
4:5   183, 216–18, 219–20, 221, 223,
   224, 261, 266, 277
4:6   xi, 4, 63, 117, 135, 153, 185, 188,
   189, 190, 194, 205, 206, 209, 212,
   213, 216, 217–25, 257, 258, 278
4:7   57, 161, 173
4:8   111, 162, 212
4:10   178
4:11   98, 169
4:12–19   5
4:12–16   6, 72
4:12   6, 162, 164
4:13   166, 167, 170, 183, 277
4:14   6, 216
4:16   6, 216
4:17   59, 68, 161, 173, 181, 185, 224,
   251, 261, 266
4:18   223
4:19   111, 173, 224
5:1   72, 162, 169, 183, 277
5:2   162, 223
5:4   153, 173, 183, 277
5:5   138, 177, 178
5:6   153, 177, 223
5:8   181, 256

5:9   6, 236
5:10   5, 54, 55, 78, 99, 153, 178, 223,
   244, 277
5:11   169
5:12   8, 178, 279
5:13   47, 73, 252, 275
5:14   244

2 Peter

1:3   78, 185
1:4   185, 229
2:4   201, 202
2:5   202
3:17   53

1 John

1:9   122
2:1   122
2:2   120
2:29   122, 133
3:2   170
3:7   122
3:8   255
3:9   133
4:7   133
4:10   120
5:1   133
5:4   133
5:18   133

2 John

1:1   46
1:13   46

Jude

6–7   201
6   200, 201
14–15   202
24   166

Revelation

1:5   89
2:7   108
2:10   201
5:2   205
5:9   88, 89, 264
8:7   89
8:8   89
12:5   256
12:10–11   256

12:10   256
14:20   89
16:3   89
16:4   89
16:6   89
17:6   89
17:14   46
18:2   201
18:12   62, 108
18:16   62
18:24   89
19:7   166
20:7   201
21:11   62
21:19   62
22:2   108
22:14   108
22:19   108

Old Testament Pseudepigrapha

1 Enoch

2–5   202
5:7   156
6:1–8   200
6:1–2   200
6:5   201
6:6   197
7:1–3   200, 203
7:1   197
7:2   197
9:7–9   197
9:7–8   200
9:9   197
10:1–22   197
10:4–14   202
10:4–6   202
10:4   203
10:12–14   203
10:12   202
10:15   197
12:3   197
12:4–6   207
12:4–5   207
12:4   197, 200, 207
13:1–10   207
13:1–2   207
13:1   202, 207
13:2   202t1, 203
13:3   207
13:9   203
14–15   207
14:1–7   207

14:5   202, 202t1, 203, 207
15:1–16   207
15:2   207
15:3   200
15:8–10   200
15:8   203
15:10   203
17–18   203–4
17:1   203
18:1–16   203
18:3   203
18:4–6   201
18:10–11   203
18:12–16   204
18:14   202t1, 203
21:1–10   203
21:6   202t1, 203
21:10   202t1, 203
38:2   122
38:3   122
39:8   156
40:9   156
54:3–4   202
56:1–4   202
56:6   122
67:1–4   202t2
67:7   203
88:1   202
106:13–15   200
106:13–14   200
106:15–18   202t2
135:2   207

2 Enoch

7   207
7:1–3   203, 204
7:2   201
50:2   156
66:6   156

4 Maccabees

3:19   89
6:6   89
15:2   159
15:8   159

4 Ezra

4   182
6:55–6   156, 182
7:9   156

7:17 156
7:96 156

Joseph and Asenath

8:10–11 130
15:4 130

Jubilees

1:22–5 133
5 207
5:1–11 197
5:6 203
7:1 200
10:1–14 197
16:18 74
22:14 156

Psalms of Solomon

14:10 156
17:25 122
17:28 122
17:31 122
17:32 122
17:42 122
18:8–9 122

Test. XII Patr.

T. Job 18 156
T. Levi 3:1–3 203
T. Naph. 3:5 200
T. Rub. 6:6 200

Qumran literature

1QH

III 6–18 131
III 20–1 131
III 22 131
VI 29 131
VII 20 131
VII 29–30 131
IX 35 131
X 27 131
XI 11 131
XVI 18 131

1QM

I 1 131
I 3 131

I 7 131
I 9 131
I 10 131
I 11 131
I 13 131
I 16 131
III 6 131
III 9 131
XIII 16 131
XIV 17 131
XVI 11 131
XVII 8 131

1QS

I 9 131
I 10 131
II 16 131
III 13–IV 26 133
III 13 131
III 19 131
III 20 131
III 21 131
III 22 131
III 24 131
III 25 131
IV 5–6 131
IX 14 131
XI 16 131

1QSa

II 11–12 131
II 11 133

4Q174[4QFlor]

I 8 131

11QT19

LXIV 7–12 108

Rabbinic Writings

Lev. Rab.

35:5 132

Midrash Pss.

2§9 133

Pesiq. Rab.

36[162a]   121
41:4   132

Pesiq. Rab. Kah.

4:6   132

Sipre Deut.

32.2.1   132
45.1.2   132

Song Rab.

1:3 §3   132
8:2 §1   131

Talmud

b. B. Bat.

16a   132

b. Šabb.

145b–146a   131

b. Sanh.

19b   132
99b   132

b. Sukkah

52b   132

b. Yebam

22a   131
48b   131
62a   131
97b   131

Other Israelite Writings

Josephus

A.J.

2.90   141
4.319   128
12.28   84
12.33   84

12.46   84
14.272   125
14.371   84
19.178   110
306   141

B.J.

1.274   84
1.325   84
1.384   84
2.200   141
4.484   128

C. Ap.

2.202   141

Philo

Abr.

46   141
56   74

Aet.

8   128
65   141
97   141

Cher.

114–115   130

Conf.

63   130
93   84

Decal.

119   141
129   141

Her.

44   84
124   84
171   141
200   130

Ios.

43   141
193   84

Leg.

1.10   141
3.180 141

Mut.

63   130
96   141
255 142

Opif.

41   141
84   130
144 101, 130

Sacr.

121 84

Sobr.

66   74

Spec.

1.209 130
1.326 141
1.77   84
2.122 84

Virt.

199   141
204–5 130

Early Christian Writings

Barnabas

5:13   108
6:2–4 64
6:2–3 67
8:5   108
12:11 108

1 Clement

5.7   100
16.17 100
33.8   100

Diognetus

9:2   122

Ignatius

  Ephesians

  12.2   95

  Smyrneans

  2   118

Justin Martyr

  Apology

  1.61.2   128

  Dialogues

  2:1   125
  17   122

  Martyrdom of Polycarp

  17.2   122
  21.1   101

Melito of Sardis

  Peri Pasch.

  94   122

Polycarp

  Philippians

  8.1   108
  8.1–2 100
  8.2   100

Clement of Alexandria

  Strom.

  5.8.49.1   100

Gregory of Nyssa

  Great Catechism

  22   259

23   259
24   259

Origen

Against Celsus

2.20   237

Comm. Rom.

1   237

Or.

18.1   100

Greek and Latin Writings

Aristophanes of Byzantium

Eq.

12   158
367   107

394   107
705   107

Frag.

38   48

Athenaeus

Deipnosophistae

5.196a   48

Diodorus of Sicily

Hist.

4.8.5   96
17.3.6   95
17.4.1   95

Diogenes Laertius

9:2   122